TEST YOUR VOCABULARY RANGE

Each of these phrases contains one italicized word. Check the closest definition of each such word. To keep your score valid, refrain, as far as possible, from wild guessing.

1. *disheveled* appearance: (a) untidy, (b) fierce, (c) foolish, (d) peculiar, (e) unhappy
2. a *baffling* problem: (a) difficult, (b) simple, (c) puzzling, (d) long, (e) new
3. *lenient* parent: (a) tall, (b) not strict, (c) wise, (d) foolish, (e) severe
4. *repulsive* personality: (a) disgusting, (b) attractive, (c) normal, (d) confused, (e) conceited
5. *audacious* attempt: (a) useless, (b) bold, (c)foolish, (d) crazy, (e) necessary
6. *parry* a blow: (a) ward off, (b) fear, (c) expect, (d) invite, (e) ignore
7. *prevalent* disease: (a) dangerous, (b) catching, (c) childhood, (d) fatal, (e) widespread
8. *ominous* report: (a) loud, (b) threatening, (c) untrue, (d) serious, (e) unpleasant
9. an *incredible* story: (a) true, (b) interesting, (c) well-known, (d) unbelievable, (e) unknown
10. an *ophthalmologist*: (a) eye doctor, (b) skin doctor, (c) foot doctor, (d) heart doctor, (e) cancer specialist
11. will *supersede* the old law: (a) enforce, (b) specify penalties for, (c) take the place of, (d) repeal, (e) continue
12. an *anonymous* donor: (a) generous, (b) stingy, (c) well-known, (d) one whose name is not known, (e) reluctant
13. performed an *autopsy*: (a) examination of living tissue, (b) examination of a corpse to determine the cause of death, (c) process in the manufacture of optical lenses, (d) operation to cure an organic disease, (e) series of questions to determine the causes of delinquent behavior
14. an *indefatigable* worker: (a) well-paid, (b) tired, (c) skillful, (d) tireless, (e) pleasant
15. a confirmed *atheist*: (a) bachelor, (b) disbeliever in God, (c) believer in religion, (d) believer in science, (e) priest

Books By Norman Lewis

Norman Lewis

Word Power Made Easy

*The Complete Handbook for
Building A Superior Vocabulary*

Expanded and Completely Revised Edition

PUBLISHED BY POCKET BOOKS NEW YORK

POCKET BOOKS, a Simon & Schuster division of
GULF & WESTERN CORPORATION
1230 Avenue of the Americas, New York, N.Y. 10020

TO:

My family and friends, who accepted, without apparent resentment and with barely audible complaint, my complete self-isolation during the many months in which I totally and shamefully neglected them while working on the revision of this book.

Especially: Mary; Margie Baldinger and the kids; Debbie and Allen Hubbert; Milton Lewis; Karen and Bob Kopfstein; Leonard Vogel, one of America's great painters, and Shirley; gourmet cooks David and Janice Potts; Seymour and Nan Prog; Ruth and Leo; Dave and Jan Hopkins; Carol and Marvin Colter; Bob Finnerty, my chess opponent, who says that winning is all that counts; Doris Garcia; Eleanor and Robert Poitou; Mary El and Dick Gayman—

Walter Garcia, Len Grandy, Don Jenkins; Sally Landsburg; Ted and Margaret Snyder; Jean Bryan; Rhoda and Ralph Duenewald; George and Phyllis Juric; Bob and Monica Myers, Tony and Kathy Garcia, Jean Kachaturian; Margie Lopez and Jo Watson—

Myrtle and Ace, Donny and Estelle, Helen and Ben, Judy and Bob, Doris and Muriel, Danny and Mary; in memoriam, Max and Frances—

Larry Scher, Chuck Nichamin, Sue Sullivan, Rosemary and Debbie Greenman, Alice Hessing, Dave and Lynn Bisset, Danny Hernandez, John Arcadi and Peggy Arcadi, Norm Ashley, Aaron Breitbart—

Lorin and Gloria Warner, Marty and Ros Chodos, Mahlon and Gwen Woirhaye, Leon and Kay East, Marijane and Paul Paulsen, Helen and Russ Hurford, Elior and Sally Kinarthy—

Carolyn Russell, Rod Sciborski, Vera Laushkin, John Hahn, Liz Johnson, Leonora Davila, Jim Hawley, Jerry Lenington, Jay Loughran, Susan Obler, Marilyn Houseman, Rita Scott, Chris Hamilton, Joan Nay, Mary Lewis, Virginia Sandoval, Hazel Haas—

The staff and all my students at Rio Hondo College—

My editor at Doubleday, Jean Anne Vincent, who so patiently and cheerfully goaded, prodded, pushed, wheedled, and cajoled me into finishing on time.

Also: I wish to thank Karen Kopfstein and Peggy Chulack for their promptness and care in typing the manuscript.

Whittier, California
January 1978

CONTENTS

PART TWO
GAINING INCREASED MOMENTUM

sophistication, etc. Excursions into expressive words that refer to ways of eating and drinking, believing and disbelieving, looking and seeing, facing the present, past, and future, and living in the city and country. How the new words you are learning have begun to influence your thinking.

A 120-item test of your achievement in *Part II*.

PART THREE
FINISHING WITH A FEELING OF COMPLETE SUCCESS

Words for poverty and wealth, direct and indirect emotions, not calling a spade a spade, banter and other light talk, animal-like contentment, homesickness, meat-eating, and different kinds of secrecy. Excursions into terms expressive of goodness, of hackneyed phraseology, of human similarity to various animals, of kinds of sound, etc. How to react to the new words you meet in your reading.

Verbs that show exhaustion, criticism, self-sacrifice, repetition, mental stagnation,

BRIEF INTERMISSIONS

HOW TO USE THIS BOOK
FOR MAXIMUM BENEFIT

1. this is not a reading book . . .

Don't read this book!

Instead, *work* with it. *Write* in it, *talk aloud* to it, *talk back* to it—use your pen or pencil, your voice, not just your eyes and mind.

Learning, *real learning,* goes on only through *active participation.*

When a new word occurs in a chapter, *say it aloud!* (The phonetic respelling will help you pronounce it correctly.)*

When you do the matching exercises, use a pen or pencil. *Write your responses!* (Check the key that immediately follows each exercise after you have filled in all the answers.)

When you do the "Yes-No," "True-False," or "Same-Opposite" exercises, use your *pen or pencil to indicate the appropriate response,* then check with the key when you have completed the whole exercise.

When you are asked to fill in words that fit definitions, *write your answers;* then check the key both to see if you have re-

---

* The system of pronunciation symbols will be thoroughly explained in Section 2 of this chapter.

sponded with the right word and also to make sure your spelling is correct.

When you do the *Review of Etymology* exercises, make sure to fill in the English word containing the prefix, root, or suffix required—use a chapter word, or any other word that comes to mind. (Coin words if you like!)

Pay special attention to the *Chapter Reviews*. Are the words still fresh in your mind? Do you remember the meaning of each root studied in the previous sessions? In these *Reviews*, you are not only testing your learning but also tightening up any areas in which you discover lacks, weaknesses, or lapses of memory.

2. master the pronunciation system!

Saying words *aloud*, and saying them *right*, is half the battle in feeling comfortable and assured with all the new words you are going to learn. Every word taught is respelled to show its pronunciation, so pay close attention to how the phonetic symbols work.

(a) *First, master the "schwa"!*

Almost every English word of two or more syllables contains one or several syllables in which the vowel sound is said *very* quickly. For example:

"*Linda* spoke to her *mother about* a *different idea* she had."

→Read the *previous sentence aloud* at *normal conversational* speed.

Read it again. Listen to how the *-a* of *Linda;* the *-er* of *mother;* the *a-* of *about;* the *-er* and *-ent* of *different;* and the *-a* of *idea* sound.

Very quick—very short! Right?

Phonetically respelled, these words are represented as:

1.	*Linda*	LIN'-də
2.	*mother*	MUTH'-ər
3.	*about*	ə-BOWT'
4.	*different*	DIF'-ər-ənt
5.	*idea*	ī-DEE'-ə

The symbol "ə," called a *schwa*, represents the quick, short vowel sound in the five words above.

Now look back at the sentence preceded by an arrow.
The italicized words are rewritten as:

1. *previous*   PREE'-vee-əs
2. *sentence*   SEN'-təns
3. *aloud*   ə-LOWD'
4. *normal*   NAWR'-məl
5. *conversational*   kon'-vər-SAY'-shən-əl

You will find ə in almost all words that are phonetically respelled throughout this book. Say the five italicized words aloud and make sure you understand how the *schwa* (ə) sounds.

(b) *Next, understand accent.*

Look at word (5) above: *conversational:* kon'-vər-SAY'-shən-əl. Note that there are *two* accent marks, one on *kon'*, another on *SAY'*. Note also that *kon'* is in lower-case letters, *SAY'* in capitals. Both syllables are stressed, but the one in capitals (*SAY'*) sounds stronger (or louder) than the one in lower case (*kon'*). Say *conversational* aloud, noting the difference.

Say these three words, taken from Chapter 3, *aloud*, noticing the variation in stress between the lower-case and the capitalized syllables:

1. *egomaniacal*   ee'-gō-mə-NĪ'-ə-kəl
2. *altercation*   awl'-tər-KAY'-shən
3. *anthropological*   an'-thrə-pə-LOJ'-ə-kəl

(c) *Be careful of the letter "S" (or "s") in phonetic respellings.* S (or s) is always *hissed*, as in *see*, *some*, *such*. After an *-n*, you will be tempted to *buzz* (or "voice") the *-s*, because final *-ns* is usually pronounced *-nz*, as in *wins*, *tons*, *owns*, etc. (Say these three words aloud—hear the *z* at the end?) *Resist the temptation!* S (or s) is *always hissed* in phonetic respellings!

Say these words aloud:

1. *ambivalence†*   am-BIV'-ə-ləns
2. *affluence*   AF'-lōō-əns
3. *opulence*   OP'-yə-ləns
4. *sentence*   SEN'-təns

† All unusual words in this chapter are taught in later chapters of the book.

(d) The symbol ī or Ī is pronounced *eye*, to rhyme with *high*, *sigh*, *my*, etc., *no matter where you find it*. For example:

1. *fights*   FĪTS
2. *spy*   SPĪ
3. *malign*   mə-LĪN′
4. *civilize*   SIV′-ə-līz′

[*I* or *i* (without the top bar) is pronounced as in *it*, *sit*, *pitch*.]

(e) *All consonants have their normal sounds.*

Except for *G* (or *g*), which is *always pronounced as in give, girl, get, go*.

1. *agree*   ə-GREE′
2. *pagan*   PAY′-gən
3. *again*   ə-GEN′

(f) *The vowel sounds are as follows:*

SYMBOL	EXAMPLE
1. A, a	*cat* (KAT)
2. E, e	*wet* (WET)
3. I, i	*sit* (SIT)
4. O, o	*knot* (NOT)
5. U, u	*nut* (NUT)
6. AH, ah	*martinet* (mahr′-tə-NET′);
7. AW, aw	*for* (FAWR); *incorrigible* (in-KAWR′-ə-jə-bəl)
8. AY, ay	*ate* (AYT); *magnate* (MAG′-nayt)
9. EE, ee	*equal* (EE′-kwəl); *clandestinely* (klan-DES′-tən-lee)
10. Ō, ō	*toe* (TŌ); *concerto* (kən-CHUR′-tō)
11. OŎ, oŏ	*book* (BOŎK); *prurient* (PROŎR′-ee-ənt)
12. OŌ, oō	*doom* (DOŌM); *blue* (BLOŌ)
13. OW, ow	*about* (ə-BOWT′)
14. OY, oy	*soil* (SOYL)
15. ING, ing	*taking* (TAYK′-ing)

(g) *TH* or *th* is pronounced as in *thing*; *TH̄* or *t̄h* is pronounced as in *this*.

3. a word (or words) on western and eastern pronunciation

In the New York City area, and in parts of New Jersey and other eastern states, the syllables *-ar*, *-er*, *-or*, *-off*, and *-aw* are pronounced somewhat differently from the way they are said in the Midwest and in the West.

In New York City, for example, the words below are generally pronounced as follows:

orange	AHR'-ənj
talk	TAWK
coffee	KAW'-fee
sorority	sə-RAHR'-ə-tee
incorrigible	in-KAHR'-ə-jə-bəl
disparage	dis-PAR'-əj (A as in HAT)
merry	MER'-ee (E as in WET)
marry	MAR'-ee (A as in HAT)
astronaut	AS'-trə-nawt'
Harry	HAR'-ee (A as in HAT)

In the Midwest and West, on the other hand, the same words are usually said approximately as follows:

orange	AWR'-ənj
talk	TOK
coffee	KOF'-ee
sorority	sə-RAWR'-ə-tee
incorrigible	in-KAWR'-ə-jə-bəl
disparage	dis-PAIR'-əj
merry	MAIR'-ee
marry	MAIR'-ee
astronaut	AS'-trə-not'
Harry	HAIR'-ee

Nothing so radical here that a person brought up in Brooklyn or the Bronx cannot understand a native of Los Angeles or San Francisco—it's just that each one thinks *the other* has an accent!

In California, for example, *Mary, merry,* and *marry* sound almost exactly alike—in New York, they are usually heard as quite different words.

(So, to be sexist for a moment, if the men at a party in Manhattan say, "Let's all make merry!", Mary doesn't feel that she is about to seduced by the males!)

In the phonetic respellings throughout the book, the western pronunciations of words with the syllables remarked on above are used. This is done largely because I myself have lived in the Los Angeles area for some fourteen years, and have had to retrain my pronunciation (having come from New York City, where I was born, and lived all my life until 1964) so that my friends and students would stop making fun of the way I speak.

Neither form of pronunciation is any better nor any more euphonious than the other. Throughout the country, pronunciation varies not only from region to region or state to state, but often from city to city! The changes are slight and subtle, but they do exist, and an expert can easily pinpoint the geographical source of a person's language patterns almost down to a few square miles in area.

If you are an Easterner, you will have no difficulty translating the pronunciations of words like *sorority, incorrigible, disparage,* and *astronaut* (all words discussed in later chapters) into your own comfortable language patterns.

4. why etymology?

Etymology (et'-ə-MOL'-ə-jee) deals with the origin or derivation of words.

When you know the meaning of a root (for example, Latin *ego,* I or self), you can better understand, and more easily remember, *all* the words built on this root.

Learn one root and you have the key that will unlock the meanings of up to ten or twenty words in which the root appears.

Learn *ego* and you can immediately get a handle on *egocentric, egomaniac, egoist, egotist,* and *alter ego.*

Learn *anthropos* (Greek, mankind), and you will quickly understand, and never forget, *anthropology, misanthropy, anthropoid, anthropocentric, anthropomorphic, philanthropy,* and *anthropo-phobia.* Meet any word with *anthropo-* in it, and you will have at least some idea of its meaning.

In the *etymological* (et'ə-mə-LOJ'-ə-kəl) approach to vocabulary building:

- You will learn about *prefixes, roots,* and *suffixes*—
- You will be able to figure out unfamiliar words by recognizing their structure, the building blocks from which they are constructed—
- You will be able to construct words correctly by learning to put these building blocks together in the proper way—and
- You will be able to derive verbs from nouns, nouns and verbs from adjectives, adjectives from nouns, etc.—and do all this correctly.

Learn how to deal with etymology and you will feel comfortable with words—you will use new words with self-assurance—you will be able to figure out thousands of words you hear or read even if you have never heard or seen these words before.

That's why the best approach to new words is through etymology‡—as you will discover for yourself as soon as you start to work on chapter 3!

5. but what are nouns, verbs, and adjectives?

You probably know.

But if you don't, you can master these parts of speech (and reference will be made to *noun forms, verb forms,* and *adjective forms* throughout the book) within the next five minutes.

(a) A *noun* is a word that can be preceded by *a, an, the, some, such,* or *my.*

An *egoist* (noun)

‡ Incidentally, Latin scholars will notice that I present a Latin verb in the first person singular, present tense (*verto,* I turn), but call it an infinitive (*verto,* to turn). I do this for two reasons: 1) *verto* is easier for a non-Latin scholar to pronounce (the actual infinitive, *vertere,* is pronounced WAIR'-tə-ray); and 2) when I studied Latin fifty years ago, the convention was to refer to a verb by using the first person singular, present tense.

If you are not a Latin scholar, you need not bother to read this footnote—if you've already done so, forget it!

Such *asceticism* (noun)

The *misogynist* (noun)

(Nouns, you will discover, often end in conventional suffixes: *-ness, -ity, -ism, -y, -ion,* etc.)

(b) A *verb* is a word that fits into the pattern, "Let us _____." A verb has a past tense.

Let us *equivocate* (verb)—past tense: *equivocated.*

Let us *alternate* (verb)—past tense: *alternated.*

Let us *philander* (verb)—past tense: *philandered.*

(Verbs, you will discover, often end in conventional suffixes: *-ate, -ize, -fy,* etc.)

(c) An *adjective* is a word that fits into the pattern, "You are very _____."

You are very *egoistic* (adjective).

You are very *introverted* (adjective).

You are very *misogynous* (adjective).

(Adjectives, you will discover, often end in conventional suffixes: *-ic, -ed, -ous, -al, -ive,* etc.)

And *adverbs,* of course, are generally formed by adding *-ly* to an adjective: *misogynous-misogynously; educational-educationally;* etc.

That's all there is to it! (Did it take more than five minutes? Maybe ten at the most?)

6. how to work for best results

If you intend to work with this book seriously (that is, if your clear intention is to add a thousand or more new words to your present vocabulary—add them permanently, unforgettably—add them so successfully that you will soon find yourself using them in speech and writing), I suggest that you give yourself every advantage by carefully following the laws of learning:

(a) *Space your learning.*

Beginning with Chapter 3, every chapter will be divided into "sessions." Each session may take one half hour to an hour and a half, depending on the amount of material and on your own speed of learning.

Do one or two sessions at a time—three if you're going strong and are all involved—and always decide when you stop *exactly when* you will return. (I remind you to do this later in the book, since such a procedure is of crucial importance.)

(b) *Do not rush—go at your own comfortable speed*.

Everyone learns at a different pace. Fast learners are no better than slow learners—it's the end result that counts, not the time it takes you to finish.

(c) *Review*.

When you start a new session, go back to the last exercise of the previous session (usually *Can you recall the words?* or *Chapter Review*), cover your answers, and test your retention—do you have quick recall after a day or so has elapsed?

(d) *Test yourself*.

You are not aiming for a grade, or putting your worth on the line, when you take the three Comprehensive Tests (Chapters 8, 13, and 17)—rather you are discovering your weaknesses, if any; deciding where repairs have to be made; and, especially, experiencing a feeling of success at work well done. (In learning, too, nothing succeeds like success!)

Use these three tests, as well as the abundant drill exercises, as aids to learning. No one is perfect, no one learns in the exact same way or at the same rate as anyone else. Find the optimum technique and speed for *your* unique learning patterns—and then give yourself every opportunity to exploit your actual, latent, and potential abilities.

But most important (*as I will remind you several times throughout the book*)—develop a routine and stick to it!

Disclaimer:

Occasionally in these pages, owing to the deficiency of the English language, I have used *he/him/his* meaning *he or she/him or her/his or her* in order to avoid awkwardness of style.

He, him, and *his* are *not* intended as exclusively masculine pronouns—they may refer to either sex or to both sexes.

Word Power
Made Easy

PART ONE

GETTING OFF TO A GOOD START

1

HOW TO TEST YOUR
PRESENT VOCABULARY

---

*Once—as a child—you were an expert, an accomplished virtuoso,
at learning new words.*

Today, by comparison, you are a rank and bumbling amateur.

Does this statement sound insulting?

It may be—but if you are the average adult, it is a statement
that is, unfortunately, only too true.

Educational testing indicates that children of ten who have
grown up in families in which English is the native language have
recognition vocabularies of over twenty thousand words—

*And that these same ten-year-olds have been learning new
words at a rate of many hundreds a year since the age of four.*

In astonishing contrast, studies show that adults who are no
longer attending school increase their vocabularies at a pace
slower than twenty-five to fifty words annually.

How do you assess your own vocabulary?

Is it quantitatively healthy?

Rich in over-all range?

Responsive to any situation in which you may find yourself?

Truly indicative of your intellectual potential?

More important, is it still growing at the same rapid clip as
when you were a child?

Or, as with most adults, has your rate of increase dropped drastically since you left school? And if so, do you now feel that your vocabulary is somewhat limited, your verbal skills not as sharp as you would like them to be?

Let us check it out.

I challenge you to a series of tests that will measure your vocabulary range, as well as your verbal speed and responsiveness.

A TEST OF VOCABULARY RANGE

Here are sixty brief phrases, each containing one italicized word; it is up to you to check the closest definition of each such word. To keep your score valid, refrain, as far as possible, from wild guessing. The key will be found at the end of the test.

1. *disheveled* appearance: (a) untidy; (b) fierce, (c) foolish, (d) peculiar, (e) unhappy
2. a *baffling* problem: (a) difficult, (b) simple, (c) puzzling, (d) long, (e) new
3. *lenient* parent: (a) tall, (b) not strict, (c) wise, (d) foolish, (e) severe
4. *repulsive* personality: (a) disgusting, (b) attractive, (c) normal, (d) confused, (e) conceited
5. *audacious* attempt: (a) useless, (b) bold, (c) foolish, (d) crazy, (e) necessary
6. *parry* a blow: (a) ward off, (b) fear, (c) expect, (d) invite, (e) ignore
7. prevalent disease: (a) dangerous, (b) catching, (c) childhood, (d) fatal, (e) widespread
8. *ominous* report: (a) loud, (b) threatening, (c) untrue, (d) serious, (e) unpleasant
9. an *incredible* story: (a) true, (b) interesting, (c) well-known, (d) unbelievable, (e) unknown
10. an *ophthalmologist:* (a) eye doctor, (b) skin doctor, (c) foot doctor, (d) heart doctor, (e) cancer specialist
11. will *supersede* the old law: (a) enforce, (b) specify penalties for, (c) take the place of, (d) repeal, (e) continue
12. an *anonymous* donor: (a) generous, (b) stingy, (c) well-known, (d) one whose name is not known, (e) reluctant

4

13. performed an *autopsy:* (a) examination of living tissue, (b) examination of a corpse to determine the cause of death, (c) process in the manufacture of optical lenses, (d) operation to cure an organic disease, (e) series of questions to determine the causes of delinquent behavior

14. an *indefatigable* worker: (a) well-paid, (b) tired, (c) skillful, (d) tireless, (e) pleasant

15. a confirmed *atheist:* (a) bachelor, (b) disbeliever in God, (c) believer in religion, (d) believer in science, (e) priest

16. endless *loquacity:* (a) misery, (b) fantasy, (c) repetitiousness, (d) ill health, (e) talkativeness

17. a *glib* talker: (a) smooth, (b) awkward, (c) loud, (d) friendly, (e) boring

18. an *incorrigible* optimist: (a) happy, (b) beyond correction or reform, (c) foolish, (d) hopeful, (e) unreasonable

19. an *ocular* problem: (a) unexpected, (b) insoluble, (c) visual, (d) continual, (e) imaginary

20. a notorious *demagogue:* (a) rabble-rouser, (b) gambler, (c) perpetrator of financial frauds, (d) liar, (e) spendthrift

21. a *naïve* attitude: (a) unwise, (b) hostile, (c) unsophisticated, (d) friendly, (e) contemptuous

22. living in *affluence:* (a) difficult circumstances, (b) countrified surroundings, (c) fear, (d) wealth, (e) poverty

23. in *retrospect:* (a) view of the past, (b) artistic balance, (c) anticipation, (d) admiration, (e) second thoughts

24. a *gourmet:* (a) seasoned traveler, (b) greedy eater, (c) vegetarian, (d) connoisseur of good food, (e) skillful chef

25. to *simulate* interest: (a) pretend, (b) feel, (c) lose, (d) stir up, (e) ask for

26. a *magnanimous* action: (a) puzzling, (b) generous, (c) foolish, (d) unnecessary, (e) wise

27. a *clandestine* meeting: (a) prearranged, (b) hurried, (c) important, (d) secret, (e) public

28. the *apathetic* citizens: (a) made up of separate ethnic groups, (b) keenly vigilant of their rights, (c) politically conservative, (d) indifferent, uninterested, uninvolved, (e) terrified

29. to *placate* his son: (a) please, (b) help, (c) find a job for, (d) make arrangements for, (e) change a feeling of hostility to one of friendliness

30. to *vacillate* continually: (a) avoid, (b) swing back and forth in indecision, (c) inject, (d) treat, (e) scold

31. a *nostalgic* feeling: (a) nauseated, (b) homesick, (c) sharp, (d) painful, (e) delighted

32. feel *antipathy:* (a) bashfulness, (b) stage fright, (c) friendliness, (d) hostility, (e) suspense

33. be more *circumspect:* (a) restrained, (b) confident, (c) cautious, (d) honest, (e) intelligent

34. an *intrepid* fighter for human rights: (a) fearless, (b) eloquent, (c) popular, (d) experienced, (e) famous

35. *diaphanous* material: (a) strong, (b) sheer and gauzy, (c) colorful, (d) expensive, (e) synthetic

36. a *taciturn* host: (a) stingy, (b) generous, (c) disinclined to conversation, (d) charming, (e) gloomy

37. to *malign* his friend: (a) accuse, (b) help, (c) disbelieve, (d) slander, (e) introduce

38. a *congenital* deformity: (a) hereditary, (b) crippling, (c) slight, (d) incurable, (e) occurring at or during birth

39. a definite *neurosis:* (a) plan, (b) emotional disturbance, (c) physical disease, (d) feeling of fear, (e) allergic reaction

40. made an *unequivocal* statement: (a) hard to understand, (b) lengthy, (c) politically motivated, (d) clear and forthright, (e) supporting

41. *vicarious* enjoyment: (a) complete, (b) unspoiled, (c) occurring from a feeling of identification with another, (d) long-continuing, (e) temporary

42. *psychogenic* ailment: (a) incurable, (b) contagious, (c) originating in the mind, (d) intestinal, (e) imaginary

43. an *anachronous* attitude: (a) unexplainable, (b) unreasonable, (c) belonging to a different time, (d) out of place, (e) unusual

44. her *iconoclastic* phase: (a) artistic, (b) sneering at tradition, (c) troubled, (d) difficult, (e) religious

45. a *tyro:* (a) dominating personality, (b) beginner, (c) accomplished musician, (d) dabbler, (e) serious student

46. a *laconic* reply: (a) immediate, (b) assured, (c) terse and meaningful, (d) unintelligible, (e) angry

47. *semantic* confusion: (a) relating to the meaning of words,

(b) pertaining to money, (c) having to do with the emotions, (d) relating to mathematics, (e) caused by inner turmoil

48. *cavalier* treatment: (a) courteous, (b) haughty and high-handed, (c) negligent, (d) affectionate, (e) expensive

49. an *anomalous* situation: (a) dangerous, (b) intriguing, (c) unusual, (d) pleasant (e) unhappy

50. *posthumous* child: (a) cranky, (b) brilliant, (c) physically weak, (d) illegitimate, (e) born after the death of the father

51. feels *enervated:* (a) full of ambition, (b) full of strength, (c) completely exhausted, (d) troubled, (e) full of renewed energy

52. shows *perspicacity:* (a) sincerity, (b) mental keenness, (c) love, (d) faithfulness, (e) longing

53. an unpopular *martinet:* (a) candidate, (b) supervisor, (c) strict disciplinarian, (d) military leader, (e) discourteous snob

54. *gregarious* person: (a) outwardly calm, (b) very sociable, (c) completely untrustworthy, (d) vicious, (e) self-effacing and timid

55. generally *phlegmatic:* (a) smug, self-satisfied, (b) easily pleased, (c) nervous, high-strung, (d) emotionally unresponsive, (e) lacking in social graces

56. an *inveterate* gambler: (a) impoverished, (b) successful, (c) habitual, (d) occasional, (e) superstitious

57. an *egregious* error: (a) outstandingly bad, (b) slight, (c) irreparable, (d) unnecessary, (e) deliberate

58. *cacophony* of a large city: (a) political administration, (b) crowded living conditions, (c) cultural advantages, (d) unpleasant noises, harsh sounds, (e) busy traffic

59. a *prurient* adolescent: (a) tall and gangling, (b) sexually longing, (c) clumsy, awkward, (d) sexually attractive, (e) soft-spoken

60. *uxorious* husband: (a) henpecked, (b) suspicious, (c) guilty of infidelity, (d) fondly and foolishly doting on his wife, (e) tightfisted, penny-pinching

---

KEY: 1–a, 2–c, 3–b, 4–a, 5–b, 6–a, 7–e, 8–b, 9–d, 10–a, 11–c, 12–d, 13–b, 14–d, 15–b, 16–e, 17–a, 18–b, 19–c, 20–a,

21–c, 22–d, 23–a, 24–d, 25–a, 26–b, 27–d, 28–d, 29–e,
30–b, 31–b, 32–d, 33–c, 34–a, 35–b, 36–c, 37–d, 38–e,
39–b, 40–d, 41–c, 42–c, 43–c, 44–b, 45–b, 46–c, 47–a,
48–b, 49–c, 50–e, 51–c, 52–b, 53–e, 54–b, 55–d, 56–c,
57–a, 58–d, 59–b, 60–d

Your score (one point for each correct choice): _____

The Meaning of Your Score:

0–11:	below average
12–35:	average
36–48:	above average
49–54:	excellent
55–60:	superior

A TEST OF VERBAL SPEED

PART 1

This is a timed test.

In no more than three minutes (time yourself, or have someone
time you), decide whether the word in column B is the *same* (or
approximately the same) in meaning as the word in column A;
opposite (or *approximately opposite*) in meaning; or whether the
two words are merely *different*.

Circle S for *same,* O for *opposite,* and D for *different.*

You will not have time to dawdle or think too long, so go as
fast as you can.

COLUMN A	COLUMN B			
1. sweet	sour	S	O	D
2. crazy	insane	S	O	D
3. stout	fat	S	O	D
4. big	angry	S	O	D
5. danger	peril	S	O	D
6. help	hinder	S	O	D

8

7. splendid	magnificent	S	O	D
8. love	hate	S	O	D
9. stand	rise	S	O	D
10. furious	violent	S	O	D
11. tree	apple	S	O	D
12. doubtful	certain	S	O	D
13. handsome	ugly	S	O	D
14. begin	start	S	O	D
15. strange	familiar	S	O	D
16. male	female	S	O	D
17. powerful	weak	S	O	D
18. beyond	under	S	O	D
19. live	die	S	O	D
20. go	get	S	O	D
21. return	replace	S	O	D
22. growl	weep	S	O	D
23. open	close	S	O	D
24. nest	home	S	O	D
25. chair	table	S	O	D
26. want	desire	S	O	D
27. can	container	S	O	D
28. idle	working	S	O	D
29. rich	luxurious	S	O	D
30. building	structure	S	O	D

PART 2

This is also a timed test.

In no more than three minutes (again, time yourself or have someone time you), write down as many *different* words as you can think of that start with the letter *D*.

Do *not* use various forms of a word, such as *do, doing, does, done, doer,* etc.

Space is provided for 125 words. You are not expected to reach that number, but write as fast as you can and see how many blanks you can fill in before your time is up.

1. _____

2. _____
3. _____
4. _____
5. _____
6. _____
7. _____
8. _____
9. _____
10. _____
11. _____
12. _____
13. _____
14. _____
15. _____
16. _____
17. _____
18. _____
19. _____
20. _____
21. _____
22. _____
23. _____
24. _____
25. _____
26. _____
27. _____
28. _____
29. _____
30. _____
31. _____
32. _____

33. _____
34. _____
35. _____
36. _____
37. _____
38. _____
39. _____
40. _____
41. _____
42. _____
43. _____
44. _____
45. _____
46. _____
47. _____
48. _____
49. _____
50. _____
51. _____
52. _____
53. _____
54. _____
55. _____
56. _____
57. _____
58. _____
59. _____
60. _____
61. _____
62. _____
63. _____

64. _____
65. _____
66. _____
67. _____
68. _____
69. _____
70. _____
71. _____
72. _____
73. _____
74. _____
75. _____
76. _____
77. _____
78. _____
79. _____
80. _____
81. _____
82. _____
83. _____
84. _____
85. _____
86. _____
87. _____
88. _____
89. _____
90. _____
91. _____
92. _____
93. _____
94. _____

95. _____
96. _____
97. _____
98. _____
99. _____
100. _____
101. _____
102. _____
103. _____
104. _____
105. _____
106. _____
107. _____
108. _____
109. _____
110. _____
111. _____
112. _____
113. _____
114. _____
115. _____
116. _____
117. _____
118. _____
119. _____
120. _____
121. _____
122. _____
123. _____
124. _____
125. _____

KEY: Part 1: 1–O, 2–S, 3–S, 4–D, 5–S, 6–O, 7–S, 8–O, 9–S, 10–S, 11–D, 12–O, 13–O, 14–S, 15–O, 16–O, 17–O, 18–D, 19–O, 20–D, 21–S, 22–D, 23–O, 24–S, 25–D, 26–S, 27–S, 28–O, 29–S, 30–S

Part 2: Any English word starting with *D* is correct unless it is merely another form of a previous word on the list.

Scoring:

PART 1

If you have up to 10 correct answers, credit your score with 25 points.

If you have 11–20 correct answers, credit your score with 50 points.

21–25 correct answers—75 points.

26–30 correct answers—100 points.

Your Score on Part 1:_____

PART 2

Up to 30 words:	25 points
31–50 words:	50 points
51–70 words:	75 points
71–125 words:	100 points

Your Score on Part 2:_____

TOTAL SCORE

On Verbal Speed:_____

The meaning of your verbal speed score:

50:	below average
75:	average
100:	above average
125–150:	excellent
175–200:	superior

14

A TEST OF VERBAL RESPONSIVENESS

PART 1

Write in the blank in column B a word starting with the letter *P* that is the *same,* or *approximately the same,* in meaning as the word given in column A.

Example: look   peer _____

Warning: Every answer *must* start with the letter *P*.

A	B		A	B
1. bucket	_____	15. stone	_____
2. trousers	_____	16. inactive	_____
3. maybe	_____	17. fussy	_____
4. forgive	_____	18. suffering	_____
5. separate	_____	19. castle	_____
6. likely	_____	20. gasp	_____
7. annoy	_____	21. fear	_____
8. good-looking	_____	22. twosome	_____
9. picture	_____	23. artist	_____
10. choose	_____	24. sheet	_____
11. ugly	_____	25. collection	_____
12. go	_____		
13. dish	_____		
14. location	_____		

PART 2

Write in the blank in column B a word starting with the letter *G* that is *opposite, approximately opposite,* or *in contrast to* the word given in column A.

Example: stop   *go*

Warning: Every answer *must* start with the letter *G*.

A	B		A	B
1. lose	_____	5. take	_____
2. midget	_____	6. moron	_____
3. special	_____	7. sad	_____
4. lady	_____	8. boy	_____

9. happy	————	18. rough	————
10. plain	————	19. bride	————
11. hello	————	20. ripe	————
12. here	————	21. unwanting	————
13. bad	————	22. unprotected	————
14. ugly	————	23. experienced	————
15. stingy	————	24. scarcity	————
16. awkward	————	25. unappreciative	————
17. little	————		

KEY, Part 1: If more than one answer is given, count as correct any word you have written that is the same as any *one* of the answers.

1–pail, pan, 2–pants, 3–perhaps, possibly, probably, 4–pardon, 5–part, 6–probable, possible, perhaps, 7–pester, 8–pretty, 9–photograph, painting, 10–pick, 11–plain, 12–proceed, 13–plate, platter, 14–place, 15–pebble, 16–passive, 17–particular, picky, 18–pain, 19–palace, 20–pant, puff, 21–panic, 22–pair, 23–painter, 24–page, 25–pack

Part 2: If more than one answer is given, count as correct any word you have written that is the same as any *one* of the answers.

1–gain, get, garner, grab, glean, grasp, grip, 2–giant, gigantic, great, gross, 3–general, 4–gentleman, 5–give, 6–genius, 7–glad, gleeful, gleesome, 8–girl, 9–gloomy, glum, grieving, grumpy, 10–gaudy, grand, grandiose, 11–goodbye, 12–gone, 13–good, 14–good-looking, 15–generous, giving, 16–graceful, 17–great, giant, gigantic, 18–gentle, 19–groom, 20–green, 21–greedy, grasping, 22–guarded, 23–green, 24–glut, gobs, 25–grateful

---

Scoring:

Score Parts 1 and 2 together. Write in the blank the *total* number of correct responses you made: ————————.

The meaning of your verbal responsiveness score:

0–10:	below average
11–20:	average
21–30:	above average
31–40:	excellent
41–50:	superior

VOCABULARY AND SUCCESS

Now you know where you stand. If you are in the below average or average group, you must consider, seriously, whether an inadequate vocabulary may be holding you back. (If you tested out on the above average, excellent, or superior level, you have doubtless already discovered the unique and far-reaching value of a rich vocabulary, and you are eager to add still further to your knowledge of words.)

Let us examine, briefly, some of the evidence that points to the close relationship between vocabulary and personal, professional, and intellectual growth.

The Human Engineering Laboratory found that the *only* common characteristic of successful people in this country is an unusual grasp of the meanings of words. The Laboratory tested the vocabularies of thousands of people in all age groups and in all walks of life—and discovered that those people drawing down the highest salaries made the highest scores. Consider very thoughtfully the explanation that the director of the Laboratory offered for the relationship between vocabulary and success:

"Why do large vocabularies characterize executives and possibly outstanding men and women in other fields? The final answer seems to be that words are the instruments by means of which men and women grasp the thoughts of others and with which they do much of their own thinking. They are the tools of thought."

There is other evidence.

At many universities, groups of freshmen were put into experimental classes for the sole purpose of increasing their knowledge of English words. *These groups did better in their sophomore, junior, and senior years than control groups of similarly endowed students who did not receive such training.*

17

And still more evidence:

At the University of Illinois, entering students were given a simple twenty-nine-word vocabulary test. The results of this test could be used, according to Professor William D. Templeman, to make an accurate prediction of future academic success—or lack of success—over the entire four year college course. "If a student has a superior vocabulary," states Professor Templeman, "it will probably follow that he will do better work academically."

And finally:

Educational research has discovered that your I.Q. is intimately related to your vocabulary. Take a standard vocabulary test and then an intelligence test—the results in both will be substantially the same.

YOU CAN INCREASE YOUR VOCABULARY

The more extensive your vocabulary, the better your chances for success, other things being equal—success in attaining your educational goals, success in moving ahead in your business or professional career, success in achieving your intellectual potential.

And you *can* increase your vocabulary—faster and easier than you may realize.

You can, in fact, accomplish a tremendous gain in less than two to three months of concentrated effort, even if you do only one session a day—in less time if you do two or more sessions a day.

Furthermore—

You can start improving your vocabulary immediately—and within a few days you can be cruising along at such a rapid rate that there will be an actual change in your thinking, in your ability to express your thoughts, and in your powers of understanding.

Does this sound as if I am promising you the whole world in a neat package with a pretty pink ribbon tied around it? I am. And I am willing to make such an unqualified promise because I have seen what happens to those of my students at New York University and at Rio Hondo College in Whittier, California, who make sincere, methodical efforts to learn more, many more, words.

HOW TO START BUILDING YOUR VOCABULARY

When you have finished working with this book, you will no longer be the same person.

You can't be.

If you honestly read every page, if you do every exercise, if you take every test, if you follow every principle, you will go through an intellectual experience that will effect a radical change in you.

For if you systematically increase your vocabulary, you will also sharpen and enrich your thinking; push back your intellectual horizons; build your self-assurance; improve your facility in handling the English language and thereby your ability to express your thoughts effectively; and acquire a deeper understanding of the world in general and of yourself in particular.

Increasing your vocabulary does not mean merely learning the definitions of large numbers of obscure words; it does not mean memorizing scores of unrelated terms. What it means—what it can only mean—is becoming acquainted with the multitudinous and fascinating phenomena of human existence for which words are, obviously, only the verbal descriptions.

Increasing your vocabulary—properly, intelligently, and systematically—means treating yourself to an all-round, liberal education.

And surely you cannot deny that such an experience will change you intellectually—

Will have a discernible effect on your methods of thinking—on your store of information—on your ability to express your ideas —on your understanding of human problems.

HOW CHILDREN INCREASE THEIR VOCABULARIES

The typical ten-year-old, you will recall, has a recognition vocabulary of over twenty thousand words—and has been learning many hundreds of new words every year since the age of four.

You were once that typical child.

You were once an accomplished virtuoso at vocabulary building.

What was your secret?

Did you spend hours every day poring over a dictionary?

Did you lull yourself to sleep at night with Webster's Unabridged?

Did you keep notebooks full of all the new words you ever heard or read?

Did you immediately look up the meaning of any new word that your parents or older members of your family used?

Such procedures would have struck you as absurd then, as absurd as they would be for you today.

You had a much better, much more effective, and considerably less self-conscious method.

Your method was the essence of simplicity: day in and day out you kept learning; you kept squeezing every possible ounce of learning out of every waking moment; you were an eternal question box, for you had a constant and insatiable desire to know and understand.

HOW ADULTS STOP BUILDING THEIR VOCABULARIES

Then, eventually, at some point in your adult life (unless you are the rare exception), you gradually lost your compulsive drive to discover, to figure out, to understand, to know.

Eventually, therefore, you gradually lost your need to increase your vocabulary—your need to learn the words that could verbalize your new discoveries, your new understanding, your new knowledge.

Roland Gelatt, in a review of Caroline Pratt's book *I Learn from Children,* describes this phenomenon as follows:

All normal human beings are born with a powerful urge to learn. Almost all of them lose this urge, even before they have reached maturity. It is only the few . . . who are so constituted that lack of learning becomes a nuisance. This is perhaps the most insidious of human tragedies.

Children are wonders at increasing their vocabularies because of their "powerful urge to learn." They do not learn solely by means of words, but as their knowledge increases, so does their vocabulary—for words are the symbols of ideas and understanding.

(If you are a parent, you perhaps remember that crucial and trying period in which your child constantly asked "Why?" The "Why?" is the child's method of finding out. How many adults that you know go about asking and thinking "Why?" How often do you yourself do it?)

The adults who "lose this urge," who no longer feel that "lack of learning becomes a nuisance," stop building their vocabularies. They stop learning, they stop growing intellectually, they stop changing. When and if such a time comes, then, as Mr. Gelatt so truly says, "This is perhaps the most insidious of human tragedies." But fortunately the process is far from irreversible.

21

If you have lost the "powerful urge to learn," you can regain it—you can regain your need to discover, to figure out, to understand, to know.

And thus you can start increasing your vocabulary at the same rate as when you were a child.

I am not spouting airy theory. For over thirty-five years I have worked with thousands of adults in my college courses in vocabulary improvement, and I can state as a fact, and without qualification, that:

If you can recapture the "powerful urge to learn" with which you were born, you can go on increasing your vocabulary at a prodigious rate—

No matter what your present age.

WHY AGE MAKES LITTLE DIFFERENCE IN VOCABULARY BUILDING

I repeat, *no matter what your present age.*

You may be laboring under a delusion common to many older people.

You may think that after you pass your twenties you rapidly and inevitably lose your ability to learn.

That is simply not true.

There is no doubt that the years up to eighteen or twenty are the best period for learning. Your own experience no doubt bears that out. And of course *for most people* more learning goes on faster up to the age of eighteen or twenty than ever after, even if they live to be older than Methuselah. (That is why vocabulary increases so rapidly for the first twenty years of life and comparatively at a snail's pace thereafter.)

But (and follow me closely)—

The fact that most learning is accomplished before the age of twenty does not mean that very little learning can be achieved beyond that age.

What *is* done by most people and what *can* be done under proper guidance and motivation are two very, very different things—as scientific experiments have conclusively shown.

22

Furthermore—

The fact that your learning ability may be best up to age twenty does not mean that it is absolutely useless as soon as your twentieth birthday is passed.

Quite the contrary.

Edward Thorndike, the famous educational psychologist, found in experiments with people of all ages that although the learning curve rises spectacularly up to twenty, it remains steady for at least another five years. After that, ability to learn (according to Professor Thorndike) drops very, very slowly up to the age of thirty-five, and drops a bit more but *still slowly* beyond that age.

And—

Right up to senility the *total* decrease in learning ability after age twenty is never more than 15 per cent!

That does not sound, I submit, as if no one can ever learn anything new after the age of twenty.

Believe me, the old saw that claims you cannot teach an old dog new tricks is a baseless, if popular, superstition.

So I repeat: no matter what your age, you can go on learning efficiently, or start learning once again if perhaps you have stopped.

You can be thirty, or forty, or fifty, or sixty, or seventy—or older.

No matter what your age, you can once again increase your vocabulary at a prodigious rate—providing you recapture the "powerful urge to learn" that is the key to vocabulary improvement.

Not the urge to learn "words"—words are only symbols of ideas.

But the urge to learn facts, theories, concepts, information, knowledge, understanding—call it what you will.

Words are the symbols of knowledge, the keys to accurate thinking. Is it any wonder then that the most successful and intelligent people in this country have the biggest vocabularies?

It was not their large vocabularies that made these people successful and intelligent, but their *knowledge*.

Knowledge, however, is gained largely through words.

In the process of increasing their knowledge, these successful people increased their vocabularies.

Just as children increase *their* vocabulary at a tremendous, phenomenal rate during those years when their knowledge is increasing most rapidly.

Knowledge is chiefly in the form of words, and from now on, in this book, you will be thinking *about,* and thinking *with,* new words and new ideas.

WHAT THIS BOOK CAN DO FOR YOU

This book is designed to get you started building your vocabulary—effectively and at jet-propelled speed—by helping you regain the intellectual atmosphere, the keen, insatiable curiosity, the "powerful urge to learn" of your childhood.

The organization of the book is based on two simple principles: 1) words are the verbal symbols of ideas, and 2) the more ideas you are familiar with, the more words you know.

So, chapter by chapter, we will start with some central idea—personality types, doctors, science, unusual occupations, liars, actions, speech habits, insults, compliments, etc.—and examine ten basic words that express various aspects of the idea. Then, using each word as a springboard, we will explore any others which are related to it in meaning or derivation, so that it is not unlikely that a single chapter may discuss, teach, and test close to one hundred important words.

Always, however, the approach will be from the idea. First there will be a "teaser preview" in which the ideas are briefly hinted at; then a "headline," in which each idea is examined somewhat more closely; next a clear, detailed paragraph or more will analyze the idea in all its ramifications; finally the word itself, which you will meet only after you are completely familiar with the idea.

In the *etymology* (derivation of words) section, you will learn what Greek or Latin root gives the word its unique meaning and what other words contain the same, or related, roots. You will thus be continually working in related fields, and there will never be any possibility of confusion from "too muchness," despite the great number of words taken up and tested in each chapter.

Successful people have superior vocabularies. People who are intellectually alive and successful in the professional or business worlds are accustomed to dealing with ideas, are constantly on the search for new ideas, build their lives and their careers on the ideas they have learned. And it is to readers whose goal is *successful* living (in the broadest meaning of the word *successful*) that this book is addressed.

A NOTE ON TIME SCHEDULES

From my experience over many years in teaching, I have become a firm believer in setting a goal for all learning and a schedule for reaching that goal.

You will discover that each chapter is divided into approximately equal sessions, and that each session will take from thirty to forty-five minutes of your time, depending on how rapidly or slowly you enjoy working—and bear in mind that everyone has an optimum rate of learning.

For best results, do one or two sessions at a time—spaced studying, with time between sessions so that you can assimilate what you have learned, is far more efficient, far more productive, than gobbling up great amounts in indigestible chunks.

Come back to the book every day, or as close to every day as the circumstances of your life permit.

Find a schedule that is comfortable for you, and then stick to it.

Avoid interrupting your work until you have completed a full session, and always decide, before you stop, *exactly when* you will plan to pick up the book again.

Working at your own comfortable rate, you will likely finish the material in two to three months, give or take a few weeks either way.

However long you take, you will end with a solid feeling of accomplishment, a new understanding of how English words work, and—most important—how to make words work for you.

3

HOW TO TALK ABOUT
PERSONALITY TYPES

(Sessions 1–3)

TEASER PREVIEW

What word best describes your personality if you:

- *are interested solely in your own welfare?*
- *constantly talk about yourself?*
- *dedicate your life to helping others?*
- *turn your mind inward?*
- *turn your mind outward?*
- *hate humanity?*
- *hate women?*
- *hate marriage?*
- *lead a lonely, austere existence?*

SESSION 1

Every human being is, in one way or another, unique.

Everyone's personality is determined by a combination of genetic and environmental factors.

Let us examine ten personality types (one of which might by chance be your very own) that result from the way culture, growth, family background, and environment interact with heredity.

And, of course, we begin not with the words, but with the ideas.

IDEAS

1. me first

Your attitude to life is simple, direct, and aboveboard—every decision you make is based on the answer to one question: "What's in it for me?" If your selfishness, greed, and ruthless desire for self-advancement hurt other people, that's too bad. "This is a tough world, pal, dog eat dog and all that, and I, for one, am not going to be left behind!"

An *egoist*

2. the height of conceit

"Now, let's see. Have you heard about all the money I'm making? Did I tell you about my latest amorous conquest? Let me give you my opinion—I know, because I'm an expert at practically everything!" You are boastful to the point of being obnoxious—you have only one string to your conversational violin, namely, *your-*

27

self; and on it you play a number of monotonous variations: what *you* think, what *you* have done, how good *you* are, how *you* would solve the problems of the world, etc. ad nauseam.

An egotist

3. let me help you

You have discovered the secret of true happiness—concerning yourself with the welfare of others. Never mind your own interests, how's the next fellow getting along?

An altruist

4. leave me alone

Like a biochemist studying a colony of bacteria under the microscope, you minutely examine your every thought, feeling, and action. Probing, futile questions like "What do other people think of me?", "How do I look?", and "Maybe I shouldn't have said that?" are your constant nagging companions, for you are unable to realize that other people do not spend as much time and energy analyzing you as you think.

You may seem unsocial, yet your greatest desire is to be liked and accepted. You may be shy and quiet, you are often moody and unhappy, and you prefer solitude or at most the company of one person to a crowd. You have an aptitude for creative work and are uncomfortable engaging in activities that require cooperation with other people. You may even be a genius, or eventually turn into one.

An introvert

5. let's do it together

You would be great as a teacher, counselor, administrator, insurance agent. You can always become interested—sincerely, vitally interested—in other people's problems. You're the life of the party, because you never worry about the effect of your actions, never inhibit yourself with doubts about dignity or propriety. You are usually happy, generally full of high spirits; you love to be with people—lots of people. Your thoughts, your interests, your whole personality are turned outward.

An *extrovert*

6. neither extreme

You have both introverted and extroverted tendencies—at different times and on different occasions. Your interests are turned, in about equal proportions, both inward and outward. Indeed, you're quite normal—in the sense that your personality is like that of most people.

An *ambivert*

7. people are no damn good

Cynical, embittered, suspicious, you hate everyone. (Especially, but never to be admitted, *yourself?*) The perfectibility of the human race? "Nonsense! No way!" The stupidity, the meanness, and the crookedness of most mortals ("Most? Probably all!")—that is your favorite theme.

A *misanthrope*

8. women are no damn good

Sometime in your dim past, you were crossed, scorned, or deeply wounded by a woman (a mother, or mother figure, perhaps?). So now you have a carefully constructed defense against further hurt —you hate *all* women.

A *misogynist*

9. "marriage is an institution—and who wants to live in an institution?"

You will not make the ultimate *legal* commitment. Members of the opposite sex are great as lovers, roommates, apartment- or house-sharers, but *not* as lawfully wedded spouses. The ties that

29

bind are too binding for you. You may possibly believe, and possibly, for yourself, be right, that a commitment is deeper and more meaningful if freedom is available without judicial proceedings.

A misogamist

10. ". . . that the flesh is heir to . . ."

Self-denial, austerity, lonely contemplation—these are the characteristics of the good life, so you claim. The simplest food and the least amount of it that will keep body and soul together, combined with abstinence from fleshly, earthly pleasures, will eventually lead to spiritual perfection—that is your philosophy.

An ascetic

USING THE WORDS

You have been introduced to ten valuable words—but in each case, as you have noticed, you have first considered the ideas that these words represent. Now *say* the words—each one is respelled phonetically so that you will be sure to pronounce it correctly.*

Say each word aloud. This is the first important step to complete mastery. As you hear a word in your own voice, think of its meaning. Are you quite clear about it? If not, reinforce your learning by rereading the explanatory paragraph or paragraphs.

Can you pronounce the words?

1.	*egoist*	EE′-gō-ist
2.	*egotist*	EE′-gō-tist
3.	*altruist*	AL′-trōō-ist
4.	*introvert*	IN′-trə-vurt′
5.	*extrovert*	EKS′-trə-vurt′
6.	*ambivert*	AM′-bə-vurt′

* See Introduction, Section 2, *Master the pronunciation system.*

30

7. *misanthrope*   MIS'-ən-thrŏp'
8. *misogynist*   mə-SOJ'-ə-nist
9. *misogamist*   mə-SOG'-ə-mist
10. *ascetic*   ə-SET'-ik

Can you work with the words?

You have taken two long steps toward mastery of the expressive words in this chapter—you have thought about the ideas behind them, and you have said them aloud.

For your third step, match each personality with the appropriate characteristic, action, or attitude.

1. egoist   a. turns thoughts inward
2. egotist   b. hates marriage
3. altruist   c. talks about accomplishments
4. introvert   d. hates people
5. extrovert   e. does not pursue pleasures of
                        the flesh
6. ambivert   f. is interested in the welfare of
                        others
7. misanthrope   g. believes in self-advancement
8. misogynist   h. turns thoughts both inward
                        and outward
9. misogamist   i. hates women
10. ascetic   j. turns thoughts outward

KEY: 1–g, 2–c, 3–f, 4–a, 5–j, 6–h, 7–d, 8–i, 9–b, 10–e

Do you understand the words?

Now that you are becoming more and more involved in these ten words, find out if they can make an immediate appeal to your understanding. Here are ten questions—can you indicate, quickly,

31

and without reference to any previous definitions, whether the correct answer to each of these questions is *yes* or *no?*

1. Is an *egoist* selfish?	YES	NO
2. Is modesty one of the characteristics of the *egotist?*	YES	NO
3. Is an *altruist* selfish?	YES	NO
4. Does an *introvert* pay much attention to himself?	YES	NO
5. Does an *extrovert* prefer solitude to companionship?	YES	NO
6. Are most normal people *ambiverts?*	YES	NO
7. Does a *misanthrope* like people?	YES	NO
8. Does a *misogynist* enjoy the company of women?	YES	NO
9. Does an *ascetic* lead a life of luxury?	YES	NO
10. Does a *misogamist* try to avoid marriage?	YES	NO

KEY: 1–yes, 2–no, 3–no, 4–yes, 5–no, 6–yes, 7–no, 8–no, 9–no, 10–yes

Can you recall the words?

You have thus far reinforced your learning by saying the words aloud, by matching them to their definitions, and by responding to meaning when they were used in context.

Can you recall each word, now, without further reference to previous material? And can you spell it correctly?

1. Who lives a lonely, austere life? 1. A_____
2. Whose interests are turned outward? 2. E_____
3. Who is supremely selfish? 3. E_____
4. Who hates people? 4. M_____
5. Whose interests are turned both inward and outward? 5. A_____

6. Who is incredibly conceited?   6. E_____
7. Who is more interested in the   7. A_____
   welfare of others than in his
   own?
8. Who hates women?   8. M_____
9. Whose interests are turned   9. I_____
   inward?
10. Who hates marriage?   10. M_____

KEY: 1–ascetic, 2–extrovert, 3–egoist, 4–misanthrope, 5–ambivert, 6–egotist, 7–altruist, 8–misogynist, 9–introvert, 10–misogamist

---

(End of Session 1)

SESSION 2

ORIGINS AND RELATED WORDS

Every word in the English language has a history—and these ten are no exception. In this section you will learn a good deal more about the words you have been working with; in addition, you will make excursions into many other words allied either in meaning, form, or history to our basic ten.

1. the ego

Egoist and *egotist* are built on the same Latin root—the pronoun *ego,* meaning *I. I* is the greatest concern in the *egoist's* mind, the most overused word in the *egotist's* vocabulary. (Keep the words differentiated in your own mind by thinking of the *t* in *talk*, and the additional *t* in *egotist*.) *Ego* itself has been taken over from Latin as an important English word and is commonly used to denote one's concept of oneself, as in, "What do you think your constant criticisms do to my *ego?*" *Ego* has also a special meaning in psychology—but for the moment you have enough problems without going into *that*.

If you are an *egocentric* (ee′-gō-SEN′-trik), you consider yourself the *center* of the universe—you are an extreme form of the *egoist*. And if you are an *egomaniac* (ee′-gō-MAY′-nee-ak), you carry *egoism* to such an extreme that your needs, desires, and interests have become a morbid obsession, a *mania*. The *egoist* or *egotist* is obnoxious, the *egocentric* is intolerable, and the *egomaniac* is dangerous and slightly mad.

Egocentric is both a noun ("What an *egocentric* her new roommate is!") and an adjective ("He is the most *egocentric* person I have ever met!").

To derive the adjective form of *egomaniac*, add *-al*, a common adjective suffix. Say the adjective aloud:

egomaniacal   ee′-gō-mə-NĪ′-ə-kəl

2. others

In Latin, the word for *other* is *alter*, and a number of valuable English words are built on this root.

Altruism (AL′-trōō-iz-əm), the philosophy practiced by *altruists*, comes from one of the variant spellings of Latin *alter*, other. *Altruistic* (al-trōō-IS′-tik) actions look toward the benefit of *others*. If you *alternate* (AWL′-tər-nayt′), you skip one and take the *other*, so to speak, as when you play golf on *alternate* (AWL′-tər-nət) Saturdays.

An *alternate* (AWL′-tər-nət) in a debate, contest, or convention is the *other* person who will take over if the original choice is unable to attend. And if you have no *alternative* (awl-TUR′-nə-tiv), you have no *other* choice.

You see how easy it is to understand the meanings of these words once you realize that they all come from the same source.

And keeping in mind that *alter* means *other,* you can quickly understand words like *alter ego, altercation,* and *alteration.*

An *alteration* (awl'-tə-RAY'-shən) is of course a change—a making into something *other.* When you *alter* (AWL'-tər) your plans, you make *other* plans.

An *altercation* (awl'-tər-KAY'-shən) is a verbal dispute. When you have an *altercation* with someone, you have a violent disagreement, a "fight" with words. And why? Because you have *other* ideas, plans, or opinions than those of the person on the *other* side of the argument. *Altercation,* by the way, is stronger than *quarrel* or *dispute*—the sentiment is more heated, the disagreement is likely to be angry or even hot-tempered, there may be recourse, if the disputants are human, to profanity or obscenity. You have *altercations,* in short, over pretty important issues, and the word implies that you get quite excited.

Alter ego (AWL'-tər EE'-gō), which combines *alter,* other, with *ego,* I, self, generally refers to someone with whom you are so close that you both do the same things, think alike, react similarly, and are, in temperament, almost mirror images of each other. Any such friend is your *other I,* your *other self,* your *alter ego.*

USING THE WORDS

Can you pronounce the words?

Digging a little into the derivation of three of our basic words, *egoist, egotist,* and *altruist,* has put us in touch with two important Latin roots, *ego,* I, self, and *alter,* other, and has made it possible for us to explore, with little difficulty, many other words derived from these roots. Pause now, for a moment, to digest these new acquisitions, and to say them *aloud.*

1. *ego*	EE'-gō
2. *egocentric*	ee-gō-SEN'-trik
3. *egomaniac*	ee-gō-MAY'-nee-ak
4. *egomaniacal*	ee'-gō-mə-NĪ'-ə-kəl

5. *altruism*	AL'-trōō-iz-əm
6. *altruistic*	al-trōō-IS'-tik
7. to *alternate* (*v.*)	AWL'-tər-nayt'
8. *alternate* (*adj.* or *noun*)	AWL'-tər-nət
9. *alternative*	awl-TUR'-nə-tiv
10. *alteration*	awl'-tər-AY'-shən
11. to *alter*	AWL'-tər
12. *altercation*	awl'-tər-KAY'-shən
13. *alter ego*	AWL'-tər EE'-gō

Can you work with the words? (I)

You have seen how these thirteen words derive from the two Latin roots *ego,* I, self, and *alter,* other, and you have pronounced them aloud and thereby begun to make them part of your active vocabulary.

Are you ready to match definitions to words?

1. ego
2. egocentric
3. altruism
4. to alternate
5. to alter
6. altercation

a. one who is excessively fixated on his own desires, needs, etc.
b. to change
c. argument
d. one's concept of oneself
e. to take one, skip one, etc.
f. philosophy of putting another's welfare above one's own

KEY: 1–d, 2–a, 3–f, 4–e, 5–b, 6–c

Can you work with the words? (II)

1. egomaniacal
2. altruistic
3. alternative

a. a change
b. other possible
c. interested in the welfare of others

4. alteration
5. alter ego
6. alternate (*adj.*)

d. one's other self
e. a choice
f. morbidly, obsessively wrapped up in oneself

KEY: 1–f, 2–c, 3–e, 4–a ,5–d, 6–b

Do you understand the words?

If you have begun to understand these thirteen words, you will be able to respond to the following questions.

1. Is rejection usually a blow to one's *ego*?	YES	NO
2. Are *egocentric* people easy to get along with?	YES	NO
3. Does an *egomaniac* have a normal personality?	YES	NO
4. Are *egomaniacal* tendencies a sign of maturity?	YES	NO
5. Is *altruism* a characteristic of selfish people?	YES	NO
6. Are *altruistic* tendencies common to egoists?	YES	NO
7. Is an *alternate* plan necessarily inferior?	YES	NO
8. Does an *alternative* allow you some freedom of choice?	YES	NO
9. Does *alteration* imply keeping things the same?	YES	NO
10. Do excitable people often engage in *altercations*?	YES	NO
11. Is your *alter ego* usually quite similar to yourself?	YES	NO

KEY: 1–yes, 2–no, 3–no, 4–no, 5–no, 6–no, 7–no, 8–yes, 9–no, 10–yes, 11–yes

---

Can you recall the words?

Have you learned these words so well that you can summon each one from your mind when a brief definition is offered? Review first if necessary; then, without further reference to previous pages, write the correct word in each blank. Make sure to check your spelling when you refer to the Key.

1. one's other self	1. A_____
2. to change	2. A_____
3. a heated dispute	3. A_____
4. excessively, morbidly obsessed with one's own needs, desires, or ambitions	4. E_____
5. unselfish; more interested in the welfare of others than in one's own	5. A_____
6. utterly involved with oneself; self-centered	6. E_____
7. a choice	7. A_____
8. one who substitutes for another	8. A_____

KEY: 1–alter ego, 2–alter, 3–altercation, 4–egomaniacal, 5–altruistic, 6–egocentric, 7–alternative, 8–alternate

(*End of Session 2*)

SESSION 3

ORIGINS AND RELATED WORDS

1. depends how you turn

Introvert, extrovert, and *ambivert* are built on the Latin verb *verto,* to turn. If your thoughts are constantly turned inward (*intro-*), you are an *introvert;* outward (*extro-*), an *extrovert;* and in both directions (*ambi-*), an *ambivert.* The prefix *ambi-,* both, is also found in *ambidextrous* (am'-bə-DEKS'-trəs), *able to use both hands with equal skill.* The noun is *ambidexterity* (am'-bə-deks-TAIR'-ə-tee).

Dexterous (DEKS'-tə-rəs) means *skillful,* the noun *dexterity* (deks-TAIR'-ə-tee) is *skill.* The ending *-ous* is a common adjective suffix (*famous, dangerous, perilous,* etc.); *-ity* is a common noun suffix (*vanity, quality, simplicity,* etc.).

(Spelling caution: Note that the letter following the *t-* in *ambidextrous* is *-r,* but that in dexterous the next letter is *-e.*)

Dexter is actually the Latin word for *right hand*—in the *ambidextrous* person, both hands are *right hands,* so to speak.

The right hand is traditionally the more skillful one; it is only within recent decades that we have come to accept that "lefties" or "southpaws" are just as normal as anyone else—and the term *left-handed* is still used as a synonym of *awkward.*

The Latin word for the *left hand* is *sinister.* This same word, in English, means *threatening, evil,* or *dangerous,* a further commentary on our early suspiciousness of left-handed persons. There may still be some parents who insist on forcing left-handed children to change (though left-handedness is inherited, and as much an integral part of its possessor as eye color or nose shape), with various unfortunate results to the child—sometimes stuttering or an inability to read with normal skill.

The French word for the *left hand* is *gauche,* and, as you would suspect, when we took this word over into English we invested it with an uncomplimentary meaning. Call someone *gauche* (GŌSH) and you imply clumsiness, generally social rather than physical. (We're right back to our age-old misconception that left-handed people are less skillful than right-handed ones.) A *gauche* remark is tactless; a *gauche* offer of sympathy is so bumbling as to be embarrassing; *gaucherie* (GŌ'-shə-ree) is an awkward, clumsy, tactless, embarrassing way of saying things or of handling situations. The *gauche* person is totally without finesse.

And the French word for the *right hand* is *droit,* which we have used in building our English word *adroit* (ə-DROYT'). Needless to say, *adroit,* like *dexterous,* means *skillful,* but especially in the exercise of the mental facilities. Like *gauche, adroit,* or its noun *adroitness,* usually is used figuratively. The *adroit* person is quick-witted, can get out of difficult spots cleverly, can handle situations ingeniously. *Adroitness* is, then, quite the opposite of *gaucherie.*

2. love, hate, and marriage

Misanthrope, misogynist, and *misogamist* are built on the Greek root *misein,* to hate. The *misanthrope* hates mankind (Greek *anthropos,* mankind); the *misogynist* hates women (Greek *gyne,* woman); the *misogamist* hates marriage (Greek *gamos,* marriage).

Anthropos, mankind, is also found in *anthropology* (an-thrə-POL'-ə-jee), the study of the development of the human race; and in *philanthropist* (fə-LAN'-thrə-pist), one who loves mankind and shows such love by making substantial financial contributions to charitable organizations or by donating time and energy to helping those in need.

The root *gyne,* woman, is also found in *gynecologist* (gīn-ə-KOL'-ə-jist *or* jin-ə-KOL'-ə-jist), the medical specialist who treats female disorders. And the root *gamos,* marriage, occurs also in *monogamy* (mə-NOG'-ə-mee), *bigamy* (BIG'-ə-mee), and *polygamy* (pə-LIG'-ə-mee).

(As we will discover later, *monos* means *one, bi-* means *two, polys* means *many.*)

So *monogamy* is the custom of only *one* marriage (at a time).

Bigamy, by etymology, is *two* marriages—in actuality, the unlawful act of contracting another marriage without divorcing one's current legal spouse.

And *polygamy,* by derivation *many* marriages, and therefore etymologically denoting plural marriage for either males *or* females, in current usage generally refers to the custom practiced in earlier times by the Mormons, and before them by King Solomon, in which the man has as many wives as he can afford financially and/or emotionally. The correct, but rarely used, term for this custom is *polygyny* (pə-LIJ'-ə-nee)—*polys,* many, plus *gyne,* woman.

What if a woman has two or more husbands, a form of marriage practiced in the Himalaya Mountains of Tibet? That custom is called *polyandry* (pol-ee-AN'-dree), from *polys* plus Greek *andros,* male.

3. making friends with suffixes

English words have various forms, using certain suffixes for nouns referring to persons, other suffixes for practices, attitudes, philosophies, etc, and still others for adjectives.

Consider:

Person	Practice, etc.	Adjective
1. misanthrope *or* misanthropist	misanthropy	misanthropic
2. misogynist	misogyny	misogynous *or* misogynistic
3. gynecologist	gynecology	gynecological
4. monogamist	monogamy	monogamous
5. bigamist	bigamy	bigamous
6. polygamist	polygamy	polygamous
7. polygynist	polygyny	polygynous
8. polyandrist	polyandry	polyandrous
9. philanthropist	philanthropy	philanthropic
10. anthropologist	anthropology	anthropological

You will note, then, that *-ist* is a common suffix for a person; *-y* for a practice, attitude, etc.; and *-ic* or *-ous* for an adjective.

4. living alone and liking it

Ascetic is from the Greek word *asketes,* monk or hermit.

A monk lives a lonely life—not for him the pleasures of the fleshpots, the laughter and merriment of convivial gatherings, the dissipation of high living. Rather, days of contemplation, study, and rough toil, nights on a hard bed in a simple cell, and the kind of self-denial that leads to a purification of the soul.

That person is an *ascetic* who leads an existence, voluntarily of course, that compares in austerity, simplicity, and rigorous hardship with the life of a monk.

The practice is *asceticism* (ə-SET′-ə-siz-əm), the adjective *ascetic*.

REVIEW OF ETYMOLOGY

Notice how efficiently you can master words by understanding their etymological structure. Stop for a moment to review the roots, prefixes, and suffixes you have studied. Can you recall a word we have discussed in this chapter that is built on the indicated prefix, root, or suffix?

PREFIX, ROOT, SUFFIX	MEANING	EXAMPLE
1. *ego*	self, I	_____
2. *alter*	other	_____
3. *intro-*	inside	_____
4. *extro-*	outside	_____
5. *verto*	turn	_____
6. *ambi-*	both	_____
7. *misein*	hate	_____
8. *anthropos*	mankind	_____
9. *gyne*	woman	_____
10. *gamos*	marriage	_____
11. *asketes*	monk	_____

12. *centrum*	center	_____
13. *mania*	madness	_____
14. *dexter*	right hand	_____
15. *sinister*	left hand	_____
16. *gauche*	left hand	_____
17. *droit*	right hand	_____
18. *monos*	one	_____
19. *bi-*	two	_____
20. *polys*	many	_____
21. *andros*	male	_____
22. *-ist*	person who (*noun suffix*)	_____
23. *-y*	Practice, custom, etc. (*noun suffix*)	_____
24. *-ous*	adjective suffix	_____
25. *-ity*	quality, condition, etc. (*noun suffix*)	_____

USING THE WORDS

Can you pronounce the words? (I)

Say each word aloud! Hear it in your own voice! *Say it often enough so that you feel comfortable with it, noting carefully from the phonetic respelling exactly how it should sound.*

Remember that the first crucial step in mastering a word is to be able to say it with ease and assurance.

1. *ambidextrous* — am-bə-DEKS′-trəs
2. *ambidexterity* — am′-bə-deks-TAIR′-ə-tee
3. *dexterous* — DEKS′-trəs
4. *dexterity* — deks-TAIR′-ə-tee
5. *sinister* — SIN′-ə-stər
6. *gauche* — GŌSH (Say the English word *go*, then quickly add -*sh*.)

43

7.	*gaucherie*	GŌ'-shə-ree
8.	*adroit*	ə-DROYT'
9.	*adroitness*	ə-DROYT'-nəss
10.	*anthropology*	an-thrə-POL'-ə-jee
11.	*anthropologist*	an-thrə-POL'-ə-jist
12.	*anthropological*	an'-thrə-pə-LOJ'-ə-kəl
13.	*philanthropist*	fə-LAN'-thrə-pist
14.	*philanthropy*	fə-LAN'-thrə-pee
15.	*philanthropic*	fil-ən-THROP'-ik
16.	*gynecologist*	gīn (*or* jin *or* jīn)-KOL'-ə-jist
17.	*gynecology*	gīn (*or* jin *or* jīn)-KOL'-ə-jee
18.	*gynecological*	gīn (*or* jin *or* jīn)-ə-kə-LOJ'-ə-kəl
19.	*monogamist*	mə-NOG'-ə-mist
20.	*monogamy*	mə-NOG'-ə-mee
21.	*monogamous*	mə-NOG'-ə-məs

Can you pronounce the words? (II)

1.	*bigamist*	BIG'-ə-mist
2.	*bigamy*	BIG'-ə-mee
3.	*bigamous*	BIG'-ə-məs
4.	*polygamist*	pə-LIG'-ə-mist
5.	*polygamy*	pə-LIG'-ə-mee
6.	*polygamous*	pə-LIG'ə-məs
7.	*polygynist*	pə-LIJ'-ə-nist
8.	*polygyny*	pə-LIJ'-ə-nee
9.	*polygynous*	pə-LIJ'-ə-nəs
10.	*polyandrist*	pol-ee-AN'-drist
11.	*polyandry*	pol-ee-AN'-dree
12.	*polyandrous*	pol-ee-AN'-drəs
13.	*misanthropist*	mis-AN'-thrə-pist
14.	*misanthropy*	mis-AN'-thrə-pee
15.	*misanthropic*	mis-ən-THROP'-ik
16.	*misogyny*	mə-SOJ'-ə-nee
17.	*misogynous*	mə-SOJ'-ə-nəs
18.	*misogynistic*	mə-soj'-ə-NIS'-tik
19.	*misogamy*	mə-SOG'-ə-mee
20.	*misogamous*	mə-SOG-ə-məs
21,	*asceticism*	ə-SET-ə-siz-əm

44

Can you work with the words? (I)

Check on your comprehension! See how successfully you can match words and meanings!

1. ambidextrous	a. evil, threatening
2. dexterous	b. hating mankind
3. sinister	c. skillful
4. gauche	d. awkward
5. misanthropic	e. capable of using both hands with equal skill

KEY: 1–e, 2–c, 3–a, 4–d, 5–b

Can you work with the words? (II)

1. anthropology	a. system of only one marriage
2. gynecology	b. hatred of women
3. monogamy	c. illegal plurality of marriages
4. bigamy	d. study of human development
5. misogyny	e. study of female ailments

KEY: 1–d, 2–e, 3–a, 4–c, 5–b

Can you work with the words? (III)

1. polygamy	a. devotion to a lonely and austere life
2. misogamy	b. skill, cleverness
3. asceticism	c. custom in which one man has many wives
4. philanthropy	d. love of mankind
5. adroitness	e. hatred of marriage

KEY: 1–c, 2–e, 3–a, 4–d, 5–b

Can you work with the words? (IV)

1. polygynist	a. student of the development of mankind
2. polyandrist	b. one who engages in charitable works
3. anthropologist	c. male with a plurality of wives
4. gynecologist	d. women's doctor
5. philanthropist	e. female with a plurality of husbands

KEY: 1–c, 2–e, 3–a, 4–d, 5–b

Do you understand the words?

1. Can *ambidextrous* people use either the left or right hand equally well?	YES	NO
2. Should a surgeon be manually *dexterous*?	YES	NO
3. Is a *sinister*-looking person frightening?	YES	NO
4. Is *gaucherie* a social asset?	YES	NO
5. Is an *adroit* speaker likely to be a successful lawyer?	YES	NO
6. Is a student of *anthropology* interested in primitive tribes?	YES	NO
7. Does a *gynecologist* have more male than female patients?	YES	NO
8. Is *monogamy* the custom in Western countries?	YES	NO
9. Is a *misogamist* likely to show tendencies toward *polygamy*?	YES	NO
10. Is a *bigamist* breaking the law?	YES	NO
11. Is a *philanthropist* generally altruistic?	YES	NO
12. Does a *misanthropist* enjoy human relationships?	YES	NO
13. Does a *misogynist* enjoy female companionship?	YES	NO

46

14. Are unmarried people necessarily *misogamous*? YES NO

15. Are bachelors necessarily *misogynous*? YES NO

16. Is *asceticism* compatible with luxurious living and the pursuit of pleasure? YES NO

17. Does a *polyandrist* have more than one husband? YES NO

KEY: 1–yes, 2–yes, 3–yes, 4–no, 5–yes, 6–yes, 7–no, 8–yes, 9–no, 10–yes, 11–yes, 12–no, 13–no, 14–no, 15–no, 16–no, 17–yes

---

Can you recall the words?

1. philosophy of living austerely	1.	A_____
2. hatred of women	2.	M_____
3. hatred of marriage	3.	M_____
4. hatred of mankind	4.	M_____
5. skillful	5.	D_____
6. awkward	6.	G_____
7. evil, threatening	7.	S_____
8. describing hatred of women (*adj.*)	8.	M_____
	or	M_____
9. skill	9.	A_____
10. pertaining to hatred of marriage. (*adj.*)	10.	M_____
11. pertaining to hatred of mankind (*adj.*)	11.	M_____
12. social custom of plural marriage	12.	P_____
	or	P_____
	or	P_____
13. unlawful state of having more than one spouse	13.	B_____
14. doctor specializing in female disorders	14.	G_____
15. custom of one marriage at a time	15.	M_____

16. one who hates the human race   16. M_____
                                          or M_____

17. able to use both hands with   17. A_____
    equal skill

18. study of mankind   18. A_____

19. one who loves mankind   19. P_____

20. skill in the use of both hands   20. A_____

KEY: 1–asceticism, 2–misogyny, 3–misogamy, 4–misanthropy, 5–dexterous, 6–gauche, 7–sinister, 8–misogynous or misogynistic, 9–adroitness, 10–misogamous, 11–misanthropic, 12–polygamy, polyandry, *or* polygyny, 13–bigamy, 14–gynecologist, 15–monogamy, 16–misanthropist *or* misanthrope, 17–ambidextrous, 18–anthropology, 19–philanthropist, 20–ambidexterity

---

CHAPTER REVIEW

A. Do you recognize the words?

1. Puts selfish desires first: (a) egoist, (b) egotist, (c) altruist
2. Is self-analytical: (a) extrovert, (b) introvert, (c) ambivert
3. Hates women: (a) misogamist, (b) misanthrope, (c) misogynist
4. One's other self: (a) altercation, (b) alter ego, (c) alteration
5. Awkward, clumsy: (a) adroit, (b) dexterous, (c) gauche
6. Plural marriage as a custom: (a) bigamy, (b) polygamy, (c) monogamy
7. Study of human development: (a) asceticism, (b) philanthropy, (c) anthropology
8. Plurality of husbands as a custom: (a) misogyny, (b) polygyny, (c) polyandry

---

KEY: 1–a, 2–b, 3–c, 4–b, 5–c, 6–b, 7–c, 8–c

B. Can you recognize roots?

ROOT	MEANING	EXAMPLE
1. *ego*	_____	egoist
2. *alter*	_____	alternative
3. *verto*	_____	introvert
4. *misein*	_____	misogynist
5. *anthropos*	_____	anthropologist
6. *gyne*	_____	gynecologist
7. *gamos*	_____	bigamy
8. *centrum*	_____	egocentric
9. *dexter*	_____	dexterous
10. *droit*	_____	adroit
11. *monos*	_____	monogamy
12. *andros*	_____	polyandry

KEY: 1–self, 2–other, 3–to turn, 4–to hate, 5–mankind, 6–woman, 7–marriage, 8–center, 9–right hand, 10–right hand, 11–one, 12–male

---

TEASER QUESTIONS FOR THE AMATEUR ETYMOLOGIST

Suppose you met the following words in your reading. Recognizing the roots on which they are constructed, could you figure out the meanings? Write your answers on the blank lines.

1. *anthropocentric:* _____

2. *andromania:* _____

3. *gynandrous:* _____

4. *monomania:* _____

5. *misandrist:* _____

(*Answers in Chapter 18.*)

STICK TO YOUR TIME SCHEDULE!

In three sessions, you have become acquainted with scores of new, vital, exciting words. You understand the ideas behind these words, their various forms and spellings, their pronunciation, their derivation, how they can be used, and exactly what they mean. I do not wish to press a point unduly, but it is possible that you have learned more new words in the short time it took you to cover this chapter than the average adult learns in an entire year. This realization should make you feel both gratified and excited.

Funny thing about time. Aside from the fact that we all, rich or poor, sick or well, have the same amount of time, exactly twenty-four hours every day (that is looking at time from a static point of view), it is also true that we can always find time for the things we enjoy doing, almost never for the things we find unpleasant (and that is looking at time from the dynamic point of view). I am not merely being philosophical—I am sure you will agree with this concept if you give it a little thought.

If you have enjoyed learning new words, accepting new challenges, gaining new understanding, and discovering the thrill of successful accomplishment, then make sure to stay with the time schedule you have set up for yourself.

A crucial factor in successful, ongoing learning is routine.

Develop a comfortable time routine, persevere against all distractions, and you will learn anything you sincerely want to learn.

So, to give yourself an edge, write here the day and hour you plan to return to your work:

DAY: _____

DATE: _____

TIME: _____

(End of Session 3)

TEST YOUR GRAMMAR

How good is your English? Have you ever said *me* and then wondered if it shouldn't have been *I*—or vice versa? Do you sometimes get a little confused about *lay* and *lie* or *who* and *whom?* Perhaps you are often a little less than certain about the distinction between *effect* and *affect, principal* and *principle, childish* and *childlike?*

Here is a series of quick tests that will show you how skillful you are in using the right word in the right place, that will give you a reliable indication of how your language ability compares with the average.

TEST I—EASY

If your English is every bit as good as average, you will have no difficulty making a proper choice in at least eight of the following ten sentences.

1. There is a beautiful moon out tonight and Estelle and I are going for a stroll—would you like to come along with (she and I, her and me?)
2. Your husband doesn't believe that you are older than (I, me).

3. Maybe we're not as rich as (they, them), but I bet we're a lot happier.
4. Does your child still (lay, lie) down for a nap after lunch?
5. When we saw Mary openly flirting with Nellie's husband, we (could, couldn't) hardly believe our eyes.
6. You should (of, have) put more vermouth into the martini.
7. Does your company (leave, let) you have as long a lunch break as you would like?
8. Harriet feels that her (brothers-in-law, brother-in-laws) are impossible to get along with.
9. "What (kind of, kind of a) car are you looking for?" asked the salesman.
10. Mrs. White was delighted that the Fennells had invited John and (she, her) to their party.

Is your English up to par? HERE ARE THE CORRECT ANSWERS

1–her and me, 2–I, 3–they, 4–lie, 5–could, 6–have, 7–let, 8–brothers-in-law, 9–kind of, 10–her

TEST II—HARDER

Choose correctly in at least seven of the following problems to consider that your skill is distinctly above average—get all ten right to conclude that you rarely, if ever, make an error in grammar.

1. What (effect, affect) has the new administration's policies had on investor confidence?
2. A feeling of one's worth is one of the (principle, principal) goals of psychological therapy.
3. There's no sense (in, of) carrying on that way.
4. I can't remember (who, whom) it was.
5. The infant (lay, laid) quietly sucking its thumb.
6. No one but (she, her) ever made a perfect score on the test.
7. In the early days of frontier history, horse thieves were (hanged, hung).
8. Neither of your responses (are, is) satisfactory.

9. Either of these two small cars, if properly maintained, (is, are) sure to give over thirty miles per gallon in highway driving.
10. Tell (whoever, whomever) is waiting to come in.

Is your English above average? HERE ARE THE CORRECT ANSWERS

1–effect, 2–principal, 3–in, 4–who, 5–lay, 6–her, 7–hanged, 8–is, 9–is, 10–whoever

TEST III—HARDEST

Now you can discover how close you are to being an expert in English. The next ten sentences are no cinch—you will be acquitting yourself creditably if you check the correct word five times out of ten. And you have every right to consider yourself an expert if you get nine or ten right.

1. We have just interviewed an applicant (who, whom) the committee believes is best qualified for the position.
2. She is one of those gifted writers who (turns, turn) out one best seller after another.
3. Don't sound so (incredulous, incredible); what I am saying is absolutely true.
4. We were totally (disinterested, uninterested) in the offer.
5. This recipe calls for two (cupsful, cupfuls) of sugar.
6. Are you trying to (infer, imply) by those words that he is not to be trusted?
7. We thought the actress to be (she, her), but we weren't sure.
8. Was it (she, her) you were talking about?
9. Your criteria (is, are) not valid.
10. "It is I who (is, am) the only friend you've got," she told him pointedly.

Are you an expert? HERE ARE THE CORRECT ANSWERS

1–who, 2–turn, 3–incredulous, 4–uninterested, 5–cupfuls, 6–imply, 7–her, 8–she, 9–are, 10–am

4

HOW TO TALK ABOUT DOCTORS

(Sessions 4–6)

TEASER PREVIEW

What is the title of the doctor who specializes in:

- *internal medicine?*
- *female ailments?*
- *pregnancy and childbirth?*
- *the treatment and care of infants and young children?*
- *skin disorders?*
- *diseases of the eye?*
- *heart problems?*
- *the brain and nervous system?*
- *mental and emotional disturbances?*

SESSION 4

In this chapter we discuss ten medical specialists—what they do, how they do it, what they are called.

IDEAS

1. what's wrong with you?

To find out what ails you and why, this specialist gives you a thorough physical examination, using an impressive array of tests: X ray, blood chemistry, urinalysis, cardiogram, and so on.

An internist

2. female troubles?

This specialist treats the female reproductive and sexual organs.

A gynecologist

3. having a baby?

This specialist delivers babies and takes care of the mother during and immediately after the period of her pregnancy.

An obstetrician

4. is your baby ill?

You know the common childhood maladies—mumps, whooping cough, chicken pox, measles. This specialist limits his practice to youngsters, taking care of babies directly after birth, supervising their diet and watching over their growth and development, giving them the series of inoculations that has done so much to decrease infant mortality, and soothing their anxious parents.

A pediatrician

5. skin clear?

You have heard the classic riddle: "What is the best use for pigskin?" Answer: "To keep the pig together." Human skin has a similar purpose: it ls, if we get down to fundamentals, what keeps us all in one piece. And our outer covering, like so many of our internal organs, is subject to diseases and infections of various kinds, running the gamut from simple acne and eczemas through impetigo, psoriasis, and cancer. There is a specialist who treats all such skin diseases.

A *dermatologist*

6. eyes okay?

The physician whose specialty is disorders of vision (myopia, astigmatism, cataracts, glaucoma, etc.) may prescribe glasses, administer drugs, or perform surgery.

An *ophthalmologist*

7. how are your bones?

This specialist deals with the skeletal structure of the body, treating bone fractures, slipped discs, clubfoot, curvature of the spine, dislocations of the hip, etc., and may correct a condition either by surgery or by the use of braces or other appliances.

An *orthopedist*

8. does your heart go pitter-patter?

This specialist treats diseases of the heart and circulatory system.

A *cardiologist*

9. is your brain working?

This physician specializes in the treatment of disorders of the brain, spinal cord, and the rest of the nervous system.

A *neurologist*

56

10. are you neurotic?

This specialist attempts to alleviate mental and emotional disturbances by means of various techniques, occasionally drugs or electroshock, more often private or group psychotherapy.

A *psychiatrist*

USING THE WORDS

Can you pronounce the words?

Words take on a new color if you hear them in your own voice; they begin to belong to you more personally, more intimately, than if you merely hear or read them. As always, therefore, *say the words aloud* to take the first, crucial step toward complete mastery.

1. *internist*	in-TURN'-ist
2. *gynecologist*	gīn (*or* jin *or* jīn)-ə-KOL'-ə-jist
3. *obstetrician*	ob-stə-TRISH'-ən
4. *pediatrician*	pee'-dee-ə-TRISH'-ən
5. *dermatologist*	dur-mə-TOL'-ə-jist
6. *ophthalmologist*	off-thal-MOL'-ə-jist
7. *orthopedist*	awr-thə-PEE'-dist
8. *cardiologist*	kahr-dee-OL'-ə-jist
9. *neurologist*	noor-OL'-ə-jist
10. *psychiatrist*	sī (*or* sə)-KĪ'-ə-trist

Can you work with the words?

Match each doctor to the field.

FIELDS	DOCTORS
1. mental or emotional disturbances	a. internist
2. nervous system	b. gynecologist

3. skin
4. diagnosis; internal organs
5. infants
6. female reproductive organs
7. eyes
8. heart
9. pregnancy, childbirth
10. skeletal system

c. obstetrician
d. pediatrician
e. dermatologist
f. ophthalmologist
g. orthopedist
h. cardiologist
i. neurologist
j. psychiatrist

KEY: 1–j, 2–i, 3–e, 4–a, 5–d, 6–b, 7–f, 8–h, 9–c, 10–g

Do you understand the words?

1. Is an *internist* an expert in diagnosis?	YES	NO
2. Is a *gynecologist* familiar with the female reproductive organs?	YES	NO
3. Does an *obstetrician* specialize in diseases of childhood?	YES	NO
4. Does a *pediatrician* deliver babies?	YES	NO
5. If you had a skin disease, would you visit a *dermatologist*?	YES	NO
6. If you had trouble with your vision would you visit an *orthopedist*?	YES	NO
7. Is an *ophthalmologist* an eye specialist?	YES	NO
8. Does a *cardiologist* treat bone fractures?	YES	NO
9. Is a *neurologist* a nerve specialist?	YES	NO
10. If you were nervous, tense, overly anxious, constantly fearful for no apparent reasons, would a *psychiatrist* be the specialist to see?	YES	NO

KEY: 1–yes, 2–yes, 3–no, 4–no, 5–yes, 6–no, 7–yes, 8–no, 9–yes, 10–yes

Can you recall the words?

Write the name of the specialist you might visit or be referred to:

1. for a suspected brain disorder   1. N_____
2. for a thorough internal checkup   2. I_____
3. if you have a skin disease   3. D_____
4. if you have a heart problem   4. C_____
5. if you are tense, fearful, insecure   5. P_____
6. if you are pregnant   6. O_____
7. for some disorder of the female reproductive organs   7. G_____
8. for a checkup for your two-month-old child   8. P_____
9. for faulty vision   9. O_____
10. for curvature of the spine   10. O_____

KEY: 1–neurologist, 2–internist, 3–dermatologist, 4–cardiologist, 5–psychiatrist, 6–obstetrician, 7–gynecologist, 8–pediatrician, 9–ophthalmologist, 10–orthopedist

---

(End of session 4)

SESSION 5

ORIGINS AND RELATED WORDS

1. inside you

Internist and *internal* derive from the same Latin root, *internus*, inside. The *internist* is a specialist in *internal* medicine, in the exploration of your *insides*. This physician determines the state of your internal organs in order to discover what's happening *within* your body to cause the troubles you're complaining of.

Do not confuse the *internist* with the *intern* (also spelled *interne*), who is a medical graduate serving an apprenticeship *inside* a hospital.

2. doctors for women

The word *gynecologist* is built on Greek *gyne,* woman, plus *logos,* science; etymologically, *gynecology* is the science (in actual use, the medical science) of women. Adjective: *gynecological* (gīn [*or* jin *or* jīn]-ə-kə-LOJ'-ə-kəl).

Obstetrician derives from Latin *obstetrix,* midwife, which in turn has its source in a Latin verb meaning *to stand*—midwives stand in front of the woman in labor to aid in the delivery of the infant.

The suffix *-ician,* as in *obstetrician, physician, musician, magician, electrician,* etc., means *expert.*

Obstetrics (ob-STET'-riks) has only within the last 150 years become a respectable specialty. No further back than 1834, Professor William P. Dewees assumed the first chair of *obstetrics* at the University of Pennsylvania and had to brave considerable medical contempt and ridicule as a result—the delivery of children was then considered beneath the dignity of the medical profession.

Adjective: *obstetric* (ob-STET'-rik) or *obstetrical* (ob-STET'-rə-kəl).

3. children

Pediatrician is a combination of Greek *paidos,* child; *iatreia,* medical healing; and *-ician,* expert.

Pediatrics (pee-dee-AT'-riks), then, is by etymology the medical healing of a child. Adjective: *pediatric* (pee-dee-AT'-rik).

(The *ped-* you see in words like *pedestal, pedal,* and *pedestrian* is from the Latin *pedis,* foot, and despite the identical spelling in English has no relationship to Greek *paidos.*)

Pedagogy (PED-ə-gō′-jee), which combines *paidos* with *agogos*, leading, is, etymologically, *the leading of children*. And to what do you lead them? To learning, to development, to growth, to maturity. From the moment of birth, infants are led by adults—they are taught, first by parents and then by teachers, to be self-sufficient, to fit into the culture in which they are born. Hence, *pedagogy*, which by derivation means *the leading of a child*, refers actually to the principles and methods of teaching. College students majoring in education take certain standard *pedagogy* courses—the history of education; educational psychology; the psychology of adolescents; principles of teaching; etc. Adjective: *pedagogical* (ped-ə-GOJ′-ə-kəl).

A *pedagogue* (PED′-ə-gog) is versed in *pedagogy*. But *pedagogue* has an unhappy history. From its original, neutral meaning of *teacher*, it has deteriorated to the point where it refers, today, to a narrow-minded, strait-laced, old-fashioned, dogmatic teacher. It is a word of contempt and should be used with caution.

Like *pedagogue*, *demagogue* (DEM′-ə-gog) has also deteriorated in meaning. By derivation a leader (*agogos*) of the people (*demos*), a *demagogue* today is actually one who attempts, in essence, to *mislead* the people, a politician who foments discontent among the masses, rousing them to fever pitch by wild oratory, in an attempt to be voted into office.

Once elected, *demagogues* use political power to further their own personal ambitions or fortunes.

Many "leaders" of the past and present, in countries around the world, have been accused of *demagoguery* (dem-ə-GOG′-ə-ree). Adjective: *demagogic* (dem-ə-GOJ′-ik).

4. skin-deep

The *dermatologist*, whose specialty is *dermatology* (dur-mə-TOL′-ə-jee), is so named from Greek *derma*, skin. Adjective: *dermatological* (dur′-mə-tə-LOJ′-ə-kəl).

See the syllables *derma* in any English word and you will know there is some reference to *skin*—for example, a *hypodermic* (hī-pə-DUR′-mik) needle penetrates *under* (Greek, *hypos*) the *skin;* the *epidermis* (ep-ə-DUR′-mis) is the outermost layer of *skin;* a *taxidermist* (TAKS′-ə-dur-mist), whose business is *taxidermy*

61

(TAKS'-ə-dur-mee), prepares, stuffs, and mounts the *skins* of animals; a *pachyderm* (PAK'-ə-durm) is an animal with an unusually thick *skin*, like an elephant, hippopotamus, or rhinoceros; and *dermatitis* (dur-mə-TĪ'-tis) is the general name for any *skin* inflammation, irritation, or infection.

5. the eyes have it

Ophthalmologist—note the *ph* preceding *th*—is from Greek *ophthalmos*, eye, plus *logos*, science or study. The specialty is *ophthalmology* (off'-thal-MOL'-ə-jee), the adjective *ophthalmological* (off'-thal-mə-LOJ'-ə-kəl).

An earlier title for this physician, still occasionally used, is *oculist* (OK'-yə-list), from Latin *oculus*, eye, a root on which the following English words are also built:

1. *ocular* (OK'-yə-lər)—an adjective that refers to the eye

2. *monocle* (MON'-ə-kəl)—a lens for one (*monos*) eye, sported by characters in old movies as a symbol of the British so-called upper class

3. *binoculars* (bə-NOK'-yə-lərz)—field glasses that increase the range of two (*bi-*) eyes

4. And, strangely enough, *inoculate* (in-OK'-yə-layt'), a word commonly misspelled with two *n's*. When you are *inoculated* against a disease, an "eye," puncture, or hole is made in your skin, through which serum is injected.

Do not confuse the *ophthalmologist* or *oculist*, a medical specialist, with two other practitioners who deal with the eye—the *optometrist* (op-TOM'-ə-trist) and *optician* (op-TISH'-ən).

Optometrists are not physicians, and do not perform surgery or administer drugs; they measure vision, test for glaucoma, and prescribe and fit glasses.

Opticians fill an *optometrist's* or *ophthalmologist's* prescription, grinding lenses according to specifications; they do not examine patients.

Optometrist combines Greek *opsis, optikos*, sight or vision, with *metron*, measurement—the *optometrist*, by etymology, is one who measures vision. The specialty is *optometry* (op-TOM'-ə-tree).

Optician is built on *opsis, optikos,* plus *-ician,* expert. The specialty is *optics* (OP'-tiks).

Adjectives: *optometric* (op-tə-MET'-rik) or *optometrical* (op-tə-MET'-rə-kəl), *optical* (OP'-tə-kəl).

REVIEW OF ETYMOLOGY

PREFIX, ROOT, SUFFIX	MEANING	ENGLISH WORD
1. *internus*	inside	_____
2. *gyne*	woman	_____
3. *obstetrix*	midwife	_____
4. *paidos*	child	_____
5. *pedis*	foot	_____
6. *agogos*	leading, leader	_____
7. *demos*	people	_____
8. *derma*	skin	_____
9. *hypos*	under	_____
10. *ophthalmos*	eye	_____
11. *oculus*	eye	_____
12. *monos*	one	_____
13. *bi-*	two	_____
14. *-ician*	expert	_____
15. *opsis, optikos*	vision, sight	_____
16. *metron*	measurement	_____

USING THE WORDS

Can you pronounce the words? (I)

1. *intern (e)*   IN'-turn
2. *gynecology*   gīn-ə-KOL'-ə-jee, jin-ə-KOL'-ə-jee, *or* jīn-ə-KOL'-ə-jee
3. *gynecological*   gīn-ə-kə-LOJ'-ə-kəl, jin-ə-kə-LOJ'-ə-kəl *or* jīn-ə-kə-LOJ-ə-kəl

4. *obstetrics*   ob-STET'-riks
5. *obstetric*   ob-STET'-rik
6. *obstetrical*   ob-STET'-rə-kəl
7. *pediatrics*   pee-dee-AT'-riks
8. *pediatric*   pee-dee-AT'-rik
9. *pedagogy*   PED'-ə-gō-jee
10. *pedagogical*   ped-ə-GOJ'-ə-kəl
11. *pedagogue*   PED'-ə-gog
12. *demagogue*   DEM'-ə-gog
13. *demagoguery*   dem-ə-GOG'-ə-ree
14. *demagogic*   dem-ə-GOJ'-ik

Can you pronounce the words? (II)

1. *dermatology*   dur-mə-TOL'-ə-jee
2. *dermatological*   dur'-mə-tə-LOJ'-ə-kəl
3. *hypodermic*   hī-pə-DURM'-ik
4. *epidermis*   ep-ə-DUR'-mis
5. *taxidermist*   TAKS'-ə-dur-mist
6. *taxidermy*   TAKS'-ə-dur-mee
7. *pachyderm*   PAK'-ə-durm
8. *dermatitis*   dur-mə-TĪ'-tis
9. *ophthalmology*   off-thal-MOL'-ə-jee
10. *ophthalmological* off'-thal-mə-LOJ'-ə-kəl
11. *oculist*   OK'-yə-list
12. *ocular*   OK'-yə-lər
13. *monocle*   MON'-ə-kəl
14. *binoculars*   bə-NOK'-yə-lərz
15. *inoculate*   in-OK'-yə-layt'
16. *optometrist*   op-TOM'-ə-trist
17. *optometry*   op-TOM'-ə-tree
18. *optometric*   op-tə-MET'-rik
19. *optometrical*   op-tə-MET'-rə-kəl
20. *optician*   op-TISH'-ən
21. *optics*   OP'-tiks
22. *optical*   OP-tə-kəl

64

Can you work with the words? (I)

1. gynecology	a. principles of teaching
2. obstetrics	b. stuffing of skins of animals
3. pediatrics	c. specialty dealing with the delivery of newborn infants
4. pedagogy	d. stirring up discontent among the masses
5. demagoguery	e. treatment of skin diseases
6. dermatology	f. specialty dealing with women's diseases
7. taxidermy	g. specialty dealing with the treatment of children

KEY: 1–f, 2–c, 3–g, 4–a, 5–d, 6–e, 7–b

Can you work with the words? (II)

1. hypodermic	a. elephant
2. epidermis	b. eye doctor
3. pachyderm	c. under the skin
4. dermatitis	d. one who measures vision
5. ophthalmologist	e. lens grinder
6. optometrist	f. outer layer of skin
7. optician	g. inflammation of the skin

KEY: 1–c, 2–f, 3–a, 4–g, 5–b, 6–d, 7–e

Do you understand the words?

1. Does a treatise on *obstetrics* deal with childbirth?   YES   NO
2. Does *gynecology* deal with the female reproductive organs?   YES   NO

3. Is *pediatrics* concerned with the diseases of old age? YES   NO

4. Does *pedagogy* refer to teaching? YES   NO

5. Is a *pedagogue* an expert teacher? YES   NO

6. Is a *demagogue* interested in the welfare of the people? YES   NO

7. Is a lion a *pachyderm*? YES   NO

8. Is the *epidermis* one of the layers of the skin? YES   NO

9. Is *dermatitis* an inflammation of one of the limbs? YES   NO

10. Is a *taxidermist* a medical practitioner? YES   NO

11. Is an *ophthalmologist* a medical doctor? YES   NO

12. Is an *optometrist* a medical doctor? YES   NO

13. Does an *optician* prescribe glasses? YES   NO

KEY: 1–yes, 2–yes, 3–no, 4–yes, 5–no, 6–no, 7–no, 8–yes, 9–no, 10–no, 11–yes, 12–no, 13–no

---

Can you recall the words?

1. specialty of child delivery   1. O_____
2. outer layer of skin   2. E_____
3. principles of teaching   3. P_____
4. thick-skinned animal   4. P_____
5. skin inflammation   5. D_____
6. one who foments political discontent   6. D_____
7. one who sells optical equipment   7. O_____
8. medical graduate serving his apprenticeship   8. I_____
9. treatment of childhood diseases   9. P_____
10. practice of stirring up political dissatisfaction for purely personal gain   10. D_____

11. one who stuffs the skins of animals	11. T_____
12. another title for *ophthalmologist*	12. O_____
13. treatment of female ailments	13. G_____
14. medical specialty relating to diseases of the eye	14. O_____
15. one-lens eyeglass	15. M_____
16. pertaining to the eye	16. O_____
17. one who measures vision	17. O_____

KEY: 1–obstetrics, 2–epidermis, 3–pedagogy, 4–pachyderm, 5–dermatitis, 6–demagogue, 7–optician, 8–intern *or* interne, 9–pediatrics, 10–demagoguery, 11–taxidermist, 12–oculist, 13–gynecology, 14–ophthalmology, 15–monocle, 16–ocular, 17–optometrist

---

(*End of Session 5*)

SESSION 6

ORIGINS AND RELATED WORDS

1. the straighteners

The *orthopedist* is so called from the Greek roots *orthos,* straight or correct, and *paidos,* child. The *orthopedist,* by etymology, straightens children. The term was coined in 1741 by the author of a textbook on the prevention of childhood diseases—at that time the correction of spinal curvature in children was a main concern of practitioners of *orthopedics* (awr-thə-PEE′-diks).

Today the specialty treats deformities, injuries, and diseases of the bones and joints (of adults as well as children, of course), often by surgical procedures.

Adjective: *orthopedic* (awr-thə-PEE'-dik).

Orthodontia (awr-thə-DON'-shə), the straightening of teeth, is built on *orthos* plus *odontos*, tooth. The *orthodontist* (awr-thə-DON'-tist) specializes in improving your "bite," retracting "buck teeth," and by means of braces and other techniques seeing to it that every molar, incisor, bicuspid, etc. is exactly where it belongs in your mouth.

Adjective: *orthodontic* (awr-thə-DON'-tik).

2. the heart

Cardiologist combines Greek *kardia*, heart, and *logos*, science.

The specialty is *cardiology* (kahr-dee-OL'-ə-jee), the adjective *cardiological* (kahr'-dee-ə-LOJ'-ə-kəl).

So a *cardiac* (KAHR'-dee-ak) condition refers to some malfunctioning of the heart; a *cardiogram* (KAHR'-dee-ə-gram') is an electrically produced record of the heartbeat. The instrument that produces this record is called a *cardiograph* (KAHR'-dee-ə-graf').

3. the nervous system

Neurologist derives from Greek *neuron*, nerve, plus *logos*, science.

Specialty: *neurology* (nŏŏr-OL'-ə-jee); adjective: *neurological* (nŏŏr-ə-LOJ'-ə-kəl).

Neuralgia (nŏŏr-AL'-ja) is acute pain along the nerves and their branches; the word comes from *neuron* plus *algos*, pain.

Neuritis (nŏŏr-Ī'-tis), is inflammation of the nerves.

Neurosis (nŏŏr-Ō'-sis), combining *neuron* with *-osis*, a suffix meaning *abnormal or diseased condition,* is not, despite its etymology, a disorder of the nerves, but rather, as described by the late Eric Berne, a psychiatrist, ". . . an illness characterized by excessive use of energy for unproductive purposes so that personality development is hindered or stopped. A man who spends most of his time worrying about his health, counting his money, plotting revenge, or washing his hands, can hope for little emotional growth."

Neurotic (nŏŏr-OT'-ik) is both the adjective form and the term for a person suffering from *neurosis*.

4. the mind

A *neurosis* is not a form of mental unbalance. A full-blown mental disorder is called a *psychosis* (sī-KŌ'-sis), a word built on Greek *psyche,* spirit, soul, or mind, plus *-osis*.

A true *psychotic* (sī-KOT'-ik) has lost contact with reality—at least with reality as most of us perceive it, though no doubt *psychotic* (note that this word, like *neurotic,* is both a noun and an adjective) people have their own form of reality.

Built on *psyche* plus *iatreia,* medical healing, a *psychiatrist* by etymology is a mind-healer. The specialty is *psychiatry* (sī- *or* sə-KĪ-ə-tree); the adjective is *psychiatric* (sī-kee-AT'-rik).

Pediatrics, as you know, is also built on *iatreia,* as is *podiatry* (pə-DĪ'-ə-tree), discussed in the next chapter, and *geriatrics* (jair'-ee-AT'-riks), the specialty dealing with the particular medical needs of the elderly. (This word combines *iatreia* with Greek *geras,* old age.)

The specialist is a *geriatrician* (jair'-ee-ə-TRISH'-ən), the adjective is *geriatric* (jair'-ee-AT'-rik).

REVIEW OF ETYMOLOGY

ROOT, SUFFIX	MEANING	ENGLISH WORD
1. *orthos*	straight, correct	_____
2. *paidos* (*ped-*)	child	_____
3. *odontos*	tooth	_____
4. *kardia*	heart	_____
5. *logos*	science; study	_____
6. *neuron*	nerve	_____
7. *algos*	pain	_____

8. *-osis*   abnormal or   _____
                      diseased condition   _____
9. *-itis*   inflammation
10. *psyche*   spirit, soul, mind   _____
11. *iatreia*   medical healing   _____
12. *geras*   old age   _____

USING THE WORDS

Can you pronounce the words (I)

1. *orthopedics*   awr-thə-PEE′-diks
2. *orthopedic*   awr-thə-PEE′-dik
3. *orthodontia*   awr-thə-DON′-shə
4. *orthodontist*   awr-thə-DON′-tist
5. *orthodontic*   awr-thə-DON′-tik
6. *cardiology*   kahr-dee-OL′-ə-jee
7. *cardiological*   kahr′-dee-ə-LOJ′-ə-kəl
8. *cardiac*   KAHR′-dee-ak
9. *cardiogram*   KAHR′-dee-ə-gram′
10. *cardiograph*   KAHR′-dee-ə-graf′

Can you pronounce the words? (II)

1. *neurology*   nŏŏr-OL′-ə-jee
2. *neurological*   nŏŏr-ə-LOJ′-ə-kəl
3. *neuralgia*   nŏŏr-AL′-jə
4. *neuritis*   nŏŏr-Ī′-tis
5. *neurosis*   nŏŏr-Ō′-sis
6. *neurotic*   nŏŏr-OT′-ik
7. *psychosis*   sī-KŌ′-sis
8. *psychotic*   sī-KOT′-ik
9. *psychiatry*   sī- *or* sə-KĪ′-ə-tree
10. *psychiatric*   sī-kee-AT′-rik
11. *geriatrics*   jair′-ee-AT′-riks
12. *geriatrician*   jair′-ee-ə-TRISH′-ən
13. *geriatric*   jair′-ee-AT′-rik

Can you work with the words? (I)

1. orthopedics
2. orthodontia

3. neuralgia
4. neuritis
5. geriatrics

a. nerve pain·
b. specialty dealing with medical problems of the elderly
c. straightening of teeth
d. inflammation of the nerves
e. treatment of skeletal deformities

KEY: 1–e, 2–c, 3–a, 4–d, 5–b

Can you work with the words? (II)

1. cardiogram
2. cardiograph
3. neurosis
4. psychosis

5. psychiatry

a. record of heart beats
b. mental unbalance
c. emotional disturbance
d. treatment of personality disorders
e. instrument for recording heartbeats

KEY: 1–a, 2–e, 3–c, 4–b, 5–d

Do you understand the words?

1. A *gynecologist's* patients are mostly men.   TRUE   FALSE
2. *Ophthalmology* is the study of eye diseases.   TRUE   FALSE
3. *Orthopedics* is the specialty dealing with the bones and joints.   TRUE   FALSE

71

4. A *cardiac* patient has a heart ailment.	TRUE	FALSE
5. A person with a bad "bite" may profit from *orthodontia*.	TRUE	FALSE
6. *Neuralgia* is a disease of the bones.	TRUE	FALSE
7. A *neurosis* is the same as a *psychosis*.	TRUE	FALSE
8. *Neuritis* is inflammation of the nerves.	TRUE	FALSE
9. *Psychiatry* is a medical specialty that deals with mental, emotional, and personality disturbances.	TRUE	FALSE
10. A *cardiograph* is a device for recording heartbeats.	TRUE	FALSE
11. *Psychiatric* treatment is designed to relieve tensions, fears, and insecurities.	TRUE	FALSE
12. A doctor who specializes in *pediatrics* has very old patients.	TRUE	FALSE
13. A *geriatrician* has very young patients.	TRUE	FALSE

KEY: 1–F, 2–T, 3–T, 4–T, 5–T, 6–F, 7–F, 8–T, 9–T, 10–T, 11–T, 12–F, 13–F

Can you recall the words?

1. specialist who straightens teeth
2. nerve pain
3. medical specialty dealing with bones and joints
4. medical specialty dealing with emotional disturbances and mental illness
5. inflammation of the nerves
6. emotional or personality disorder
7. mentally unbalanced
8. pertaining to the heart
9. specialty dealing with medical problems of the elderly

1. O_____
2. N_____
3. O_____
4. P_____
5. N_____
6. N_____
7. P_____
8. C_____
9. G_____

10. instrument that records heart action

10. C_____

11. record produced by such an instrument

11. C_____

CHAPTER REVIEW

A. Do you recognize the words?

1. Specialist in female ailments:
   (a) obstetrician, (b) gynecologist, (c) dermatologist
2. Specialist in children's diseases:
   (a) orthopedist, (b) pediatrician, (c) internist
3. Specialist in eye diseases:
   (a) cardiologist, (b) opthalmologist, (c) optician
4. Specialist in emotional disorders:
   (a) neurologist, (b) demagogue, (c) psychiatrist
5. Pertaining to medical treatment of the elderly:
   (a) neurological, (b) obstetric, (c) geriatric
6. Straightening of teeth:
   (a) orthodontia, (b) orthopedic, (c) optometry
7. Personality disorder:
   (a) neuritis, (b), neuralgia, (c) neurosis
8. Mentally unbalanced:
   (a) neurotic, (b) psychotic, (c) cardiac
9. Principles of teaching:
   (a) demagoguery, (b) pedagogy, (c) psychosis

B. Can you recognize roots?

ROOT	MEANING	EXAMPLE
1. *internus*	_____	internist
2. *paidos (ped-)*	_____	pediatrician
3. *pedis*	_____	pedestrian
4. *agogos*	_____	pedagogue
5. *demos*	_____	demagogue
6. *derma*	_____	dermatologist
7. *hypos*	_____	hypodermic
8. *ophthalmos*	_____	ophthalmologist
9. *oculus*	_____	monocle
10. *opsis, optikos*	_____	optician
11. *metron*	_____	optometrist
12. *orthos*	_____	orthopedist
13. *odontos*	_____	orthodontist
14. *kardia*	_____	cardiologist
15. *logos*	_____	anthropologist
16. *neuron*	_____	neurologist
17. *algos*	_____	neuralgia
18. *psyche*	_____	psychiatrist
19. *iatreia*	_____	psychiatry
20. *geras*	_____	geriatrics

KEY: 1–inside, 2–child, 3–foot, 4–leading, 5–people, 6–skin, 7–under, 8–eye, 9–eye, 10–view, vision, sight, 11–measurement, 12–straight, correct, 13–tooth, 14–heart, 15–science, study, 16–nerve, 17–pain, 18–mind, 19–medical healing, 20–old age

---

TEASER QUESTIONS FOR THE AMATEUR ETYMOLOGIST

1. Thinking of the roots *odontos* and *paidos* (spelled *ped-* in English), figure out the meaning of *pedodontia*: _____

2. Recall the roots *kardia* and *algós*. What is the meaning of *cardialgia*? _____

_____

3. Of *odontalgia*? _____

_____

4. *Nostos* is the Greek word for a *return* (home). Can you combine this root with *algos*, pain, to construct the English word meaning *homesickness*? _____

_____

(*Answers in Chapter 18*)

TWO KEYS TO SUCCESS: SELF-DISCIPLINE AND PERSISTENCE

You can achieve a superior vocabulary in a phenomenally short time—given self-discipline and persistence.

The greatest aid in building self-discipline is, as I have said, a matter of devising a practical and comfortable schedule for yourself and then *keeping to that schedule*.

Make sure to complete *at least* one session each time you pick up the book, and always decide exactly when you will continue with your work before you put the book down.

There may be periods of difficulty—then is the time to exert the greatest self-discipline, the most determined persistence.

For every page that you study will help you attain a mastery over words; every day that you work will add to your skill in understanding and using words.

(*End of Session 6*)

―――――*Brief Intermission Two*―――――

RANDOM NOTES ON MODERN USAGE

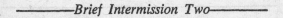

English grammar is confusing enough as it is—what makes it doubly confounding is that it is slowly but continually changing.

This means that some of the strict rules you memorized so painfully in your high school or college English courses may no longer be completely valid.

Following such outmoded principles, you may think you are speaking "perfect" English, and instead you may sound stuffy and pedantic.

The problem boils down to this: If grammatical usage is gradually becoming more liberal, where does educated, unaffected, informal speech end? And where does illiterate, ungrammatical speech begin?

The following notes on current trends in modern usage are intended to help you come to a decision about certain controversial expressions. As you read each sentence, pay particular attention to the italicized word or words. Does the usage square with your own language patterns? Would you be willing to phrase your thought in just terms? Decide whether the sentence is right or wrong, then compare your conclusion with the opinion given in the explanatory paragraphs that follow the test.

TEST YOURSELF

1. If you drink too many vodka martinis,   RIGHT   WRONG
   you will surely *get* sick.
2. Have you *got* a dollar?   RIGHT   WRONG
3. No one loves you except *I*.   RIGHT   WRONG
4. Please *lay* down.   RIGHT   WRONG
5. *Who* do you love?   RIGHT   WRONG
6. Neither of these cars *are* worth the   RIGHT   WRONG
   money.
7. The judge sentenced the murderer to be   RIGHT   WRONG
   hung.
8. Mother, *can* I go out to play?   RIGHT   WRONG
9. Take two *spoonsful* of this medicine   RIGHT   WRONG
   every three hours.
10. Your words seem to *infer* that Jack is a RIGHT   WRONG
    liar.
11. I *will* be happy to go to the concert   RIGHT   WRONG
    with you.
12. It is *me*.   RIGHT   WRONG
13. Go *slow*.   RIGHT   WRONG
14. Peggy and Karen are *alumni* of the   RIGHT   WRONG
    same high school.
15. I *would* like to ask you a question.   RIGHT   WRONG

1. If you drink too many vodka martinis, you will surely *get* sick.

RIGHT. The puristic objection is that *get* has only one meaning—namely, *obtain*. However, as any modern dictionary will attest, *get* has scores of different meanings, one of the most respectable of which is *become*. You can *get* tired, *get* dizzy, *get* drunk, or *get* sick—and your choice of words will offend no one but a pedant.

2. Have you *got* a dollar?

RIGHT. If purists get a little pale at the sound of *"get* sick," they turn chalk white when they hear *have got* as a substitute for *have.* But the fact is that *have got* is an established American form of expression. Jacques Barzun, noted author and literary critic, says: *"Have you got* is good idiomatic English—I use it in speech without thinking about it and would write it if colloquialism seemed appropriate to the passage."

3. No ones loves you except *I.*

WRONG. In educated speech, *me* follows the preposition *except.* This problem is troublesome because, to the unsophisticated, the sentence sounds as if it can be completed to "No one loves you, except *I* do," but current educated usage adheres to the technical rule that a preposition requires an objective pronoun (*me*).

4. Please *lay* down.

WRONG. Liberal as grammar has become, there is still no sanction for using *lay* with the meaning of *recline. Lay* means to place, as in *"Lay* your hand on mine." *Lie* is the correct choice.

5. *Who* do you love?

RIGHT. "The English language shows some disposition to get rid of *whom* altogether, and unquestionably it would be a better language with *whom* gone." So wrote Janet Rankin Aiken, of Columbia University, way back in 1936. Today, many decades later, the "disposition" has become a full-fledged force.

The rules for *who* and *whom* are complicated, and few educated speakers have the time, patience, or expertise to bother with them. Use the democratic *who* in your everyday speech whenever it sounds right.

6. Neither of these cars *are* worth the money.

WRONG. The temptation to use *are* in this sentence is, I admit, practically irresistible. However, "neither of" means "neither *one* of" and *is,* therefore, is the preferable verb.

7. The judge sentenced the murderer to be *hung.*

WRONG. A distinction is made, in educated speech, between *hung* and *hanged.* A picture is *hung,* but a person is *hanged*—that is, if such action is intended to bring about an untimely demise.

8. Mother, *can* I go out to play?

RIGHT. If you insist that your child say *may,* and nothing but *may,* when asking for permission, you may be considered puristic. *Can* is not discourteous, incorrect, or vulgar—and the newest editions of the authoritative dictionaries fully sanction the use of *can* in requesting rights, privileges, or permission.

9. Take two *spoonsful* of this medicine every three hours.

WRONG. There is a strange affection, on the part of some people, for *spoonsful* and *cupsful,* even though *spoonsful* and *cupsful* do not exist as acceptable words. The plurals are *spoonfuls* and *cupfuls.*

I am taking for granted, of course, that you are using one spoon and filling it twice. If, for secret reasons of your own, you prefer to take your medicine in two separate spoons, you may then properly speak of "two *spoons full* (not *spoonsful*) of medicine."

10. Your words seem to *infer* that Jack is a liar.

WRONG. *Infer* does not mean *hint* or *suggest. Imply* is the proper word; to *infer* is to draw a conclusion from another's words.

11. I *will* be happy to go to the concert with you.

RIGHT. In informal speech, you need no longer worry about the technical and unrealistic distinctions between *shall* and *will.* The theory of modern grammarians is that *shall-will* differences were simply invented out of whole cloth by the textbook writers of the 1800s. As the editor of the scholarly *Modern Language Forum* at the University of California has stated, "The artificial distinction between *shall* and *will* to designate futurity is a superstition that has neither a basis in historical grammar nor the sound sanction of universal usage."

12. It is *me.*

RIGHT. This "violation" of grammatical "law" has been completely sanctioned by current usage. When the late Winston Churchill made a nationwide radio address from New Haven, Connecticut, many, many years ago, his opening sentence was: "This is *me,* Winston Churchill." I imagine that the purists who were listening fell into a deep state of shock at these words, but of course Churchill was simply using the kind of down-to-earth English that had long since become standard in informal educated speech.

13. Go *slow*.

RIGHT. "Go *slow*" is not, and never has been, incorrect English—every authority concedes that *slow* is an adverb as well as an adjective. Rex Stout, well-known writer of mystery novels and creator of Detective Nero Wolfe, remarked: "Not only do I use and approve of the idiom *Go slow,* but if I find myself with people who do not, I leave quick."

14. Peggy and Karen are *alumni* of the same high school.

WRONG. As Peggy and Karen are obviously women, we call them *alumnae* (ə-LUM'-nee); only male graduates are *alumni* (ə-LUM'-nī).

15. I *would* like to ask you a question.

RIGHT. In current American usage, *would* may be used with *I,* though old-fashioned rules demand *I should.*

Indeed, in modern speech, *should* is almost entirely restricted to expressing probability, duty, or responsibility.

As in the case of the charitable-looking dowager who was approached by a seedy character seeking a handout.

"Madam," he whined, "I haven't eaten in five days."

"My good man," the matron answered with great concern, "you should force yourself!"

5

HOW TO TALK ABOUT
VARIOUS PRACTITIONERS

(Sessions 7–10)

TEASER PREVIEW

What practitioner:

- *is a student of human behavior?*
- *follows the techniques devised by Sigmund Freud?*
- *straightens teeth?*
- *measures vision?*
- *grinds lenses?*
- *treats minor ailments of the feet?*
- *analyzes handwriting?*
- *deals with the problems of aging?*
- *uses manipulation and massage as curative techniques?*

SESSION 7

An ancient Greek mused about the meaning of life, and *philosophy* was born. The first Roman decided to build a road instead of cutting a path through the jungle, and *engineering* came into existence. One day in primitive times, a human being lent to another whatever then passed for money and got back his original investment plus a little more—and *banking* had started.

Most people spend part of every workday at some gainful employment, honest or otherwise, and in so doing often contribute their little mite to the progress of the world.

We explore in this chapter the ideas behind people's occupations—and the words that translate these ideas into verbal symbols.

IDEAS

1. behavior

By education and training, this practitioner is an expert in the dark mysteries of human behavior—what makes people act as they do, why they have certain feelings, how their personalities were formed—in short, what makes them tick. Such a professional is often employed by industries, schools, and institutions to devise means for keeping workers productive and happy, students well-adjusted, and inmates contented. With a state license, this person may also do private or group therapy.

A psychologist

2. worries, fears, conflicts

This practitioner is a physician, psychiatrist, or psychologist who has been specially trained in the techniques devised by Sigmund Freud, encouraging you to delve into that part of your mind called "the unconscious." By reviewing the experiences, traumas, feelings, and thoughts of your earlier years, you come to a better understanding of your present worries, fears, conflicts, repressions, insecurities, and nervous tensions—thus taking the first step in coping with them. Treatment, consisting largely in listening to, and helping you to interpret the meaning of, your free-flowing ideas, is usually given in frequent sessions that may well go on for a year or more.

A psychoanalyst

3. teeth

This practitioner is a dentist who has taken postgraduate work in the straightening of teeth.

An orthodontist

4. eyes

This practitioner measures your vision and prescribes the type of glasses that will give you a new and more accurate view of the world.

An optometrist

5. glasses

This practitioner grinds lenses according to the specifications prescribed by your optometrist or ophthalmologist, and may also deal in other kinds of optical goods.

An optician

6. bones and blood vessels

This practitioner is a member of the profession that originated in 1874, when Andrew T. Still devised a drugless technique of curing diseases by massage and other manipulative procedures, a technique based on the theory that illness may be caused by the undue pressure of displaced bones on nerves and blood vessels.

Training is equal to that of physicians, and in most states these practitioners may also use the same methods as, and have the full rights and privileges of, medical doctors.

An *osteopath*

7. joints and articulations

The basic principle of this practitioner's work is the maintenance of the structural and functional integrity of the nervous system. Treatment consists of manipulating most of the articulations of the body, especially those connected to the spinal column. Licensed and legally recognized in forty-five states, this professional has pursued academic studies and training that parallel those of the major healing professions.

A *chiropractor*

8. feet

This practitioner treats minor foot ailments—corns, calluses, bunions, fallen arches, etc., and may perform minor surgery.

A *podiatrist*

9. writing

This practitioner analyzes handwriting to determine character, personality, or aptitudes, and is often called upon to verify the authenticity of signatures, written documents, etc.

A *graphologist*

10. getting old

This social scientist deals with the financial, economic, sexual, social, retirement, and other non-medical problems of the elderly.

A *gerontologist*

USING THE WORDS

Can you pronounce the words?

1.	*psychologist*	sī-KOL'-ə-jist
2.	*psychoanalyst*	sī-kō-AN'-ə-list
3.	*orthodontist*	awr-thə-DON'-tist
4.	*optometrist*	op-TOM'-ə-trist
5.	*optician*	op-TISH'-ən
6.	*osteopath*	OS'-tee-ə-path
7.	*chiropractor*	KĪ'-rə-prək'-tər
8.	*podiatrist*	pə-DĪ'-ə-trist
9.	*graphologist*	graf-OL'-ə-jist
10.	*gerontologist*	jair'-ən-TOL'-ə-jist

Can you work with the words?

PRACTITIONERS

INTERESTS

1. psychologist	a. vision
2. psychoanalyst	b. "the unconscious"
3. orthodontist	c. bones and blood vessels
4. optometrist	d. lenses and optical instruments
5. optician	e. feet
6. osteopath	f. teeth
7. chiropractor	g. problems of aging
8. podiatrist	h. joints of the spine
9. graphologist	i. handwriting
10. gerontologist	j. behavior

KEY: 1–j, 2–b, 3–f, 4–a, 5–d, 6–c, 7–h, 8–e, 9–i, 10–g

Do you understand the words?

1. A *psychologist* must also be a physician.

TRUE   FALSE

2. A *psychoanalyst* follows Freudian techniques.   TRUE   FALSE

3. An *orthodontist* specializes in straightening teeth.   TRUE   FALSE

4. An *optometrist* prescribes and fits glasses.   TRUE   FALSE

5. An *optician* may prescribe glasses.   TRUE   FALSE

6. An *osteopath* may use massage and other manipulative techniques.   TRUE   FALSE

7. A *chiropractor* has a medical degree.   TRUE   FALSE

8. A *podiatrist* may perform major surgery.   TRUE   FALSE

9. A *graphologist* analyzes character from handwriting.   TRUE   FALSE

10. A *gerontologist* is interested in the non-medical problems of adolescence.   TRUE   FALSE

KEY: 1–F, 2–T, 3–T, 4–T, 5–F, 6–T, 7–F, 8–F, 9–T, 10–F

Can you recall the words?

1. delves into the unconscious   1. P_____

2. uses either massage and manipulation or other standard medical procedures to treat illness   2. O_____

3. takes care of minor ailments of the feet   3. P_____

4. straightens teeth   4. O_____

5. analyzes handwriting   5. G_____

6. grinds lenses and sells optical goods   6. O_____

7. deals with the non-medical problems of aging   7. G_____

8. manipulates articulations connected to the spinal column   8. C_____

9. studies and explains human
behavior

9. P_____

10. measures vision and prescribes
glasses

10. O_____

KEY: 1–psychoanalyst, 2–osteopath, 3–podiatrist, 4–orthodontist,
5–graphologist, 6–optician, 7–gerontologist, 8–chiropractor, 9–psychologist, 10–optometrist

---

(End of Session 7)

SESSION 8

ORIGINS AND RELATED WORDS

1. the mental life

Psychologist is built upon the same Greek root as *psychiatrist*—*psyche*, spirit, soul, or mind. In *psychiatrist*, the combining form is *iatreia*, medical healing. In *psychologist*, the combining form is *logos*, science or study; a *psychologist*, by etymology, is one who studies the mind.

The field is *psychology* (sī-KOL′-ə-jee), the adjective *psychological* (sī′-kə-LOJ′-ə-kəl).

Psyche (SĪ′-kee) is also an English word in its own right—it designates the mental life, the spiritual or non-physical aspect of one's existence. The adjective *psychic* (SĪ′-kik) refers to phenomena or qualities that cannot be explained in purely physical terms. People may be called *psychic* if they seem to possess a sixth sense, a special gift of mind reading, or any mysterious aptitudes that cannot be accounted for logically. A person's disturbance is *psychic* if it is emotional or mental, rather than physical.

Psyche combines with the Greek *pathos,* suffering or disease, to form *psychopathic* (sī-kə-PATH'-ik), an adjective that describes someone suffering from a severe mental or emotional disorder. The noun is *psychopathy* (sī'-KOP'-ə-thee).*

The root *psyche* combines with Greek *soma,* body, to form *psychosomatic* (sī'-kō-sə-MAT'-ik), an adjective that delineates the powerful influence that the mind, especially the unconscious, has on bodily diseases. Thus, a person who fears the consequence of being present at a certain meeting will suddenly develop a bad cold or backache, or even be injured in a traffic accident, so that his appearance at this meeting is made impossible. It's a real cold, it's far from an imaginary backache, and of course one cannot in any sense doubt the reality of the automobile that injured him. Yet, according to the *psychosomatic* theory of medicine, his unconscious made him susceptible to the cold germs, caused the backache, or forced him into the path of the car.

A *psychosomatic* disorder actually exists insofar as symptoms are concerned (headache, excessive urination, pains, paralysis, heart palpitations), yet there is no organic cause within the body. The cause is within the *psyche,* the mind. Dr. Flanders Dunbar, in *Mind and Body,* gives a clear and exciting account of the interrelationship between emotions and diseases.

Psychoanalysis (sī'-kō-ə-NAL'-ə-sis) relies on the technique of deeply, exhaustively probing into the unconscious, a technique developed by Sigmund Freud. In oversimplified terms, the general principle of *psychoanalysis* is to guide the patient to an awareness of the deep-seated, unconscious causes of anxieties, fears, conflicts, and tension. Once found, exposed to the light of day, and thoroughly understood, claim the *psychoanalysts,* these causes may vanish like a light snow that is exposed to strong sunlight.

Consider an example: You have asthma, let us say, and your

* *Psychopathy* is usually characterized by antisocial and extremely egocentric behavior. A *psychopath* (SĪ'-kə-path'), sometimes called a *psychopathic personality,* appears to be lacking an inner moral censor, and often commits criminal acts, without anxiety or guilt, in order to obtain immediate gratification of desires. Such a person may be utterly lacking in sexual restraint, or addicted to hard drugs. Some psychologists prefer the label *sociopath* (SŌ'-shee-ə-path' *or* SŌ'-see-ə-path') for this type of personality to indicate the absence of a social conscience.

doctor can find no physical basis for your ailment. So you are referred to a *psychoanalyst* (or *psychiatrist* or clinical *psychologist* who practices *psychoanalytically* oriented therapy).

With your therapist you explore your past life, dig into your unconscious, and discover, let us say for the sake of argument, that your mother or father always used to set for you impossibly high goals. No matter what you accomplished in school, it was not good enough—in your mother's or father's opinion (and such opinions were always made painfully clear to you), you could do better if you were not so lazy. As a child you built up certain resentments and anxieties because you seemed unable to please your parent—and (this will sound farfetched, but it is perfectly possible) as a result you became asthmatic. How else were you going to get the parental love, the approbation, the attention you needed and that you felt you were not receiving?

In your sessions with your therapist, you discover that your asthma is emotionally, rather than organically, based—your ailment is *psychogenic* (sī'-kō-JEN'-ik), of *psychic* origin, or (the terms are used more or less interchangeably although they differ somewhat in definition) *psychosomatic,* resulting from the interaction of mind and body. (*Psychogenic* is built on *psyche* plus Greek *genesis,* birth or origin.)

And your treatment? No drugs, no surgery—these may help the body, not the emotions. Instead, you "work out" (this is the term used in *psychoanalytic* [sī-kō-an'-ə-LIT'-ik] parlance) early trauma in talk, in remembering, in exploring, in interpreting, in reliving childhood experiences. And if your asthma is indeed *psychogenic* (or *psychosomatic*), therapy will very likely help you; your attacks may cease, either gradually or suddenly.

Freudian therapy is less popular today than formerly; many newer therapies—Gestalt, bioenergetics, transactional analysis, to name only a few—claim to produce quicker results.

In any case, *psychotherapy* (sī-kō-THAIR'-ə-pee) of one sort or another is the indicated treatment for *psychogenic* (or *psychosomatic*) disorders, or for any personality disturbances. The practitioner is a *psychotherapist* (sī-kō-THAIR'-ə-pist) or *therapist,* for short; the adjective is *psychotherapeutic* (sī-kō-thair'-ə-PYOO'-tik).

REVIEW OF ETYMOLOGY

ROOT, SUFFIX	MEANING	ENGLISH WORD
1. *psyche*	spirit, soul, mind	_____
2. *iatreia*	medical healing	_____
3. *-ic*	adjective suffix	_____
4. *soma*	body	_____
5. *genesis*	birth, origin	_____
6. *pathos*	suffering, disease	_____

USING THE WORDS

Can you pronounce the words?

1. *psychology*	sī-KOL'-ə-jee
2. *psychological*	sī'-kə-LOJ'-ə-kəl
3. *psyche*	SĪ'-kee
4. *psychic*	SĪ'-kik
5. *psychopathic*	sī-kə-PATH'-ik
6. *psychopathy*	sī-KOP'-ə-thee
7. *psychopath*	SĪ'-kə-path
8. *psychosomatic*	sī'-kō-sə-MAT'-ik
9. *psychoanalysis*	sī'-kō-ə-NAL'-ə-sis
10. *psychoanalytic*	sī-kō-an'-ə-LIT'-ik
11. *psychogenic*	sī-kō-JEN'-ik
12. *psychotherapy*	sī-kō-THAIR'-ə-pee
13. *psychotherapist*	sī-kō-THAIR'-ə-pist
14. *psychotherapeutic*	sī-kō-thair'-ə-PYOO'-tik

Can you work with the words?

1. psychology   a. mental or emotional disturb-
                                  ance

2. psyche

3. psychic

4. psychopathy

5. psychosomatic

6. psychoanalysis

7. psychogenic

8. psychotherapy

9. psychopath

b. psychological treatment based on Freudian techniques

c. general term for psychological treatment

d. originating in the mind or emotions

e. one's inner or mental life, or self-image

f. study of the human mind and behavior

g. describing the interaction of mind and body

h. pertaining to the mind; extrasensory

i. person lacking in social conscience or inner censor

KEY: 1–f, 2–e, 3–h, 4–a, 5–g, 6–b, 7–d, 8–c, 9–i

Do you understand the words?

1. *Psychological* treatment aims at sharpening the intellect. TRUE FALSE

2. *Psychic* phenomena can be explained on rational or physical grounds TRUE FALSE

3. *Psychopathic* personalities are normal and healthy. TRUE FALSE

4. A *psychosomatic* symptom is caused by organic disease. TRUE FALSE

5. Every therapist uses *psychoanalysis*. TRUE FALSE

6. A *psychogenic* illness originates in the mind or emotions. TRUE FALSE

7. A *psychotherapist* must have a medical degree. TRUE FALSE

8. *Psychoanalytically* oriented therapy uses Freudian techniques.   TRUE   FALSE
9. A *psychopath* is often a criminal.   TRUE   FALSE

KEY: 1–F, 2–F, 3–F, 4–F, 5–F, 6–T, 7–F, 8–T, 9–T

Can you recall the words?

1. one's inner or mental life, or self-image   1. P_____
2. the adjective that denotes the interactions, especially in illness, between mind and body   2. P_____
3. mentally or emotionally disturbed   3. P_____
4. study of behavior   4. P_____
5. extrasensory   5. P_____
6. treatment by Freudian techniques   6. P_____
7. pertaining to the study of behavior (*adj.*)   7. P_____
8. of mental or emotional origin   8. P_____
9. general term for treatment of emotional disorders   9. P_____
10. antisocial person   10. P_____

KEY: 1–psyche, 2–psychosomatic, 3–psychopathic, 4–psychology, 5–psychic, 6–psychoanalysis, 7–psychological, 8–psychogenic, 9–psychotherapy, 10–psychopath

---

(*End of Session 8*)

SESSION 9

ORIGINS AND RELATED WORDS

1. the whole tooth

Orthodontist, as we discovered in Chapter 4, is built on *orthos,* straight, correct, plus *odontos,* tooth.

A *pedodontist* (pee′-dō-DON′-tist) specializes in the care of children's teeth—the title is constructed from *paidos,* child, plus *odontos.* The specialty: *pedodontia* (pee′-dō-DON′-sha); the adjective: *pedodontic* (pee′-dō-DON′-tik).

A *periodontist* (pair′-ee-ō-DON′-tist) is a gum specialist—the term combines *odontos* with the prefix *peri-,* around, surrounding. (As a quick glance in the mirror will tell you, the gums surround the teeth, more or less.)

Can you figure out the word for the specialty?

_____

For the adjective? _____

An *endodontist* (en′-dō-DON′-tist) specializes in work on the pulp of the tooth and in root-canal therapy—the prefix in this term is *endo-,* from Greek *endon,* inner, within.

Try your hand again at constructing words. What is the specialty? _____. And the adjective?

_____.

The prefix *ex-,* out, combines with *odontos* to form *exodontist* (eks′-ō-DON′-tist). What do you suppose, therefore, is the work in which this practitioner specializes? _____.
And the term for the specialty? _____.
For the adjective? _____

2. measurement

The *optometrist*, by etymology, measures vision—the term is built on *opsis, optikos*, view, vision, plus *metron*, measurement.

Metron is the root in many other words:

1. *thermometer* (thər-MOM'-ə-tər)—an instrument to measure heat (Greek *therme*, heat).

2. *barometer* (bə-ROM'-ə-ter)—an instrument to measure atmospheric pressure (Greek *baros*, weight); the adjective is *barometric* (bair'-ə-MET'-rik).

3. *sphygmomanometer* (sfig'-mō-mə-NOM'-ə-tər)—a device for measuring blood pressure (Greek *sphygmos*, pulse).

4. *metric* system—a decimal system of weights and measures, long used in other countries and now gradually being adopted in the United States.

3. bones, feet, and hands

Osteopath combines Greek *osteon*, bone, with *pathos*, suffering, disease. *Osteopathy* (os'-tee-OP'-ə-thee), you will recall, was originally based on the theory that disease is caused by pressure of the bones on blood vessels and nerves. An *osteopathic* (os'-tee-ə-PATH'-ik) physician is *not* a bone specialist, despite the misleading etymology—and should not be confused with the *orthopedist*, who is.

The *podiatrist* (Greek *pous, podos*, foot, plus *iatreia*, medical healing) practices *podiatry* (pə-DĬ'-ə-tree). The adjective is *podiatric* (pō'-dee-AT'-rik).

The root *pous, podos* is found also in:

1. *octopus* (OK'-tə-pəs), the eight-armed (or, as the etymology has it, eight-footed) sea creature (Greek *okto*, eight).

2. *platypus* (PLAT'-ə-pəs), the strange water mammal with a duck's bill, webbed feet, and a beaver-like tail that reproduces by laying eggs (Greek *platys*, broad, flat—hence, by etymology, a flatfoot!).

3. *podium* (PŌ'-dee-əm), a speaker's platform, etymologically a place for the feet. (The suffix *-ium* often signifies "place where," as in *gymnasium, stadium, auditorium*, etc.)

4. *tripod* (TRĪ'-pod), a three-legged (or "footed") stand for a camera or other device (*tri-*, three).

5. *chiropodist* (kə-ROP'-ə-dist), earlier title for a *podiatrist*, and still often used. The specialty is *chiropody* (kə-ROP'-ə-dee).

Chiropody combines *podos* with Greek *cheir*, hand, spelled *chiro-* in English words. The term was coined in the days before labor-saving machinery and push-button devices, when people worked with their hands and developed calluses on their upper extremities as well as on their feet. Today most of us earn a livelihood in more sedentary occupations, and so we may develop calluses on less visible portions of our anatomy.

Chiropractors heal with their hands—the specialty is *chiropractic* (kī'-rō-PRAK'-tik).

Cheir (*chiro-*), hand, is the root in *chirography* (kī-ROG'-rə-fee). Recalling the *graph-* in *graphologist*, can you figure out by etymology what *chirography* is? _____

An expert in writing by hand, or in penmanship (a lost art in these days of electronic word-processing),† would be a *chirographer* (kī-ROG'-rə-fər); the adjective is *chirographic* (kī'-rō-GRAF'-ik).

If the suffix *-mancy* comes from a Greek word meaning *foretelling* or *prediction*, can you decide what *chiromancy* (KĪ'-rō-man'-see) must be? _____.

The person who practices *chiromancy* is a *chiromancer* (KĪ'-rō-man'-sər); the adjective is *chiromantic* (kī'-rō-MAN'-tik).

REVIEW OF ETYMOLOGY

PREFIX, ROOT, SUFFIX	MEANING	ENGLISH WORD
1. *orthos*	straight, correct	_____
2. *odontos*	tooth	_____
3. *paidos* (*ped-*)	child	_____
4. *-ic*	adjective suffix	_____
5. *peri-*	around, surrounding	_____
6. *endo-*	inner, within	_____

† But see *calligrapher* in the next session.

7. *ex-*	out	_____
8. *opsis, optikos*	vision	_____
9. *metron*	measurement	_____
10. *therme*	heat	_____
11. *baros*	weight	_____
12. *sphygmos*	pulse	_____
13. *osteon*	bone	_____
14. *pathos*	suffering, disease	_____
15. *pous, podos*	foot	_____
16. *okto*	eight	_____
17. *platys*	broad, flat	_____
18. *-ium*	place where	_____
19. *tri-*	three	_____
20. *cheir* (*chiro-*)	hand	_____
21. *mancy*	prediction	_____
22. *iatreia*	medical healing	_____

USING THE WORDS

Can you pronounce the words? (I)

1. *pedodontist*	pee′-dō-DON′-tist
2. *pedodontia*	pee′-dō-DON′-shə
3. *pedodontic*	pee′-dō-DON′-tik
4. *periodontist*	pair′-ee-ō-DON′-tist
5. *periodontia*	pair′-ee-ō-DON′-shə
6. *periodontic*	pair′-ee-ō-DON′-tik
7. *endodontist*	en′-dō-DON′-tist
8. *endodontia*	en′-dō-DON′-shə
9. *endodontic*	en′-dō-DON′-tik
10. *exodontist*	eks′-ō-DON′-tist
11. *exodontia*	eks′-ō-DON′-shə
12. *exodontic*	eks′-ō-DON′-tik
13. *thermometer*	thər-MOM′-ə-tər
14. *barometer*	bə-ROM′-ə-tər
15. *barometric*	bair′-ə-MET′-rik
16. *sphygmomanometer*	sfig′-mō-mə-NOM′-ə-tər

96

Can you pronounce the words? (II)

1. *osteopathy* — os'-tee-OP'-ə-thee
2. *osteopathic* — os'-tee-ə-PATH'-ik
3. *podiatry* — pə-DĬ'-ə-tree
4. *podiatric* — pō'-dee-AT'-rik
5. *octopus* — OK'-tə-pəs
6. *platypus* — PLAT'-ə-pəs
7. *podium* — PŌ'-dee-əm
8. *tripod* — TRĬ'-pod
9. *chiropodist* — kə-ROP'-ə-dist
10. *chiropody* — kə-ROP'-ə-dee
11. *chiropractic* — kī'-rō-PRAK'-tik
12. *chirography* — kī-ROG'-rə-fee
13. *chirographer* — kī-ROG'-rə-fər
14. *chirographic* — kī'-rə-GRAF'-ik
15. *chiromancy* — KĪ'-rə-man'-see
16. *chiromancer* — KĪ'-rə-man'-sər
17. *chiromantic* — kī'-rə-MAN'-tik

Can you work with the words? (I)

1. orthodontia   a. dental specialty involving the pulp and root canal
2. pedodontia   b. instrument that measures atmospheric pressure
3. periodontia   c. specialty arising from the theory that pressure of the bones on nerves and blood vessels may cause disease
4. endodontia   d. specialty of child dentistry
5. exodontia   e. blood-pressure apparatus
6. barometer   f. treatment of minor ailments of the foot
7. sphygmomanometer   g. instrument to measure heat
8. osteopathy   h. specialty of tooth extraction
9. podiatry   i. specialty of tooth straightening

10. thermometer   j. specialty of the gums

Can you work with the words? (II)

1. octopus   a. speaker's platform
2. platypus   b. maintenance of integrity of
                                      the nervous system by ma-
                                      nipulation and massage
3. podium   c. palm reading
4. chiropody   d. eight-armed sea creature
5. chiropractic   e. handwriting
6. chirography   f. treatment of minor ailments
                                      of the foot
7. chiromancy   g. egg-laying mammal with
                                      webbed feet

KEY: 1–d, 2–g, 3–a, 4–f, 5–b, 6–e, 7–c

Do you understand the words?

1. *Orthodontia* is a branch of dentistry.	TRUE	FALSE
2. Doctors use *sphygmomanometers* to check blood pressure.	TRUE	FALSE
3. *Osteopathic* physicians may use standard medical procedures.	TRUE	FALSE
4. *Chiropractic* deals with handwriting.	TRUE	FALSE
5. *Chiropody* and *podiatry* are synonymous terms.	TRUE	FALSE
6. A *podium* is a place from which a lecture might be delivered.	TRUE	FALSE
7. A *pedodontist* is a foot doctor.	TRUE	FALSE
8. A *periodontist* is a gum specialist.	TRUE	FALSE
9. A *endodontist* does root-canal therapy.	TRUE	FALSE
10. An *exodontist* extracts teeth.	TRUE	FALSE

11. A *barometer* measures heat.	TRUE	FALSE
12. An *octopus* has eight arms.	TRUE	FALSE
13. A *platypus* is a land mammal.	TRUE	FALSE
14. A *tripod* has four legs.	TRUE	FALSE
15. A *chirographer* is an expert at penmanship.	TRUE	FALSE
16. A *chiromancer* reads palms.	TRUE	FALSE

KEY: 1–T, 2–T, 3–T, 4–F, 5–T, 6–T, 7–F, 8–T, 9–T, 10–T, 11–F, 12–T, 13–F, 14–F, 15–T, 16–T

Do you recall the words? (I)

1. pertaining to child dentistry (*adj.*)   1. P_____
2. pertaining to treatment of the foot (*adj.*)   2. P_____
3. blood-pressure apparatus   3. S_____
4. three-legged stand   4. T_____
5. pertaining to the treatment of diseases by manipulation to relieve pressure of the bones on nerves and blood vessels (*adj.*)   5. O_____
6. pertaining to handwriting (*adj.*)   6. C_____
7. gum specialist   7. P_____
8. treatment of ailments of the foot   8. P_____ *or* C_____
9. stand for a speaker   9. P_____
10. dentist specializing in treating the pulp of the tooth or in doing root-canal therapy   10. E_____

KEY: 1–pedodontic, 2–podiatric, 3–sphygmomanometer, 4–tripod, 5–osteopathic, 6–chirographic, 7–periodontist, 8–podiatry *or* chiropody, 9–podium, 10–endodontist

---

Can you recall the words? (II)

1. pertaining to the specialty of tooth extraction (*adj.*)
2. pertaining to the measurement of atmospheric pressure (*adj.*)
3. palm reading (*noun*)
4. handwriting
5. the practice of manipulating bodily articulations to relieve ailments
6. egg-laying mammal
7. eight-armed sea creature
8. instrument to measure heat

1. E_____
2. B_____
3. C_____
4. C_____
5. C_____

6. P_____
7. O_____
8. T_____

KEY: 1—exodontic, 2—barometric, 3—chiromancy, 4—chirography, 5—chiropractic, 6—platypus, 7—octopus, 8—thermometer

(*End of Session 9*)

SESSION 10

ORIGINS AND RELATED WORDS

1. writing and writers

The Greek verb *graphein*, to write, is the source of a great many English words.

We know that the *graphologist* analyzes handwriting, the term combining *graphein* with *logos*, science, study. The specialty is *graphology* (grə-FOL'-ə-jee), the adjective *graphological* (graf'-ə-LOJ'-ə-kəl).

Chirographer is built on *graphein* plus *cheir* (*chiro*-), hand.

Though *chirography* may be a lost art, *calligraphy* (kə-LIG′-rə-fee) is enjoying a revival. For centuries before the advent of printing, *calligraphy*, or penmanship as an artistic expression, was practiced by monks.

A *calligrapher* (kə-LIG′-rə-fər) is called upon to design and write announcements, place cards, etc., as a touch of elegance. The adjective is *calligraphic* (kal′-ə-GRAF′-ik).

Calligraphy combines *graphein* with Greek *kallos*,‡ beauty, and so, by etymology, means *beautiful writing*.

If a word exists for artistic handwriting, there must be one for the opposite—bad, scrawly, or illegible handwriting. And indeed there is—*cacography* (kə-KOG′-rə-fee), combining *graphein* with Greek *kakos*, bad, harsh.

By analogy with the forms of *calligraphy*, can you write the word for:

One who uses bad or illegible handwriting?

_____

Pertaining to, or marked by, bad handwriting (*adjective*)?

_____

Graphein is found in other English words:

1. *cardiograph* (discussed in Chapter 4)—etymologically a "heart writer" (*kardia*, heart).

2. *photograph*—etymologically, "written by light" (Greek *photos*, light).

3. *phonograph*—etymologically, a "sound writer" (Greek *phone*, sound).

4. *telegraph*—etymologically a "distance writer" (Greek *tele-*, distance).

5. *biography*—etymologically "life writing" (Greek, *bios*, life).

(Many of these new roots will be discussed in greater detail in later chapters.)

2. aging and the old

We know that a *geriatrician* specializes in the medical care of the elderly. The Greek word *geras*, old age, has a derived form,

‡ An entrancing word that also derives from *kallos* is *callipygian* (kal′-ə PIJ′-ee-ən), an adjective describing a shapely or attractive rear end, or a person so endowed—the combining root is *pyge*, buttocks.

geron, old man, the root in *gerontologist.* The specialty is *gerontology* (jair′-ən-TOL′-ə-jee), the adjective is *gerontological* (jair′-ən-tə-LOJ′-ə-kəl).

The Latin word for *old* is *senex,* the base on which *senile, senescent, senior,* and *senate* are built.

1. *senile* (SEE′-nīl)—showing signs of the physical and/or mental deterioration that generally marks very old age. The noun is *senility* (sə-NIL′-ə-tee).

2. *senescent* (sə-NES′-ənt)—aging, growing old. (Note the same suffix in this word as in *adolescent,* growing into an adult, *convalescent,* growing healthy again, and *obsolescent,* growing or becoming obsolete.) The noun is *senescence* (sə-NES′-əns).

3. *senior* (SEEN′-yər)—older. Noun: *seniority* (seen-YAWR′-ə-tee).

4. *senate* (SEN′-ət)—originally a council of older, and presumably wiser, citizens.

REVIEW OF ETYMOLOGY

PREFIX, ROOT, SUFFIX	MEANING	ENGLISH WORD
1. *graphein*	to write	_____
2. *cheir (chiro-)*	hand	_____
3. *kallos*	beauty	_____
4. *-er*	one who	_____
5. *-ic*	adjective suffix	_____
6. *pyge*	buttocks	_____
7. *kakos*	bad, harsh	_____
8. *kardia*	heart	_____
9. *photos*	light	_____
10. *tele-*	distance	_____
11. *bios*	life	_____
12. *geras*	old age	_____
13. *geron*	old man	_____
14. *senex*	old	_____
15. *-escent*	growing, becoming	_____

USING THE WORDS

Can you pronounce the words?

1. *graphology*	grə-FOL'-ə-jee
2. *graphological*	graf'-ə-LOJ'-ə-kəl
3. *calligraphy*	kə-LIG'-rə-fee
4. *calligrapher*	kə-LIG'-rə-fər
5. *calligraphic*	kal'-ə-GRAF'-ik
6. *callipygian*	kal'-ə-PIJ'-ee-ən
7. *cacography*	kə-KOG'-rə-fee
8. *cacographer*	kə-KOG'-rə-fər
9. *cacographic*	kak'-ə-GRAF'-ik
10. *gerontology*	jair'-ən-TOL'-ə-jee
11. *gerontological*	jair'-ən-tə-LOJ'-ə-kəl
12. *senile*	SEE'-nīl
13. *senility*	sə-NIL'-ə-tee
14. *senescent*	sə-NES'-ənt
15. *senescence*	sə-NES'-əns

Can you work with the words?

1. graphology	a.	possessed of beautiful buttocks
2. calligraphy	b.	science of the social, economic, etc. problems of the aged
3. callipygian	c.	condition of aging or growing old
4. cacography	d.	deteriorated old age
5. gerontology	e.	analysis of handwriting
6. senility	f.	ugly, bad, illegible handwriting
7. senescence	g.	beautiful handwriting; handwriting as an artistic expression

KEY: 1–e, 2–g, 3–a, 4–f, 5–b, 6–d, 7–c

Do you understand the words?

1.	*Graphology* analyzes the grammar, spelling, and sentence structure of written material.	TRUE	FALSE
2.	A *calligrapher* creates artistic forms out of alphabetical symbols.	TRUE	FALSE
3.	Tight slacks are best worn by those of *callipygian* anatomy.	TRUE	FALSE
4.	*Cacographic* writing is easy to read.	TRUE	FALSE
5.	*Gerontology* aims to help old people live more comfortably.	TRUE	FALSE
6.	*Senile* people are old but still vigorous and mentally alert.	TRUE	FALSE
7.	In a society dedicated to the worship of youth, *senescence* is not an attractive prospect.	TRUE	FALSE

KEY: 1–F, 2–T, 3–T, 4–F, 5–T, 6–F, 7–T

Can you recall the words?

1.	pertaining to the study of the non-medical problems of the aged (*adj.*)	1. G_____
2.	growing old (*adj.*)	2. S_____
3.	pertaining to handwriting as an artistic expression (*adj.*)	3. C_____
4.	one who uses ugly, illegible handwriting	4. C_____
5.	mentally and physically deteriorated from old age	5. S_____
6.	pertaining to the analysis of handwriting (*adj.*)	6. G_____

7. possessed of beautiful or shapely   7. C_____
   buttocks

KEY: 1–gerontological, 2–senescent, 3–calligraphic, 4–cacogra-
     pher, 5–senile, 6–graphological, 7–callipygian

CHAPTER REVIEW

A. Do you recognize the words?

1. Practitioner trained in Freudian techniques: (a) psychologist, (b) psychoanalyst, (c) psychotherapist
2. Foot doctor: (a) podiatrist, (b) osteopath, (c) chiropractor
3. Handwriting analyst: (a) graphologist, (b) chirographer, (c)
   cacographer
4. Mentally or emotionally disturbed: (a) psychological, (b)
   psychopathic, (c) psychic
5. Originating in the emotions: (a) psychic, (b) psychogenic,
   (c) psychoanalytic
6. Describing bodily ailments tied up with the emotions: (a)
   psychosomatic, (b) psychopathic, (c) psychiatric
7. Gum specialist: (a) periodontist, (b) pedodontist, (c) endodontist
8. Specialist in tooth extraction: (a) orthodontist, (b) exodontist,
   (c) endodontist
9. Blood-pressure apparatus: (a) barometer, (b) thermometer,
   (c) sphygmomanometer
10. Prediction by palm reading: (a) chirography, (b) chiropody,
    (c) chiromancy
11. Possessed of a shapely posterior: (a) calligraphic, (b) calli-
    pygian, (c) adolescent
12. Artistic handwriting: (a) calligraphy, (b) chirography, (c)
    graphology
13. Growing old: (a) senile, (b) geriatric, (c) senescent
14. Medical specialty dealing with the aged: (a) gerontology,
    (b) geriatrics, (c) chiropractic

15. Antisocial person who may commit criminal acts: (a) psychopath, (b) sociopath, (c) osteopath

---

KEY: 1–b, 2–a, 3–a, 4–b, 5–b, 6–a, 7–a, 8–b, 9–c, 10–c, 11–b, 12–a, 13–c, 14–b, 15–a *and* b

---

B. Can you recognize roots?

ROOT	MEANING	EXAMPLE
1. *psyche*		psychiatry
2. *iatreia*		podiatry
3. *soma*		psychosomatic
4. *pathos*		osteopath
5. *orthos*		orthodontia
6. *paidos (ped-)*		pedodontist
7. *odontos*		exodontist
8. *pous, podos*		platypus
9. *cheir (chiro-)*		chiropodist
10. *okto*		octopus
11. *graphein*		graphology
12. *kallos*		calligraphy
13. *pyge*		callipygian
14. *kakos*		cacography
15. *photos*		photography
16. *tele-*		telegraph
17. *bios*		biography
18. *geras*		geriatrics
19. *geron*		gerontology
20. *senex*		senate

KEY: 1–mind, 2–medical healing, 3–body, 4–disease, 5–straight, correct, 6–child, 7–tooth, 8–foot, 9–hand, 10–eight, 11–to write, 12–beauty, 13–buttocks, 14–bad, ugly, 15–light, 16–distance, 17–life, 18–old age, 19–old man, 20–old.

TEASER QUESTIONS FOR THE AMATEUR ETYMOLOGIST

1. Latin *octoginta* is a root related to Greek *okto,* eight. How old is an *octogenarian* (ok'-tə-jə-NAIR'-ee-ən)? _____
_____.

2. You are familiar with *kakos,* bad, harsh, as in *cacography,* and with *phone,* sound, as in *phonograph.* Can you construct a word ending in the letter *y* that means *harsh, unpleasant sound?* _____. (Can you pronounce it?)

3. Using *callipygian* as a model, can you construct a word to describe an ugly, unshapely rear end? _____
_____. (Can you pronounce it?)

4. Using the prefix *tele-,* distance, can you think of the word for a field glass that permits the viewer to see great distances? _____. How about a word for the instrument that transmits sound over a distance? _____
_____. Finally, what is it that makes it possible for you to view happenings that occur a great distance away? _____
_____.

(*Answers in Chapter 18*)

BECOMING WORD-CONSCIOUS

Perhaps, if you have been working as assiduously with this book as I have repeatedly counseled, you have noticed an interesting phenomenon.

This phenomenon is as follows: You read a magazine article and suddenly you see one or more of the words you have recently learned. Or you open a book and there again are some of the words you have been working with. In short, all your reading seems to call to your attention the very words you've been studying.

Why? Have I, with uncanny foresight, picked words which have suddenly and inexplicably become popular among writers? Obviously, that's nonsense.

The change is in you. You have now begun to be alert to words, you have developed what is known in psychology as a "mind-set" toward certain words. Therefore, whenever these words occur in your reading you take special notice of them.

The same words occurred before—and just as plentifully—but since they presented little communication to you, you reacted to them with an unseeing eye, with an ungrasping mind. You were figuratively, and almost literally, blind to them.

Do you remember when you bought, or contemplated buying, a new car? Let's say it was a Toyota. Suddenly you began to see Toyotas all around you—you had a Toyota "mind-set."

It is thus with anything new in your life. Development of a "mind-set" means that the new experience has become very real, very important, almost vital.

If you have become suddenly alert to the new words you have been learning, you're well along toward your goal of building a superior vocabulary. *You are beginning to live in a new and different intellectual atmosphere—nothing less!*

On the other hand, if the phenomenon I have been describing has not yet occurred, do not despair. It will. I am alerting you to its possibilities—recognize it and welcome it when it happens.

(*End of Session 10*)

HOW GRAMMAR CHANGES

If you think that grammar is an exact science, get ready for a shock. Grammar is a science, all right—but it is most inexact. There are no inflexible laws, no absolutely hard and fast rules, no unchanging principles. Correctness varies with the times and depends much more on geography, on social class, and on collective human caprice than on the restrictions found in textbooks.

In mathematics, which is an exact science, five and five make ten the country over—in the North, in the South, in the West; in Los Angeles and Coral Gables and New York. There are no two opinions on the matter—we are dealing, so far as we know, with a universal and indisputable fact.

In grammar, however, since the facts are highly susceptible to change, we have to keep an eye peeled for trends. What are educated people saying these days? Which expressions are generally used and accepted on educated levels, which others are more or less restricted to the less educated levels of speech? The answers to these questions indicate the trend of usage in the United States, and if such trends come in conflict with academic rules, then the rules are no longer of any great importance.

Grammar follows the speech habits of the majority of educated people—not the other way around. That is the important point to keep in mind.

The following notes on current trends in modern usage are intended to help you come to a decision about certain controversial expressions. As you read each sentence, pay particular attention to the italicized word or words. Does the usage square with your own language patterns? Would you be willing to phrase your thoughts in just such terms? Decide whether the sentence is right or wrong, then compare your conclusion with the opinions given following the test.

TEST YOURSELF

1. Let's keep this between you and *I*.	RIGHT	WRONG
2. I'm your best friend, *ain't* I?	RIGHT	WRONG
3. Five and five *is* ten.	RIGHT	WRONG
4. I never saw a man get so *mad*.	RIGHT	WRONG
5. Every one of his sisters *are* unmarried.	RIGHT	WRONG
6. He visited an *optometrist* for an eye operation.	RIGHT	WRONG
7. Do you *prophecy* another world war?	RIGHT	WRONG
8. *Leave* us not mention it.	RIGHT	WRONG
9. If you expect to *eventually succeed,* you must keep trying.	RIGHT	WRONG

1. Let's keep this between you and *I*.

WRONG. Children are so frequently corrected by parents and teachers when they say *me* that they cannot be blamed if they begin to think that this simple syllable is probably a naughty word. Dialogues such as the following are certainly typical of many households.

"Mother, can me and Johnnie go out and play?"

"No, dear, not until you say it correctly. You mean 'May Johnnie and I go out to play?'"

"Who wants a jelly apple?"

"Me!"

"Then use the proper word."

(The child becomes a little confused at this point—there seem to be so many "proper" and "improper" words.)

110

"Me, *please!*"

"No, dear, not *me*."

"Oh. *I*, please?"

(This sounds terrible to a child's ear. It completely violates his sense of language, but he does want the jelly apple, so he grudgingly conforms.)

"Who broke my best vase?"

"It wasn't me!"

"Is that good English, Johnnie?"

"Okay, it wasn't I. But honest, Mom, it wasn't me—I didn't even touch it!"

And so, if the child is strong enough to survive such constant corrections, he decides that whenever there is room for doubt, it is safer to say *I*.

Some adults, conditioned in childhood by the kind of misguided censorship detailed here, are likely to believe that "between you and *I*" is the more elegant form of expression, but most educated speakers, obeying the rule that a preposition governs the objective pronoun, say "between you and *me*."

2. I'm your best friend, *ain't* I?

WRONG. As linguistic scholars have frequently pointed out, it is unfortunate that *ain't I?* is unpopular in educated speech, for the phrase fills a long-felt need. *Am I not?* is too prissy for down-to-earth people; *amn't I?* is ridiculous; and *aren't I,* though popular in England, has never really caught on in America. With a sentence like the one under discussion you are practically in a linguistic trap—there is no way out unless you are willing to choose between appearing illiterate, sounding prissy, or feeling ridiculous.

"What is the matter with *ain't I?* for *am I not?*" language scholar Wallace Rice once wrote. "Nothing whatever, save that a number of minor grammarians object to it. *Ain't I?* has a pleasant sound once the ears are unstopped of prejudice." Mr. Rice has a valid point there, yet educated people avoid *ain't I?* as if it were catching. In all honesty, therefore, I must say to you: don't use *ain't I?*, except humorously. What is a safe substitute? Apparently none exists, so I suggest that you manage, by some linguistic calisthenics, to avoid having to make a choice. Otherwise you may find yourself in the position of being damned if you do and damned if you don't.

3. Five and five *is* ten.

RIGHT. But don't jump to the conclusion that "five and five *are* ten" is wrong—both verbs are equally acceptable in this or any similar construction. If you prefer to think of "five-and-five" as a single mathematical concept, say *is*. If you find it more reasonable to consider "five and five" a plural idea, say *are*. The teachers I've polled on this point are about evenly divided in preference, and so, I imagine, are the rest of us. Use whichever verb has the greater appeal to your sense of logic.

4. I never saw a man get so *mad*.

RIGHT. When I questioned a number of authors and editors about their opinion of the acceptability of *mad* as a synonym for *angry*, the typical reaction was: "Yes, I say *mad*, but I always feel a little guilty when I do."

Most people do say *mad* when they are sure there is no English teacher listening; it's a good sharp word, everybody understands exactly what it means, and it's a lot stronger than *angry*, though not quite as violent as *furious* or *enraged*. In short, *mad* has a special implication offered by no other word in the English language; as a consequence, educated people use it as the occasion demands and it is perfectly correct. So correct, in fact, that every authoritative dictionary lists it as a completely acceptable usage. If you feel guilty when you say *mad*, even though you don't mean *insane*, it's time you stopped plaguing your conscience with trivialities.

5. Every one of his sisters *are* unmarried.

WRONG. *Are* is perhaps the more logical word, since the sentence implies that he has more than one sister and they are all unmarried. In educated speech, however, the tendency is to make the verb agree with the subject, even if logic is violated in the process—and the better choice here would be *is*, agreeing with the singular subject, *every one*.

6. He visited an *optometrist* for an eye operation.

WRONG. If the gentleman in question did indeed need an operation, he went to the wrong doctor. In most states, optometrists are forbidden by law to perform surgery or administer drugs—they may only prescribe and fit glasses. And they are not medical doctors. The M.D. who specializes in the treatment of eye diseases, and who may operate when necessary, is an *ophthalmologist*. (See Chapter 4.)

7. Do you *prophecy* another world war?

WRONG. Use *prophecy* only when you mean *prediction,* a noun. When you mean *predict,* a verb, as in this sentence, use *prophesy.* This distinction is simple and foolproof. Therefore we properly say: "His *prophecy* (*prediction*) turned out to be true," but "He really seems able to *prophesy* (*predict*) political trends." There is a distinction also in the pronunciation of these two words. *Prophecy* is pronounced PROF′-ə-see; *prophesy* is pronounced PROF′-ə-sī′.

8. *Leave* us not mention it.

WRONG. On the less sophisticated levels of American speech, *leave* is a popular substitute for *let.* On educated levels, the following distinction is carefully observed: *let* means *allow; leave* means *depart.* (There are a few idiomatic exceptions to this rule, but they present no problem.) "*Let* me go" is preferable to "*Leave* me go" even on the most informal of occasions, and a sentence like "*Leave* us not mention it" is not considered standard English.

9. If you expect to *eventually succeed,* you must keep trying.

RIGHT. We have here, in case you're puzzled, an example of that notorious bugbear of academic grammar, the "split infinitive." (An infinitive is a verb preceded by *to: to succeed, to fail, to remember.*)

Splitting an infinitive is not at all difficult—you need only insert a word between the *to* and the verb: *to eventually succeed, to completely fail, to quickly remember.*

Now that you know how to split an infinitive, the important question is, is it legal to do so? I am happy to be able to report to you that it is not only legal, it is also ethical, moral, and sometimes more effective than to not split it. Benjamin Franklin, Washington Irving, Nathaniel Hawthorne, Theodore Roosevelt, and Woodrow Wilson, among many others, were unconscionable infinitive splitters. And modern writers are equally partial to the construction.

To bring this report up to the minute, I asked a number of editors about their attitude toward the split infinitive. Here are two typical reactions.

An editor at Doubleday and Company: "The restriction against the split infinitive is, to my mind, the most artificial of all grammatical rules. I find that most educated people split infinitives regularly in their speech, and only eliminate them from their writing when they rewrite and polish their material."

An editor at *Reader's Digest:* "I want to defend the split infinitive. The construction adds to the strength of the sentence—it's compact and clear. This is to loudly say that I split an infinitive whenever I can catch one."

And here, finally, is the opinion of humorist James Thurber, as quoted by Rudolf Flesch in *The Art of Plain Talk:* "Word has somehow got around that the split infinitive is always wrong. This is of a piece with the outworn notion that it is always wrong to strike a lady."

I think the evidence is conclusive enough—it is perfectly correct to consciously split an infinitive whenever such an act increases the strength or clarity of your sentence.

6

HOW TO TALK ABOUT
SCIENCE AND SCIENTISTS

(Sessions 11–13)

TEASER PREVIEW

What scientist:

- *is interested in the development of the human race?*
- *is a student of the heavens?*
- *explores the physical qualities of the earth?*
- *studies all living matter?*
- *is a student of plant life?*
- *is a student of animal life?*
- *is professionally involved in insects?*
- *is a student of language?*
- *is a student of the psychological effects of words?*
- *studies the culture, structure, and customs of different societies?*

SESSION 11

A true scientist lives up to the etymological meaning of his title "one who knows." Anything scientific is based on facts—observable facts that can be recorded, tested, checked, and verified.

Science, then, deals with human knowledge—as far as it has gone. It has gone very far indeed since the last century or two, when we stopped basing our thinking on guesses, wishes, theories that had no foundation in reality, and concepts of how the world *ought* to be; and instead began to explore the world as it *was,* and not only the world but the whole universe. From Galileo, who looked through the first telescope atop a tower in Pisa, Italy, through Pasteur, who watched microbes through a microscope, to Einstein, who deciphered riddles of the universe by means of mathematics, we have at last begun to fill in a few areas of ignorance.

Who are some of the more important explorers of knowledge—and by what terms are they known?

IDEAS

1. whither mankind?

The field is all mankind—how we developed in mind and body from primitive cultures and early forms.

An anthropologist

2. what's above?

The field is the heavens and all that's in them—planets, galaxies, stars, and other universes.

An astronomer

3. and what's below?

The field is the comparatively little and insignificant whirling ball on which we live—the earth. How did our planet come into being, what is it made of, how were its mountains, oceans, rivers, plains, and valleys formed, and what's down deep if you start digging?

A geologist

4. what is life?

The field is all living organisms—from the simplest one-celled amoeba to the amazingly complex and mystifying structure we call a human being. Plant or animal, flesh or vegetable, denizen of water, earth, or air—if it lives and grows, this scientist wants to know more about it.

A biologist

5. flora

Biology classifies life into two great divisions—plant and animal. This scientist's province is the former category—flowers, trees, shrubs, mosses, marine vegetation, blossoms, fruits, seeds, grasses, and all the rest that make up the plant kingdom.

A botanist

6. and fauna

Animals of every description, kind, and condition, from birds to bees, fish to fowl, reptiles to humans, are the special area of exploration of this scientist.

A zoologist

7. and all the little bugs

There are over 650,000 different species of insects, and millions of individuals of every species—and this scientist is interested in every one of them.

An entomologist

8. tower of Babel

This linguistic scientist explores the subtle, intangible, elusive uses of that unique tool that distinguishes human beings from all other forms of life—to wit: language. This person is, in short, a student of linguistics, ancient and modern, primitive and cultured, Chinese, Hebrew, Icelandic, Slavic, Teutonic, and every other kind spoken now or in the past by human beings, not excluding that delightful hodgepodge known as "pidgin English," in which a piano is described as "big box, you hit 'um in teeth, he cry," and in which Hamlet's famous quandary, "To be or not to be, that is the question . . . ," is translated into "Can do, no can do—how fashion?"

A philologist

9. what do you really mean?

This linguistic scientist explored the subtle, intangible, elusive relationship between language and thinking, between meaning and words; and is interested in determining the psychological causes and effects of what people say and write.

A semanticist

10. who are your friends and neighbors?

This scientist is a student of the ways in which people live together, their family and community structures and customs, their housing, their social relationships, their forms of government, and their layers of caste and class.

A sociologist

USING THE WORDS

Can you pronounce the words?

1.	*anthropologist*	an'-thrə-POL'-ə-jist
2.	*astronomer*	ə-STRON'-ə-mər
3.	*geologist*	jee-OL'-ə-jist
4.	*biologist*	bī-OL'-ə-jist
5.	*botanist*	BOT'-ə-nist
6.	*zoologist*	zō-OL'-ə-jist
7.	*entomologist*	en'-tə-MOL'-ə-jist
8.	*philologist*	fə-LOL'-ə-jist
9.	*semanticist*	sə-MAN'-tə-sist
10.	*sociologist*	sō-shee-OL'-ə-jist *or* sō'-see-OL'-ə-jist

Can you work with the words?

SCIENTIST	PROFESSIONAL FIELD
1. anthropologist	a. community and family life
2. astronomer	b. meanings and psychological effects of words
3. geologist	c. development of the human race
4. biologist	d. celestial phenomena
5. botanist	e. language
6. zoologist	f. insect forms
7. entomologist	g. the earth
8. philologist	h. all forms of living matter
9. semanticist	i. animal life
10. sociologist	j. plant life

KEY: 1–c, 2–d, 3–g, 4–h, 5–j, 6–i, 7–f, 8–e, 9–b, 10–a

Can you recall the words?

1.	insects	1. E_____
2.	language	2. P_____
3.	social conditions	3. S_____
4.	history of development of mankind	4. A_____
5.	meanings of words	5. S_____
6.	plants	6. B_____
7.	the earth	7. G_____
8.	the heavenly bodies	8. A_____
9.	all living things	9. B_____
10.	animals	10. Z_____

KEY: 1–entomologist, 2–philologist, 3–sociologist, 4–anthropologist, 5–semanticist, 6–botanist, 7–geologist, 8–astronomer, 9–biologist, 10–zoologist

---

(End of Session 11)

SESSION 12

ORIGINS AND RELATED WORDS

1. people and the stars

Anthropologist is constructed from roots we are familiar with—*anthropos,* mankind, and *logos,* science, study.

The science is *anthropology* (an′-thrə-POL′-ə-jee). Can you write the adjective form of this word? _____
_____. (Can you pronounce it?)

Astronomer is built on Greek *astron,* star, and *nomos,* arrangement, law, or order. The *astronomer* is interested in the arrangement of stars and other celestial bodies. The science is *astronomy* (ə-STRON'-ə-mee), the adjective is *astronomical* (as'-trə-NOM'-ə-kəl), a word often used in a non-heavenly sense, as in "the *astronomical* size of the national debt." *Astronomy* deals in such enormous distances (the sun, for example, is 93,000,000 miles from the earth, and light from stars travels toward the earth at 186,000 miles per *second*) that the adjective *astronomical* is applied to any tremendously large figure.

Astron, star, combines with *logos* to form *astrology* (ə-STROL'-ə-jee), which assesses the influence of planets and stars on human events. The practitioner is an *astrologer* (ə-STROL'-ə-jər). Can you form the adjective? _____. (Can you pronounce it?)

By etymology, an *astronaut* (AS'-trə-not') is a sailor among the stars (Greek *nautes*, sailor). This person is termed with somewhat less exaggeration a *cosmonaut* (KOZ'-mə-not')by the Russians (Greek, *kosmos*, universe). *Nautical* (NOT'-ə-kəl), relating to sailors, sailing, ships, or navigation, derives also from *nautes*, and *nautes* in turn is from Greek *naus*, ship—a root used in *nausea* (etymologically, ship-sickness or seasickness!).

Aster (AS'-tər) is a star shaped flower. *Asterisk* (AS'-tə-risk), a star-shaped symbol (*), is generally used in writing or printing to direct the reader to look for a footnote. *Astrophysics* (as'-trə-FIZ'-iks) is that branch of physics dealing with heavenly bodies.

Disaster (də-ZAS'-tər) and *disastrous* (də-ZAS'-trəs) also come from *astron*, star. In ancient times it was believed that the stars ruled human destiny; any misfortune or calamity, therefore, happened to someone because the stars were in opposition. (*Dis-*, a prefix of many meanings, in this word signifies *against*.)

Nomos, arrangement, law, or order, is found in two other interesting English words.

For example, if you can make your own laws for yourself, if you needn't answer to anyone else for what you do, in short, if you are independent, then you enjoy *autonomy* (aw-TON'-ə-mee), a word that combines *nomos*, law, with *autos*, self. *Autonomy*, then, is self-law, self-government. The fifty states in our nation are fairly *autonomous* (aw-TON'-ə-məs), but not completely so. On the other hand, in most colleges each separate department is pretty much *autonomous*. And of course, one of the big reasons for the revolution of 1776 was that America wanted *autonomy*, rather than control by England.

You know the instrument that beginners at the piano use to guide their timing? A pendulum swings back and forth, making an audible click at each swing, and in that way governs or orders the measure (or timing) of the player. Hence it is called a *metronome* (MET′-rə-nōm′), a word that combines *nomos* with *metron*, measurement.

2. the earth and its life

Geologist derives from Greek *ge* (*geo-*), earth. The science is *geology* (jee-OL′-ə-jee). Can you write the adjective? _____. (Can you pronounce it?)

Geometry (jee-OM′-ə-tree)—*ge* plus *metron*—by etymology "measurement of the earth," is that branch of mathematics treating of the measurement and properties of solid and plane figures, such as angles, triangles, squares, spheres, prisms, etc. (The etymology of the word shows that this ancient science was originally concerned with the measurement of land and spaces on the earth.)

The mathematician is a *geometrician* (jee′-ə-mə-TRISH′-ən), the adjective is *geometric* (jee′-ə-MET′-rik).

Geography (jee-OG′-rə-fee) is writing about (*graphein*, to write), or mapping, the earth. A practitioner of the science is a *geographer* (jee-OG′-rə-fər), the adjective is *geographic* (jee-ə-GRAF′-ik).

(The name *George* is also derived from *ge* (*geo-*), earth, plus *ergon*, work—the first George was an earth-worker or farmer.)

Biologist combines *bios*, life, with *logos*, science, study. The science is *biology* (bī-OL′-ə-jee). The adjective? _____

Bios, life, is also found in *biography* (bī-OG′-rə-fee), writing about someone's *life; autobiography* (aw′-tə-bī-OG′-rə-fee), the story of one's *life* written by *oneself;* and *biopsy* (BĪ′-op-see), a medical examination, or view (*opsis, optikos,* view, vision), generally through a microscope, of living tissue, frequently performed when cancer is suspected. A small part of the tissue is cut from the affected area and under the microscope its cells can be investigated for evidence of malignancy. A *biopsy* is contrasted with an *autopsy* (AW'-top-see), which is a medical examination of a corpse in order to discover the cause of death. Th *autos* in *autopsy* means, as you know, *self*—in an *autopsy*, etymologically speaking, the surgeon or pathologist determines, by actual view or sight rather than by theorizing (i.e., "by viewing or seeing for oneself"), what brought the corpse to its present grievous state.

Botanist is from Greek *botane,* plant. The field is *botany* (BOT'-ə-nee); the adjective is *botanical* (bə-TAN'-ə-kəl).

Zoologist is from Greek *zoion,* animal. The science is *zoology.* The adjective? _____. The combination of the two *o*'s tempts many people to pronounce the first three letters of these words in one syllable, thus: *zoo.* However, the two *o*'s should be separated, as in *co-operate,* even though no hyphen is used in the spelling to indicate such separation. Say zō-OL'-ə-jist, zō-OL'-ə-jee, zō'-ə-LOJ'-ə-kəl. *Zoo,* a park for animals, is a shortened form of *zoological gardens,* and is, of course, pronounced in one syllable.

The *zodiac* (ZŌ'-dee-ak) is a diagram, used in astrology, of the paths of the sun, moon, and planets; it contains, in part, Latin names for various animals—*scorpio,* scorpion; *leo,* lion; *cancer,* crab; *taurus,* bull; *aries,* ram; and *pisces,* fish. Hence its derivation from *zoion,* animal.

The adjective is *zodiacal* (zō-DĪ'-ə-kəl).

REVIEW OF ETYMOLOGY

PREFIX, ROOT	MEANING	ENGLISH WORD
1. *anthropos*	mankind	_____
2. *logos*	science, study	_____
3. *astron*	star	_____
4. *nautes*	sailor	_____
5. *naus*	ship	_____
6. *dis-*	against	_____
7. *nomos*	arrangement, law, order	_____
8. *autos*	self	_____

123

9. *metron*	measurement	_____
10. *ge (geo-)*	earth	_____
11. *graphein*	to write	_____
12. *bios*	life	_____
13. *opsis, optikos*	view, vision, sight	_____
14. *botane*	plant	_____
15. *zoion*	animal	_____

USING THE WORDS

Can you pronounce the words? (I)

1. *anthropology*	an'-thrə-POL'-ə-jee
2. *anthropological*	an'-thrə-pə-LOJ'-ə-kəl
3. *astronomy*	ə-STRON'-ə-mee
4. *astronomical*	as'-trə-NOM'-ə-kəl
5. *astrology*	ə-STROL'-ə-jee
6. *astrological*	as'-trə-LOJ'-ə-kəl
7. *astronaut*	AS'-trə-not'
8. *cosmonaut*	KOZ'-mə-not'
9. *nautical*	NOT'-ə-kəl
10. *aster*	AS'-tər
11. *asterisk*	AS'-tə-risk
12. *disaster*	də-ZAS'-tər
13. *disastrous*	də-ZAS'-trəs

Can you pronounce the words? (II)

1. *geology*	jee-OL'-ə-jee
2. *geological*	jee'-ə-LOJ'-ə-kəl
3. *geometry*	jee-OM'-ə-tree
4. *geometrician*	jee'-ə-mə-TRISH'-ən
5. *geometric*	jee-ə-MET'-rik
6. *geography*	jee-OG'-rə-fee
7. *geographer*	jee-OG'-rə-fər

124

8. geographical	jee'-ə-GRAF'-ə-kəl
9. biology	bī-OL'-ə-jee
10. biological	bī'-ə-LOJ'-ə-kəl
11. biography	bī-OG'-rə-fee
12. biographer	bī-OG'-rə-fər
13. biographical	bī'-ə-GRAF'-ə-kəl

Can you pronounce the words? (III)

1. autonomy	aw-TON'-ə-mee
2. autonomous	aw-TON'-ə-məs
3. metronome	MET'-rə-nōm'
4. autobiography	aw'-tə-bī-OG'-rə-fee
5. autobiographer	aw'-tə-bī-OG'-rə-fər
6. autobiographical	aw-tə-bī'-ə-GRAF'-ə-kəl
7. biopsy	BĪ'-op-see
8. autopsy	AW'-top-see
9. botany	BOT'-ə-nee
10. botanical	bə-TAN'-ə-kəl
11. zoology	zō-OL'-ə-jee
12. zoological	zō-ə-LOJ'-ə-kəl
13. zodiac	ZŌ'-dee-ak
14. zodiacal	zō-DĪ'-ə-kəl

Can you work with the words? (I)

1. anthropology	a. theory of the influence of planets and stars on human events
2. astronomy	b. science of earth-mapping
3. astrology	c. science of all living matter
4. geology	d. science of human development
5. biology	e. science of plants
6. geometry	f. science of the composition of the earth
7. botany	g. science of animal life

125

| 8. zoology | h. science of the heavens |
| 9. geography | i. mathematical science of figures, shapes, etc. |

Can you work with the words? (II)

1. autopsy	a. "sailor among the stars"
2. biopsy	b. star-shaped flower
3. biography	c. story of one's own life
4. autobiography	d. dissection and examination of a corpse to determine the cause of death
5. zodiac	e. great misfortune
6. astronaut	f. "sailor of the universe"
7. cosmonaut	g. story of someone's life
8. aster	h. diagram of paths of sun, moon, and planets
9. disaster	i. instrument to measure musical time
10. autonomy	j. self-rule
11. metronome	k. examination of living tissue

Do you understand the words?

1. Are *anthropological* studies concerned with plant life?	YES	NO
2. Are *astronomical* numbers extremely small?	YES	NO
3. Is an *astrologer* interested in the time and date of your birth?	YES	NO
4. Are *nautical* maneuvers carried on at sea?	YES	NO

126

5. Does a *disastrous* earthquake take a huge toll of life and property? YES NO
6. Do *geological* investigations sometimes determine where oil is to be found? YES NO
7. Does a *geometrician* work with mathematics? YES NO
8. Do *geographical* shifts in population sometimes affect the economy of an area? YES NO
9. Does a *biographical* novel deal with the life of a real person? YES NO
10. Is *botany* a biological science? YES NO
11. Is the United States politically *autonomous*? YES NO
12. Is a *biopsy* performed on a dead body? YES NO
13. Is a *metronome* used in the study of mathematics? YES NO
14. Is an *autopsy* performed to correct a surgical problem? YES NO
15. Does an author write an *autobiography* about someone else's life? YES NO

KEY: 1–no, 2–no, 3–yes, 4–yes, 5–yes, 6–yes, 7–yes, 8–yes, 9–yes, 10–yes, 11–yes, 12–no, 13–no, 14–no, 15–no

---

Can you recall the words? (I)

1. pertaining to the science of animals (*adj.*)
2. pertaining to the science of plants (*adj.*)
3. dissection of a corpse to determine the cause of death
4. story of one's life, self-written
5. pertaining to the science of all living matter (*adj.*)
6. science of the measurement of figures

1. Z_____
2. B_____
3. A_____
4. A_____
5. B_____
6. G_____

7. pertaining to the science of the earth's composition (*adj.*)

7. G_____

8. branch of physics dealing with the composition of celestial bodies

8. A_____

9. star-shaped flower

9. A_____

10. very high in number; pertaining to the science of the heavens (*adj.*)

10. A_____

11. science of heavenly bodies

11. A_____

12. science of the development of mankind

12. A_____

13. person who believes human events are influenced by the paths of the sun, moon, and planets

13. A_____

KEY: 1–zoological, 2–botanical, 3–autopsy, 4–autobiography, 5–biological, 6–geometry, 7–geological, 8–astrophysics, 9–aster, 10–astronomical, 11–astronomy, 12–anthropology, 13–astrologer

---

Can you recall the words? (II)

1. microscopic examination of living tissue

1. B_____

2. self-government

2. A_____

3. time measurer for music

3. M_____

4. voyager among the stars

4. A_____

5. traveler through the universe

5. C_____

6. great misfortune

6. D_____

7. mapping of the earth (*noun*)

7. G_____

8. self-governing (*adj.*)

8. A_____

9. diagram used in astrology

9. Z_____

10. pertaining to such a diagram (*adj.*)

10. Z_____

11. pertaining to ships, sailing, etc.

11. N_____

12. star-shaped symbol   12. A_____
13. story of a person's life   13. B_____

KEY: 1–biopsy, 2–autonomy, 3–metronome, 4–astronaut, 5–cosmonaut, 6–disaster, 7–geography, 8–autonomous, 9–zodiac, 10–zodiacal, 11–nautical, 12–asterisk, 13–biography

---

(End of Session 12)

SESSION 13

ORIGINS AND RELATED WORDS

1. cutting in and out

Flies, bees, beetles, wasps, and other insects are segmented creatures—head, thorax, and abdomen. Where these parts join, there appears to the imaginative eye a "cutting in" of the body.

Hence the branch of zoology dealing with insects is aptly named *entomology,* from Greek *en-,* in, plus *tome,* a cutting. The adjective is *entomological* (en'-tə-mə-LOJ'-ə-kəl).

(The word *insect* makes the same point—it is built on Latin *in-* in, plus *sectus,* a form of the verb meaning *to cut.*)

The prefix *ec-,* from Greek *ek-,* means *out.* (The Latin prefix, you will recall, is *ex-.*) Combine *ec-* with *tome* to derive the words for surgical procedures in which parts are "cut out," or removed: *tonsillectomy* (the tonsils), *appendectomy* (the appendix), *mastectomy* (the breast), *hysterectomy* (the uterus), *prostatectomy* (the prostate), etc.

Combine *ec-* with Greek *kentron,* center (the Latin root, as we have discovered, is *centrum*), to derive *eccentric* (ək-SEN'-trik)—*out of the center,* hence deviating from the normal in behavior, attitudes, etc., or unconventional, odd, strange. The noun is *eccentricity* (ek'-sən-TRIS'-ə-tee).

129

2. more cuts

The Greek prefix *a-* makes a root negative; the *atom* (AT′-əm) was so named at a time when it was considered the smallest possible particle of an element, that is, one that could *not* be cut any further. (We have long since split the atom, of course, with results, as in most technological advances, both good and evil.) The adjective is *atomic* (ə-TOM′-ik).

The Greek prefix *ana-* has a number of meanings, one of which is *up,* as in *anatomy* (ə-NAT′-ə-mee), originally the *cutting up* of a plant or animal to determine its structure, later the bodily structure itself. The adjective is *anatomical* (an′-ə-TOM′-ə-kəl).

Originally any book that was part of a larger work of many volumes was called a *tome* (TŌM)—etymologically, a part *cut* from the whole. Today, a *tome* designates, often disparagingly, an exceptionally large book, or one that is heavy and dull in content.

The Greek prefix *dicha-*, in two, combines with *tome* to construct *dichotomy* (dī-KOT′-ə-mee), a splitting in two, a technical word used in astronomy, biology, botany, and the science of logic. It is also employed as a non-technical term, as when we refer to the *dichotomy* in the life of a man who is a government clerk all day and a night-school teacher after working hours, so that his life is, in a sense, split into two parts. The verb is *dichotomize* (dī-KOT′-ə-mīz′); the adjective is *dichotomous* (dī-KOT′-ə-məs). *Dichotomous* thinking is the sort that divides everything into two parts—good and bad; white and black; Democrats and Republicans; etc. An unknown wit has made this classic statement about *dichotomous* thinking: "There are two kinds of people: those who divide everything into two parts, and those who do not."

Imagine a book, a complicated or massive report, or some other elaborate document—now figuratively cut on or through it so that you can get to its essence, the very heart of the idea contained in it. What you have is an *epitome* (ə-PIT′-ə-mee), a condensation of the whole. (From *epi-*, on, upon, plus *tome*.)

An *epitome* may refer to a summary, condensation, or abridgment of language, as in "Let me have an *epitome* of the book," or "Give me the *epitome* of his speech."

More commonly, *epitome* and the verb *epitomize* (ə-PIT'-ə-mīz') are used in sentences like "She is the *epitome* of kindness," or "That one act *epitomizes* her philosophy of life." If you cut everything else away to get to the *essential* part, that part is a representative cross-section of the whole. So a woman who is the *epitome* of kindness stands for all people who are kind; and an act that *epitomizes* a philosophy of life represents, by itself, the complete philosophy.

3. love and words

Logos, we know, means *science* or *study;* it may also mean *word* or *speech*, as it does in *philolog*y (fə-LOL'-ə-jee), etymologically *the love of words* (from Greek *philein*, to love, plus *logos*), or what is more commonly called *linguistics* (ling-GWIS'-tiks), the science of language, a term derived from Latin *lingua*, tongue.

·Can you write, and pronounce, the adjective form of *philology?*

_____.

4. more love

Philanthropy (fə-LAN'-thrə-pee) is by etymology the love of mankind—one who devotes oneself to *philanthropy* is a *philanthropist* (fə-LAN'-thrə-pist), as we learned in Chapter 3; the adjective is *philanthropic* (fil-ən-THROP'-ik).

The verb *philander* (fə-LAN'-dər), to "play around" sexually, be promiscuous, or have extramarital relations, combines *philein* with *andros*, male. (*Philandering*, despite its derivation, is not of course exclusively the male province. The word is, in fact, derived from the proper name conventionally given to male lovers in plays and romances of the 1500s and 1600s.) One who engages in the interesting activities catalogued above is a *philanderer* (fə-LAN'-dər-ər).

By etymology, *philosophy* is the love of wisdom (Greek *sophos*, wise); *Philadelphia* is the City of Brotherly Love (Greek *adelphos*, brother); *philharmonic* is the love of music or harmony (Greek *harmonia*, harmony); and a *philter*, a rarely used word, is a love potion. Today we call whatever arouses sexual desire an *aphrodisiac* (af'-rə-DIZ'-ee-ak'), from Aphrodite, the Greek goddess of love and beauty.

Aphrodisiac is an adjective as well as a noun, but a longer adjective form, *aphrodisiacal* (af'-rə-də-ZĪ'-ə-kəl), is also used.

A *bibliophile* (BIB'-lee-ə-fīl') is one who loves books as collectibles, admiring their binding, typography, illustrations, rarity, etc.—in short, a book collector. The combining root is Greek *biblion*, book.

An *Anglophile* (ANG'-glə-fīl') admires and is fond of the British people, customs, culture, etc. The combining root is Latin *Anglus*, English.

5. words and how they affect people

The *semanticist* is professionally involved in *semantics* (sə-MAN'-tiks). The adjective is *semantic* (sə-MAN'-tik) or *semantical* (sə-MAN'-tə-kəl).

Semantics, like *orthopedics*, *pediatrics*, and *obstetrics*, is a singular noun despite the *-s* ending. Semantics *is*, not *are*, an exciting study. However, this rule applies only when we refer to the word as a science or area of study. In the following sentence, *semantics* is used as a plural: "The *semantics* of your thinking *are* all wrong."

Two stimulating and highly readable books on the subject, well worth a visit to the library to pick up, are *Language in Thought and Action*, by S. I. Hayakawa, and *People in Quandaries*, by Dr. Wendell Johnson.

6. how people live

The profession of the *sociologist* is *sociology* (sō'-shee-OL'-ə-jee *or* sō-see-OL'-ə-jee). Can you write, and pronounce, the adjective? _____.

Sociology is built on Latin *socius*, companion,* plus *logos*, sci-

---

* *Companion* itself has an interesting etymology—Latin *com*-, with, plus *panis*, bread. If you are social, you enjoy breaking bread with companions. *Pantry* also comes from *panis*, though far more than bread is stored there.

ence, study. *Socius* is the source of such common words as *associate, social, socialize, society, sociable,* and *antisocial;* as well as *asocial* (ay-SŌ'-shəl), which combines the negative prefix *a-* with *socius.*

The *antisocial* person actively dislikes people, and often behaves in ways that are detrimental or destructive to society or the social order (*anti-,* against).

On the other hand, someone who is *asocial* is withdrawn and self-centered, avoids contact with others, and feels completely indifferent to the interests or welfare of society. The *asocial* person doesn't want to "get involved."

REVIEW OF ETYMOLOGY

PREFIX, ROOT	MEANING	ENGLISH WORD
1. *en-*	in	_____
2. *tome*	a cutting	_____
3. *in-*	in	_____
4. *sectus*	cut	_____
5. *kentron* (*centrum*)	center	_____
6. *a-*	not, negative	_____
7. *ana-*	up	_____
8. *dicha-*	in two	_____
9. *epi-*	on, upon	_____
10. *logos*	word, speech	_____
11. *lingua*	tongue	_____
12. *philein*	to love	_____
13. *sophos*	wise	_____
14. *adelphos*	brother	_____
15. *biblion*	book	_____
16. *Anglus*	English	_____
17. *socius*	companion	_____
18. *anti-*	against	_____

USING THE WORDS

Can you pronounce the words? (I)

1. *entomology* — en'-tə-MOL'-ə-jee
2. *entomological* — en'-tə-mə-LOJ'-ə-kəl
3. *eccentric* — ək-SEN'-trik
4. *eccentricity* — ək'-sən-TRIS'-ə-tee
5. *atom* — AT'-əm
6. *atomic* — ə-TOM'-ik
7. *anatomy* — ə-NAT'-ə-mee
8. *anatomical* — an'-ə-TOM'-ə-kəl
9. *tome* — TŌM
10. *dichotomy* — dī-KOT'-ə-mee
11. *dichotomous* — dī-KOT'-ə-məs
12. *dichotomize* — dī-KOT'-ə-mīz'

Can you pronounce the words? (II)

1. *epitome* — ə-PIT'-ə-mee
2. *epitomize* — ə-PIT'-ə-mīz'
3. *philology* — fə-LOL'-ə-jee
4. *philological* — fil'-ə-LOJ'-ə-kəl
5. *linguistics* — ling-GWIS'-tiks
6. *philanthropy* — fə-LAN'-thrə-pee
7. *philanthropist* — fə-LAN'-thrə-pist
8. *philanthropic* — fil'-ən-THROP'-ik
9. *philander* — fə-LAN'-dər
10. *philanderer* — fə-LAN'-dər-ər

Can you pronounce the words? (III)

1. *philter* — FIL'-tər
2. *aphrodisiac* — af'-rə-DIZ'-ee-ak'
3. *aphrodisiacal* — af'-rə-də-ZĪ'-ə-kəl
4. *bibliophile* — BIB'-lee-ə-fīl'
5. *Anglophile* — ANG'-glə-fīl'
6. *semantics* — sə-MAN'-tiks

134

7. *semantic*	sə-MAN'-tik
8. *semantical*	sə-MAN'-tə-kəl
9. *sociology*	sō'-shee-OL'-ə-jee *or*
	sō'-see-OL'-ə-jee
10. *sociological*	sō'-shee-ə-LOJ'-ə-kəl *or*
	sō'-see-ə-LOJ'-ə-kəl
11. *asocial*	ay-SŌ'-shəl

Can you work with the words? (I)

1. entomology	a.	physical structure
2. eccentricity	b.	summary; representation of the whole
3. anatomy	c.	science of the meanings and effects of words
4. dichotomy	d.	linguistics
5. epitome	e.	science dealing with insects
6. philology	f.	science of social structures and customs
7. semantics	g.	charitable works
8. sociology	h.	that which causes sexual arousal
9. aphrodisiac	i.	strangeness; oddness; unconventionality
10. philanthropy	j.	condition or state of being split into two parts

---

KEY: 1–e, 2–i, 3–a, 4–j, 5–b, 6–d, 7–c, 8–f, 9–h, 10–g

Can you work with the words? (II)

1. dichotomize	a.	dull, heavy book
2. epitomize	b.	love potion; aphrodisiac
3. philander	c.	pertaining to the study of language
4. philter	d.	one fond of British people, customs, etc.

5. bibliophile	e. pertaining to the science of group cultures, conventions, etc.
6. Anglophile	f. to split in two
7. asocial	g. withdrawn from contact with people
8. tome	h. book collector
9. philological	i. to summarize
10. sociological	j. to engage in extramarital sex

KEY: 1–f, 2–i, 3–j, 4–b, 5–h, 6–d, 7–g, 8–a, 9–c, 10–e

Do you understand the words?

1.	Is a *philanderer* likely to be faithful to a spouse?	YES	NO
2.	Did Dr. Jekyll-Mr. Hyde lead a *dichotomous* existence?	YES	NO
3.	Is an egoist the *epitome* of selfishness?	YES	NO
4.	Is a *philanthropist* antisocial?	YES	NO
5.	Is an *aphrodisiac* intended to reduce sexual interest?	YES	NO
6.	Is a *bibliophile's* chief aim the enjoyment of literature?	YES	NO
7.	Does a *philologist* understand etymology?	YES	NO
8.	Is a *semanticist* interested in more than the dictionary meanings of words?	YES	NO
9.	Is an *asocial* person interested in improving social conditions?	YES	NO
10.	Is a light novel considered a *tome?*	YES	NO

KEY: 1–no, 2–yes, 3–yes, 4–no, 5–no, 6–no, 7–yes, 8–yes, 9–no, 10–no

---

Can you recall the words?

1. pertaining to the study of social customs (*adj.*)   1. S_____

2. pertaining to the psychological effects of words (*adj.*)   2. S_____
        or S_____

3. lover and collector of books   3. B_____

4. make love promiscuously   4. P_____

5. pertaining to the science of linguistics (*adj.*)   5. P_____

6. pertaining to the study of insects (*adj.*)   6. E_____

7. one who admires British customs   7. A_____

8. smallest particle, so-called   8. A_____

9. pertaining to the structure of a body (*adj.*)   9. A_____

10. a dull, heavy book   10. T_____

11. split in two (*adj.*)   11. D_____

12. to split in two   12. D_____

13. a condensation, summary, or representation of the whole   13. E_____

14. to stand for the whole; to summarize   14. E_____

15. pertaining to charitable activities (*adj.*)   15. P_____

16. out of the norm; odd   16. E_____

17. one who "plays around"   17. P_____

18. arousing sexual desire (*adj.*)   18. A_____
        or A_____

19. science of the manner in which groups function   19. S_____

20. self-isolated from contact with people   20. A_____

KEY: 1–sociological, 2–semantic *or* semantical, 3–bibliophile, 4–philander, 5–philological, 6–entomological, 7–Anglophile, 8–atom, 9–anatomical, 10–tome, 11–dichotomous,

12–dichotomize, 13–epitome, 14–epitomize, 15–philanthropic, 16–eccentric, 17–philanderer, 18–aphrodisiac *or* aphrodisiacal, 19–sociology, 20–asocial

CHAPTER REVIEW

A. Do you recognize the words?

1. Student of the stars and other heavenly phenomena: (a) geologist, (b) astronomer, (c) anthropologist
2. Student of plant life: (a) botanist, (b) zoologist, (c) biologist
3. Student of insect life: (a) sociologist, (b) entomologist, (c) etymologist
4. Student of the meaning and psychology of words: (a) philologist, (b) semanticist, (c) etymologist
5. Analysis of living tissue: (a) autopsy, (b) biopsy, (c) autonomy
6. That which arouses sexual desire: (a) zodiac, (b) bibliophile, (c) aphrodisiac
7. Self-governing: (a) autobiographical, (b) autonomous, (c) dichotomous
8. Part that represents the whole: (a) epitome, (b) dichotomy, (c) metronome
9. One who physically travels in space: (a) astronomer, (b) astrologer, (c) astronaut
10. One who has extramarital affairs: (a) cosmonaut, (b) philanderer, (c) philanthropist

KEY: 1–b, 2–a, 3–b, 4–b, 5–b, 6–c, 7–b, 8–a, 9–c, 10–b

B. Can you recognize roots?

ROOT	MEANING	EXAMPLE
1. *anthropos*	_____	anthropology
2. *logos*	_____	philology

3. *astron*	_____	astronomy
4. *nautes*	_____	astronaut
5. *nomos*	_____	metronome
6. *autos*	_____	autonomy
7. *ge (geo-)*	_____	geology
8. *graphein*	_____	biography
9. *opsis, optikos*	_____	autopsy
10. *zoion*	_____	zodiac
11. *tome*	_____	entomology
12. *sectus*	_____	insect
13. *lingua*	_____	linguistics
14. *philein*	_____	philanthropy
15. *sophos*	_____	philosophy
16. *biblion*	_____	bibliophile
17. *Anglus*	_____	Anglophile
18. *socius*	_____	sociology
19. *logos*	_____	biology
20. *bios*	_____	biopsy

KEY: 1–mankind, 2–word, speech, 3–star, 4–sailor, 5–law, order, arrangement, 6–self, 7–earth, 8–to write, 9–view, vision, sight, 10–animal, 11–a cutting, 12–cut, 13–tongue, 14–to love, 15–wise, 16–book, 17–English, 18–companion, 19–science, study, 20–life

TEASER QUESTION FOR THE AMATEUR ETYMOLOGIST

1. Recalling the root *sophos,* wise, and thinking of the English word *moron,* write the name given to a second-year student in high school or college: _____. Etymologically, what does this word mean? _____

2. Based on the root *sophos,* what word means *worldly-wise?* _____.

3. Thinking of *bibliophile,* define *bibliomaniac:* _____
_____
_____.

4. These three words, based on *lingua,* tongue, use prefixes we have discussed. Can you define each one?

    (a) monolingual   _____

    (b) bilingual   _____

    (c) trilingual   _____

Can you, now, guess at the meaning of *multilingual?* _____

_____

_____.

How about *linguist?* _____

_____.

What do you suppose the Latin root *multus* means? _____

_____. (Think of *multitude.*)

5. With *Anglophile* as your model, can you figure out what country and its people, customs, etc. each of the following admires?

    (a) Francophile   _____

    (b) Russophile   _____

    (c) Hispanophile _____

    (d) Germanophile _____

    (e) Nipponophile _____

    (f) Sinophile   _____

6. Using roots you have learned, and with *bibliophile* as your model, can you construct a word for:

    (a) one who loves males: _____

    (b) one who loves women: _____

    (c) one who loves children: _____

    (d) one who loves animals: _____

    (e) one who loves plants: _____

(*Answers in Chapter 18*)

WHERE TO GET NEW IDEAS

People with superior vocabularies, I have submitted, are the people with ideas. The words they know are verbal symbols of the ideas they are familiar with—reduce one and you must reduce the other, for ideas cannot exist without verbalization. Freud once had an idea—and had to coin a whole new vocabulary to make his idea clear to the world. Those who are familiar with Freud's theories know all the words that explain them—the *unconscious*, the *ego*, the *id*, the *superego*, *rationalization*, *Oedipus complex*, and so on. Splitting the atom was once a new idea—anyone familiar with it knew something about *fission*, *isotope*, *radioactive*, *cyclotron*, etc.

Remember this: your vocabulary indicates the alertness and range of your mind. The words you know show the extent of your understanding of what's going on in the world. The size of your vocabulary varies directly with the degree to which you are growing intellectually.

You have covered so far in this book several hundred words. Having learned these words, you have begun to think of an equal number of new ideas. A new word is not just another pattern of syllables with which to clutter up your mind—a new word is a new idea to help you think, to help you understand the thoughts of others, to help you express your own thoughts, to help you live a richer intellectual life.

Realizing these facts, you may become impatient. You will begin to doubt that a book like this can cover all the ideas that an alert and intellectually mature adult wishes to be acquainted with. Your doubt is well-founded.

One of the chief purposes of this book is to get you started, to give you enough of a push so that you will begin to gather momentum, to stimulate you enough so that you will want to start gathering your own ideas.

Where can you gather them? From good books on new topics.

How can you gather them? By reading on a wide range of new subjects.

Reference has repeatedly been made to psychology, psychiatry, and psychoanalysis in these pages. If your curiosity has been piqued by these references, here is a good place to start. In these fields there is a tremendous and exciting literature—and you can read as widely and as deeply as you wish.

What I would like to do is offer a few suggestions as to where you might profitably begin—how far you go will depend on your own interest.

I suggest, first, half a dozen older books (older, but still immensely valuable and completely valid) available at any large public library.

The Human Mind, by Karl A. Menninger
Mind and Body, by Flanders Dunbar
The Mind in Action, by Eric Berne
Understandable Psychiatry, by Leland E. Hinsie
A General Introduction to Psychoanalysis, by Sigmund Freud
Emotional Problems of Living, by O. Spurgeon English and Gerald H. J. Pearson

Next, I suggest books on some of the newer approaches in psychology. These are available in inexpensive paperback editions as well as at your local library.

I Ain't Well—But I Sure Am Better, by Jess Lair, Ph.D.
The Disowned Self, by Nathaniel Brandon
A Primer of Behavioral Psychology, by Adelaide Bry
I'm OK—You're OK, by Thomas A. Harris, M.D.
Freedom to Be and *Man the Manipulator,* by Everett L. Shostrum
Games People Play, by Eric Berne, M.D.
Love and Orgasm, Pleasure and *The Language of the Body,* by Alexander Lowen, M.D.
The Transparent Self, by Sydney M. Jourard
Don't Say Yes When You Want to Say No, by Herbert Fensterheim and Jean Baer
Gestalt Therapy Verbatim, by Frederick S. Perls
Born to Win, by Muriel James and Dorothy Jongeward
Joy and *Here Comes Everybody,* by William C. Schutz
The Fifty-Minute Hour, by Robert Lindner

(End of Session 13)

HOW TO AVOID BEING A PURIST

Life, as you no doubt realize, is complicated enough these days. Yet puristic textbooks and English teachers with puristic ideas are striving to make it still more complicated. Their contribution to the complexity of modern living is the repeated claim that many of the natural, carefree, and popular expressions that most of us use every day are "bad English," "incorrect grammar," "vulgar," or "illiterate."

In truth, many of the former restrictions and "thou shalt nots" of academic grammar are now outmoded—most educated speakers quite simply ignore them.

Students in my grammar classes at Rio Hondo College are somewhat nonplused when they discover that correctness is not determined by textbook rules and cannot be enforced by schoolteacher edict. They invariably ask: "Aren't you going to draw the line somewhere?"

It is neither necessary nor possible for any one person to "draw the line." That is done—and quite effectively—by the people themselves, by the millions of educated people throughout the nation.

Of course certain expressions may be considered "incorrect" or "illiterate" or "bad grammar"—not because they violate puristic

143

rules, but only because they are rarely if ever used by educated speakers.

Correctness, in short, is determined by current educated usage.

The following notes on current trends in modern usage are intended to help you come to a decision about certain controversial expressions. As you read each sentence, pay particular attention to the italicized word or words. Does the usage square with your own language patterns? Would you be willing to phrase your thoughts in just such terms? Decide whether the sentence is "right" or "wrong," then compare your conclusions with the opinions given after the test.

TEST YOURSELF

1. Let's not walk any *further* right now.	RIGHT	WRONG
2. Some people admit that their *principle* goal in life is to become wealthy.	RIGHT	WRONG
3. What a *nice* thing to say!	RIGHT	WRONG
4. He's *pretty* sick today.	RIGHT	WRONG
5. I feel *awfully* sick.	RIGHT	WRONG
6. Are you going to invite Doris and *I* to your party?	RIGHT	WRONG

1. Let's not walk any *further* right now.

RIGHT. In the nineteenth century, when professional grammarians attempted to Latinize English grammar, an artificial distinction was drawn between *farther* and *further*, to wit: *farther* refers to space, *further* means *to a greater extent* or *additional*. Today, as a result, many teachers who are still under the forbidding influence of nineteenth-century restrictions insist that it is incorrect to use one word for the other.

To check on current attitudes toward this distinction, I sent the test sentence above to a number of dictionary editors, authors, and professors of English, requesting their opinion of the acceptability of *further* in reference to actual distance. Sixty out of eighty-seven professors, over two thirds of those responding, accepted the

144

usage without qualification. Of twelve dictionary editors, eleven accepted *further*, and in the case of the authors, thirteen out of twenty-three accepted the word as used. A professor of English at Cornell University remarked: "I know of no justification for any present-day distinction between *further* and *farther*"; and a consulting editor of the Funk and Wagnalls dictionary said, "There is nothing controversial here. As applied to spatial distance, *further* and *farther* have long been interchangeable."

Perhaps the comment of a noted author and columnist is most to the point: "I like both *further* and *farther*, as I have never been able to tell which is which or why one is any farther or further than the other."

2. Some people admit that their *principle* goal in life is to become wealthy.

WRONG. In speech, you can get *principal* and *principle* confused as often as you like, and no one will ever know the difference—both words are pronounced identically. In writing, however, your spelling will give you away.

There is a simple memory trick that will help you if you get into trouble with these two words. *Rule* and *principle* both end in *-le*—and a princip*le* is a ru*le*. On the other hand, *principal* contains an *a*, and so does *main*—and princip*a*l means m*a*in. Get these points straight and your confusion is over.

Heads of schools are called *principals*, because they are the *main* person in that institution of learning. The money you have in the bank is your *principal*, your *main* financial assets. And the stars of a play are *principals*—the *main* actors.

Thus, "Some people admit that their *principal* (main) goal in life is to become wealthy," but "Such a *principle* (rule) is not guaranteed to lead to happiness."

3. What a *nice* thing to say!

RIGHT. Purists object to the popular use of *nice* as a synonym for *pleasant, agreeable,* or *delightful*. They wish to restrict the word to its older and more erudite meaning of *exact* or *subtle*. You will be happy to hear that they aren't getting anywhere.

When I polled a group of well-known authors on the acceptability in everyday speech of the popular meaning of *nice*, their opinions were unanimous; not a single dissenting voice, out of the twenty-three authors who answered, was raised against the usage. One writer responded: "It has been right for about 150 years . . ."

Editors of magazines and newspapers questioned on the same point were just a shade more conservative. Sixty out of sixty-nine accepted the usage. One editor commented: "I think we do not have to be nice about *nice* any longer. No one can eradicate it from popular speech as a synonym for *pleasant,* or *enjoyable,* or *kind,* or *courteous.* It is a workhorse of the vocabulary, and properly so."

The only valid objection to the word is that it is *overworked* by some people, but this shows a weakness in vocabulary rather than in grammar.

As in the famous story of the editor who said to her secretary: "There are two words I wish you would stop using so much. One is 'nice' and the other is 'lousy.'"

"Okay," said the secretary, who was eager to please. "What are they?"

4. He's *pretty* sick today.

RIGHT. One of the purist's pet targets of attack is the word *pretty* as used in the sentence under discussion. Yet all modern dictionaries accept such use of *pretty,* and a survey made by a professor at the University of Wisconsin showed that the usage is established English.

5. I feel *awfully* sick.

RIGHT. Dictionaries accept this usage in informal speech and the University of Wisconsin survey showed that it is established English.

The great popularity of *awfully* in educated speech is no doubt due to the strong and unique emphasis that the word gives to an adjective—substitute *very, quite, extremely,* or *severely* and you considerably weaken the force.

On the other hand, it is somewhat less than cultivated to say "I feel *awful* sick," and the wisdom of using *awfully* to intensify a *pleasant* concept ("What an *awfully* pretty child"; "That book is *awfully* interesting") is perhaps still debatable, though getting less and less so as the years go on.

6. Are you going to invite Doris and *I* to your party?

WRONG. Some people are almost irresistibly drawn to the pronoun *I* in constructions like this one. However, not only does such use of *I* violate a valid and useful grammatical principle, but, more important, it is rarely heard in educated speech. The meaning of the sentence is equally clear no matter which form of the pronoun is employed, of course, but the use of *I*, the less popular choice, may stigmatize the speaker as uneducated.

Consider it this way: You would normally say, "Are you going to invite *me* to your party?" It would be wiser, therefore, to say, "Are you going to invite Doris and *me* to your party?"

7

HOW TO TALK
ABOUT LIARS AND LYING

(Sessions 14–17)

TEASER PREVIEW

What kind of liar are you if you:

- *have developed a reputation for falsehood?*
- *are particularly skillful?*
- *cannot be reformed?*
- *have become habituated to your vice?*
- *started to lie from the moment of your birth?*
- *always lie?*
- *cannot distinguish fact from fancy?*
- *suffer no pangs of conscience?*
- *are suspiciously smooth and fluent in your lying?*
- *tell vicious lies?*

SESSION 14

It was the famous Greek philosopher and cynic Diogenes who went around the streets of Athens, lantern in hand, looking for an honest person.

This was over two thousand years ago, but I presume that Diogenes would have as little success in his search today. Lying seems to be an integral weakness of mortal character—I doubt that few human beings would be so brash as to claim that they have never in their lives told at least a partial untruth. Indeed, one philologist goes so far as to theorize that language must have been invented for the sole purpose of deception. Perhaps so. It is certainly true that animals seem somewhat more honest than humans, maybe because they are less gifted mentally.

Why do people lie? To increase their sense of importance, to escape punishment, to gain an end that would otherwise be denied them, out of long-standing habit, or sometimes because they actually do not know the difference between fact and fancy. These are the common reasons for falsification. No doubt there are other, fairly unique, motives that impel people to distort the truth. And, to come right down to it, can we always be certain what is true and what is false?

If lying is a prevalent and all-too-human phenomenon, there would of course be a number of interesting words to describe different types of liars.

Let us pretend (not to get personal, but only to help you become personally involved in the ideas and words) that you are a liar.

The question is, what kind of liar *are* you?

IDEAS

1. you don't fool even some of the people

Everybody knows your propensity for avoiding facts. You have built so solid and unsavory a reputation that only a stranger is likely to be misled—and then, not for long.

A *notorious* liar

2. to the highest summits of artistry

Your ability is top-drawer—rarely does anyone lie as convincingly or as artistically as you do. Your skill has, in short, reached the zenith of perfection. Indeed, your mastery of the art is so great that your lying is almost always crowned with success—and you have no trouble seducing an unwary listener into believing that you are telling gospel truth.

A *consummate* liar

3. beyond redemption or salvation

You are impervious to correction. Often as you may be caught in your fabrications, there is no reforming you—you go right on lying despite the punishment, embarrassment, or unhappiness that your distortions of truth may bring upon you.

An *incorrigible* liar

4. too old to learn new tricks

You are the victim of firmly fixed and deep-rooted habits. Telling untruths is as frequent and customary an activity as brushing your teeth in the morning, or having toast and coffee for breakfast, or lighting up a cigarette after dinner (if you are a smoker). And almost as reflexive.

An *inveterate* liar

5. an early start

You have such a long history of persistent falsification that one can only suspect that your vice started when you were reposing in your mother's womb. In other words, and allowing for a great deal of exaggeration for effect, you have been lying from the moment of your birth.

A *congenital* liar

6. no letup

You never stop lying. While normal people lie on occasion, and often for special reasons, you lie continually—not occasionally or even frequently, but over and over.

A *chronic* liar

7. a strange disease

You are not concerned with the difference between truth and falsehood; you do not bother to distinguish fact from fantasy. In fact, your lying is a disease that no antibiotic can cure.

A *pathological* liar

8. no regrets

You are completely without a conscience. No matter what misery your fabrications may cause your innocent victims, you never feel the slightest twinge of guilt. Totally unscrupulous, you are a dangerous person to get mixed up with.

An *unconscionable* liar

9. smooth!

Possessed of a lively imagination and a ready tongue, you can distort facts as smoothly and as effortlessly as you can say your name. But you do not always get away with your lies.

151

Ironically enough, it is your very smoothness that makes you suspect: your answers are too quick to be true. Even if we can't immediately catch you in your lies, we have learned from unhappy past experience not to suspend our critical faculties when you are talking. We admire your nimble wit, but we listen with a skeptical ear.

A *glib* liar

10. outstanding!

Lies, after all, are bad—they are frequently injurious to other people, and may have a particularly dangerous effect on you as a liar. At best, if you are caught you suffer some embarrassment. At worst, if you succeed in your deception your character becomes warped and your sense of values suffers. Almost all lies are harmful; some are no less than vicious.

If you are one type of liar, *all* your lies are vicious—calculatedly, predeterminedly, coldly, and advisedly vicious. In short, your lies are so outstandingly hurtful that people gasp in amazement and disgust at hearing them.

An *egregious* liar

In this chapter the ten basic words revolve rather closely around a central core. Each one, however, has a distinct, a unique meaning, a special implication. Note the differences.

TYPE OF LIAR	SPECIAL IMPLICATION
1. *notorious*	*famous*—or *infamous*—for lying; tendency to falsify is *well-known*
2. *consummate*	great *skill*
3. *incorrigible*	too far gone to be *reformed*— *impervious to rehabilitation*
4. *inveterate*	lying has become a *deep-rooted habit*
5. *congenital*	lying had *very early beginnings*—as if *from birth*

6. *chronic*	*over and over*
7. *pathological*	an irresistible *compulsion* to lie—often for no rational reason; lying is a *disease*
8. *unconscionable*	*lack of regret or remorse*
9. *glib*	great *smoothness*
10. *egregious*	*viciousness* of the lies

These ten expressive adjectives, needless to say, are not restricted to lying or liars. Note their general meanings:

1. *notorious*	well-known for some bad quality—a *notorious* philanderer
2. *consummate*	perfect, highly skilled—*consummate* artistry at the keyboard
3. *incorrigible*	beyond reform—an *incorrigible* optimist
4. *inveterate*	long-accustomed, deeply habituated—an *inveterate* smoker (this adjective, like *notorious,* usually has an unfavorable connotation)
5. *congenital*	happening at or during birth—a *congenital* deformity
6. *chronic*	going on for a long time, or occurring again and again—*chronic* appendicitis
7. *pathological*	diseased—a *pathological* condition
8. *unconscionable*	without pangs of conscience—*unconscionable* cruelty to children
9. *glib*	smooth, suspiciously fluent—a *glib* witness
10. *egregious*	outstandingly bad or vicious—an *egregious* error

With the exception of *consummate* and *congenital,* all ten adjectives have strongly derogatory implications and are generally used to describe people, characteristics, or conditions we disapprove of.

153

USING THE WORDS

Can you pronounce the words?

1.	*notorious*	nə-TAWR'-ee-əs
2.	*consummate*	kən-SUM•ət
3.	*incorrigible*	in-KAWR'-ə-jə-bəl
4.	*inveterate*	in-VET'-ə-rət
5.	*congenital*	kən-JEN'-ə-təl
6.	*chronic*	KRON'-ik
7.	*pathological*	path'-ə-LOJ'-ə-kəl
8.	*unconscionable*	un-KON'-shə-nə-bəl
9.	*glib*	GLIB
10.	*egregious*	ə-GREE'-jəs

Can you work with the words?

1.	notorious	a.	beyond reform
2.	consummate	b.	continuing over a long period of time; recurring
3.	incorrigible	c.	diseased
4.	inveterate	d.	from long-standing habit
5.	congenital	e.	suspiciously smooth
6.	chronic	f.	without conscience or scruples
7.	pathological	g.	outstandingly bad or vicious
8.	unconscionable	h.	unfavorably known
9.	glib	i.	from birth
10.	egregious	j.	finished, perfect, artistic

KEY: 1–h, 2–j, 3–a, 4–d, 5–i, 6–b, 7–c, 8–f, 9–e, 10–g

Do you understand the words?

1.	Do people become *notorious* for good acts?	YES	NO
2.	Is Beethoven considered a *consummate* musical genius?	YES	NO
3.	If a criminal is truly *incorrigible,* is there any point in attempting rehabilitation?	YES	NO
4.	Does an *inveterate* smoker smoke only occasionally?	YES	NO
5.	Is a *congenital* deformity one that occurs late in life?	YES	NO
6.	Is a *chronic* invalid ill much of the time?	YES	NO
7.	Is a *pathological* condition normal and healthy?	YES	NO
8.	If a person commits an *unconscionable* act of cruelty, is there any regret, remorse, or guilt?	YES	NO
9.	Is a *glib* talker awkward and hesitant in speech?	YES	NO
10.	Is an *egregious* error very bad?	YES	NO

KEY: 1–no, 2–yes, 3–no, 4–no, 5–no, 6–yes, 7–no, 8–no, 9–no, 10–yes

Can you recall the words?

1. outstandingly vicious; so bad as to be in a class by itself   1. E_____
2. starting at birth   2. C_____
3. happening over and over again; continuing for a long time   3. C_____

4. widely and unfavorably known (as for antisocial acts, character weaknesses, immoral or unethical behavior, etc.)

4. N_____

5. beyond correction

5. I_____

6. smooth and persuasive; unusually, almost suspiciously, fluent

6. G_____

7. long addicted to a habit

7. I_____

8. perfect in the practice of an art; extremely skillful

8. C_____

9. unscrupulous; entirely without conscience

9. U_____

10. diseased

10. P_____

KEY: 1–egregious, 2–congenital, 3–chronic, 4–notorious, 5–incorrigible, 6–glib, 7–inveterate, 8–consummate, 9–unconscionable, 10–pathological

---

Can you use the words?

As a result of the tests you are taking, you are becoming more and more familiar with these ten valuable and expressive words. Now, as a further check on your learning, write the word that best fits each blank.

1. This person has gambled, day in and day out, for as long as anyone can remember—gambling has become a deep-rooted habit.

    1. An _____ gambler

2. Born with a clubfoot

    2. A _____ deformity

3. Someone known the world over for criminal acts

    3. A _____ criminal

4. An invading army kills, maims, and tortures without mercy, compunction, or regret.

    4. _____ acts of cruelty

5. The suspect answers the detective's questions easily, fluently, almost too smoothly.

    5. _____ responses

6. A person reaches the acme of perfection as an actress or actor.

    6. A _____ performer

7. No one can change someone's absurdly romantic attitude toward life.

    7. An _____ romantic

8. A mistake so bad that it defies description

    8. An _____ blunder

9. Drunk almost all the time, again and again and again—periods of sobriety are few and very, very far between

    9. A _____ alcoholic

10. Doctors find a persistent, dangerous infection in the bladder

    10. A _____ condition

KEY: 1–inveterate, 2–congenital, 3–notorious, 4–unconscionable, 5–glib, 6–consummate, 7–incorrigible, 8–egregious, 9–chronic, 10–pathological

---

(End of Session 14)

SESSION 15

ORIGINS AND RELATED WORDS

1. well-known

"Widely but unfavorably known" is the common definition for *notorious*. Just as a *notorious* liar is well-known for unreliable statements, so a *notorious* gambler, a *notorious* thief, or a *notori-*

157

ous killer has achieved a wide reputation for some form of antisocial behavior. The noun is *notoriety* (nō-tə-RĪ'-ə-tee).

The derivation is from Latin *notus,* known, from which we also get *noted.* It is an interesting characteristic of some words that a change of syllables can alter the emotional impact. Thus, an admirer of certain business executives will speak of them as *"noted industrialists";* these same people's enemies will call them *"notorious* exploiters."* Similarly, if we admire a man's or a woman's unworldliness, we refer to it by the complimentary term *childlike;* but if we are annoyed by the trait, we describe it, derogatively, as *childish.* Change "-like" to "-ish" and our emotional tone undergoes a complete reversal.

2. plenty of room at the top

The top of a mountain is called, as you know, the *summit,* a word derived from Latin *summus,* highest, which also gives us the mathematical term *sum,* as in addition. A *consummate* artist has reached the very highest point of perfection; and to *consummate* (KON'-sə-mayt') a marriage, a business deal, or a contract is, etymologically, to bring it to the highest point; that is, to put the final touches to it, to bring it to completion.

[Note how differently *consummate* (kən-SUM'-ət), the adjective, is pronounced from the verb to *consummate* (KON'-sə-mayt')].

Nouns are formed from adjectives by the addition of the noun suffix *-ness: sweet—sweetness; simple—simpleness; envious—enviousness;* etc.

Many adjectives, however, have alternate noun forms, and the adjective *consummate* is one of them. To make a noun out of *consummate,* add either *-ness* or *-acy; consummateness* (kən-SUM'-ət-nəs) or *consummacy* (kən-SUM'-ə-see).

Verbs ending in *-ate* invariably tack on the noun suffix *-ion* to form nouns: *create—creation; evaluate—evaluation;* etc.

Can you write the noun form of the verb to *consummate?*

158

3. no help

Call people *incorrigible* (in-KAWR'-ə-jə-bəl) if they do anything to excess, and if all efforts to correct or reform them are to no avail. Thus, one can be an *incorrigible* idealist, an *incorrigible* criminal, an *incorrigible* optimist, or an *incorrigible* philanderer. The word derives from Latin *corrigo*, to correct or set straight, plus the negative prefix *in-*. (This prefix, depending on the root it precedes, may be negative, may intensify the root, as in *invaluable*, or may mean *in*.)

The noun is *incorrigibility* (in-kawr'-ə-jə-BIL'-ə-tee) or, alternatively, *incorrigibleness*.

4. veterans

Inveterate, from Latin *vetus*, old,* generally indicates disapproval.

Inveterate gamblers have grown old in the habit, etymologically speaking; *inveterate* drinkers have been imbibing for so long that they, too, have formed old, well-established habits; and *inveterate* liars have been lying for so long, and their habits are by now so deep-rooted, that one can scarcely remember (the word implies) when they ever told the truth.

The noun is *inveteracy* (in-VET'-ər-ə-see) or *inveterateness*.

A *veteran* (VET'-ə-rən), as of the Armed Forces, grew older serving the country; otherwise a *veteran* is an old hand at the game (and therefore skillful). The word is both a noun and an adjective: a *veteran* at (or in) swimming, tennis, police work, business, negotiations, diplomacy—or a *veteran* actor, teacher, diplomat, political reformer.

---

* Latin *senex*, source of *senile* and *senescent*, also, you will recall, means *old*. In *inveterate*, *in-* means *in*; it is not the negative prefix found in *incorrigible*.

159

5. birth

Greek *genesis,* birth or origin, a root we discovered in discussing *psychogenic* (Chapter 5), is the source of a great many English words.

Genetics (jə-NET′-iks) is the science that treats of the transmission of hereditary characteristics from parents to offspring. The scientist specializing in the field is a *geneticist* (jə-NET′-ə-sist), the adjective is *genetic* (jə-NET′-ik). The particle in the chromosome of the germ cell containing a hereditary characteristic is a *gene* (JEEN).

Genealogy (jeen′-ee-AL′-ə-jee) is the study of family trees or ancestral origins (*logos,* study). The practitioner is a *genealogist* (jeen′-ee-AL′-ə-jist). Can you form the adjective? _____. (And can you pronounce it?)

The *genital* (GEN′-ə-təl), or sexual, organs are involved in the process of conception and birth. The *genesis* (JEN′-ə-sis) of anything—a plan, idea, thought, career, etc.—is its beginning, birth, or origin, and *Genesis,* the first book of the Old Testament, describes the creation, or birth, of the universe.

Congenital is constructed by combining the prefix *con-,* with or together, and the root *genesis,* birth.

So a *congenital* defect, deformity, condition, etc. occurs during the nine-month birth process (or period of gestation, to become technical). *Hereditary* (hə-RED′-ə-tair′-ee) characteristics, on the other hand, are acquired at the moment of conception. Thus, eye color, nose shape, hair texture, and other such qualities are *hereditary;* they are determined by the *genes* in the germ cells of the mother and father. But a thalidomide baby resulted from the use of the drug by a pregnant woman, so the deformities were *congenital.*

Congenital is used both literally and figuratively. Literally, the word generally refers to some medical deformity or abnormality occurring during gestation. Figuratively, it wildly exaggerates, for effect, the very early existence of some quality: *congenital* liar, *congenital* fear of the dark, etc.

REVIEW OF ETYMOLOGY

PREFIX, ROOT	MEANING	ENGLISH WORD
1. *notus*	known	_____
2. *summus*	highest	_____
3. *corrigo*	to correct, set straight	_____
4. *vetus*	old	_____
5. *senex*	old	_____
6. *genesis*	birth, origin	_____
7. *logos*	science, study	_____
8. *in-*	negative prefix	_____

USING THE WORDS

Can you pronounce the words?

1. *notoriety* — nō-tə-RĪ′-ə-tee
2. *to consumate (v.)* — KON′-sə-mayt′
3. *consummacy* — kən-SUM′-ə-see
4. *consummation* — kon′-sə-MAY′-shən
5. *incorrigibility* — in-kawr′-ə-jə-BIL′-ə-tee
6. *inveteracy* — in-VET′-ə-rə-see
7. *veteran* — VET′-ə-rən
8. *genetics* — jə-NET′-iks
9. *geneticist* — jə-NET′-ə-sist
10. *genetic* — jə-NET′-ik
11. *gene* — JEEN
12. *genealogy* — jee′-nee-AL′-ə-jee
13. *genealogist* — jee′-nee-AL′-ə-jist
14. *genealogical* — jee′-nee-ə-LOJ′-ə-kəl
15. *genital* — JEN′-ə-təl
16. *genesis* — JEN′-ə-sis
17. *hereditary* — hə-RED′-ə-tair′-ee

Can you work with the words?

1. notoriety	a. state of artistic height
2. to consummate (*v.*)	b. state of being long established in a habit
3. consummacy	c. beginning, origin
4. incorrigibility	d. science of heredity
5. inveteracy	e. bring to completion; top off
6. genetics	f. study of ancestry
7. genealogy	g. referring to characteristics passed on to offspring by parents
8. genital	h. referring to reproduction, or to the reproductive or sexual organs
9. genesis	i. ill fame
10. hereditary	j. particle that transmits hereditary characteristics
11. gene	k. state of being beyond reform or correction

KEY: 1–i, 2–e, 3–a, 4–k, 5–b, 6–d, 7–f, 8–h, 9–c, 10–g, 11–j

Do you understand the words?

1. Does *notoriety* usually come to perpetrators of mass murders?　　YES　NO

2. Is the product of a *consummately* skillful counterfeiter likely to be taken as genuine?　　YES　NO

3. Is *incorrigibility* in a criminal a sign that rehabilitation is possible?　　YES　NO

4. Is a *geneticist* interested in your parents' characteristics?　　YES　NO

5. Does *inveteracy* suggest that a habit is new?　　YES　NO

6. When you *consummate* a deal, do you back out of it? YES NO
7. Is a *veteran* actress long experienced at her art? YES NO
8. Do *genes* determine heredity? YES NO
9. Is a *genealogist* interested in your family origins? YES NO
10. Are the *genital* organs used in reproduction? YES NO
11. Is the *genesis* of something the final point? YES NO
12. Are *hereditary* characteristics derived from parents? YES NO

KEY: 1–yes, 2–yes, 3–no, 4–yes, 5–no, 6–no, 7–yes, 8–yes, 9–yes, 10–yes, 11–no, 12–yes

Can you recall the words?

1. sexual; reproductive
2. to complete
3. wide and unfavorable reputation
4. particle in the chromosome of a cell that transmits a characteristic from parent to offspring
5. completion
6. inability to be reformed
7. the science that deals with the transmission of characteristics from parents to children
8. referring to a quality or characteristic that is inherited (*adj.*)
9. beginning or origin

1. G_____
2. C_____
3. N_____

4. G_____

5. C_____
6. I_____
7. G_____

8. H_____

9. G_____

10. student of family roots or origins	10. G_____
11. height of skill or artistry	11. C_____
	or C_____
12. transmitted by heredity	12. G_____
13. quality of a habit that has been established over many years	13. I_____
	or I_____
14. a person long experienced at a profession, art, or business	14. V_____
15. pertaining to a study of family origins (*adj.*)	15. G_____

KEY: 1–genital, 2–consummate, 3–notoriety, 4–gene, 5–consummation, 6–incorrigibility, 7–genetics, 8–hereditary, 9–genesis, 10–genealogist, 11–consummacy *or* consummateness, 12–genetic, 13–inveteracy *or* inveterateness, 14–veteran, 15–genealogical

---

(*End of Session 15*)

SESSION 16

ORIGINS AND RELATED WORDS

1. of time and place

A *chronic* liar lies constantly, again and again and again; a *chronic* invalid is ill time after time, frequently, repeatedly. The derivation of the word is Greek *chronos,* time. The noun form is *chronicity* (krə-NIS'-ə-tee).

An *anachronism* (ə-NAK'-rə-niz-əm) is someone or something out of time, out of date, belonging to a different era, either earlier or later. (The prefix *ana-* like *a-*, is negative.) The adjective is *anachronous* (ə-NAK'-rə-nəs) or *anachronistic* (ə-nak'-rə-NIS'-tik).

Wander along Fifty-ninth Street and Central Park in Manhattan some Sunday. You will see horse-drawn carriages with top-hatted coachmen—a vestige of the 1800s. Surrounded by twentieth-century motorcars and modern skyscrapers, these romantic vehicles of a bygone era are *anachronous*.

Read a novel in which a scene is supposedly taking place in the nineteenth century and see one of the characters turning on a TV set. An *anachronism!*

Your friend talks, thinks, dresses, and acts as if he were living in the time of Shakespeare. Another *anachronism!*

Science fiction is deliberately *anachronous*—it deals with phenomena, gadgetry, accomplishments far off (possibly) in the future.

An *anachronism* is out of *time;* something out of *place* is *incongruous* (in-KONG'-grōō-əs), a word combining the negative prefix *in-*, the prefix *con-*, with or together, and a Latin verb meaning to *agree* or *correspond.*

Thus, it is *incongruous* to wear a sweater and slacks to a formal wedding; it is *anachronous* to wear the wasp waist, conspicuous bustle, or powdered wig of the eighteenth century. The noun form of *incongruous* is *incongruity* (in-kəng-GRŌŌ'-ə-tee).

Chronological (kron-ə-LOJ'-ə-kəl), in correct time order, comes from *chronos*. To tell a story *chronologically* is to relate the events in the time order of their occurrence. *Chronology* (krə-NOL'-ə-jee) is the science of time order and the accurate dating of events (*logos,* science)—the expert in this field is a *chronologist* (krə-NOL'-ə-jist)—or a list of events in the time order in which they have occurred or will occur.

A *chronometer* (krə-NOM'-ə-tər), combining *chronos* with *metron,* measurement, is a highly accurate timepiece, especially one used on ships. *Chronometry* (krə-NOM'-ə-tree) is the measurement of time—the adjective is *chronometric* (kron'-ə-MET'-rik).

Add the prefix *syn-*, together, plus the verb suffix *-ize*, to *chronos*, and you have constructed *synchronize* (SIN'-krə-nīz'), etymologically *to time together,* or to move, happen, or cause to happen, at the same time or rate. If you and your friend *synchro-*

nize your watches, you set them at the same time. If you *synchronize* the activity of your arms and legs, as in swimming, you move them at the same time or rate. The adjective is *synchronous* (SIN'-krə-nəs); the noun form of the verb *synchronize* is *synchronization* (sin'-krə-nə-ZAY'-shən).

2. disease, suffering, feeling

Pathological is *diseased* (a *pathological* condition)—this meaning of the word ignores the root *logos,* science, study.

Pathology (pə-THOL'-ə-jee) *is* the science or study of disease —its nature, cause, cure, etc. However, another meaning of the noun ignores *logos,* and *pathology* may be any morbid, diseased, or abnormal physical condition or conditions; in short, simply *disease,* as in "This case involves so many kinds of *pathology* that several different specialists are working on it."

A *pathologist* (pə-THOL'-ə-jist) is an expert who examines tissue, often by autopsy or biopsy, to diagnose disease and interpret the abnormalities in such tissue that may be caused by specific diseases.

Pathos occurs in some English words with the additional meaning of *feeling.* If you feel or suffer with someone, you are *sympathetic* (sim-pə-THET'-ik)—*sym-* is a respelling before the letter *p* of the Greek prefix *syn-,* with or together. The noun is *sympathy* (SIM'-pə-thee), the verb *sympathize* (SIM'-pə-thīz). Husbands, for example, so the story goes, may have *sympathetic* labor pains when their wives are about to deliver.

The prefix *anti-,* you will recall, means *against.* If you experience *antipathy* (an-TIP'-ə-thee) to people or things, you feel *against* them—you feel strong dislike or hostility. The adjective is *antipathetic* (an'-tə-pə-THET'-ik), as in "an *antipathetic* reaction to an authority figure."

But you may have *no* feeling at all—just indifference, lack of any interest, emotion, or response, complete listlessness, especially when some reaction is normal or expected. Then you are *apathetic* (ap-ə-THET'-ik); *a-,* as you know, is a negative prefix. The noun is *apathy* (AP'-ə-thee), as in voter *apathy,* student *apathy,* etc.

166

On the other hand, you may be so sensitive or perceptive that you not only share the feelings of another, but you also *identify* with those feelings, in fact experience them yourself as if momentarily you were that other person. What you have, then, is *empathy* (EM′-pə-thee); you *empathize* (EM′-pə-thīz′), you are *empathetic* (em-pə-THET′-ik), or, to use an alternate adjective, *empathic* (em-PATH′-ik). *Em-* is a respelling before the letter *p* of the Greek prefix *en-*, in.

Someone is *pathetic* (pə-THET′-ik) who is obviously suffering —such a person may arouse sympathy or pity (or perhaps *antipathy?*) in you. A *pathetic* story is about suffering and, again, is likely to arouse sadness, sorrow, or pity.

Some interesting research was done many years ago by Dr. J. B. Rhine and his associates at Duke University on extrasensory perception; you will find an interesting account of Rhine's work in his book *The Reach of the Mind*. What makes it possible for two people separated by miles of space to communicate with each other without recourse to messenger, telephone, telegraph, or postal service? It can be done, say the believers in *telepathy* (tə-LEP′-ə-thee), also called *mental telepathy*, though they do not yet admit to knowing how. How can one person read the mind of another? Simple—by being *telepathic* (tel-ə-PATH′-ik), but no one can explain the chemistry or biology of it. *Telepathy* is built by combining *pathos*, feeling, with the prefix *tele-*, distance, the same prefix we found in *telephone, telegraph, telescope*.

Telepathic (tel-ə-PATH′-ik) communication occurs when people can *feel* each other's thoughts from a distance, when they have ESP.

REVIEW OF ETYMOLOGY

PREFIX, ROOT, SUFFIX	MEANING	ENGLISH WORD
1. *chronos*	time	_____
2. *ana-, a-*	negative prefix	_____
3. *con-*	with, together	_____

4. *in-*	negative prefix	_____
5. *logos*	science, study	_____
6. *metron*	measurement	_____
7. *syn-, sym-*	with, together	_____
8. *-ize*	verb suffix	_____
9. *pathos*	disease, suffering, feeling	_____
10. *anti-*	against	_____
11. *en-, em-*	in	_____
12. *tele-*	distance	_____

USING THE WORDS

Can you pronounce the words? (I)

1. *chronicity*	krə-NIS′-ə-tee
2. *anachronism*	ə-NAK′-rə-niz-əm
3. *anachronous*	ə-NAK′-rə-nəs
4. *anachronistic*	ə-nak′-rə-NIS′-tik
5. *incongruous*	in-KONG′-grōō-əs
6. *incongruity*	in′-kəng-GRŌŌ′-ə-tee
7. *chronological*	kron′-ə-LOJ′-ə-kəl
8. *chronology*	krə-NOL′-ə-jee
9. *chronologist*	krə-NOL′-ə-jist
10. *chronometer*	krə-NOM′-ə-tər
11. *chronometry*	krə-NOM′-ə-tree
12. *chronometric*	kron′-ə-MET′-rik
13. *synchronize*	SIN′-krə-nīz′
14. *synchronization*	sin′-krə-nə-ZAY′-shən
15. *synchronous*	SIN′-krə-nəs

Can you pronounce the words? (II)

1. *pathology*	pə-THOL′-ə-jee
2. *pathologist*	pə-THOL′-ə-jist
3. *sympathy*	SIM′-pə-thee

168

4. *sympathetic*   sim-pə-THET'-ik
5. *sympathize*   SIM'-pə-thīz
6. *antipathy*   an-TIP'-ə-thee
7. *antipathetic*   an'-tə-pə-THET'-ik
8. *apathy*   AP'-ə-thee
9. *apathetic*   ap-ə-THET'-ik
10. *empathy*   EM'-pə-thee
11. *empathize*   EM'-pə-thīz'
12. *empathetic*   em-pə-THET'-ik
13. *empathic*   em-PATH'-ik
14. *pathetic*   pə-THET'-ik
15. *telepathy*   tə-LEP'-ə-thee
16. *telepathic*   tel'-ə-PATH'-ik

Can you work with the words? (I)

1. chronicity
2. anachronism
3. incongruity
4. chronology
5. chronometer
6. chronometry
7. synchronization
8. pathology
9. sympathy
10. telepathy

a. something, or state of being, out of place
b. timepiece; device that measures time very accurately
c. condition of continual or repeated recurrence
d. act of occurring, or of causing to occur, at the same time
e. calendar of events in order of occurrence
f. something, or someone, out of time
g. measurement of time
h. a sharing or understanding of another's feeling
i. ESP; communication from a distance
j. disease; study of disease

KEY: 1–c, 2–f, 3–a, 4–e, 5–b, 6–g, 7–d, 8–j, 9–h, 10–i

169

Can you work with the words? (II)

1. pathologist
2. antipathy
3. apathy
4. empathy
5. synchronize
6. empathize
7. anachronous
8. incongruous
9. synchronous
10. pathetic
11. telepathic

a. identification with another's feelings
b. share another's feelings so strongly as to experience those feelings oneself
c. out of time
d. one who examines tissue to diagnose disease
e. occurring at the same time or rate
f. relating to extrasensory perception
g. suffering; arousing sympathy or pity
h. lack of feeling; non-responsiveness
i. out of place
j. happen, or cause to happen, at the same time or rate
k. hostility; strong dislike

KEY: 1–d, 2–k, 3–h, 4–a, 5–j, 6–b, 7–c, 8–i, 9–e, 10–g, 11–f

Do you understand the words?

1. Are these dates in *chronological* order?   YES   NO
   1492, 1941, 1586
2. Is *pathology* the study of healthy tissue?   YES   NO
3. Is *telepathic* communication carried on   YES   NO
   by telephone?
4. Does a *sympathetic* response show an   YES   NO
   understanding of another's feelings?
5. Is one *antipathetic* to things, ideas, or   YES   NO
   people one finds agreeable?
6. Do *apathetic* people react strongly?   YES   NO

170

7. Does an *empathic* response show identification with the feelings of another? — YES NO

8. Is a swimsuit *incongruous* attire at a formal ceremony? — YES NO

9. Is an *anachronistic* attitude up to date? — YES NO

10. Are *synchronous* movements out of time with one another? — YES NO

KEY: 1–no, 2–no, 3–no, 4–yes, 5–no, 6–no, 7–yes, 8–yes, 9–no, 10–no

Can you recall the words?

1. in order of time — 1. C_____
2. out of place — 2. I_____
3., 4. out of time (two forms) — 3. A_____
   — 4. A_____
5. something, or state of being, out of place — 5. I_____
6. lack of feeling — 6. A_____
7. measurer of time — 7. C_____
8. study of disease — 8. P_____
9. feeling of hostility or dislike — 9. A_____
10. to occur, or cause to occur, at the same time or rate — 10. S_____
11. evoking sorrow or pity — 11. P_____
12. something out of time — 12. A_____
13. state of recurring again and again — 13. C_____
14. extransensory perception — 14. T_____
15. one who examines tissue to diagnose disease — 15. P_____
16. identification with the feelings of another — 16. E_____
17. happening at the same time or rate (*adj.*) — 17. S_____

171

18. skillful at thought transference without sensory communication   18. T_____

19. calendar of events in time sequence   19. C_____

20. referring to the measurement of time (*adj.*)   20. C_____

KEY: 1–chronological, 2–incongruous, 3, 4–anachronous, anachronistic, 5–incongruity, 6–apathy, 7–chronometer, 8–pathology, 9–antipathy, 10–synchronize, 11–pathetic, 12–anachronism, 13–chronicity, 14–telepathy, 15–pathologist, 16–empathy, 17–synchronous, 18–telepathic, 19–chronology, 20–chronometric

---

(*End of Session 16*)

SESSION 17

ORIGINS AND RELATED WORDS

1. knowing

Psychopaths commit antisocial and *unconscionable* acts—they are not troubled by *conscience,* guilt, remorse, etc. over what they have done.

Unconscionable and *conscience* are related in derivation—the first word from Latin *scio,* to know, the second from Latin *sciens,* knowing, and both using the prefix *con-,* with, together.

Etymologically, then, your *conscience* is your knowledge *with* a moral sense of right and wrong; if you are *unconscionable,* your conscience is not (*un-*) working, or you have no conscience. The noun form is *unconscionableness* or *unconscionability* (un-kon'-shə-nə-BIL'-ə-tee).

Conscious, also from *con-* plus *scio,* is knowledge or awareness of one's emotions or sensations, or of what's happening around one.

Science, from *sciens,* is systematized *knowledge* as opposed, for example, to belief, faith, intuition, or guesswork.

Add Latin *omnis,* all, to *sciens,* to construct *omniscient* (om-NISH'-ənt), all-knowing, possessed of infinite knowledge. The noun is *omniscience* (om-NISH'-əns).

Add the prefix *pre-,* before, to *sciens,* to construct *prescient* (PREE'-shənt)—knowing about events *before* they occur, i.e., psychic, or possessed of unusual powers of prediction. The noun is *prescience* (PREE'-shəns).

And, finally, add the negative prefix *ne-* to *sciens* to produce *nescient* (NESH'-ənt), not knowing, or ignorant. Can you, by analogy with the previous two words, write the noun form of *nescient?* _____ (Can you pronounce it?)

2. fool some of the people . . .

Glib is from an old English root that means *slippery. Glib* liars or *glib* talkers are smooth and slippery; they have ready answers, fluent tongues, a persuasive air—but, such is the implication of the word, they fool only the most *nescient,* for their smoothness lacks sincerity and conviction.

The noun is *glibness.*

3. herds and flocks

Egregious (remember the pronunciation? ə-GREE'-jəs) is from Latin *grex, gregis,* herd or flock. An *egregious* lie, act, crime, mistake, etc. is so exceptionally vicious that it conspicuously stands *out* (*e-,* a shortened form of the prefix *ex-,* out) from the *herd* or *flock* of other bad things.

The noun is *egregiousness* (ə-GREE'-jəs-nəs).

A person who enjoys companionship, who, etymologically, likes to be with the herd, who reaches out for friends and is happiest when surrounded by people—such a person is *gregarious* (grə-GAIR′-ee-əs).

Extroverts are of course *gregarious*—they prefer human contact, conversation, laughter, interrelationships, to solitude.

The suffix *-ness,* as you know, can be added to an adjective to construct a noun form. Write the noun for *gregarious:*

_____

Add the prefix *con-,* with, together, to *grex, gregis,* to get the verb *congregate* (KONG′-grə-gayt′); add the prefix *se-,* apart, to build the verb *segregate* (SEG′-rə-gayt′); add the prefix *ad-,* to, toward (*ad-* changes to *ag-* before a root starting with *g-*), to construct the verb *aggregate* (AG-rə-gayt′).

Let's see what we have. When people gather *together* in a *herd* or *flock,* they (write the verb) _____.
The noun is *congregation* (cong′-grə-GAY′-shən), one of the meanings of which is a religious "flock."

Put people or things apart from the *herd,* and you (write the verb) _____ them. Can you construct the noun by adding the suitable noun suffix?

_____.

Bring individual items to or toward the *herd* or *flock,* and you (write the verb) _____ them. What is the noun form of this verb? _____

The verb *aggregate* also means *to come together to or toward the herd,* that is, *to gather into a mass or whole,* or by extension, *to total or amount to.* So *aggregate,* another noun form, pronounced AG′-rə-gət, is a group or mass of individuals considered as a whole, a *herd,* or a *flock,* as in the phrase "people in the *aggregate* . . ."

REVIEW OF ETYMOLOGY

PREFIX, ROOT, SUFFIX	MEANING	ENGLISH WORD
1. *grex, gregis*	herd, flock	_____
2. *e-, ex-*	out	_____

3. *-ness*	noun suffix	_____
4. *con-*	with, together	_____
5. *ad-, ag-*	to, toward	_____
6. *un-*	negative prefix	_____
7. *scio*	to know	_____
8. *sciens*	knowing	_____
9. *omnis*	all	_____
10. *pre-*	before	_____
11. *ne-*	negative prefix	_____
12. *se-*	apart	_____
13. *-ion*	noun suffix added to verbs	_____

USING THE WORDS

Can you pronounce the words?

1.	*unconscionability*	un-kon'-shə-nə-BIL'-ə-tee
2.	*omniscient*	om-NISH'-ənt
3.	*omniscience*	om-NISH'-əns
4.	*prescient*	PREE'-shənt
5.	*prescience*	PREE'-shəns
6.	*nescient*	NESH'-ənt
7.	*nescience*	NESH'-əns
8.	*glibness*	GLIB'-nəs
9.	*egregiousness*	ə-GREE'-jəs-nəs
10.	*gregarious*	grə-GAIR'-ee-əs
11.	*gregariousness*	grə-GAIR'-ee-əs-nəs
12.	*congregate*	KONG'-grə-gayt'
13.	*congregation*	kong'-grə-GAY'-shən
14.	*segregate*	SEG'-rə-gayt'
15.	*segregation*	seg'-rə-GAY'-shən
16.	*aggregate* (*v.*)	AG'-rə-gayt
17.	*aggregate* (*n.*)	AG'-rə-gət
18.	*aggregation*	ag'-rə-GAY'-shən

Can you work with the words?

1. unconscionability	a. ignorance
2. omniscience	b. outstanding badness or viciousness
3. prescience	c. religious group; a massing together
4. nescience	d. total; mass; whole
5. glibness	e. exclusion from the herd; a setting apart
6. egregiousness	f. infinite knowledge
7. gregariousness	g. friendliness; enjoyment of mixing with people
8. congregation	h. lack of conscience
9. segregation	i. suspiciously smooth fluency
10. aggregate (*n.*)	j. foreknowledge

KEY: 1–h, 2–f, 3–j, 4–a, 5–i, 6–b, 7–g, 8–c, 9–e, 10–d

Do you understand the words?

1. Is *unconscionability* one of the signs of the psychopath?	YES	NO
2. Can anyone be truly *omniscient?*	YES	NO
3. Does a *prescient* fear indicate some knowledge of the future?	YES	NO
4. Is *nescience* a result of learning?	YES	NO
5. Does *glibness* make someone sound sincere and trustworthy?	YES	NO
6. Is *egregiousness* an admirable quality?	YES	NO
7. Do *gregarious* people enjoy parties?	YES	NO
8. Do spectators *congregate* at sports events?	YES	NO
9. Do we often *segregate* hardened criminals from the rest of society?	YES	NO

10. Is an *aggregation* of problems a whole   YES   NO
    mass of problems?

KEY: 1–yes, 2–no, 3–yes, 4–no, 5–no, 6–no, 7–yes, 8–yes, 9–yes,
     10–yes

Can you recall the words?

1. enjoying groups and   1. G_____
   companionship
2. ignorant   2. N_____
3. state of *not* being held back   3. U_____
   from antisocial behavior by   *or* U_____
   one's conscience
4. having knowledge of an event   4. P_____
   before it occurs (*adj.*)
5. a religious "flock"   5. C_____
6. a total, whole, or mass   6. A_____
                                             or A_____
7. to separate from the rest   7. S_____
8. suspiciously smooth fluency   8. G_____
9. all-knowing (*adj.*)   9. O_____
10. to come together into a group   10. C_____
    or mass

KEY: 1–gregarious, 2–nescient, 3–unconscionability *or* uncon-
     scionableness, 4–prescient, 5–congregation, 6–aggregate *or*
     aggregation, 7–segregate, 8–glibness, 9–omniscient, 10–con-
     gregate

CHAPTER REVIEW

A. Do you recognize the words?

1. Highly skilled:
   (a) consummate, (b) inveterate, (c) notorious

2. Beyond reform:
   (a) inveterate, (b) incorrigible, (c) glib
3. Dating from birth:
   (a) inveterate, (b) congenital, (c) psychopathic
4. Outstandingly bad:
   (a) egregious, (b) unconscionable, (c) chronic
5. Science of heredity:
   (a) pathology, (b) genetics, (c) orthopedics
6. Out of time:
   (a) incongruous, (b) anachronous, (c) synchronous
7. Study of disease:
   (a) pathology, (b) telepathy, (c) antipathy
8. Fond of company, friends, group activities, etc.:
   (a) apathetic, (b) gregarious, (c) chronological
9. Indifferent:
   (a) antipathetic, (b) pathetic, (c) apathetic
10. Long accustomed in habit:
    (a) incorrigible, (b) notorious, (c) inveterate
11. Study of family ancestry:
    (a) genealogy, (b) genetics, (c) genesis
12. To complete, finish, top off:
    (a) synchronize, (b) consummate, (c) empathize
13. Accurate timepiece:
    (a) anachronism, (b) chronology, (c) chronometer
14. Identification with the feelings of another:
    (a) sympathy, (b) apathy, (c) empathy
15. Thought transference; extrasensory perception:
    (a) telepathy, (b) empathy, (c) omniscience
16. Ignorance:
    (a) omniscience, (b) prescience, (c) nescience
17. To gather into a group:
    (a) congregate, (b) segregate, (c) synchronize

KEY: 1–a, 2–b, 3–b, 4–a, 5–b, 6–b, 7–a, 8–b, 9–c, 10–c, 11–a, 12–b, 13–c, 14–c, 15–a, 16–c, 17–a

B. Can you recognize roots?

ROOT	MEANING	EXAMPLE
1. *notus*	_____	notorious
2. *summus*	_____	summit
3. *corrigo*	_____	incorrigible
4. *vetus*	_____	veteran
5. *senex*	_____	senile
6. *genesis*	_____	congenital
7. *logos*	_____	genealogy
8. *chronos*	_____	chronic
9. *metron*	_____	chronometer
10. *pathos*	_____	pathology
	_____	pathetic
	_____	empathy
11. *grex, gregis*	_____	gregarious
12. *scio*	_____	unconscionable
13. *sciens*	_____	prescience
14. *omnis*	_____	omniscient

KEY: 1–known, 2–highest, 3–to correct, set straight, 4–old, 5–old, 6–birth, 7–science, study, 8–time, 9–measurement, 10–disease, suffering, feeling, 11–herd, flock, 12–to know, 13–knowing, 14–all

TEASER QUESTIONS FOR THE AMATEUR ETYMOLOGIST

1. "She was one of many *notables* who attended the convention." Recognizing that the italicized word is built on the root *notus,* can you define the noun *notable* in the context of *known?*

_____
_____.

2. *Notify* and *notice* derive from the same root. Can you define these two words, again in the context of *known? Notify:* _____. *Notice:* _____.

179

What do you suppose the verb suffix *-fy* of *notify* means? (Think also of *simplify, clarify, liquefy,* etc.) _____.

3. You are familiar with the roots *chronos* and *graphein*. Suppose you came across the word *chronograph* in your reading. Can you make an educated guess as to the meaning? _____

_____

4. Recognizing the root *genesis* in the verb *generate,* how would you define the word? _____

_____

How about *regenerate?* _____

_____

What do you suppose the prefix *re-* means? _____

_____

5. Recognizing the root *omnis* in *omnipotent* and *omnipresent,* can you define the words?

  Omnipotent: _____
  Omnipresent: _____

Recalling how we formed a noun from the adjective *omniscient,* write the noun forms of:

  Omnipotent: _____.
  Omnipresent: _____.

6. Think of the negative prefix in *anachronism;* think next of the noun *aphrodisiac.* Can you construct a word for *that which reduces or eliminates sexual desire?* _____.

(*Answers in Chapter 18*)

FOUR LASTING BENEFITS

You know by now that it is easy to build your vocabulary if you work diligently and intelligently. Diligence is important—to come to the book occasionally is to learn new words and ideas in an aimless fashion, rather than in the continuous way that characterizes the natural, uninterrupted, intellectual growth of a child. (You will recall that children are top experts in increasing their vocabularies.) And an intelligent approach is crucial—new words can be completely understood and permanently remembered only as symbols of vital ideas, never if memorized in long lists of isolated forms.

If you have worked diligently and intelligently, you have done much more than merely learned a few hundred new words. Actually, I needn't tell you what else you've accomplished, since, if you really have accomplished it, you can feel it for yourself; but it may be useful if I verbalize the feelings you may have.

In addition to learning the meanings, pronunciation, background, and use of 300–350 valuable words, you have:

1. *Begun to sense a change in your intellectual atmosphere.* (You have begun to do your thinking with many of the words, with many of the ideas behind the words. You have begun to use the words in your speech and writing, and have become alert to their appearance in your reading.)

2. *Begun to develop a new interest in words as expressions of ideas.*

3. *Begun to be aware of the new words you hear and that you see in your reading.*

4. *Begun to gain a new feeling for the relationship between words.* (For you realize that many words are built on roots from other languages and are related to other words which derive from the same roots.)

Now, suppose we pause to see how successful your learning has been.

In the next chapter, I offer you a comprehensive test on the first part of your work.

(*End of Session 17*)

8

HOW TO CHECK YOUR PROGRESS

Comprehensive Test I

SESSION 18

If you have worked diligently thus far, you have:

1. Become acquainted, or perhaps reacquainted, with approximately 300–350 expressive words—
2. Learned scores of important Latin and Greek prefixes, roots, and suffixes—
3. Set up valuable habits of self-discipline and self-directed learning—
4. Explored your attitudes toward grammar and current usage, meanwhile erasing any confusion you may once have felt about specific problems of correctness in your use of words—
5. And, finally, taken good, long steps toward your ultimate goal, namely, the development of a better, richer, more expressive—in short, *superior*—vocabulary.

Here is your chance both to review and to check your learning.

(Bear in mind that without careful and periodic review, a significant amount of learning is lost.)

Methods of scoring your achievement on this test, and the meaning of your results, will be explained at the end of the chapter.

I etymology

ROOT	MEANING	EXAMPLE
1. *ego*		egoism
2. *misein*		misanthrope
3. *gamos*		bigamy
4. *gyne*		gynecology
5. *derma*		dermatology
6. *orthos*		orthodontia
7. *psyche*		psychotic
8. *neuron*		neurology
9. *logos*		biology
10. *bios*		biopsy
11. *opsis, optikos*		autopsy, optical
12. *algos*		neuralgia
13. *agogos*		demagogue
14. *pedis*		pedestrian
15. *paidos (ped-)*		pediatrician
16. *demos*		democracy
17. *oculus*		oculist
18. *iatreia*		podiatrist
19. *metron*		optometrist
20. *geras*		geriatrics
21. *soma*		psychosomatic
22. *pathos*		osteopath
23. *odontos*		exodontist
24. *pous, podos*		octopus, podium
25. *cheir (chiro-)*		chirography

II more etymology

ROOT	MEANING	EXAMPLE
1. *graphein*	_____	graphology
2. *kallos*	_____	calligrapher
3. *pyge*	_____	callipygian
4. *kakos*	_____	cacophony
5. *senex*	_____	senescent
6. *anthropos*	_____	anthropology
7. *astron*	_____	astronomy
8. *nautes*	_____	astronaut
9. *ge* (*geo-*)	_____	geology
10. *zoion*	_____	zodiac
11. *lingua*	_____	bilingual
12. *philein*	_____	Philadelphia
13. *biblion*	_____	bibliophile
14. *autos*	_____	autonomous
15. *socius*	_____	asocial
16. *notus*	_____	notorious
17. *summus*	_____	consummate
18. *vetus*	_____	inveterate
19. *genesis*	_____	congenital
20. *chronos*	_____	chronic
21. *pathos*	_____	empathy
22. *grex, gregis*	_____	egregious
23. *sciens*	_____	prescient
24. *omnis*	_____	omniscient
25. *nomos*	_____	metronome

III same or opposite?

1. egoistic—altruistic	S	O
2. misanthropic—philanthropic	S	O
3. misogamous—polygamous	S	O
4. dexterous—skillful	S	O
5. sinister—threatening	S	O
6. optical—visual	S	O
7. notorious—infamous	S	O

8. consummate (*adj.*)—unskilled   S   O
9. chronic—acute   S   O
10. glib—halting   S   O
11. ophthalmologist—oculist   S   O
12. geriatric—pediatric   S   O
13. endodontist—exodontist   S   O
14. calligraphy—cacography   S   O
15. astronaut—cosmonaut   S   O
16. biopsy—autopsy   S   O
17. dichotomous—cut in two   S   O
18. congenital—hereditary   S   O
19. veteran—"old hand"   S   O
20. anachronous—timely   S   O

IV matching

I	II
1. dislikes women	a. entomologist
2. is pathologically self-interested	b. taxidermist
3. studies the development of the human race	c. egomaniac
4. is an expert on insects	d. bibliophile
5. collects books	e. ophthalmologist
6. mounts and stuffs animal skins	f. psychopath
7. is an eye doctor	g. philologist
8. is a student of linguistics	h. anthropologist
9. has "split off" from reality	i. psychotic
10. commits antisocial acts without guilt or pangs of conscience	j. misogynist

V more matching

I	II
1. delivers babies	a. pediatrician
2. treats female ailments	b. cardiologist

3. treats infants   c. psychiatrist
4. treats skin diseases   d. podiatrist
5. treats skeletal deformities   e. dermatologist
6. is a heart specialist   f. periodontist
7. treats mental or emotional   g. obstetrician
    disturbances
8. treats disorders of the   h. neurologist
    nervous system
9. treats minor ailments of   i. orthopedist
    the feet
10. treats ailments of the   j. gynecologist
    gums

VI recall a word

1. ruthless; without conscience   1. U_____
2. suspiciously fluent or smooth   2. G_____
3. outstandingly bad; vicious   3. E_____
4. out of place   4. I_____
5. study of the family tree;   5. G_____
    specialty of tracing ancestry
6. science of heredity   6. G_____
7. in correct order of time   7. C_____
8. socially awkward   8. G_____
9. record of heart action   9. C_____
10. equally skillful with both the   10. A_____
    right and left hand
11. social scientist who deals with   11. G_____
    the problems of aging
12. extrasensory perception   12. T_____
13. branch of dentistry specializing   13. P_____
    in the care of children's teeth
14. blood-pressure apparatus   14. S_____
15. growing old (*adj.*)   15. S_____
16. palm reader   16. C_____
17. that which arouses sexual   17. A_____
    desire
18. representation of the whole   18. E_____
19. diseased; pertaining to the   19. P_____
    study of disease (*adj.*)

20. measurement of time   20. C_____
21. hostility; strong dislike;   21. A_____
    aversion
22. to occur, or cause to occur, at   22. S_____
    the same time or rate
23. ignorant   23. N_____
24. knowledge of an occurrence   24. P_____
    beforehand
25. enjoying being with the herd;   25. G_____
    liking companionship
26. to identify strongly with the   26. E_____
    feelings of another
27. instrument to measure   27. B_____
    atmospheric pressure
28. to separate from the herd   28. S_____
29. possessed of shapely buttocks   29. C_____
30. ugly, illegible handwriting   30. C_____

KEY: A correct answer counts one point. Score your points for
     each part of the test, then add for a total.

I
1–I, self, 2–to hate, 3–marriage, 4–woman, 5–skin, 6–straight,
correct, 7–mind, soul, spirit, 8–nerve, 9–science, study, 10–life,
11–view, sight, vision, 12–pain, 13–leading, 14–foot, 15–child,
16–people, 17–eye, 18–medical healing, 19–measurement, 20–old
age, 21–body, 22–disease, 23–tooth, 24–foot, 25–hand

Your score: _____

II
1–to write, 2–beauty, 3–buttock, 4–harsh, ugly, bad, 5–old,
6–mankind, 7–star, 8–sailor, 9–earth, 10–animal, 11–tongue,
12–to love, 13–book, 14–self, 15–companion, 16–known, 17–highest, 18–old, 19–birth (beginning, origin), 20–time, 21–feeling,
22–herd, flock, 23–knowing, 24–all, 25–law, order, arrangement

Your score: _____

III

1–O, 2–O, 3–O, 4–S, 5–S, 6–S, 7–S, 8–O, 9–O, 10–O, 11–S, 12–O, 13–O, 14–O, 15–S, 16–O, 17–S, 18–O, 19–S, 20–O

Your score: _____

IV

1–j, 2–c, 3–h, 4–a, 5–d, 6–b, 7–e, 8–g, 9–i, 10–f

Your score: _____

V

1–g, 2–j, 3–a, 4–e, 5–i, 6–b, 7–c, 8–h, 9–d, 10–f

Your score: _____

VI

1–unconscionable, 2–glib, 3–egregious, 4–incongruous, 5–genealogy, 6–genetics, 7–chronological, 8–gauche, 9–cardiogram, 10–ambidextrous, 11–gerontologist, 12–telepathy, 13–pedodontia, 14–sphygmomanometer, 15–senescent, 16–chiromancer, 17–aphrodisiac, 18–epitome, 19–pathological, 20–chronometry, 21–antipathy, 22–synchronize, 23–nescient, 24–prescience, 25–gregarious, 26–empathize, 27–barometer, 28–segregate, 29–callipygian, 30–cacography

Your score: _____

Your total score: _____

Significance of Your Total Score:

100–120: Masterly work; you are ready to move right along.

80– 99: Good work; this review was useful to you.

65– 79: Average work; you're getting a good deal out of your study, but perhaps you should review thoroughly after each session.

50– 64: Barely acceptable; work harder.

35– 49: Poor; further review is suggested before you go on.

0– 34: You can do much better if you really try; continue with firmer resolve and more determination.

PART TWO

GAINING INCREASED
MOMENTUM

9

HOW TO TALK
ABOUT ACTIONS

(Sessions 19–23)

TEASER PREVIEW

What verb means to:

- *belittle?*
- *be purposely confusing?*
- *tickle someone's fancy?*
- *flatter fulsomely?*
- *prohibit some food or activity?*
- *make unnecessary?*
- *work against?*
- *spread slander?*
- *give implicit forgiveness for a misdeed?*
- *change hostility to friendliness?*

SESSION 19

Verbs are incalculably useful to you.

Every sentence you think, say, read, or write contains an implied or expressed verb, for it is the verb that carries the action, the movement, the force of your ideas.

As a young child, you used verbs fairly early.

Your first words, of course, were probably *nouns,* as you identified the things or people around you.

Mama, Dada, doll, baby, bottle, etc. perhaps were the first standard syllables you uttered, for naming concrete things or real persons is the initial step in the development of language.

Soon there came the ability to express *intangible* ideas, and then you began to use simple verbs—*go, stop, stay, want, eat, sleep,* etc.

As you gained maturity, your verbs expressed ideas of greater and greater complexity; as an adult you can describe the most involved actions in a few simple syllables—if you have a good store of useful verbs at your command.

The richer and more extensive your vocabulary of verbs, the more accurately and expressively you can communicate your understanding of actions, reactions, attitudes, and emotions.

Let's be specific.

IDEAS

1. playing it down

Ready to go back thirty or more years? Consider some post-World War II American political history:

Harry Truman couldn't win the 1948 election. The pollsters said so, the Republicans heartily agreed, even the Democrats, some in high places, believed it. Mr. Truman himself was perhaps the only voter in the country who was not entirely convinced.

Came the first Tuesday after the first Monday in November—well, if you were one of those who stayed up most of the night listening to the returns, and then kept your ear to the radio most of the next day, you recall how you reacted to the unique Truman triumph.

It was no mean accomplishment, thought many people. Pure accident, said others. If one out of twelve voters in a few key states had changed his ballot, Harry could have gone back to selling ties, one Republican apologist pointed out. It wasn't anything Truman did, said another; it was what Dewey didn't do. No credit to Truman, said a third; it was the farmers—or labor—or the Republicans who hadn't bothered to vote—or the ingenious miscounting of ballots. No credit to Truman, insisted a fourth; it was Wallace's candidacy—it was the Democrats—it was Republican overconfidence—it was sunspots—it was the Communists—it was the civil service workers who didn't want to lose their cushy jobs —it was really Roosevelt who won the election.

Anyway Harry didn't accomplish a thing—he was just a victim of good fortune.

What were the apologists for Dewey's failure doing?

They were *disparaging* Truman's achievement.

2. playing it safe

Willing to look at some more history of the late 1940s?

Of course, Dewey did campaign, in his own way, for the presidency. As the Republican aspirant, he had to take a stand on the controversial Taft-Hartley Act.

Was he for it? He was for that part of it which was *good*. Naturally, he was against any of the provisions which were *bad*. Was he for it? The answer was *yes*—and also *no*. Take whichever answer you wanted most to hear.

What was Dewey doing?

He was *equivocating*.

3. enjoying the little things

Have you ever gone through a book that was so good you kept hugging yourself mentally as you read? Have you ever seen a play or motion picture that was so charming that you felt sheer delight as you watched? Or perhaps you have had a portion of pumpkin-chiffon pie, light and airy and mildly flavored, and with a flaky, delicious crust, that was the last word in gustatory enjoyment?

Now notice the examples I have used. I have not spoken of books that grip you emotionally, of plays and movies that keep you on the edge of your seat in suspense, or of food that satisfies a ravenous hunger. These would offer quite a different, perhaps more lasting and memorable, type of enjoyment. I have detailed, rather, mental or physical stimuli that excite enjoyably but not too sharply—a delightful novel, a charming play, a delicious dessert.

How do such things affect you?

They *titillate* you.

4. playing it way up

You know how the teen-agers of an earlier generation adored, idolized, and overwhelmed Frank Sinatra, Elvis Presley, the Beatles?

And of course you know how certain people fall all over visiting celebrities—best-selling authors, much publicized artists, or famous entertainers. They show them ingratiating, almost servile attention, worship and flatter them fulsomely.*

How do we say it in a single word?

They *adulate* such celebrities.

5. accentuating the negative

What does the doctor say to you if you have low blood sugar? "No candy, no pastries, no chocolate marshmallow cookies, no ice

---

* *Fulsome* (FOOL'-səm) does not mean, despite its appearance, *fully* or *completely*, but rather, *offensive because of excessiveness or insincerity*, often in reference to compliments, praise, admiration, or flattery.

194

cream!", your morale dropping lower and lower as each favorite goody is placed on the forbidden list.

What, in one word, is the doctor doing?

> The doctor is *proscribing* harmful
> items in your diet.

6. accentuating the affirmative

You are warm, friendly, enthusiastic, outgoing, easy to please; you are quick to show appreciation, yet accept, without judgment or criticism, the human weaknesses of others.

You are a fascinating talker, an even better listener.

You believe in, and practice, honest self-disclosure; you feel comfortable with yourself and therefore with everyone else; and you have a passionate interest in experiencing, in living, in relating to people.

Need you have any fears about making friends? Obviously not.

> Your characteristics and temperament
> *obviate* such fears.

7. playing it wrong

Theodor Reik, in his penetrating book on psychoanalysis *Listening with the Third Ear,* talks about neurotic people who unconsciously wish to fail. In business interviews they say exactly the wrong words, they do exactly the wrong things, they seem intent (as, *unconsciously,* they actually are) on insuring failure in every possible way, though consciously they are doing their best to court success.

What effect does such a neurotic tendency have?

> It *militates* against success.

8. playing it dirty

"Harry?" *He's a closet alcoholic.* Maud? *She's sleeping around* —and her stupid husband doesn't suspect a thing. Bill? *He's embezzling from his own company.* Paul? *He's a child molester.*

195

Sally? You don't know that *she's a notorious husband-beater?*"

What is this character doing?

He's *maligning* everyone.

9. giving the benefit of any doubt

Do you think it's all right to cheat on your income taxes? At least just a little? It's wrong, of course, but doesn't everybody do it?

How do you feel about marital infidelity? Are you inclined to overlook the occasional philandering of the male partner, since, after all, to invent a cliché, men are essentially polygamous by nature?

If your answers are in the affirmative, how are you reacting to such legal or ethical transgressions?

You *condone* them.

10. changing hostility

Unwittingly you have done something that has aroused anger and resentment in your best friend. You had no desire to hurt him, yet he makes it obvious that he feels pretty bitter about the whole situation. (Perhaps you failed to invite him to a gathering he wanted to come to; or you neglected to consult him before making a decision on a matter in which he felt he should have some say.) His friendship is valuable to you and you wish to restore yourself in his good graces. What do you do?

You try to *placate* him.

USING THE WORDS

Can you pronounce the words?

1. *disparage*	dis-PAIR'-əj
2. *equivocate*	ee-KWIV'-ə-kayt'
3. *titillate*	TIT'-ə-layt'

4. *adulate*   AJ'-ə-layt'
5. *proscribe*   prō-SKRĪB'
6. *obviate*   OB'-vee-ayt'
7. *militate*   MIL'-ə-tayt
8. *malign*   mə-LĪN'
9. *condone*   kən-DŌN'
10. *placate*   PLAY'-kayt'

Can you work with the words?

1. disparage	a.	flatter lavishly
2. equivocate	b.	work against
3. titillate	c.	prohibit
4. adulate	d.	forgive
5. proscribe	e.	change hostility to friendliness
6. obviate	f.	purposely talk in such a way as to be vague and misleading
7. militate	g.	slander
8. malign	h.	play down
9. condone	i.	make unnecessary
10. placate	j.	tickle; stimulate pleasurably

KEY: 1–h, 2–f, 3–j, 4–a, 5–c, 6–i, 7–b, 8–g, 9–d, 10–e

Do you understand the words?

1. Do you normally *disparage* something you admire?   YES   NO
2. Do you *equivocate* if you think it unwise to take a definite stand?   YES   NO
3. Do pleasant things *titillate* you?   YES   NO
4. Do emotionally mature people need constant *adulation*?   YES   NO
5. Is sugar *proscribed* for diabetics?   YES   NO
6. Does a substantial fortune *obviate* financial fears?   YES   NO

7. Does a worker's inefficiency often *militate* against his keeping his job? YES NO
8. Do people enjoy being *maligned*? YES NO
9. Do we generally *condone* the faults of those we love? YES NO
10. Can you sometimes *placate* a person by apologizing? YES NO

KEY: 1–no, 2–yes, 3–yes, 4–no, 5–yes, 6–yes, 7–yes, 8–no, 9–yes, 10–yes

Can you use the words?

In this exercise you gain the value of actually writing a new word as a meaningful solution to a problem. To think about a word, to say it, to write it, to use it—that is the road to word mastery. Write the verb that best fits each situation.

1. You've been asked to take a stand on a certain issue, but you don't have the courage to be either definitely for or against.
   You _____.

2. You spread around an unpleasant story that you know will blacken someone's reputation.
   You _____ that person.

3. Your friend is justifiably angry—you asked him to go to a party with you, ignored him all evening, and then finally left with someone else. What must you do if you wish to restore the relationship?
   You must try to _____ him.

4. You virtually worship your therapist. You express your admiration in lavish flattery; you praise her in such excessive terms that she appears devoid of all human frailty.
   You _____ her.

5. You are crowding 260 on the scales, so your doctor warns against high-calorie meals, rich desserts, second helpings, excessive carbohydrates, etc.
   The doctor _____ these foods.

198

6. Your child Johnnie has smacked the neighbor's kid—entirely without provocation, you are forced to admit. But after all, you think, tomorrow the other kid will, with equal lack of provocation, probably smack Johnnie.

   You _____ Johnnie's behavior.

7. When your son, understandably expecting praise, mentions the three B's and two A's he earned in his courses, you respond, callously, "Is that the best you can do? What stopped you from getting *all* A's?"

   You _____ his accomplishment.

8. You have run out of cash and plan to go to the bank to make a withdrawal; then unexpectedly you discover a twenty-dollar bill you secreted in your desk drawer months ago.

   Your find _____ a trip to the bank.

9. You are the soul of honesty, but unfortunately, you have a sneaky, thievish, sinister look—and no one ever trusts you.

   Your appearance _____ against you.

10. The centerfold of *Playboy* or *Playgirl* provides a mild and agreeable stimulation.

    The centerfold _____ you.

KEY: 1–equivocate, 2–malign, 3–placate, 4–adulate, 5–proscribes, 6–condone, 7–disparage, 8–obviates, 9–militates, 10–titillates

---

Can you recall the words?

1. change hostility into friendliness
2. make unnecessary
3. belittle
4. overlook or forgive a transgression
5. tickle; delight; stimulate pleasurably
6. spread malicious rumors about

1. P_____
2. O_____
3. D_____
4. C_____
5. T_____
6. M_____

7. purposely use language
   susceptible of opposite
   interpretations
8. act to disadvantage of
9. forbid
10. worship; flatter fulsomely

7. E_____
8. M_____
9. P_____
10. A_____

KEY: 1–placate, 2–obviate, 3–disparage, 4–condone, 5–titillate,
     6–malign, 7–equivocate, 8–militate (against), 9–proscribe,
     10–adulate

(End of Session 19)

SESSION 20

ORIGINS AND RELATED WORDS

1. equality

If you play golf, you know that each course or hole has a certain *par*, the number of strokes allowed according to the results achieved by expert players. Your own accomplishment on the course will be at *par*, above *par*, or below *par*.

Similarly, some days you may feel up to *par*, other days below *par*.

Par is from a Latin word meaning *equal*. You may try, when you play golf, to *equal* the expert score; and some days you may, or may not, feel *equal* to your usual self.

When we speak of *parity* payments to farmers, we refer to payments that show an *equality* to earnings for some agreed-upon year.

So when you *disparage*, you lower someone's *par*, or feeling of *equality,* (*dis-* as you know, may be a negative prefix). The noun is *disparagement* (dis-PAIR'-əj-mənt), the adjective *disparaging* (dis-PAIR'-əj-ing), as in "Why do you always make *disparaging* remarks about me?"

Parity (PAIR'-ə-tee) as a noun means *equality; disparity* (dis-PAIR'-ə-tee) means a lack of *equality,* or a difference. We may speak, for example, of the *disparity* between someone's promise and performance; or of the *disparity* between the rate of vocabulary growth of a child and of an adult. The adjective *disparate* (DIS'-pə-rət) indicates *essential* or *complete* difference or inequality, as in "Our philosophies are so *disparate* that we can never come to any agreement on action."

The word *compare* and all its forms (*comparable, comparative,* etc.) derive from *par,* equal. Two things are *compared* when they have certain *equal* or similar qualities, (*con-, com-,* together, with).

Pair and *peer* are also from *par.* Things (shoes, socks, gloves, etc.) in *pairs* are *equal* or similar; your *peers* are those *equal* to you, as in age, position, rank, or ability. Hence the expression "to be judged by a jury of one's *peers.*"

(British *peers,* however, such is the contradiction of language, were *nobles.*)

2. how to say yes and no

Equivocate is built on another Latin word meaning *equal*— *aequus* (the spelling in English is always *equ-*)—plus *vox, vocis,* voice.

When you *equivocate* (ə-KWIV'-ə-kayt'), you seem to be saying both *yes* and *no* with *equal voice.* An *equivocal* (ə-KWIV'-ə-kəl) answer, therefore, is by design vague, indefinite, and susceptible of contradictory interpretations, quite the opposite of an *unequivocal* (un'-ə-KWIV'-ə-kəl) response, which says *Yes!* or *No!,* and no kidding. Professional politicians are masters of *equivocation* (ə-kwiv'-ə-KAY'-shən)—they are, on most vital issues, mugwumps; they sit on a fence with their *mugs* on one side and their *wumps* on the other. You will often hear candidates for office say, publicly, that they *unequivocally* promise, if elected, to . . . ; and then they start *equivocating* for all they are worth, like people

201

who say, "Let me be perfectly *frank* with you"—and then promptly and glibly lie through their teeth.

3. statements of various kinds

Do not confuse *equivocal* with *ambiguous* (am'-BIG'-yŏŏ-əs). An *equivocal* statement is purposely, deliberately (and with malice aforethought) couched in language that will be deceptive; an *ambiguous* statement is *accidentally* couched in such language. *Equivocal* is, in short, purposely *ambiguous*.

You will recall that *ambi-*, which we last met in *ambivert* and *ambidextrous,* is a root meaning *both;* anything *ambiguous* may have *both* one meaning and another meaning. If you say, "That sentence is the height of *ambiguity*," you mean that you find it vague because it admits of both affirmative and negative interpretations, or because it may mean two different things. *Ambiguity* is pronounced am'-bə-GYŎŎ-ə-tee.

Another type of statement or word contains the possibility of two interpretations—one of them suggestive, risqué, or sexy. Such a statement or word is a *double entendre.* This is from the French and translates literally as *double meaning.* Give the word as close a french pronunciation as you can—DŎŎB'-ləhn-TAHN'-drə. (The *n*'s are nasalized, the *r* somewhat throaty, and the final syllable is barely audible.)

REVIEW OF ETYMOLOGY

PREFIX, ROOT, SUFFIX	MEANING	ENGLISH WORD
1. *par*	equal	_____
2. *-ment*	noun suffix attached to verbs	_____
3. *-ity*	noun suffix attached to adjectives	_____
4. *dis-*	negative prefix	_____
5. *con-, com-*	with, together	_____
6. *aequus (equ-)*	equal	_____

7. *vox, vocis*	voice	_____
8. *-ate*	verb suffix	_____
9. *-ion*	noun suffix attached to verbs ending in *-ate*	_____
10. *-ous*	adjective suffix	_____
11. *ambi-*	both	_____

USING THE WORDS

Can you pronounce the words?

1. *parity* — PAIR′-ə-tee
2. *disparity* — dis-PAIR′-ə-tee
3. *disparate* — DIS′-pə-rət
4. *disparagement* — dis-PAIR′-əj-mənt
5. *disparaging* — dis-PAIR′-əj-ing
6. *peer* — PEER
7. *equivocate* — ə-KWIV′-ə-kayt′
8. *equivocation* — ə-kwiv′-ə-KAY′-shən
9. *equivocal* — ə-KWIV′-ə-kəl
10. *unequivocal* — un′-ə-KWIV′-ə-kəl
11. *ambiguous* — am-BIG′-yŏŏ-əs
12. *ambiguity* — am′-bə-GYŎŌ′-ə-tee
13. *double entendre* — DOOB′-ləhn-TAHN′-drə

Can you work with the words?

1. parity
2. disparity

   a. belittlement
   b. act of being deliberately vague or indirectly deceptive; statement that is deceptive or purposely open to contrary interpretations

3. disparagement

   c. quality of being open to mis-interpretation; statement with this quality

203

4. peer

    d. statement or word with two meanings, one of them risqué, indelicate, or of possible sexual connotation

5. equivocation

    e. inequality

6. ambiguity

    f. equality

7. double entendre

    g. one's equal

KEY: 1–f, 2–e, 3–a, 4–g, 5–b, 6–c, 7–d

Do you understand the words?

1. Is there a *disparity* in age between a grandfather and his granddaughter? YES NO
2. Is an *equivocal* statement clear and direct? YES NO
3. Is an *unequivocal* answer vague and misleading? YES NO
4. Are politicians often masters of *equivocation?* YES NO
5. Are *ambiguous* sentences somewhat confusing? YES NO
6. Are people with *disparate* perceptions of life likely to experience reality in the same way? YES NO
7. Is a *disparaging* look one of admiration? YES NO
8. When people *equivocate,* are they evading the issue? YES NO
9. Is the deliberate use of *double entendres* likely to shock puritanical people? YES NO
10. Are supervisors and their subordinates *peers?* YES NO

KEY: 1–yes, 2–no, 3–no, 4–yes, 5–yes, 6–no, 7–no, 8–yes, 9–yes, 10–no

---

Can your recall the words?

1. accidentally vague   1. A_____
2. purposely vague   2. E_____
3. equality   3. P_____
4. word or statement one meaning   4. D_____
   of which may be interpreted as   _____
   risqué
5. lack of equality   5. D_____
6. belittlement   6. D_____
7. clear; direct; capable of only   7. U_____
   one interpretation
8. essentially or widely unequal or 8. D_____
   different
9. one's equal in age, rank, etc.   9. P_____
10. to use words in a calculated   10. E_____
    effort to mislead or to be
    ambiguous

KEY: 1–ambiguous, 2–equivocal, 3–parity, 4–double entendre,
     5–disparity, 6–disparagement, 7–unequivocal, 8–disparate,
     9–peer, 10–equivocate

(End of Session 20)

SESSION 21

ORIGINS AND RELATED WORDS

1. more on equality

The root *aequus,* spelled *equ-* in English words, is a building
block of:

1. *equity* (EK′-wə-tee)—justice, fairness; i.e., equal treatment.

(By extension, stocks in the financial markets are *equities,* and the value of your home or other property over and above the amount of the mortgage you owe is your *equity* in it.) The adjective is *equitable* (EK'-wə-tə-bəl).

2. *inequity* (in-EK'-wə-tee)—injustice, unfairness (*equity* plus the negative prefix *in-*). Adjective: *inequitable* (in-EK'-wə-tə-bəl).

3. *iniquity* (in-IK'-wə-tee)—by one of those delightful surprises and caprices characteristic of language, the change of a single letter (*e* to *i*), extends the meaning of a word far beyond its derivation and original denotation. Injustice and unfairness are sinful and wicked, especially if you naïvely believe that life is fair. So a "den of *iniquity*" is a place where vice flourishes; an *iniquity* is a sin or vice, or an egregiously immoral act; and *iniquity* is wickedness, sinfulness. Adjective: *iniquitous* (in-IK'-wə-təs).

4. *equinox* (EE'-kwə-noks')—etymologically, "equal night," a combination of *aequus* and *nox, noctis,* night. The *equinox,* when day and night are of equal length, occurs twice a year: about March 21, and again about September 21 or 22. (The adjective is *equinoctial*—ee'-kwə-NOK'-shəl.) *Nocturnal* (nok-TURN'-əl), derived from *nox, noctis,* describes people, animals, or plants that are active or flourish at night rather than during daylight hours. Cats and owls are *nocturnal,* as is the moonflower, whose blossoms open at night; not to mention "night people," whose biorhythms are such that they function better after the sun goes down, and who like to stay up late and sleep well into midmorning. A *nocturne* (NOK'-turn) is a musical composition of dreamy character (i.e., night music), or a painting of a night scene.

5. *equanimity* (ee'-kwə-NIM'-ə-tee *or* ek'-wə-NIM'-ə-tee)—etymologically *aequus* plus *animus,* mind, hence "equal mind." Maintain your *equanimity,* your evenness of temper, your composure, your coolness or calmness, when everyone around you is getting excited or hysterical, and you will probably be considered an admirable person, though one might wonder what price you pay for such emotional control. (Other words built on *animus,* mind, will be discussed in Chapter 12.)

6. *Equability* (ee'-kwə-BIL'-ə-tee *or* ek'-wə-BIL'-ə-tee)—a close synonym of *equanimity.* A person of *equable* (EE'-kwə-bəl

or EK'-wə-bəl) temperament is characteristically calm, serene, unflappable, even-tempered.

7. *equilibrium* (ee'-kwə-LIB'-ree-əm)—by derivation *aequus* plus *libra*, balance, weight, pound, hence "equal balance." *Libra* (LĬ'-brə) is the seventh sign of the zodiac, represented by a pair of scales. Now you know, in case the question has been bothering you, why the abbreviation for the word *pound* is *lb.* and why the symbol for the British *pound*, the monetary unit, is £. *Equilibrium* is a state of *physical* balance, especially between opposing forces. When you are very drunk you may have difficulty keeping your *equilibrium*—the force of gravity is stronger than your ability to stay upright. An *equilibrist* (ə-KWIL'-ə-brist), as you might guess, is a professional tightrope walker—a performer successfully defying the law of gravity (when sober) by *balancing* on a thin overhead wire.

The *equator* divides the earth into *equal* halves, and words like *equation*, *equivalent*, *equidistant*, *equiangular*, and *equilateral* (from Latin *latus*, *lateris*, side) are self-explanatory.

2. not to be confused with horses

Equestrian (ə-KWES'-tree-ən) is someone on a horse (as *pedestrian* is someone on foot); an *equestrienne* (ə-kwes'-tree-EN') is a woman on a horse (if you *must* make the distinction); and *equine* (EE'-kwīn) is like a horse, as in appearance or characteristics, or descriptive of horses.

Equestrian is also an adjective referring to horseback riding, as an *equestrian* statue; and *equine* is also a noun, i.e., a horse.

So the *equ-* in these words, from Latin *equus*, horse, is not to be confused with the *equ-* in the words of the previous section—that *equ-* is from *aequus*, equal. (Remember, also, not to confuse the *ped-* in *pedestrian*, from Latin *pedis*, foot, with the *ped-* in *pediatrician*, from Greek *paidos*, child.)

3. hear voices?

Equivocal, you will recall, combines *aequus* with *vox*, *vocis*, voice; and *vox*, *vocis* combines with *fero*, to bear or carry, to form *vociferous* (vō-SIF'-ər-əs), etymologically "carrying (much) voice," hence loud, noisy, clamorous, as *vociferous* demands (not at all quiet or subtle), or the *vociferous* play of young children ("Please! Try to be quiet so Dad can get his work done!"), though unfortunately TV addiction has abnormally eliminated child noises, at least during the program breaks between commercials. (*Vociferous* will be discussed at greater length in Chapter 10.)

If you are *vocal* (VŌ'-kəl), you express yourself readily and freely by voice; *vocal* sounds are voiced; *vocal* music is sung; and you know what your *vocal* cords are for.

To *vocalize* (VŌ'-kə-līz') is to give voice to ("*Vocalize* your anger, don't hold it in!"), or to sing the *vocals* (or voice parts) of music. (Can you write the noun form of the verb *vocalize*?
_____.) A *vocalist* (VŌ'-kə-list) is a singer. And *Magnavox* (*vox* plus *magnus*, large) is the trade name for a brand of radios and TV sets.

REVIEW OF ETYMOLOGY

PREFIX, ROOT, SUFFIX	MEANING	ENGLISH WORD
1. *aequus* (*equ-*)	equal	_____
2. *in-*	negative prefix	_____
3. *nox, noctis*	night	_____
4. *animus*	mind	_____
5. *-ity*	noun suffix	_____
6. *libra*	balance, weight, pound	_____
7. *-ist*	person who	_____
8. *latus, lateris*	side	_____
9. *equus*	horse	_____
10. *-ine*	like, descriptive of	_____
11. *pedis*	foot	_____
12. *paidos* (*ped-*)	child	_____
13. *vox, vocis*	voice	_____
14. *fero*	to bear, carry	_____
15. *magnus*	large	_____

USING THE WORDS

Can you pronounce the words? (I)

1.	equity	EK'-wə-tee
2.	equitable	EK'-wə-tə-bəl
3.	inequity	in-EK'-wə-tee
4.	inequitable	in-EK'-wə-tə-bəl
5.	iniquity	in-IK'-wə-tee
6.	iniquitous	in-IK'-wə-təs
7.	equinox	EE'-kwə-noks'
8.	equinoctial	ee'-kwə-NOK'-shəl
9.	nocturnal	nok-TURN'-əl
10.	nocturne	NOK'-turn

Can you pronounce the words? (II)

1.	equanimity	ee'-kwə (or ek'-wə) -NIM'-ə-tee
2.	equability	ee'-kwə (or ek'-wə) -BIL'-ə-tee
3.	equable	EE'-kwə-bəl or EK'-wə-bəl
4.	equilibrium	ee'-kwə-LIB'-ree-əm
5.	equilibrist	ee-KWIL'-ə-brist
6.	equilateral	ee-kwə-LAT'-ər-əl
7.	equestrian	ə-KWES'-tree-ən
8.	equine	EE'-kwīn
9.	vociferous	vō-SIF'-ər-əs
10.	vocal	VŌ'-kəl
11.	vocalize	VŌ'-kə-līz'
12.	vocalization	vō'-kə-lə-ZAY'-shən
13.	vocalist	VŌ'-kə-list

Can you work with the words? (I)

1. equity   a. time when night and day are of equal length

2. inequity

    b. balance of mind; composure; calmness under trying circumstances

3. iniquity

    c. horseback rider

4. equinox

    d. a horse

5. nocturne

    e. sinfulness; wickedness; immoral act; sin

6. equanimity

    f. unfairness, injustice

7. equilibrium

    g. tightrope walker

8. equestrian

    h. singer

9. equilibrist

    i. fairness, justice

10. equine

    j. balance, especially between opposing forces

11. vocalist

    k. night music

KEY: 1–i, 2–f, 3–e, 4–a, 5–k, 6–b, 7–j, 8–c, 9–g, 10–d, 11–h

Can you work with the words? (II)

1. equitable

    a. descriptive of time when night and day are of equal length

2. inequitable

    b. give voice to; sing

3. iniquitous

    c. having equal sides

4. equinoctial

    d. using, or referring to, the voice; freely expressing by voice

5. nocturnal

    e. noisy, loud, clamorous

6. equable

    f. calm, unruffled, even-tempered

7. equilateral

    g. fair, just

8. vociferous

    h. referring or pertaining to, or active at, night

9. vocal

    i. sinful, wicked, immoral

10. vocalize

    j. unfair, unjust

KEY: 1–g, 2–j, 3–i, 4–a, 5–h, 6–f, 7–c, 8–e, 9–d, 10–b

Do you understand the words?

1.	Is life always *equitable*?	YES	NO
2.	Does the cynic expect more *inequity* than *equity* in life?	YES	NO
3.	Do ethical people practice *iniquity*?	YES	NO
4.	Does the *equinox* occur once a month?	YES	NO
5.	Are *nocturnal* animals active at night?	YES	NO
6.	If you generally preserve your *equanimity,* do you often get very excited?	YES	NO
7.	Is it easy to maintain your *equilibrium* on icy ground?	YES	NO
8.	Is *equability* the mark of a calm, even-tempered person?	YES	NO
9.	Does an *equilateral* triangle have equal sides?	YES	NO
10.	Is an *equine* a dog?	YES	NO
11.	If you demand something *vociferously,* do you make a lot of noise?	YES	NO
12.	If you are *vocal,* do you have difficulty expressing yourself?	YES	NO
13.	Is a *vocalist* the same as an instrumentalist?	YES	NO

KEY: 1–no, 2–yes, 3–no, 4–no, 5–yes, 6–no, 7–no, 8–yes, 9–yes, 10–no, 11–yes, 12–no, 13–no

Can you recall the words? (I)

1. to give voice to; to express aloud; to sing 1. V_____

2. tightrope walker 2. E_____

3. active or flourishing at night 3. N_____

4. descriptive or characteristic of, or like, a horse 4. E_____

5. referring to the voice; skillful or fluent in expressing by voice
6. calm and unflappable in temperament
7. wicked, sinful
8. night music
9. fairness, justice

5. V_____
6. E_____
7. I_____
8. N_____
9. E_____

KEY: 1–vocalize, 2–equilibrist, 3–nocturnal, 4–equine, 5–vocal, 6–equable, 7–iniquitous, 8–nocturne, 9–equity

---

Can you recall the words? (II)

1. loud, noisy, clamorous
2. person on horseback

3. calmness or evenness of temper

4. unfair, unjust
5. sin; wickedness; grossly immoral behavior
6. time when day and night are of equal length
7. fair, just, evenhanded
8. physical balance; balance between opposing forces
9. having equal sides
10. singer

1. V_____
2. E_____
   or E_____
3. E_____
   or E_____
4. I_____
5. I_____
6. E_____
7. E_____
8. E_____
9. E_____
10. V_____

KEY: 1–vociferous, 2–equestrian or equestrienne, 3–equanimity or equability, 4–inequitable, 5–iniquity, 6–equinox, 7–equitable, 8–equilibrium, 9–equilateral, 10–vocalist

---

(End of Session 21)

SESSION 22

ORIGINS AND RELATED WORDS

1. how to tickle

Titillate comes from a Latin verb meaning *to tickle,* and may be used both literally and figuratively. That is (literally), you can *titillate* by gentle touches in strategic places; you are then causing an actual (and always very pleasant) physical sensation. Or you can (figuratively) *titillate* people, or their minds, fancies, palates (and this is the more common use of the word), by charm, brilliance, wit, promises, or in any other way your imagination can conceive.

Titillation (tit'-ə-LAY'-shən) has the added meaning of light sexual stimulation. (Note that both noun and verb are spelled with a double *l, not* a double *t.*)

2. how to flatter

A *compliment* is a pleasant and courteous expression of praise; *flattery* is stronger than a compliment and often considered insincere. *Adulation* (aj'-ə-LAY'-shən) is flattery and worship carried to an excessive, ridiculous degree. There are often public figures (entertainers, musicians, government officials, etc.) who receive widespread *adulation,* but those not in the public eye can also be *adulated,* as a teacher by students, a wife by husband (and vice versa), a doctor by patients, and so on. (The derivation is from a Latin verb meaning *to fawn upon.*)

The adjective *adulatory* (aj'-ə-lə-TAWR'-ee) ends in *-ory,* a suffix we are meeting for the first time in these pages. (Other adjective suffixes: *-al, -ic, -ical, -ous.*)

3. ways of writing

Proscribe, to forbid, is commonly used for medical, religious, or legal prohibitions.

A doctor *proscribes* a food, drug, or activity that might prove harmful to the patient. The church *proscribes,* or announces a *proscription* (prō-SKRIP′-shən) against, such activities as may harm its parishioners. The law *proscribes* behavior detrimental to the public welfare.

Generally, one might concede, *proscribed* activities are the most pleasant ones—as Alexander Woolcott once remarked, if something is pleasurable, it's sure to be either immoral, illegal, or fattening.

The derivation is the prefix *pro-,* before, plus *scribo, scriptus,* to write. In ancient Roman times, a man's name was written on a public bulletin board if he had committed some crime for which his property or life was to be forfeited; Roman citizens in good standing would thereby know to avoid him. In a similar sense, the doctor writes down those foods or activities that are likely to commit crimes against the patient's health—in that way the patient knows to avoid them.

Scribo, scriptus is the building block of scores of common English words: *scribe, scribble, prescribe, describe, subscribe, script, the Scriptures, manuscript, typescript,* etc. *Describe* uses the prefix *de-,* down—to *describe* is, etymologically, "to write down" about. *Manuscript,* combining *manus,* hand (as in *manual* labor), with *scriptus,* is something handwritten—the word was coined before the invention of the typewriter. *The Scriptures* are holy writings. To *subscribe* (as to a magazine) is to write one's name *under* an order or contract (*sub-,* under, as in *subway, subsurface,* etc.); to *subscribe* to a philosophy or a principle is figuratively to write one's name *under* the statement of such philosophy or principle.

To *inscribe* is to write *in* or *into* (a book, for example, or metal or stone). A *postscript* is something written after (Latin *post,* after) the main part is finished.

Note how *-scribe* verbs change to nouns and adjectives:

VERB	NOUN	ADJECTIVE
prescribe	prescription	prescriptive
subscribe	subscription	subscriptive

Can you follow the pattern?

describe _____ _____
inscribe _____ _____
proscribe _____ _____

4. it's obvious

You are familiar with the word *via,* by way of, which is from the Latin word for *road.* (The *Via Appia* was one of the famous highways of ancient Roman times.) When something is *obvious,* etymologically it is right there in the middle of the road where no one can fail to see it—hence, easily seen, not hidden, conspicuous. And if you meet an obstacle in the road and dispose of it forthwith, you are doing what *obviate* says. Thus, if you review your work daily in some college subject, frenzied "cramming" at the end of the semester will be *obviated.* A large and steady income *obviates* fears of financial insecurity; leaving for work early will *obviate* worry about being late. *To obviate,* then, is to make unnecessary, to do away with, to prevent by taking effective measures or steps against (an occurrence, a feeling, a requirement, etc.). The noun is *obviation* (ob'-vee-AY'-shən).

Surprisingly, *via,* road, is the root in the English word *trivial* (*tri-,* three). Where three roads intersect, you are likely to find busy traffic, lots of people, in short a fairly public place, so you are not going to talk of important or confidential matters, lest you be overheard. You will, instead, talk of *trivial* (TRIV'-ee-əl) things —whatever is unimportant, without great significance; you will confine your conversation to *trivialities* (triv'-ee-AL'-ə-teez) or to *trivia* (also a plural noun, pronounced TRIV'-ee-ə), insignificant trifles.

5. war

Militate derives from *militis,* one of the forms of the Latin noun meaning *soldier* or *fighting man.* If something *militates* against you, it fights against you, i.e., works to your disadvantage. Thus, your timidity may *militate* against your keeping your friends. (*Militate* is always followed by the preposition *against* and, like *obviate*, never takes a personal subject—*you* don't *militate* against anyone, but some habit, action, tendency, etc. *militates* against someone or something.)

The adjective *militant* (MIL′-ə-tənt) comes from the same root. A *militant* reformer is one who fights for reforms; a *militant* campaign is one waged aggressively and with determination. The noun is *militancy* (MIL′-ə-tən-see), and *militant* is also a noun for the person—"Sally is a *militant* in the Women's Liberation movement."

Military and *militia* also have their origin in *militis.*

6. first the bad news

Built on Latin *malus*, bad, evil, to *malign* is to speak evil about, to defame, to slander. *Malign* is also an adjective meaning *bad, harmful, evil, hateful,* as in "the *malign* influence of his unconscious will to fail." Another adjective form is *malignant* (mə-LIG′-nənt), as in "a *malignant* glance," i.e., one showing deep hatred, or "a *malignant* growth," i.e., one that is cancerous (bad).

The noun of *malignant* is *malignancy* (mə-LIG′-nən-see), which, medically, is a cancerous growth, or, generally, the condition, state, or attitude of harmfulness, hatefulness, evil intent, etc. The noun form of the adjective *malign* is *malignity* (mə-LIG′-nə-tee).

Observe how we can construct English words by combining *malus* with other Latin roots.

Add the root *dico, dictus,* to say or tell, to form *malediction* (mal′-ə-DIK′-shən), a curse, i.e., an evil saying. Adjective: *maledictory* (mal′-ə-DIK′-tə-ree).

Add the root *volo,* to wish, to will, or to be willing, and we can construct the adjective *malevolent* (mə-LEV′-ə-lent), wishing evil or harm—a *malevolent* glance, attitude, feeling, etc. The noun is *malevolence* (mə-LEV′-ə-ləns).

Add the root *facio, factus,* to do or make (also spelled, in English words, *fec-, fic-, factus,* or, as a verb ending, *-fy*), to form the adjective *maleficent* (mə-LEF′-ə-sənt), doing harm or evil, or causing hurt—*maleficent* acts, deeds, behavior.

Can you figure out, and pronounce, the noun form of *maleficent?* _____

A *malefactor* (MAL'-ə-fak'-tər) is a wrongdoer, an evildoer, a criminal—a *malefactor* commits a *malefaction* (mal'-ə-FAK'-shən), a crime, an evil deed.

French is a "Romance" language, that is, a language based on Roman or Latin (as are, also, Spanish, Portuguese, Italian, and Romanian), and so Latin *malus* became French *mal*, bad, the source of *maladroit* (mal'-ə-DROYT'), clumsy, bungling, awkward, unskillful, etymologically, having a "bad right hand." (See *adroit*, Chapter 3.) The noun is *maladroitness*. Also from French *mal: malaise* (mə-LAYZ'), an indefinite feeling of bodily discomfort, as in a mild illness, or as a symptom preceding an illness; etymologically, "bad ease," just as *disease* (dis-ease) is "lack of ease."

Other common words that you are familiar with also spring from Latin *malus: malicious, malice, malady;* and the same *malus* functions as a prefix in words like *maladjusted, malcontent, malpractice, malnutrition,* etc., all with the connotation of *badness.*

And what's the *good* news? See Session 23.

REVIEW OF ETYMOLOGY

PREFIX, ROOT, SUFFIX	MEANING	ENGLISH WORD
1. -ory	adjective suffix	
2. scribo, scriptus	to write	
3. de-	down	
4. manus	hand	
5. sub-	under	
6. in-	in, into	
7. post	after	
8. via	road	
9. tri-	three	
10. militis	soldier	
11. malus	bad, evil	
12. dico, dictus	to say, tell	
13. volo	to wish	

14. *facio (fec-, fic-, fy)*   to do, make   _____
15. *-ence, -ancy*   noun suffix   _____

WORKING WITH THE WORDS

Can you pronounce the words? (I)

1. *titillation*   tit'-ə-LAY'-shən
2. *adulation*   aj'-ə-LAY'-shən
3. *adulatory*   AJ'-ə-lə-tawr'-ee
4. *proscription*   prō-SKRIP'-shən
5. *proscriptive*   prō-SKRIP'-tiv
6. *obviation*   ob'-vee-AY'-shən
7. *trivial*   TRIV'-ee-əl
8. *trivialities*   triv'-ee-AL'-ə-teez
9. *trivia*   TRIV'-ee-ə
10. *militant*   MIL'-ə-tənt
11. *militancy*   MIL'-ə-tən-see
12. *malign (adj.)*   mə-LĪN'
13. *malignity*   mə-LIG'-nə-tee
14. *malignant*   mə-LIG'-nənt
15. *malignancy*   mə-LIG'-nən-see

Can you pronounce the words? (II)

1. *malediction*   mal'-ə-DIK'-shən
2. *maledictory*   mal'-ə-DIK'-tə-ree
3. *malevolent*   mə-LEV'-ə-lənt
4. *malevolence*   mə-LEV'-ə-ləns
5. *maleficent*   mə-LEF'-ə-sənt
6. *maleficence*   mə-LEF'-ə-səns
7. *malefactor*   MAL'-ə-fak'-tər
8. *malefaction*   mal'-ə-FAK'-shən
9. *maladroit*   mal'-ə-DROYT'
10. *maladroitness*   mal'-ə-DROYT'-nəs
11. *malaise*   mə-LAYZ'

218

Can you work with the words? (I)

1. titillation		a.	prohibition
2. adulation		b.	hatefulness; harmfulness
3. proscription		c.	clumsiness
4. militancy		d.	quality of wishing evil; ill-will
5. malignity		e.	prevention; fact or act of making unnecessary or of doing away with
6. malediction		f.	worship; excessive flattery
7. maladroitness		g.	vague feeling of bodily discomfort
8. obviation		h.	pleasurable stimulation; tickling
9. malevolence		i.	a curse
10. malaise		j.	aggressiveness

KEY: 1–h, 2–f, 3–a, 4–j, 5–b, 6–i, 7–c, 8–e, 9–d, 10–g

Can you work with the words? (II)

1. adulatory		a.	aggressive; "fighting"
2. proscriptive		b.	of no great consequence
3. militant		c.	bearing ill-will; wishing harm
4. malign		d.	of the nature of curses
5. trivial		e.	clumsy, awkward
6. maledictory		f.	worshipful, adoring
7. malevolent		g.	bad, harmful, hurtful
8. maladroit		h.	relating or pertaining to prohibitions

KEY: 1–f, 2–h, 3–a, 4–g, 5–b, 6–d, 7–c, 8–e

219

Do you understand the words?

1. Does a *malignant* look indicate kindly feelings?   YES   NO
2. Is a cancer sometimes called a *malignancy*?   YES   NO
3. Are *trivialties* important?   YES   NO
4. If your house is cluttered with *trivia*, are these objects of great value?   YES   NO
5. Do people enjoy having *maledictions* hurled at them?   YES   NO
6. Is a *maleficent* act likely to cause harm or hurt?   YES   NO
7. Does *maladroitness* show skill?   YES   NO
8. Is a *malefactor* a wrongdoer?   YES   NO
9. Does an *adulatory* attitude show exaggerated admiration?   YES   NO
10. Is *militancy* the same as passiveness?   YES   NO

KEY: 1–no, 2–yes, 3–no, 4–no, 5–no, 6–yes, 7–no, 8–yes, 9–yes, 10–no

---

Can you recall the words? (I)

1. clumsy, awkward	1. M_____
2. bearing ill-will; wishing harm	2. M_____
3. pleasurable stimulation	3. T_____
4. a person aggressively fighting for a cause	4. M_____
5. prohibition against something injurious	5. P_____
6. excessive flattery; exaggerated admiration	6. A_____
7. vague feeling of general physical discomfort	7. M_____
8. a criminal; a wrongdoer	8. M_____

9. a curse
10. a crime; bad or evil act or behavior

9. M_____
10. M_____

Can you recall the words? (II)

1. fact or act of making unnecessary or of taking effective steps toward prevention
2. aggressive attitude
3. harmful, hurtful, bad

4. unimportant, insignificant
5. unimportant, insignificant things; trifles

6. cursing; of the nature of, or relating to, curses (adj.)
7. worshipful

1. O_____

2. M_____
3. M_____
   or M_____
   or M_____
4. T_____
5. T_____
   or T_____
6. M_____

7. A_____

(*End of Session 22*)

SESSION 23

ORIGINS AND RELATED WORDS

1. so now what's the good news?

Malus is *bad; bonus* is *good*. The adverb from the Latin adjective *bonus* is *bene,* and *bene* is the root found in words that contrast with the *mal-* terms we studied in the previous session.

So *benign* (bə-NĪN′) and *benignant* (bə-NIG′-nənt) are kindly, good-natured, not harmful, as in *benign* neglect, a *benign* judge, a *benign* tumor (not cancerous), a *benignant* attitude to malefactors and scoundrels. The corresponding nouns are *benignity* (bə-NIG′-nə-tee) and *benignancy* (bə-NIG′-nən-see).

A *malediction* is a curse; a *benediction* (ben′-ə-DIK′-shən) is a blessing, a "saying good." The adjective is *benedictory* (ben′-ə-DIK′-tə-ree).

In contrast to *maleficent* is *beneficent* (bə-NEF′-ə-sənt), doing good. The noun? _____.

In contrast to *malefactor* is *benefactor* (BEN′-ə-fak′-tər), one who does good things for another, as by giving help, providing financial gifts or aid, or coming to the rescue when someone is in need. If you insist on making sexual distinctions, a woman who so operates is a *benefactress* (BEN′-ə-fak′-trəs). And, of course, the person receiving the *benefaction* (ben-ə-FAK′-shən), the recipient of money, help, etc., is a *beneficiary* (ben′-ə-FISH′-ər-ee *or* ben-ə-FISH′-ee-air-ee). *Benefit* and *beneficial* are other common words built on the combination of *bene* and a form of *facio,* to do or make.

So let others be *malevolent* toward you—confuse them by being *benevolent* (bə-NEV′-ə-lənt)—wish them well. (Turn the other cheek? Why not?) The noun? _____.

The adjective *bonus,* good, is found in English *bonus,* extra payment, theoretically—but not necessarily—for some good act:

in *bonbon,* a candy (a "good-good," using the French version of the Latin adjective); and in *bona fide* (BŌ'-nə-FĪD' *or* BŌ'-nə-FĪ'-dee), etymologically, "in good faith," hence valid, without pretense, deception, or fraudulent intent—as a *bona fide* offer, a *bona fide* effort to negotiate differences, etc. *Fides* is Latin for *faith* or *trust,* as in *fidelity* (fə-DEL'-ə-tee), faithfulness; *Fido,* a stereotypical name for a dog, one's faithful friend; *infidel* (IN'-fə-dəl), one who does *not* have the right faith or religion (depending on who is using the term), or one who has *no* religion (Latin *in-,* not); and *infidelity* (in'-fə-DEL'-ə-tee), unfaithfulness, especially to the marriage vows.

2. say, do, and wish

Benediction and *malediction* derive from *dico, dictus,* to say, tell. *Dictate, dictator, dictation, dictatorial* (dik'-tə-TAWR'-ee-əl) —words that signify telling others what to do ("Do as I say!")— are built on *dico,* as is *predict,* to tell beforehand, i.e., to say that something will occur before it actually does (*pre-,* before, as in *prescient*).

The brand name *Dictaphone* combines *dico* with *phone,* sound; *contradict,* to say against, or to make an opposite statement ("Don't *contradict* me!"; "That *contradicts* what I know") combines *dico* with *contra-,* against, opposite; and *addiction,* etymologically "a saying to or toward," or the compulsion to say "yes" to a habit, combines *dico* with *ad-,* to, toward.

Facio, factus, to do or make (as in *malefactor, benefactor*), has, as noted, variant spellings in English words: *fec-, fic-,* or, as a verb ending, *-fy.*

Thus *factory* is a place where things are *made* (*-ory,* place where); a *fact* is something *done* (i.e., something that occurs, or exists, or is, therefore, true); *fiction,* something *made* up or invented; *manufacture,* to *make* by hand (*manus,* hand, as in *manuscript, manual*), a word coined before the invention of machinery; *artificial, made* by human art rather than occurring in nature, as *artificial* flowers, etc.; and *clarify, simplify, liquefy, magnify* (to *make* clear, simple, liquid, larger) among hundreds of other *-fy* verbs.

Volo, to wish, to will, to be willing (as in *malevolent, benevo-*

lent), occurs in *voluntary, involuntary, volunteer,* words too familiar to need definition, and each quite obviously expressing *wish* or *willingness.* Less common, and from the same root, is *volition* (vō-LISH'-ən), the act or power of willing or wishing, as in "of her own *volition,*" i.e., *voluntarily,* or "against her *volition.*"

3. if you please!

Placate is built on the root *plac-* which derives from two related Latin verbs meaning, 1) *to please,* and 2) *to appease, soothe,* or *pacify.*

If you succeed in *placating* an angry colleague, you turn that person's hostile attitude into one that is friendly or favorable. The noun is *placation* (play-KAY'-shən), the adjective either *placative* (PLAK'-ə-tiv or PLAY'-kə-tiv) or *placatory* (PLAK'-ə-taw-ree or PLAY'-kə-taw-ree). A more *placatory* attitude to those you have offended may help you regain their friendship; when husband and wife, or lovers, quarrel, one of them finally makes a *placative* gesture if the war no longer fulfills his or her neurotic needs—one of them eventually will wake up some bright morning in a *placatory* mood.

But then, such is life, the other one may at that point be *implacable* (im-PLAK'-ə-bəl or im-PLAY'-kə-bəl)—*im-* is a respelling of *in-,* not, before the letter *p.* One who *can* be soothed, whose hostility *can* be changed to friendliness, is *placable* (PLAK'-ə-bəl or PLAY'-kə-bəl).

Implacable has taken on the added meaning of *unyielding to entreaty or pity;* hence, *harsh, relentless,* as "The governor was *implacable* in his refusal to grant clemency."

The noun form of *implacable* is *implacability* (im-plak'-ə-BIL'-ə-tee or im-play'-kə-BIL'-ə-tee). Can you write (and pronounce) the noun derived from *placable?* ───────────────────

If you are *placid* (PLAS'-id), you are calm, easygoing, serene, undisturbed—etymologically, you are pleased with things as they are. Waters of a lake or sea, or the emotional atmosphere of a place, can also be *placid.* The noun is *placidity* (plə-SID'-ə-tee).

If you are *complacent* (kəm-PLAY-sənt), you are pleased with yourself (*com-,* from *con-,* with, together); you may, in fact, such is one common connotation of the word, be smug, *too* pleased with your position or narrow accomplishments, too easily self-satisfied, and the hour of reckoning may be closer than you realize. (Humans, as you know, are delighted to be critical of the contentment of others.)

The noun is *complacence* (kəm-PLAY'-səns) or *complacency* (kəm-PLAY'-sən-see).

4. how to give—and forgive

To *condone* is to forgive, overlook, pardon, or be uncritical of (an offense, or of an antisocial or illegal act). You yourself might or might not indulge in such behavior or commit such an offense, but you feel no urge to protest, or to demand censure or punishment for someone else who does. You may *condone* cheating on one's income tax, shoplifting from a big, impersonal supermarket, or exceeding the speed limit, though you personally observe the law with scrupulousness. (Not everyone, however, is so charitable or forgiving.) The noun is *condonation* (kon'-dō-NAY'-shən).

Condone is built on Latin *dono*, to give, the root found in *donor*, one who gives; *donate*, to give; and *donation*, a gift.

REVIEW OF ETYMOLOGY

PREFIX, ROOT, SUFFIX	MEANING	ENGLISH WORD
1. *bonus, bene*	good, well	_____
2. *fides*	faith	_____
3. *dico, dictus*	to say, tell	_____
4. *pre-*	before, beforehand	_____
5. *phone*	sound	_____
6. *contra-*	against, opposite	_____
7. *ad-*	to, toward	_____
8. *facio, factus, fec-, fic-, -fy*	to make or do	_____
9. *-ory*	place where	_____
10. *manus*	hand	_____
11. *volo*	to wish, to will, to be willing	_____

12. *plac-*	to please, appease, soothe, pacify	_____
13. *-ive*	adjective suffix	_____
14. *-ory*	adjective suffix	_____
15. *im-* (*in-*)	not; negative prefix	_____
16. *com-* (*con-*)	with, together	_____
17. *dono*	to give	_____

USING THE WORDS

Can you pronounce the words? (I)

1.	*benign*	bə-NĪN′
2.	*benignity*	bə-NIG′-nə-tee
3.	*benignant*	bə-NIG′-nənt
4.	*benignancy*	bə-NIG′-nən-see
5.	*benediction*	ben′-ə-DIK′-shən
6.	*benedictory*	ben′-ə-DIK′-tə-ree
7.	*beneficent*	bə-NEF′-ə-sənt
8.	*beneficence*	bə-NEF′-ə-səns
9.	*benefactor*	BEN′-ə-fak′-tər
10.	*benefaction*	ben′-ə-FAK′-shən
11.	*beneficiary*	ben′-ə-FISH′-ər-ee *or* ben′-ə-FISH′-ee-air-ee
12.	*benevolent*	bə-NEV′-ə-lənt
13.	*benevolence*	bə-NEV′-ə-ləns
14.	*bona fide*	BŌ′-nə FĪD′ *or* BŌ′-nə FĪ′-dee
15.	*fidelity*	fə-DEL′-ə-tee
16.	*infidelity*	in′-fə-DEL′-ə-tee
17.	*infidel*	IN′-fə-dəl

Can you pronounce the words? (II)

1.	*dictatorial*	dik′-tə-TAWR′-ee-əl
2.	*volition*	vō-LISH′-ən
3.	*placation*	play-KAY′-shən
4.	*placative*	PLAK′-ə-tiv *or* PLAY′-kə-tiv

22

5. *placatory*	PLAK'-ə-tawr-ee *or* PLAY'-kə-tawr-ee
6. *placable*	PLAK'-ə-bəl *or* PLAY'-kə-bəl
7. *implacable*	im-PLAK'-ə-bəl *or* im-PLAY'-kə-bəl
8. *placability*	plak'-ə-BIL'-ə-tee *or* play'-kə-BIL'-ə-tee
9. *implacability*	im-plak'-ə-BIL'-ə-tee *or* im-play'-kə-BIL'-ə-tee
10. *placid*	PLAS'-id
11. *placidity*	plə-SID'-ə-tee
12. *complacent*	kəm-PLAY'-sənt
13. *complacence*	kəm-PLAY'-səns
14. *complacency*	kəm-PLAY'-sən-see
15. *condonation*	kon'-dō-NAY'-shən

Can you work with the words? (I)

1. benign		a.	wishing good things (for another); well disposed
2. benedictory		b.	domineering; giving orders in a manner permitting no refusal
3. benevolent		c.	not to be soothed or pacified; unyielding to pity or entreaty
4. bona fide		d.	tending, or intended, to pacify, to soothe, or to change hostility to friendliness
5. dictatorial		e.	kindly, good-natured; not cancerous
6. placatory		f.	calm, unruffled, undisturbed
7. implacable		g.	self-satisfied; smug
8. placid		h.	of the nature of, or relating to, blessings
9. complacent		i.	in good faith; sincere; valid

KEY: 1–e, 2–h, 3–a, 4–i, 5–b, 6–d, 7–c, 8–f, 9–g

Can you work with the words? (II)

1. benevolence
2. benefaction
3. beneficiary

4. infidelity
5. volition
6. placation
7. fidelity

8. condonation

9. placidity
10. complacency

a. recipient of money, kindness, etc.
b. free will
c. act of overlooking, or of forgiving, an offense or transgression
d. faithfulness
e. self-satisfaction; smugness
f. calmness
g. act of pacifying, or of turning hostility or anger into friendly feelings
h. attitude of wishing good things for another
i. faithlessness
j. good deed; act of charity or kindness

KEY: 1–h, 2–j, 3–a, 4–i, 5–b, 6–g, 7–d, 8–c, 9–f, 10–e

Do you understand the words? (I)

1. Are *benedictions* given in houses of worship? — YES NO
2. Is it pleasant to be the recipient of a *beneficent* act? — YES NO
3. Are kind people *benevolent*? — YES NO
4. Do *placatory* gestures often heal wounds and soothe disgruntled friends? — YES NO
5. Are some unambitious people *complacent*? — YES NO
6. Does *benignity* show malice? — YES NO
7. Is a *benefaction* an act of philanthropy? — YES NO
8. Is an *implacable* foe of corruption likely to *condone* corrupt acts? — YES NO

9. Is a *bona fide* offer made insincerely?   YES   NO
10. Does a *benignant* attitude indicate   YES   NO
    hostility?

KEY: 1–yes, 2–yes, 3–yes, 4–yes, 5–yes, 6–no, 7–yes, 8–no,
     9–no, 10–no

Do you understand the words? (II)

1. benign—hateful   SAME   OPPOSITE
2. benignant—kindly   SAME   OPPOSITE
3. benediction—malediction   SAME   OPPOSITE
4. benefactor—evildoer   SAME   OPPOSITE
5. beneficiary—giver   SAME   OPPOSITE
6. benevolent—well disposed   SAME   OPPOSITE
7. bona fide—valid   SAME   OPPOSITE
8. fidelity—unfaithfulness   SAME   OPPOSITE
9. infidel—true believer   SAME   OPPOSITE
10. dictatorial—submissive   SAME   OPPOSITE
11. placative—pacifying   SAME   OPPOSITE
12. implacable—unyielding   SAME   OPPOSITE
13. placid—calm   SAME   OPPOSITE
14. complacent—discontented   SAME   OPPOSITE
15. condonation—forgiveness   SAME   OPPOSITE

KEY: 1–O, 2–S, 3–O, 4–O, 5–O, 6–S, 7–S, 8–O, 9–O, 10–O,
     11–S, 12–S, 13–S, 14–O, 15–S

Can you recall the words?

1. tending to give orders   1. D_____
2. act of overlooking (an offense,   2. C_____
   etc.)
3. unyieldingly hostile; beyond   3. I_____
   soothing; relentless; pitiless
4. intended to soothe or   4. P_____
   pacify (*adj.*)   *or* P_____

229

5. one's desire, wishes, or unforced will

5. V_____

6. calmness

6. P_____

7. self-satisfaction; smugness

7. C_____
   or C_____

8. non-believer in the "true" religion

8. I_____

9. kindly; well disposed

9. B_____
   or B_____
   or B_____

10. unfaithfulness

10. I_____

11. involving a blessing (*adj.*)

11. B_____

12. doing something good or kind (*adj.*)

12. B_____

13. faithfulness

13. F_____

14. sincere; valid; in good faith

14. B_____

15. one who does something good, kind, or charitable (for another)

15. B_____

16. a kind or charitable deed

16. B_____

17. recipient of kindness, gift, etc.

17. B_____

18. able to be soothed or pacified

18. P_____

KEY: 1–dictatorial, 2–condonation, 3–implacable, 4–placatory *or* placative, 5–volition, 6–placidity, 7–complacence *or* complacency, 8–infidel, 9–benign, benignant, *or* benevolent, 10–infidelity, 11–benedictory, 12–beneficent, 13–fidelity, 14–bona fide, 15–benefactor, 16–benefaction, 17–beneficiary, 18–placable

---

CHAPTER REVIEW

A. Do you recognize the words?

1. To belittle:
   (a) titillate, (b) disparage, (c) adulate

2. To be purposely confusing:
   (a) equivocate, (b) obviate, (c) proscribe
3. To work to the disadvantage of:
   (a) malign, (b) militate, (c) placate
4. To slander:
   (a) malign, (b) condone, (c) placate
5. Lack of equality:
   (a) parity, (b) disparity, (c) ambiguity
6. Phrase that may have two interpretations, one of them indelicate or off-color:
   (a) equivocation, (b) ambiguity, (c) double entendre
7. Hateful:
   (a) malignant, (b) benignant, (c) malaise
8. Ill will:
   (a) malaise, (b) malevolence, (c) maleficence
9. Kindly:
   (a) benevolent, (b) placid, (c) complacent
10. Inflexibly hostile:
    (a) implacable, (b) placatory, (c) militant
11. Giving orders imperiously:
    (a) benedictory, (b) dictatorial, (c) adulatory
12. Self-satisfaction:
    (a) complacency, (b) placation, (c) placidity

KEY: 1–b, 2–a, 3–b, 4–a, 5–b, 6–c, 7–a, 8–b, 9–a, 10–a, 11–b, 12–a

---

B. Can you recognize roots?

ROOT	MEANING	EXAMPLE
1. *par*	_____	parity
2. *aequus (equ-)*	_____	equivocal
3. *vox, vocis*	_____	vocal
4. *nox, noctis*	_____	nocturnal
5. *libra*	_____	equilibrist
6. *latus, lateris*	_____	equilateral
7. *equus*	_____	equine

8. *pedis*	_____	pedestrian
9. *paidos (ped-)*	_____	pedagogue
10. *fero*	_____	vociferous
11. *magnus*	_____	magnify
12. *scribo, scriptus*	_____	proscribe
13. *manus*	_____	manuscript
14. *post*	_____	postscript
15. *via*	_____	trivial
16. *militis*	_____	militate
17. *malus*	_____	malefactor
18. *dico, dictus*	_____	dictatorial
19. *volo*	_____	volition
20. *facio (fec-, fic-, -fy)*	_____	benefactor
		fiction
		simplify
21. *bonus*	_____	bona fide
22. *fides*	_____	fidelity
23. *phone*	_____	Dictaphone
24. *plac-*	_____	placate
25. *dono*	_____	donation

KEY: 1–equal, 2–equal, 3–voice, 4–night, 5–balance, 6–side, 7–horse, 8–foot, 9–child, 10–carry, bear, 11–large, 12–write, 13–hand, 14–after, 15–road, 16–soldier, 17–bad, 18–say, tell, 19–wish, 20–do, make, 21–good, 22–faith, 23–sound, 24–please, soothe, pacify, 25–give

---

TEASER QUESTIONS FOR THE AMATEUR ETYMOLOGIST

1. Keeping in mind the roots *animus* in *equanimity* and *magnus* in *Magnavox* or *magnify*, can you combine these two roots to form a noun meaning, etymologically, *largeness of mind*? _____. Can you figure out the adjective form, ending in *-ous*, of the noun you have constucted? _____.

2. If *equilateral* means *equal-sided,* can you construct an adjective meaning *two-sided?* _____.

3. *Trans-* is a prefix meaning *across.* Build a verb meaning *to write across* (from one form or language to another): _____. What is the noun derived from this verb? _____.

4. What disease was so named on the erroneous assumption that it was caused by "bad air?" _____.

5. *Facio* may appear in English words as *fec-.* Using the prefix *con-,* together, can you form a noun sometimes used as a synonym for candy, cake, or ice cream (etymologically, "something made together")? _____.

(*Answers in Chapter 18*)

THE THRILL OF RECOGNITION

You have been adding, over the past twenty-three sessions, hundreds of words to your vocabulary; you have been learning hundreds of prefixes, roots, and suffixes that make it possible for you to figure out the meaning of many unfamiliar words you may come across in your reading.

As time goes on and you notice more and more of the words you have studied whenever you read, or whenever you listen to lectures, the radio, or TV, the thrill of recognition plus the immediate comprehension of complex ideas will provide a dividend of incalculable value.

You will hear these words in conversation, and you will begin to use them yourself, unself-consciously, whenever something you want to say is best expressed by one of the words that exactly verbalizes your thinking. Another priceless dividend!

So keep on! You are involved in a dividend-paying activity that will eventually make you intellectually rich.

(*End of Session 23*)

HOW TO SPEAK NATURALLY

Consider this statement by Louis Bromfield, a noted author: "If I, as a novelist, wrote dialogue for my characters which was meticulously grammatical, the result would be the creation of a speech which rendered the characters pompous and unreal."

And this one by Jacques Barzun, former literary critic for *Harper's:* "Speech, after all, is in some measure an expression of character, and flexibility in its use is a good way to tell your friends from the robots."

Consider also this puckish remark by the late Clarence Darrow: "Even if you do learn to speak correct English, who are you going to speak it to?"

These are typical reactions of professional people to the old restrictions of formal English grammar. Do the actual teachers of English feel the same way? Again, some typical statements:

"Experts and authorities do not make decisions and rules, by logic or otherwise, about correctness," said E. A. Cross, then Professor of English at the Greeley, Colorado, College of Education. "All they can do is observe the customs of cultivated and educated people and report their findings."

"Grammar is only an analysis after the facts, a post-mortem on usage," said Stephen Leacock in *How To Write.* "Usage comes first and usage must rule."

One way to discover current trends in usage is to poll a cross

234

section of people who use the language professionally, inquiring as to their opinion of the acceptability, in everyday speech, of certain specific and controversial expressions. A questionnaire I prepared recently was answered by eighty-two such people—thirty-one authors, seven book reviewers, thirty-three editors, and eleven professors of English. The results, some of which will be detailed below, may possibly prove startling to you if you have been conditioned to believe, as most of us have, that correct English is rigid, unchangeable, and exclusively dependent on grammatical rules.

TEST YOURSELF

1.	Californians boast of the *healthy* climate of their state.	RIGHT	WRONG
2.	Her new novel is not *as* good as her first one.	RIGHT	WRONG
3.	We *can't* hardly believe it.	RIGHT	WRONG
4.	This is *her*.	RIGHT	WRONG
5.	*Who* are you waiting for?	RIGHT	WRONG
6.	Please take care of *whomever* is waiting.	RIGHT	WRONG
7.	*Whom* would you like to be if you weren't yourself?	RIGHT	WRONG
8.	My wife has been *robbed*.	RIGHT	WRONG
9.	Is this *desert* fattening?	RIGHT	WRONG

1. Californians boast of the *healthy* climate of their state.

RIGHT. There is a distinction, says formal grammar, between *healthy* and *healthful*. A person can be *healthy*—I am still quoting the rule—if he possesses good health. But climate must be *healthful*, since it is *conducive* to health. This distinction is sometimes observed in writing but rarely in everyday speech, as you have probably noticed. Even the dictionaries have stopped splitting hairs—they permit you to say *healthy* no matter which of the two meanings you intend.

"*Healthy* climate" was accepted as current educated usage by twenty-six of the thirty-three editors who answered the questionnaire, six of the seven book reviewers, nine of the eleven professors of English, and twenty of the thirty-one authors. The earlier distinction, in short, is rapidly becoming obsolete.

2. Her new novel is not *as* good as her first one.

RIGHT. If you have studied formal grammar, you will recall that after a negative verb the "proper" word is *so,* not *as.* Is this rule observed by educated speakers? Hardly ever.

In reference to the sentence under discussion, author Thomas W. Duncan remarked: "I always say—and write—*as,* much to the distress of my publisher's copyreader. But the fellow is a wretched purist."

The tally on this use of *as* showed seventy-four for, only eight against.

3. We *can't* hardly believe it.

WRONG. Of the eighty-two professional people who answered my questionnaire, seventy-six rejected this sentence; it is evident that *can't hardly* is far from acceptable in educated speech. Preferred usage: We *can* hardly believe it.

4. This is *her.*

WRONG. This substitution of *her* where the rule requires *she* was rejected by fifty-seven of my eighty-two respondents. Paradoxically enough, although "It's *me*" and "This is *me*" are fully established in educated speech, "This is *her*" still seems to be condemned by the majority of cultivated speakers. Nevertheless, the average person, I imagine, may feel a bit uncomfortable saying "This is *she*"—it sounds almost too sophisticated.

This is more than an academic problem. If the voice at the other end of a telephone conversation makes the opening move with "I'd like to speak to Jane Doe [your name, for argument's sake]," you are, unfortunately, on the horns of a very real dilemma. "This is *she*" may sound prissy—"This is *her*" may give the impression that you're uneducated. Other choices are equally doubtful. "Talking!" is suspiciously businesslike if the call comes to your home, and "I am Jane Doe!" may make you feel like the opening line of a high school tableau. The need for a decision arises several times in a busy day—and, I am sorry to report, the English language is just deficient enough not to be of much help. I wonder how it would be if you just grunted affably?

5. *Who* are you waiting for?

RIGHT. *Formal grammar* not only requires *whom* but demands that the word order be changed to: "For whom are you waiting?" (Just try talking with such formality on everyday occasions and see how long you'll keep your friends.)

Who is the normal, popular form as the first word of a sentence, no matter what the grammatical construction; and an opinion by Kyle Crichton, a well-known magazine editor, is typical of the way many educated people feel. Mr. Crichton says: "The most loathsome word (to me at least) in the English language is *whom*. You can always tell a half-educated buffoon by the care he takes in working the word in. When he starts it, I know I am faced with a pompous illiterate who is not going to have me long as company."

The score for acceptance of the sentence as it stands (with *who*) was sixty-six out of eighty-two. If, like most unpedantic speakers, you prefer *who* to *whom* for informal occasions, or if you feel as strongly about *whom* as Mr. Crichton does, you will be happy to hear that modern trends in English are all on your side.

6. Please take care of *whomever* is waiting.

WRONG. *Whomever* is awkward and a little silly in this sentence and brings to mind Franklin P. Adams' famous remark on grammar: "'Whom are you?' asked Cyril, for he had been to night school." It is also contrary to grammatical rule. People who are willing to be sufficiently insufferable to use *whomever* in this construction have been tempted into error by the adjacent word *of*. They believe that since they are following a preposition with an objective pronoun they are speaking impeccable grammar. In actuality, however, *whomever* is not the object of the preposition *of* but the subject of the verb *is waiting*. Preferable form: Please take care of *whoever* is waiting.

7. *Whom* would you like to be if you weren't yourself?

WRONG. Here is another and typical example of the damage which an excessive reverence for *whom* can do to an innocent person's speech. Judged by grammatical rule, *whom* is incorrect in this sentence (the verb *to be* requires *who*); judged by normal speech patterns, it is absurd. This use of *whom* probably comes from an abortive attempt to sound elegant.

8. My wife has been *robbed*.

RIGHT—if something your wife owns was taken by means of thievery. However, if your wife herself was kidnapped, or in some way talked into leaving you, she was *stolen,* not *robbed*. To *rob* is to abscond with the contents of something—to *steal* is to walk off with the thing itself. Needless to say, both forms of activity are highly antisocial and equally illegal.

9. Is this *desert* fattening?

WRONG. The *dessert* that is fattening is spelled with two *s*'s. With one *s*, it's a desert, like the Sahara. Remember the two *s*'s in dessert by thinking how much you'd like *two* portions, if only your waistline permitted.

10

HOW TO TALK
ABOUT VARIOUS SPEECH HABITS

(Sessions 24–27)

TEASER PREVIEW

What adjective describes people who:

- *are disinclined to conversation?*
- *are brief and to the point in their speech?*
- *are blocked or incoherent in their speech?*
- *show by their speech that they are trite and unimaginative?*
- *use more words than necessary?*
- *are forcefully compelling and logical in their speech?*
- *talk rapidly and fluently?*
- *are noisy and clamorous?*
- *are talkative?*

SESSION 24

Perhaps some of your richest and most satisfying experiences have been with people to whom you can just talk, talk, talk. As you speak, previously untapped springs of ideas and emotions begin to flow; you hear yourself saying things you never thought you knew.

What kinds of people might you find yourself in conversation with? In this chapter we start by examining ten types, discovering the adjective that aptly describes each one.

IDEAS

1. saying little

There are some people who just don't like to talk. It's not that they prefer to listen. Good listeners hold up their end of the conversation delightfully—with appropriate facial expressions; with empathetic smiles, giggles, squeals, and sighs at just the right time; and with encouraging nods or phrases like "Go on!", "Fantastic!", "And then what happened?"

These people like neither to talk nor to listen—they act as if conversation is a bore, even a painful waste of time. Try to engage them, and the best you may expect for your efforts is a vacant stare, a noncommittal grunt, or an impatient silence. Finally, in frustration, you give up, thinking. "Are they self-conscious? Do they hate people? Do they hate *me?*"

The adjective: taciturn

2. saying little—meaning much

There is a well-known anecdote about Calvin Coolidge, who, when he was President, was often called (though probably not to his face) "Silent Cal":

A young newspaperwoman was sitting next to him at a banquet, so the story goes, and turned to him mischievously.

"Mr. Coolidge," she said, "I have a bet with my editor that I can get you to say more than two words to me this evening."

"You lose," Coolidge rejoined simply.

The adjective: *laconic*

3. when the words won't come

Under the pressure of some strong emotion—fear, rage, anger, for example—people may find it difficult, or even impossible, to utter words, to get their feelings unjumbled and untangled enough to form understandable sentences. They undoubtedly have a lot they want to say, but the best they can do is sputter!

The adjective: *inarticulate*

4. much talk, little sense

Miss Bates, a character in *Emma,* a novel by Jane Austen:

"So obliging of you! No, we should not have heard, if it had not been for this particular circumstance, of her being able to come here so soon. My mother is so delighted! For she is to be three months with us at least. Three months, she says so, positively, as I am going to have the pleasure of reading to you. The case is, you see, that the Campbells are going to Ireland. Mrs. Dixon has persuaded her father and mother to come over and see her directly. I was going to say, but, however, different countries, and so she wrote a very urgent letter to her mother, or her father, I declare I do not know which it was, but we shall see presently in Jane's letter . . ."

The adjective: *garrulous*

5. unoriginal

Some people are completely lacking in originality and imagination—and their talk shows it. Everything they say is trite, hack-

241

neyed, commonplace, humorless—their speech patterns are full of clichés and stereotypes, their phraseology is without sparkle.

The adjective: *banal*

6. words, words, words!

They talk and talk and talk—it's not so much the quantity you object to as the repetitiousness. They phrase, rephrase, and re-rephrase their thoughts—using far more words than necessary, overwhelming you with words, drowning you with them, until your only thought is how to escape, or maybe how to die.

The adjective: *verbose*

7. words in quick succession

They are rapid, fluent talkers, the words seeming to roll off their tongues with such ease and lack of effort, and sometimes with such copiousness, that you listen with amazement.

The adjective: *voluble*

8. words that convince

They express their ideas persuasively, forcefully, brilliantly, and in a way that calls for wholehearted assent and agreement from an intelligent listener.

The adjective: *cogent*

9. the sound and the fury

Their talk is loud, noisy, clamorous, vehement. What may be lacking in content is compensated for in force and loudness.

The adjective: *vociferous*

10. quantity

They talk a lot—a *whole* lot. They may be voluble, vociferous, garrulous, verbose, but never inarticulate, taciturn, or laconic. No matter. It's the quantity and continuity that are most conspicuous. "Were you vaccinated with a phonograph needle?" is the question you are tempted to ask as you listen.

The adjective: *loquacious*

These ten words revolve around the idea of varying kinds and ways of talking and not talking. Many of the adjectives are close in meaning, but each contains its unique difference.

QUALITY	ADJECTIVE
1. silence, unresponsiveness	taciturn
2. economy, brevity, meaningfulness	laconic
3. awkwardness, sputtering, incoherence	inarticulate
4. rambling chatter	garrulous
5. hackneyed, unoriginal phraseology	banal
6. wordiness, repetitiousness	verbose
7. fluency, rapidity	voluble
8. logic, clarity, persuasiveness	cogent
9. noise, vehemence	vociferous
10. talkativeness	loquacious

USING THE WORDS

Can you pronounce the words?

1. *taciturn*	TAS'-ə-turn
2. *laconic*	lə-KON'-ik
3. *inarticulate*	in'-ahr-TIK'-yə-lət
4. *garrulous*	GAIR'-ə-ləs
5. *banal*	BAY'-nəl
6. *verbose*	vər-BŌS'
7. *voluble*	VOL'-yə-bəl
8. *cogent*	KŌ'-jənt
9. *vociferous*	vō-SIF'-ər-əs
10. *loquacious*	lō-KWAY'-shəs

243

Can you work with the words?

1. taciturn
2. laconic
3. inarticulate
4. garrulous
5. banal
6. verbose
7. voluble
8. cogent

9. vociferous

10. loquacious

a. chattering meaninglessly
b. wordy
c. trite, hackneyed, unoriginal
d. fluent and rapid
e. noisy, loud
f. sputtering unintelligibly
g. talkative
h. brilliantly compelling, persuasive
i. unwilling to engage in conversation
j. using few words packed with meaning

KEY: 1–i, 2–j, 3–f, 4–a, 5–c, 6–b, 7–d, 8–h, 9–e, 10–g

Do you understand the words?

1. Do *taciturn* people usually make others feel comfortable and welcome?	YES	NO
2. Does a *laconic* speaker use more words than necessary?	YES	NO
3. Does rage make some people *inarticulate*?	YES	NO
4. Is it interesting to listen to *garrulous* old men?	YES	NO
5. Do *banal* speakers show a great deal of originality?	YES	NO
6. Is *verbose* a complimentary term?	YES	NO
7. Is it easy to be *voluble* when you don't know the subject you are talking about?	YES	NO
8. Do unintelligent people usually make *cogent* statements?	YES	NO
9. Is a *vociferous* demand ordinarily made by a shy, quiet person?	YES	NO

10. Do *loquacious* people spend more time   YES   NO
talking than listening?

KEY: 1–no, 2–no, 3–yes, 4–no, 5–no, 6–no, 7–no, 8–no, 9–no, 10–yes

Can you recall the words?

Do you know that new nerve patterns are formed by repeated actions? As a very young child, you tied your shoelaces and buttoned your clothing with great concentration—the activity was directed, controlled, purposeful, exciting. As you grew older and more skillful, you tied and buttoned with scarcely a thought of what you were doing. Your fingers flew about their task almost automatically—for the habit had formed a nerve pattern and the action needed little if any conscious attention.

That's simple enough to understand. If you do not remember your own experiences, you can observe the phenomenon of struggling with a skill, mastering it, and finally making it a self-starting habit by watching any young child. Or you can simply take my word for it.

You need not take my word for the way a mastery of new words is acquired. You can see in yourself, as you work with this book, how adding words to your vocabulary is exactly analogous to a child's mastery of shoelacing. First you struggle with the concepts; then you eventually master them; finally, by frequent work with the new words (now you see the reason for the great number of exercises, the repetitious writing, saying, thinking) you build up new nerve patterns and you begin to use the new words with scarcely any consciousness of what you are doing.

Watch this common but important phenomenon closely as you do the next exercise. Your total absorption of the material so far has given you complete mastery of our ten basic words. Prove that you are beginning to form new nerve patterns in relation to these words by writing the one that fits each brief definition. The more quickly you think of the word that applies, the surer you can be that using these words will soon be as automatic and unself-conscious as putting on your shoes or buttoning/zipping yourself up in the morning.

1. talkative	1. L_____	
2. noisy, vehement, clamorous	2. V_____	
3. incoherent; sputtering	3. I_____	
4. gabbing ceaselessly and with little meaning	4. G_____	
5. disinclined to conversation	5. T_____	
6. talking in hackneyed phraseology	6. B_____	
7. showing a fine economy in the use of words	7. L_____	
8. forceful and convincing	8. C_____	
9. talking rapidly and fluently	9. V_____	
10. using more words than necessary	10. V_____	

KEY: 1–loquacious, 2–vociferous, 3–inarticulate, 4–garrulous, 5–taciturn, 6–banal, 7–laconic, 8–cogent, 9–voluble, 10–verbose

(End of Session 24)

SESSION 25

ORIGINS AND RELATED WORDS

1. about keeping one's mouth shut

If you let your mind play over some of the *taciturn* people you know, you will realize that their abnormal disinclination to conversation makes them seem morose, sullen, and unfriendly. Cal Coolidge's *taciturnity* was world-famous, and no one, I am sure, ever conceived of him as cheerful, overfriendly, or particularly sociable. There are doubtless many possible causes of such verbal rejection of the world: perhaps lack of self-assurance, feelings of inadequacy or hostility, excessive seriousness or introspection, or just plain having nothing to say. Maybe, in Coolidge's case, he was saving up his words—after he did not "choose to run" in 1928, he wrote a daily column for the New York *Herald Tribune* at a rumored price of two dollars a word—and, according to most critics (probably all Democrats), he had seemed wiser when he kept silent. Coolidge hailed from New England, and *taciturnity* (tas-ə-TURN'-ə-tee) in that part of the country, so some people say, is considered a virtue. Who knows, the cause may be geographical and climatic, rather than psychological.

Taciturn is from a Latin verb *taceo*, to be silent, and is one of those words whose full meaning cannot be expressed by any other combination of syllables. It has many synonyms, among them *silent, uncommunicative, reticent, reserved, secretive, close-lipped,* and *close-mouthed;* but no other word indicates the *permanent, habitual,* and *temperamental* disinclination to talk implied by *taciturn.*

2. better left unsaid

Tacit (TAS'-it) derives also from *taceo.*

Here is a man dying of cancer. He suspects what his disease is, and everyone else, of course, knows. Yet he never mentions the dread word, and no one who visits him ever breathes a syllable of it in his hearing. It is *tacitly* understood by all concerned that the word will remain forever unspoken.

(Such a situation today, however, may or may not be typical—there appears to be a growing tendency among physicians and family to be open and honest with people who are dying.)

Consider another situation:

An executive is engaging in extracurricular activities with her secretary. Yet during office time they are as formal and distant as any two human beings can well be. Neither of them ever said to the other, "Now, look here, we may be lovers after five o'clock,

247

but between nine and five we must preserve the utmost decorum, okay?" Such speech, such a verbal arrangement, is considered unnecessary—so we may say that the two have a *tacit* agreement (i.e., nothing was ever actually *said*) to maintain a complete employer-employee relationship during office hours.

Anything *tacit,* then, is unspoken, unsaid, not verbalized. We speak of a *tacit* agreement, arrangement, acceptance, rejection, assent, refusal, etc. A person is never called *tacit.*

The noun is *tacitness* (TAS'-it-nəs). (Bear in mind that you can transform any adjective into a noun by adding *-ness,* though in many cases there may be a more sophisticated, or more common, noun form.)

Changing the *a* of the root *taceo* to *i,* and adding the prefix *re-,* again, and the adjective suffix *-ent,* we can construct the English word *reticent* (RET'-ə-sənt).

Someone is *reticent* who prefers to keep silent, whether out of shyness, embarrassment, or fear of revealing what should not be revealed. (The idea of "againness" in the prefix has been lost in the current meaning of the word.)

We have frequently made nouns out of *-ent* adjectives. Write two possible noun forms of *reticent:* _____, or, less commonly, _____.

3. talk, talk, talk!

Loquacious people love to talk. This adjective is not necessarily a put-down, but the implication, when you so characterize such people, is that you wish they would pause for breath once in a while so that *you* can get your licks in. The noun is *loquacity* (lō-KWAS'-ə-tee), or, of course, *loquaciousness.*

The word derives from Latin *loquor,* to speak, a root found also in:

1. *soliloquy* (sə-LIL'-ə-kwee)—a speech to oneself (*loquor* plus *solus,* alone), or, etymologically, a speech when alone.

We often talk to ourselves, but usually silently, the words going through our minds but not actually passing our lips. The term *so-*

liloquy is commonly applied to utterances made in a play by characters who are speaking their thoughts aloud so the audience won't have to guess. The *soliloquist* (sə-LIL'-ə-kwist) may be alone; or other members of the cast may be present on stage, but of course they don't hear what's being said, because they're not supposed to know. Eugene O'Neill made novel uses of *soliloquies* in *Mourning Becomes Electra*—the characters made honest disclosures of their feelings and thoughts to the audience, but kept the other players in the dark.

The verb is to *soliloquize* (sə-LIL'-ə-kwīz').

2. A *ventriloquist* (ven-TRIL'-ə-kwist) is one who can throw his voice. A listener thinks the sound is coming from some source other than the person speaking. The combining root is Latin *venter, ventris,* belly; etymologically, *ventriloquism* (ven-TRIL'-ə-kwiz-əm) is the art of "speaking from the belly." The adjective is *ventriloquistic* (ven-tril'-ə-KWIS'-tik). Can you figure out how the verb will end? Write the verb: _____.

3. *Colloquial* (kə-LŌ'-kwee-əl) combines *loquor,* to speak, with the prefix *con-*. (*Con-* is spelled *col-* before a root starting with *l; cor-* before a root starting with *r; com-* before a root starting with *m, p,* or *b.*) When people speak together they are engaging in conversation—and their language is usually more informal and less rigidly grammatical than what you might expect in writing or in public addresses. *Colloquial* patterns are perfectly correct—they are simply informal, and suitable to everyday conversation.

A *colloquialism* (kə-LŌ'-kwee-ə-liz-əm), therefore, is a *conversational-style* expression, like "He hasn't got any" or "Who are you going with?" as contrasted to the formal or literary "He has none" or "With whom are you going?" *Colloquial* English is the English you and I talk on everyday occasions—it is not slangy, vulgar, or illiterate.

4. A *circumlocution* (sur-kəm-lō-KYOO'-shən) is, etymologically, a "talking around" (*circum-,* around). Any way of expressing an idea that is roundabout or indirect is *circumlocutory* (sur'-kəm-LOK'-yə-tawr'-ee)—you are now familiar with the common adjective suffix *-ory.*

REVIEW OF ETYMOLOGY

PREFIX, ROOT, SUFFIX	MEANING	ENGLISH WORD
1. *taceo*	to be silent	_____
2. *-ity*	noun suffix	_____
3. *-ness*	noun suffix	_____
4. *-ent*	adjective suffix	_____
5. *-ence, -ency*	noun suffix	_____
6. *re-*	again	_____
7. *loquor*	to speak	_____
8. *solus*	alone	_____
9. *-ist*	one who	_____
10. *-ize*	verb suffix	_____
11. *venter, ventris*	belly	_____
12. *-ic*	adjective suffix	_____
13. *-ous*	adjective suffix	_____
14. *con-, col-, com-, cor-*	with, together	_____
15. *-al*	adjective suffix	_____
16. *-ism*	noun suffix	_____

WORKING WITH THE WORDS

Can you pronounce the words?

1. *taciturnity*	tas-ə-TURN′-ə-tee
2. *tacit*	TAS′-it
3. *tacitness*	TAS′-ət-nəs
4. *reticent*	RET′-ə-sənt
5. *reticence*	RET′-ə-səns
6. *reticency*	RET′-ə-sən-see

250

7. *loquaciousness*	lō-KWAY′-shəs-nəs
8. *loquacity*	lō-KWAS′-ə-tee
9. *soliloquy*	sə-LIL′-ə-kwee
10. *soliloquist*	sə-LIL′-ə-kwist
11. *soliloquize*	sə-LIL′-ə-kwīz′
12. *ventriloquist*	ven′-TRIL′-ə-kwist
13. *ventriloquism*	ven-TRIL′-ə-kwiz-əm
14. *ventriloquistic*	ven-tril′-ə-KWIS′-tik
15. *ventriloquize*	ven-TRIL′-ə-kwīz′
16. *colloquial*	kə-LŌ′-kwee-əl
17. *colloquialism*	kə-LŌ′-kwee-ə-liz-əm
18. *circumlocution*	sur′-kəm-lō-KYŌŌ′-shən
19. *circumlocutory*	sur′-kəm-LOK′-yə-tawr′-ee

Can you work with the words?

1. taciturnity	a. unwillingness to talk, or disclose, out of fear, shyness, reserve, etc.
2. tacitness	b. talking, or a speech, "to oneself"
3. reticence	c. art of throwing one's voice
4. loquacity	d. unwillingness to engage in conversation
5. soliloquy	e. informal expression used in everyday conversation
6. ventriloquism	f. state of being understood though not actually expressed
7. colloquialism	g. a talking around; method of talking indirectly or in a roundabout way
8. circumlocution	h. talkativeness

KEY: 1–d, 2–f, 3–a, 4–h, 5–b, 6–c, 7–e, 8–g

Do you understand the words?

1. A *tacit* understanding is put into words.	TRUE	FALSE
2. Inhibited people are seldom *reticent* about expressing anger.	TRUE	FALSE
3. A *soliloquist* expresses his thoughts aloud.	TRUE	FALSE
4. A *ventriloquistic* performance on stage involves a dummy who appears to be talking.	TRUE	FALSE
5. A *colloquial* style of writing is ungrammatical.	TRUE	FALSE
6. *Circumlocutory* speech is direct and forthright.	TRUE	FALSE
7. *Inarticulate* people are generally given to *loquaciousness*.	TRUE	FALSE
8. A *soliloquy* is a dialogue.	TRUE	FALSE

KEY: 1–F, 2–F, 3–T, 4–T, 5–F, 6–F, 7–F, 8–F

Can you recall the words?

1. to speak to oneself	1. S_____
2. to throw one's voice	2. V_____
3. unwillingness to engage in conversation	3. T_____
4. unspoken	4. T_____
5. referring to an indirect, roundabout style of expression (*adj.*)	5. C_____
6. suitable for informal conversation	6. C_____
7. talkativeness	7. L_____
	or L_____
8. reluctance to express one's feelings or thoughts	8. R_____
	or R_____

252

9. a speech to oneself, especially   9. S_____
   in a play
10. an indirect, roundabout   10. C_____
    expression

KEY: 1–soliloquize, 2–ventriloquize, 3–taciturnity, 4–tacit, 5–circumlocutory, 6–colloquial, 7–loquaciousness *or* loquacity, 8–reticence *or* reticency, 9–soliloquy, 10–circumlocution

---

(End of Session 25)

SESSION 26

ORIGINS AND RELATED WORDS

1. a Spartan virtue

In ancient Sparta, originally known as *Laconia,* the citizens were long-suffering, hard-bitten, stoical, and military-minded, and were even more noted for their economy of speech than Vermonters, if that is possible. Legend has it that when Philip of Macedonia was storming the gates of Sparta (or Laconia), he sent a message to the besieged king saying, "If we capture your city we will burn it to the ground." A one-word answer came back: "If." It was now probably Philip's turn to be speechless, though history does not record his reaction.

It is from the name *Laconia* that we derive our word *laconic*—pithy, concise, economical in the use of words almost to the point of curtness; precisely the opposite of *verbose.*

Like the man who was waiting at a lunch counter for a ham sandwich. When it was ready, the clerk inquired politely, "Will you eat it here, or take it with you?"

"Both," was the *laconic* reply.

Or like the woman who was watching a lush imbibing dry martinis at a Third Avenue bar in New York City. The drunk downed the contents of each cocktail glass at one gulp, daintily nibbled and swallowed the bowl, then finally turned the glass over and ate the base. The stem he threw into a corner. This amazing gustatory feat went on for half an hour, until a dozen stems were lying shattered in the corner, and the drunk had chewed and swallowed enough bowls and bases to start a glass factory. He suddenly turned to the lady and asked belligerently, "I suppose you think I'm cuckoo, don't you?" "Sure—the stem is the best part," was the *laconic* answer.

(It was doubtless this same gentleman, in his accustomed state of intoxication, who found himself painfully weaving his way along Wilshire Boulevard in Beverly Hills, California—he had somehow gotten on a TWA jetliner instead of the subway—when he realized, almost too late, that he was going to bump into a smartly dressed young woman who had just stepped out of her Mercedes-Benz to go window-shopping along the avenue. He quickly veered left, but by some unexplainable magnetic attraction the woman veered in the same direction, again making collision apparently inevitable. With an adroit maneuver, the drunk swung to the right—the lady, by now thoroughly disoriented, did the same. Finally both jammed on the brakes and came to a dead stop, face to face, and not six inches apart; and as the alcoholic fumes assailed the young lady's nostrils, she sneered at the reeking, swaying man, as much in frustration as in contempt: "Oh! How gauche!" "Fine!" was his happy response. "How goesh with you?" This answer, however, is not *laconic*, merely confused.)

We have learned that *-ness*, *-ity*, and *-ism* are suffixes that transform adjectives into nouns—and all three can be used with *laconic*:

  . . . with characteristic *laconicness* (lə-KON'-ək-nəs)
  . . . her usual *laconicity* (lak'-ə-NIS'-ə-tee)
  . . . his habitual *laconism* (LAK'-ə-niz-əm)
  . . . with, for him, unusual *laconicism* (lə-KON'-ə-siz-əm)

A *laconism* is also the expression itself that is pithy and concise, as the famous report from a naval commander in World War II: "Saw sub, sank same."

2. brilliant

Cogent is a term of admiration. A *cogent* argument is well put, convincing, hardly short of brilliant. *Cogency* (KŌ′-jən-see) shows a keen mind, an ability to think clearly and logically. The word derives from the Latin verb *cogo*, to drive together, compel, force. A *cogent* argument *compels* acceptance because of its logic, its persuasiveness, its appeal to one's sense of reason.

3. back to talk

You will recall that *loquor*, to speak, is the source of *loquacity*, *soliloquy*, *ventriloquism*, *colloquialism*, *circumlocution*. This root is also the base on which *eloquent* (EL′-ə-kwənt), *magniloquent* (mag-NIL′-ə-kwənt), and *grandiloquent* (gran-DIL′-ə-kwənt) are built.

The *eloquent* person speaks *out* (*e-*, from *ex-*, out), is vividly expressive, fluent, forceful, or persuasive in language ("the prosecutor's *eloquent* plea to the jury"). The word is partially synonymous with *cogent*, but *cogent* implies irresistible logical reasoning and intellectual keenness, while *eloquent* suggests artistic expression, strong emotional appeal, the skillful use of language to move and arouse a listener.

Magniloquent (*magnus*, large) and *grandiloquent* (*grandis*, grand) are virtually identical in meaning. *Magniloquence* or *grandiloquence* is the use of high-flown, grandiose, even pompous language; of large and impressive words; of lofty, flowery, or over-elegant phraseology. Home is *a place of residence;* wife is *helpmate, helpmeet,* or *better half;* women are *the fair sex;* children are *offspring* or *progeny;* a doctor is a *member of the medical fraternity;* people are the *species Homo sapiens,* etc., etc.

Loquacious, verbose, voluble, and *garrulous* people are all talkative; but each type, you will recall, has a special quality.

If you are *loquacious,* you talk a lot because you *like* to talk and doubtless have a lot to say.

If you are *verbose,* you smother your ideas with excess words, with such an overabundance of words that your listener either drops into a state of helpless confusion or falls asleep.

If you are *voluble,* you speak rapidly, fluently, glibly, without hesitation, stutter, or stammer; you are vocal, verbal, and highly articulate.

If you are *garrulous,* you talk constantly, and usually aimlessly and meaninglessly, about trifles. We often hear the word used in "a *garrulous* old man" or "a *garrulous* old woman," since in very advanced age the mind may wander and lose the ability to discriminate between the important and the unimportant, between the interesting and the dull.

Verbose is from Latin *verbum,* word—the *verbose* person is wordy.

Voluble comes from Latin *volvo, volutus,* to roll—words effortlessly roll off the *voluble* speaker's tongue.

And *garrulous* derives from Latin *garrio,* to chatter—a *garrulous* talker chatters away like a monkey.

The suffix *-ness* can be added to all these adjectives to form nouns. Alternate noun forms end in *-ity:*

verbosity	(vər-BOS′-ə-tee)
volubility	(vol′-yə-BIL′-ə-tee)
garrulity	(gə-ROOL′-ə-tee)

4. at large

We discovered *magnus,* large, big, great, in Chapter 9, in discussing *Magnavox* (etymologically, "big voice"), and find it again in *magniloquent* (etymologically, "talking big"). The root occurs in a number of other words:

1. *Magnanimous* (mag-NAN′-ə-məs)—big-hearted, generous, forgiving (etymologically, "great-minded"). (*Magnus* plus *animus,* mind.) We'll discuss this word in depth in Chapter 12.

2. *Magnate* (MAG′-nayt)—a person of great power or influence, a big wheel, as a business *magnate.*

3. *Magnify*—to make larger, or make seem larger (*magnus* plus *-fy* from *facio,* to make), as in "*magnify* your problems."

4. *Magnificent*—*magnus* plus *fic-,* from *facio.*

5. *Magnitude*—*magnus* plus the common noun suffix *-tude,* as in *fortitude, multitude, gratitude,* etc.

6. *Magnum* (as of champagne or wine)—a large bottle, generally two fifths of a gallon.

7. *Magnum opus* (MAG′-nəm Ō′-pes)—etymologically, a "big work"; actually, the greatest work, or masterpiece, of an artist, writer, or composer. *Opus* is the Latin word for *work;* the plural of *opus* is used in the English word *opera*, etymologically, "a number of works," actually a musical drama containing overture, singing, and other forms of music, i.e., many musical works. The verb form *opero*, to work, occurs in *operate, co-operate, operator,* etc.

5. words, words, words!

Latin *verbum* is *word*. A *verb* is the important word in a sentence; *verbatim* (vər-BAY′-tim) is word-for-word (a *verbatim* report).

Verbal (VUR′-bəl), ending in the adjective suffix *-al*, may refer either to a *verb*, or to words in general (a *verbal* fight); or it may mean, loosely, *oral* or *spoken*, rather than written (*verbal* agreement or contract); or, describing people ("she is quite *verbal*"), it may refer to a ready ability to put feelings or thoughts into words.

Working from *verbal*, can you add a common verb suffix to form a word meaning *to put into words?* _____

Verbiage (VUR′-bee-əj) has two meanings: an excess of words ("Such *verbiage!*"); or a style or manner of using words (medical *verbiage*, military *verbiage*).

6. roll on, and on!

Volvo, volutus, to roll, the source of *voluble*, is the root on which many important English words are based.

Revolve (rə-VOLV′)—roll again (and again), or keep turning round. Wheels *revolve*, the earth *revolves* around the sun, the cylinder of a revolver *revolves*. (The prefix is *re-*, back or again.)

The noun is *revolution* (rev-ə-LOO′-shən), which can be one such complete rolling, or, by logical extension, a radical change of any sort (TV was responsible for a *revolution* in the entertainment industry), especially political (the American, or French,

Revolution). The adjective *revolutionary* (rev'-ə-LOO'-shən-air'-ee) introduces us to a new adjective suffix, *-ary,* as in *contrary, disciplinary, stationary, imaginary,* etc. (But *-ary* is sometimes also a noun suffix, as in *dictionary, commentary,* etc.)

Add different prefixes to *volvo* to construct two more English words:

1. *involve*—etymologically, "roll in" ("I didn't want to get *involved!*"). Noun: *involvement.*

2. *evolve* (ə-VOLV')—etymologically, "roll out" (*e-,* out); hence to unfold, or gradually develop ("The final plan *evolved* from some informal discussions"; "The political party *evolved* from a group of interested citizens who met frequently to protest government actions").

By analogy with the forms derived from *revolve,* can you construct the noun and adjective of *evolve?* Noun: _____ _____. Adjective: _____.

REVIEW OF ETYMOLOGY

PREFIX, ROOT, SUFFIX	MEANING	ENGLISH WORD
1. *Laconia*	Sparta	_____
2. *-ness*	noun suffix	_____
3. *-ism*	noun suffix	_____
4. *-ity*	noun suffix	_____
5. *e- (ex-)*	out	_____
6. *-ent*	adjective suffix	_____
7. *-ence*	noun suffix	_____
8. *magnus*	big	_____
9. *grandis*	grand	_____
10. *verbum*	word	_____
11. *volvo, volutus*	to roll	_____
12. *garrio*	to chatter	_____
13. *animus*	mind	_____
14. *-fy*	to make	_____
15. *-tude*	noun suffix	_____
16. *opus*	work	_____

258

17.	*opero*	to work	_____
18.	*-al*	adjective suffix	_____
19.	*-ize*	verb suffix	_____
20.	*re-*	again, back	_____
21.	*-ary*	adjective suffix	_____
22.	*in-*	in	_____

USING THE WORDS

Can you pronounce the words? (I)

1.	*laconicity*	lak'-ə-NIS'-ə-tee
2.	*laconism*	LAK'-ə-niz-əm
3.	*laconicism*	lə-KON'-ə-siz-əm
4.	*eloquent*	EL'-ə-kwənt
5.	*eloquence*	EL'-ə-kwəns
6.	*magniloquent*	mag-NIL'-ə-kwənt
7.	*magniloquence*	mag-NIL'-ə-kwəns
8.	*grandiloquent*	gran-DIL'-ə-kwənt
9.	*grandiloquence*	gran-DIL'-ə-kwəns
10.	*verbosity*	vər-BOS'-ə-tee
11.	*volubility*	vol'-yə-BIL'-ə-tee
12.	*garrulity*	gə-ROO'-lə-tee
13.	*cogency*	KŌ'-jən-see

Can you pronounce the words? (II)

1.	*magnanimous*	mag-NAN'-ə-məs
2.	*magnate*	MAG'-nayt
3.	*magnum opus*	MAG'-nəm Ō'-pəs
4.	*verbatim*	vər-BAY'-tim
5.	*verbal*	VUR'-bəl
6.	*verbalize*	VUR'-bə-līz'
7.	*verbiage*	VUR'-bee-əj
8.	*revolve*	rə-VOLV'
9.	*revolution*	rev'-ə-LOO'-shən
10.	*revolutionary*	rev'-ə-LOO'shə-nair'-ee

11.	*evolve*	ə-VOLV′
12.	*evolution*	ev′-ə-LOO′-shən
13.	*evolutionary*	ev′-ə-LOO′-shə-nair′-ee

Can you work with the words? (I)

1.	laconicity	a.	floweriness, pompousness, or elegance in speech
2.	eloquence	b.	incessant chatter with little meaning
3.	magniloquence	c.	big wheel; important or influential person
4.	verbosity	d.	great artistic work; masterpiece
5.	volubility	e.	a gradual unfolding or development; "a rolling out"
6.	garrulity	f.	"a rolling round"; radical change; political upheaval
7.	magnum opus	g.	great economy in speech
8.	magnate	h.	fluency, ease, and/or rapidity of speech
9.	revolution	i.	great, artistic, or emotional expressiveness
10.	evolution	j.	wordiness
11.	cogency	k.	persuasiveness through logic; keen-mindedness in reasoning

---

KEY: 1–g, 2–i, 3–a, 4–j, 5–h, 6–b, 7–d, 8–c, 9–f, 10–e, 11–k

Can you work with the words? (II)

1.	laconism	a.	word for word
2.	verbiage	b.	to put into words
3.	verbalize	c.	causing, or resulting from, radical change; new and totally different

4. verbal

5. verbatim

6. revolutionary

7. evolutionary

8. grandiloquent

9. eloquent

10. magnanimous

d. resulting or developing gradually from (something)

e. expressive; emotionally moving

f. pithiness or economy of expression; word or phrase packed with meaning

g. big-hearted; generous, forgiving

h. referring or pertaining to, or involving, words; oral, rather than written

i. using flossy, flowery, elegant, or impressive phraseology

j. wordiness; style or manner of using words; type of words

KEY: 1–f, 2–j, 3–b, 4–h, 5–a, 6–c, 7–d, 8–i, 9–e, 10–g

Do you understand the words?

1.	Is *laconicism* characteristic of a verbose speaker?	YES	NO
2.	Does a *magniloquent* speaker use short, simple words?	YES	NO
3.	Does a frog *evolve* from a tadpole?	YES	NO
4.	Is an *eloquent* speaker interesting to listen to?	YES	NO
5.	Do verbose people use a lot of *verbiage*?	YES	NO
6.	Is *volubility* characteristic of an inarticulate person?	YES	NO
7.	Does *verbosity* show a careful and economical use of words?	YES	NO
8.	Is a *verbal* person usually inarticulate?	YES	NO
9.	Is a *magnun opus* one of the lesser works of a writer, artist, or composer?	YES	NO

261

10. Is a *magnanimous* person selfish and   YES   NO
petty-minded?

KEY: 1–no, 2–no, 3–yes, 4–yes, 5–yes, 6–no, 7–no, 8–no, 9–no, 10–no

---

Can you recall the words?

1. gradually unfolding, resulting, or developing (*adj.*) — 1. E_____
2. causing, or resulting from, radical change (*adj.*) — 2. R_____
3. quality of conciseness and economy in the use of words — 3. L_____
or L_____
or L_____
or L_____
4. expressiveness in the use of words — 4. E_____
5. turn round and round — 5. R_____
6. important person, as in the commercial world — 6. M_____
7. unselfish; generous; noble in motive; big-hearted; forgiving — 7. M_____
8. using words easily; vocal; articulate; referring to, or involving, words; oral, rather than written — 8. V_____
9. style of word usage; type of words; overabundance of words — 9. V_____
10. wordiness; quality of using excess words — 10. V_____
11. elegance in word usage — 11. M_____
or G_____
12. quality of chattering on and on about trivia, or with little meaning — 12. G_____
13. fluency and ease in speech — 13. V_____

14. word for word
15. masterpiece; great artistic work
16. persuasiveness and forcefulness in speech or writing through closely reasoned logic

14. V_____
15. M_____O____
16. C_____

(*End of Session 26*)

SESSION 27

ORIGINS AND RELATED WORDS

1. front and back—and uncles

The *ventriloquist* appears to talk from the belly (*venter, ventris* plus *loquor*) rather than through the lips (or such was the strange perception of the person who first used the word).

Venter, ventris, belly, is the root on which *ventral* (VEN′-trəl) and *ventricle* are built.

The *ventral* side of an animal, for example, is the front or anterior side—the belly side.

A *ventricle* (VEN′-trə-kəl) is a hollow organ or cavity, or, logically enough, belly, as one of the two chambers of the heart, or one of the four chambers of the brain. The *ventricles* of the heart are the lower chambers, and receive blood from the *auricles,* or upper chambers. The *auricle* (AW′-rə-kəl), so named because it is somewhat ear-shaped (Latin *auris,* ear), receives blood from the veins; the *auricles* send the blood into the *ventricles,* which in turn pump the blood into the arteries. (It's all very complicated, but fortunately it works.)

The adjective form of *ventricle* is *ventricular* (ven-TRIK'-yə-lər), which may refer to a *ventricle,* or may mean *having a belly-like bulge.*

Now that you see how *ventricular* is formed from *ventricle,* can you figure out the adjective of *auricle?* _____.
How about the adjective of *vehicle?* _____.
Of *circle?* _____.

No doubt you wrote *auricular* (aw-RIK'-yə-lər), *vehicular,* and *circular,* and have discovered that nouns ending in *-cle* from adjectives ending in *-cular.*

So you can now be the first person on your block to figure out the adjective derived from:

clavicle: _____
cuticle: _____
vesicle: _____
testicle: _____
uncle: _____

The answers of course are *clavicular, cuticular, vesicular, testicular*—and for *uncle* you have every right to shout "No fair!" (But where is it written that life is fair?)

The Latin word for *uncle* (actually, uncle on the mother's side) is *avunculus,* from which we get *avuncular* (ə-VUNG'-kyə-lər), referring to an uncle.

Now what about an uncle? Well, traditional or stereotypical uncles are generally kindly, permissive, indulgent, protective—and often give helpful advice. So anyone who exhibits one or more of such traits to another (usually younger) person is *avuncular* or acts in an *avuncular* capacity.

So, at long last, to get back to *ventral.* If there's a front or belly side, anatomically, there must be a reverse—a back side. This is the *dorsal* (DAWR'-səl) side, from Latin *dorsum,* the root on which the verb *endorse* (en-DAWRS') is built.

If you *endorse* a check, you sign it on the back side; if you *endorse* a plan, an idea, etc., you *back* it, you express your approval or support. The noun is *endorsement* (en-DAWRS′-mənt).

2. the noise and the fury

Vociferous derives from Latin *vox, vocis,* voice (a root you met in Chapter 9), plus *fero,* to bear or carry. A *vociferous* rejoinder carries a lot of voice—i.e., it is vehement, loud, noisy, clamorous, shouting. The noun is *vociferousness* (vō-SIF′-ə-rəs-nəs); the verb is to *vociferate* (vō-SIF′-ə-rayt′). Can you form the noun derived from the verb? _____.

3. to sleep or not to sleep—that is the question

The root *fero* is found also in *somniferous* (som-NIF′-ə-rəs), carrying, bearing, or bringing sleep. So a *somniferous* lecture is so dull and boring that it is sleep-inducing.

Fero is combined with *somnus,* sleep, in *somniferous.* (The suffix -*ous* indicates what part of speech? _____
_____.)

Tack on the negative prefix *in-* to *somnus* to construct *insomnia* (in-SOM′-nee-ə), the abnormal inability to fall asleep when sleep is required or desired. The unfortunate victim of this disability is an *insomniac* (in-SOM′-nee-ak), the adjective is *insomnious* (in-SOM′-nee-əs). (So -*ous,* in case you could not answer the question in the preceding paragraph, is an *adjective* suffix.)

Add a different adjective suffix to *somnus* to derive *somnolent* (SOM′-nə-lənt), sleepy, drowsy. Can you construct the noun form of *somnolent?* _____ *or* _____
_____.

Combine *somnus* with *ambulo,* to walk, and you have *somnambulism* (som-NAM′-byə-liz-əm), walking in one's sleep. With your increasing skill in using etymology to form words, write the term for the person who is a sleepwalker. _____.
_____. Now add to the word you wrote a two-letter adjective suffix we have learned, to form the adjective: _____
_____.

4. a walkaway

An *ambulatory* (AM'-byə-lə-taw'-ree) patient, as in a hospital or convalescent home, is finally well enough to get out of bed and walk around. A *perambulator* (pə-RAM'-byə-lay'-tər), a word used more in England than in the United States, and often shortened to *pram,* is a baby carriage, a vehicle for walking an infant through the streets (*per-,* through). To *perambulate* (pə-RAM'-byə-layt') is, etymologically, "to walk through"; hence, to stroll around. Can you write the noun form of this verb?

_____.

To *amble* (AM'-bəl) is to walk aimlessly; an *ambulance* is so called because originally it was composed of two stretcher-bearers who *walked* off the battlefield with a wounded soldier; and a *preamble* (PREE'-am-bəl) is, by etymology, something that "walks before" (*pre-,* before, beforehand), hence an introduction or introductory statement, as the *preamble* to the U. S. Constitution ("We the people . . ."), a *preamble* to the speech, etc; or any event that is introductory or preliminary to another, as in "An increase in inflationary factors in the economy is often a *preamble* to a drop in the stock market."

5. back to sleep

Somnus is one Latin word for sleep—*sopor* is another. A *soporific* (sop'-ə-RIF'-ik) lecture, speaker, style of delivery, etc. will put the audience to sleep (*fic-* from *facio,* to make), and a *soporific* is a sleeping pill.

6. noun suffixes

You know that *-ness* can be added to any adjective to construct the noun form. Write the noun derived from *inarticulate:*
_____. *Inarticulate* is a combination of the negative prefix *in-* and Latin *articulus,* a joint. The *inarticulate* person has trouble joining words together coherently. If you are quite *articulate* (ahr-TIK'-yə-lət), on the other hand, you join your words together easily, you are verbal, vocal, possibly even

voluble. The verb to *articulate* (ahr-TIK'-yə-layt') is to join (words), i.e., to express your vocal sounds—as in "Please *articulate* more clearly." Can you write the noun derived from the verb *articulate*? _____.

Another, and very common, noun suffix attached to adjectives is, as you have discovered, *-ity*. So the noun form of *banal* is either *banalness*, or, more commonly, *banality* (bə-NAL'-ə-tee).

Bear in mind, then, that *-ness* and *-ity* are common noun suffixes attached to adjectives, and *-ion* (or *-ation*) is a noun suffix frequently affixed to verbs (to *articulate—articulation*; to *vocalize—vocalization*; to *perambulate—perambulation*).

REVIEW OF ETYMOLOGY

PREFIX, ROOT, SUFFIX	MEANING	ENGLISH WORD
1. *venter, ventris*	belly	_____
2. *loquor*	to speak	_____
3. *auris*	ear	_____
4. *avunculus*	uncle	_____
5. *dorsum*	back	_____
6. *vox, vocis*	voice	_____
7. *fero*	to carry, bear	_____
8. *somnus*	sleep	_____
9. *-ous*	adjective suffix	_____
10. *in-*	negative suffix	_____
11. *ambulo*	to walk	_____
12. *-ory*	adjective suffix	_____
13. *per-*	through	_____
14. *pre-*	before, beforehand	_____
15. *sopor*	sleep	_____
16. *fic- (facio)*	to make or do	_____
17. *-ness*	noun suffix	_____
18. *-ity*	noun suffix	_____
19. *-ion (-ation)*	noun suffix attached to verbs	_____
20. *-ent*	adjective suffix	_____
21. *-ence, -ency*	noun suffix	_____

267

USING THE WORDS

Can you pronounce the words? (I)

1. *ventral*	VEN'-trəl
2. *ventricle*	VEN'-trə-kəl
3. *auricle*	AWR'-ə-kəl
4. *ventricular*	ven-TRIK'-yə-lər
5. *auricular*	aw-RIK'-yə-lər
6. *avuncular*	ə-VUNG'-kyə-lər
7. *dorsal*	DAWR'-səl
8. *endorse*	en-DAWRS'
9. *endorsement*	en-DAWRS'-mənt
10. *vociferousness*	vō-SIF'-ə-rəs-nəs
11. *vociferate*	vō-SIF'-ə-rayt'
12. *vociferation*	vō-sif'-ə-RAY'-shən

Can you pronounce the words? (II)

1. *somniferous*	som-NIF'-ər-əs
2. *insomnia*	in-SOM'-nee-ə
3. *insomniac*	in-SOM'-nee-ak'
4. *insomnious*	in-SOM'-nee-əs
5. *somnolent*	SOM'-nə-lənt
6. *somnolence*	SOM'-nə-ləns
7. *somnolency*	SOM'-nə-lən-see
8. *somnambulism*	som-NAM'-byə-liz-əm
9. *somnambulist*	som-NAM'-byə-list
10. *somnambulistic*	som-nam'-byə-LIST'-ik

Can you pronounce the words? (III)

1. *ambulatory*	AM'-byə-lə-tawr'-ee
2. *perambulator*	pə-RAM'-byə-lay'-tər
3. *perambulate*	pə-RAM'-byə-layt'
4. *perambulation*	pə-ram'-byə-LAY'-shən
5. *amble*	AM'-bəl
6. *preamble*	PREE'-am-bəl

7. *soporific*   sop-ə-RIF'-ik
8. *inarticulateness*   in'-ahr-TIK'-yə-lət-nəs
9. *articulate*   ahr-TIK'-yə-lət
10. *banality*   bə-NAL'-ə-tee

Can you work with the words? (I)

1. ventral	a. unable to fall asleep
2. dorsal	b. pertaining to sleepwalking
3. somniferous	c. drowsy
4. insomnious	d. able to walk, after being bed-ridden
5. somnolent	e. verbal, vocal
6. somnambulistic	f. like an uncle; kindly; protective
7. ambulatory	g. pertaining to one of the chambers of the heart
8. articulate	h. referring to the front or belly side
9. ventricular, auricular	i. sleep-inducing
10. avuncular	j. referring to the back side

KEY: 1–h, 2–j, 3–i, 4–a, 5–c, 6–b, 7–d, 8–e, 9–g, 10–f

Can you work with the words? (II)

1. ventricle, auricle	a. inability to fall asleep
2. endorsement	b. sleepwalking
3. vociferousness	c. introduction; preliminary or introductory occurrence
4. insomnia	d. incoherence; sputtering; inability to get words out
5. somnolence	e. chamber of the heart
6. somnambulism	f. sleeping pill
7. perambulator	g. support; approval
8. preamble	h. lack of originality; lack of imagination
9. soporific	i. drowsiness

269

10. inarticulateness
11. banality

j. baby buggy; stroller
k. loudness; clamorousness

KEY: 1–e, 2–g, 3–k, 4–a, 5–i, 6–b, 7–j, 8–c, 9–f, 10–d, 11–h

Can you work with the words? (III)

1. endorse
2. vociferate
3. insomniac
4. somnolency
5. somnambulist

6. perambulate
7. amble

8. soporific
9. insomnious

a. one who cannot fall asleep
b. sleepwalker
c. walk aimlessly
d. stroll through; walk around
e. to sign on the back; support; approve of
f. drowsiness
g. say loudly and with great vehemence
h. causing sleep
i. wakeful; unable to fall asleep

KEY: 1–e, 2–g, 3–a, 4–f, 5–b, 6–d, 7–c, 8–h, 9–i

Do you understand the words?

1. Does an *insomniac* often need a *soporific*?	YES	NO
2. Does a *somnambulist* always stay in bed when asleep?	YES	NO
3. Are *ambulatory* patients bedridden?	YES	NO
4. Does a *preamble* come after another event?	YES	NO
5. Are *articulate* people verbal?	YES	NO
6. Does *banality* show creativeness?	YES	NO
7. Does an *avuncular* attitude indicate affection and protectiveness?	YES	NO
8. Is *vociferation* habitual with quiet, shy people?	YES	NO
9. Is a *somnolent* person wide awake?	YES	NO

270

10. Is a *somniferous* speaker stimulating   YES   NO
and exciting?

Can you recall the words?

1. lack of imagination or   1. B_____
originality in speech, actions,
or style of life; hackneyed or
trite phraseology
2. sleep-inducing   2. S_____
                           or S_____
3. unable to fall asleep (*adj.*)   3. I_____
4. verbal, vocal, speaking   4. A_____
fluently
5. acting like an uncle   5. A_____
6. referring to the front; anterior   6. V_____
7. referring to the back; posterior   7. D_____
8. approve of; support; sign on   8. E_____
the back of
9. shout vehemently   9. V_____
10. one who cannot fall asleep   10. I_____
11. drowsy; sleepy   11. S_____
12. sleepwalker   12. S_____
13. now able to walk, though   13. A_____
previously bedridden
14. walk aimlessly   14. A_____
15. introduction; introductory   15. P_____
event
16. incoherence   16. I_____

CHAPTER REVIEW

A. Do you recognize the words?

1. Disinclined to conversation:
    (a) loquacious, (b) laconic, (c) taciturn
2. Trite:
    (a) inarticulate, (b) banal, (c) verbose
3. Rapid and fluent:
    (a) voluble, (b) verbose, (c) garrulous
4. Forceful and compelling:
    (a) vociferous, (b) cogent, (c) laconic
5. Unspoken:
    (a) verbatim, (b) eloquent, (c) tacit
6. Using elegant and impressive words:
    (a) verbose, (b) grandiloquent, (c) colloquial
7. Back:
    (a) dorsal, (b) ventral, (c) somniferous
8. Sleep-inducing:
    (a) soporific, (b) somnolent, (c) ventral
9. Inability to fall asleep:
    (a) somnambulism, (b) ambulatory, (c) insomnia
10. Talkativeness:
    (a) reticence, (b) ventriloquism, (c) loquacity
11. Expressing indirectly or in a roundabout way:
    (a) circumlocutory, (b) colloquial, (c) laconic
12. Elegance in expression:
    (a) magniloquence, (b) grandiloquence, (c) verbiage
13. Wordiness:
    (a) laconism, (b) cogency, (c) verbosity
14. Big-hearted, generous, unselfish:
    (a) grandiloquent, (b) magnanimous, (c) garrulous
15. Causing radical changes:
    (a) evolutionary, (b) revolutionary, (c) ventricular
16. To shout vehemently:
    (a) endorse, (b) perambulate, (c) vociferate

17. Like an uncle:
   (a) ventricular, (b) auricular, (c) avuncular
18. Drowsy:
   (a) somniferous, (b) somnolent, (c) soporific
19. Sleepwalking:
   (a) insomnia, (b) somnolency, (c) somnambulism
20. Introduction:
   (a) preamble, (b) perambulator, (c) evolution

KEY: 1–c, 2–b, 3–a, 4–b, 5–c, 6–b, 7–a, 8–a, 9–c, 10–c, 11–a,
   12–a *and* b, 13–c, 14–b, 15–b, 16–c, 17–c, 18–b, 19–c,
   20–a

B. Can you recognize roots?

ROOT	MEANING	EXAMPLE
1. *taceo*	_____	taciturn
2. *loquor*	_____	loquacity
3. *solus*	_____	soliloquize
4. *venter, ventris*	_____	ventral
5. *magnus*	_____	magniloquent
6. *grandis*	_____	grandiloquent
7. *verbum*	_____	verbatim
8. *volvo, volutus*	_____	revolution
9. *garrio*	_____	garrulous
10. *animus*	_____	magnanimous
11. *opus*	_____	magnum opus
12. *opero*	_____	operator
13. *auris*	_____	auricle
14. *avunculus*	_____	avuncular
15. *dorsum*	_____	dorsal
16. *vox, vocis*	_____	vociferate
17. *fero*	_____	somniferous
18. *ambulo*	_____	preamble

273

19. *sopor*   ————————— soporific
20. *somnus*   ————————— somnolency

KEY: 1–to be silent, 2–to speak, 3–alone, 4–belly, 5–big, large, great, 6–grand, 7–word, 8–to roll, 9–to chatter, 10–mind, 11–work, 12–to work, 13–ear, 14–uncle, 15–back, 16–voice, 17–to carry or bear, 18–to walk, 19–sleep, 20–sleep

---

TEASER QUESTIONS FOR THE AMATEUR ETYMOLOGIST

1. The present participle (or *-ing* form) of the Latin verb *opero*, to work, is *operans*, working. The form *operandi* means *of working*. Can you figure out the literal meaning of the phrase *modus operandi*, sometimes used to signify the characteristic methods or procedures used by certain criminals? ————————

————————————————————————————

2. *Circum-*, we have learned, is a prefix meaning *around*, as in *circumlocution, circumference, circumcision, circumnavigation*, etc. Thinking of the root *scribo, scriptus*, to write, can you figure out the word meaning *writing, or written material, around* (the edge of something)? ————————————————

————————————

3. You know the roots *somnus* and *loquor*. Can you combine these two roots to form an adjective meaning *talking in one's sleep*? ————————————————————————. Can you write the noun form of this adjective? ————————————

————————

4. We have discovered *auris*, ear, as in *auricle*. Can you figure out the specialty of the physician called an *aurist*?

---

5. *Verbal*, from *verbum*, refers to words; *oral*, from *os, oris*, the mouth, refers to spoken words or sounds. Can you analyze *aural* and decide on its meaning? _____

_____

6. A *somnambulist* walks in his sleep. What does a *noctambulist* do? _____

_____

7. *Soporific*, combining *sopor*, sleep, with *fic-* (from *facio*), to make, means *inducing or causing sleep*. Use *somnus*, another root for sleep, to construct a word that has the same form and meaning as *soporific*: _____

8. *Perambulate* is *to walk through*. Use another Latin prefix to construct a verb meaning *to walk around*. _____

_____

(*Answers in Chapter 18*)

BECOMING ALERT TO NEW IDEAS

Some chapters back I suggested that since words are symbols of ideas, one of the most effective means of building your vocabulary is to read books that deal with new ideas. Along that line, I further suggested that the fields of psychology, psychiatry, and psychoanalysis would be good starting points, and I mentioned a number of exciting books to work with.

Needless to say, you will not wish to neglect other fields, and so I want to recommend, at this point, highly readable books in additional subjects. All these books will increase your familiarity with the world of ideas—all of them, therefore, will help you build a superior vocabulary.

SEMANTICS

Language in Thought and Action, by S. I. Hayakawa
People in Quandaries, by Wendell Johnson

EDUCATION AND LEARNING

How to Survive in Your Native Land, by James Herndon
Education and the Endangered Individual, by Brian V. Hill
How Children Fail and *What Do I Do Monday?,* by John Holt
Teaching Human Beings, by Jeffrey Schrank
Education and Ecstasy, by George B. Leonard
Human Teaching for Human Learning, by George Isaac Brown

SEX, LOVE, MARRIAGE

Couple Therapy, by Gerald Walker Smith and Alice I. Phillips
Your Fear of Love, by Marshall Bryant Hodge
Sexual Suicide, by George F. Gilder
Intimacy, by Gina Allen and Clement G. Martin, M.D.
How to Live with Another Person, by David Viscott, M.D.
Pairing, by George R. Bach and Ronald M. Deutsch
The Intimate Enemy, by George R. Bach and Peter Wyden
The Rape of the Ape, by Allan Sherman (Humor)
The Hite Report, by Shere Hite
Sex in Human Loving, by Eric Berne, M.D.

WOMEN, FEMINISM, ETC.

Rebirth of Feminism, by Judith Hole and Ellen Levine
The Way of All Women, by M. Esther Harding
Knowing Woman, by Irene Claremont de Castillejo
Sexist Justice, by Karen De Crow
Our Bodies, Our Selves, by The Boston Women's Health Book
  Collective

CHILDREN, CHILD-RAISING, ETC.

Between Parent and Child and *Between Parent and Teenager,*
  by Dr. Haim Ginott
Children Who Hate, by Fritz Redl and David Wineman
Parent Effectiveness Training, by Dr. Thomas Gordon
How to Parent, by Dr. Fitzhugh Dodson
Escape from Childhood, by John Holt
One Little Boy, by Dorothy W. Baruch

HEALTH

Save Your Life Diet Book, by David Reuben, M.D.
Folk Medicine, by D. C. Jarvis, M.D.
Get Well Naturally, by Linda Clark
Let's Eat Right to Keep Fit, by Adelle Davis

PHILOSOPHY

The Way of Zen and *What Does It Matter?,* by Alan W. Watts
Love's Body, by Norman O. Brown

BUSINESS, ECONOMICS, FINANCE

The Affluent Society, by John Kenneth Galbraith
Parkinson's Law, by C. Northcote Parkinson
The Peter Principle, by Laurence J. Peter
Up the Organization, by Robert Townsend

SOCIOLOGY

Passages, by Gail Sheehy
Future Shock, by Alvin Toffler
Hard Times, by Studs Terkel
Roots, by Alex Haley

DEATH AND DYING

Life After Life, by Raymond A. Moody, Jr., M.D.
On Death and Dying, by Elizabeth Kubler Ross

All but one or two of these stimulating and informative books are available in inexpensive paperback editions—most of them can be found in any large public library. Any one of them will provide an evening of entertainment and excitement far more rewarding than watching TV, will possibly open for you new areas of knowledge and understanding, and will undoubtedly contain so many of the words you have learned in this book that you will again and again experience the delicious shock of recognition that I spoke of in an earlier chapter.

Additionally, you may encounter words you have never seen before that are built on roots you are familiar with—*and you will then realize how simple it is to figure out the probable meaning of even the most esoteric term once you have become an expert in roots, prefixes, and suffixes.*

(End of Session 27)

—————Brief Intermission Six—————

DO YOU ALWAYS
USE THE PROPER WORD?

The fact is that grammar is getting more liberal every day. Common usage has put a stamp of approval on many expressions which your grandmother would not have dared utter in her most intimate conversation—not if she believed she was in the habit of using good English. *It is me; have you got a cold?; it's a nice day; can I have another piece of cake?; she is a most aggravating child; will everybody please remove their hats*—all these today represent perfectly correct grammar for everyday conversation. Modern grammar research reports that these expressions have become universal in educated speech.

However, such a liberal policy does not mean that all bars are down. Only a person whose speech borders on the illiterate would make such statements as: *can you learn me to swim?; he don't live here no more; we ain't working so good; me and my husband are glad to see you.* There are still certain minimum essentials of good English that the cultivated speaker carefully observes.

Is your grammar as good as the next person's? Here's a quick test by which you can measure your ability.

Check the preferable choice in each sentence, then compare your results with the key at the end. Allowing 4 per cent for each correct answer, consider 92–100 excellent, 76–88 good, 68–72 average.

1. What (a–effect, b–affect) does Farrah Fawcett-Majors have on you?
2. What's the sense (a–in, b–of) looking for a needle in a haystack?
3. She won't (a–leave, b–let) us meet her new boy friend.
4. What (a–kind of, b–kind of a) dress do you want?
5. Her (a–principle, b–principal) objection to neurotics is that they are difficult to live with.
6. The murderer was (a–hanged, b–hung) two hours before the governor's pardon arrived.
7. Many men feel great affection for their (a–mother-in-laws, b–mothers-in-law).
8. For a light cake, use two (a–spoonfuls, b–spoonsful) of baking powder.
9. Everyone likes you but (a–she, b–her).
10. Sally sent a gift for (a–him and me, b–he and I).
11. The criteria you are using (a–is, b–are) not valid.
12. The cost of new houses (a–is, b–are) finally stabilizing.
13. Irene as well as her husband (a–has, b–have) come to see you.
14. (a–Is, b–Are) either of your sisters working?
15. As soon as the editor or her secretary (a–comes, b–come) in, let me know.
16. One or two of her features (a–is, b–are) very attractive.
17. Can you visit Mary and (a–I, b–me) tonight?
18. He is totally (a–uninterested, b–disinterested) in your personal affairs.
19. She (a-laid, b-lay) on the beach while her son splashed at the water's edge.
20. (a–Who, b–Whom) would you rather be if you weren't yourself?
21. You should not (a–have, b–of) spoken so harshly.
22. She is one of those women who (a–believes, b–believe) that husbands should share in doing housework and taking care of the children.
23. Was it you who (a–was, b–were) here yesterday?

24. What we need in this country (a–is, b–are) honest politicians.
25. I'm smarter than Gladys, but she's richer than (a–I, b–me).

KEY: 1–a, 2–a, 3–b, 4–a, 5–b, 6–a, 7–b, 8–a, 9–b, 10–a, 11–b,
12–a, 13–a, 14–a, 15–a, 16–b, 17–b, 18–a, 19–b, 20–a,
21–a, 22–b, 23–b, 24–a, 25–a

---

11

HOW TO INSULT
YOUR ENEMIES

(*Sessions 28–31*)

_____

TEASER PREVIEW

What do you call a person who:

- *insists on complete and blind obedience?*
- *toadies to the rich or influential?*
- *dabbles in the fine arts?*
- *is a loud-mouthed, quarrelsome woman?*
- *has a one-track mind?*
- *sneers at other people's cherished traditions?*
- *does not believe in God?*
- *has imaginary ailments?*

_____

SESSION 28

There are few of us who do not need warm and nourishing relationships to lead a fulfilled life.

Psychology makes clear that loving and being loved are important elements in emotional health, but also points out the necessity for expressing, rather than repressing, our hostilities. (You know how good you feel once you blow off steam? And how much closer you can become attached to someone once you directly and honestly vent your anger, resentment, or irritation instead of bottling it up and seething in fury?)

It is a mark of your own emotional maturity if you can *accept* hostility as well as dish it out. So let us pretend, in order to encourage you to become personally involved in the introductory ten words of this chapter, that each paragraph in the next few pages accurately describes *you*. What label exactly fits your personality?

IDEAS

1. slave driver

You make everyone toe the mark—right down to the last centimeter. You exact blind, unquestioning obedience; demand the strictest conformity to rules, however arbitrary or tyrannical; and will not tolerate the slightest deviation from your orders. You are, in short, the very epitome of the army drill sergeant.

> You are a *martinet*.

2. bootlicker

You toady to rich or influential people, catering to their vanity, flattering their ego. You are the personification of the traditional

283

ward heeler, you out-yes the Hollywood yes men. And on top of all these unpleasant characteristics, you're a complete hypocrite. All your servile attentions and unceasing adulation spring from your own selfish desires to get ahead, not out of any sincere admiration. You cultivate people of power or property so that you can curry favor at the opportune moment.

You are a *sycophant*.

3. dabbler

Often, though not necessarily, a person of independent income, you engage superficially in the pursuit of one of the fine arts—painting, writing, sculpturing, composing, etc. You do this largely for your own amusement and not to achieve any professional competence; nor are you at all interested in monetary rewards. Your artistic efforts are simply a means of passing time pleasantly.

You are a *dilettante*.

4. battle-ax

You are a loud-mouthed, shrewish, turbulent woman; you're quarrelsome and aggressive, possessing none of those gentle and tender qualities stereotypically associated with femininity. You're strong-minded, unyielding, sharp-tongued, and dangerous. You can curse like a stevedore and yell like a fishwife—and often do.

You are a *virago*.

5. superpatriot

Anything you own or belong to is better—simply because you own it or belong to it, although you will be quick to find more justifiable explanations. Your religion, whatever it may be, is far superior to any other; your political party is the only honest one; your neighborhood puts all others in the city in the shade; members of your own sex are more intelligent, more worthy, more emotionally secure, and in every way far better than people of the opposite sex; your car is faster, more fun to drive, and gets better gas mileage than any other, no matter in what price range; and of course your country and its customs leave nothing to be desired, and inhabitants of other nations are in comparison barely civilized. In short, you are exaggeratedly, aggressively, absurdly, and excessively devoted to your own affiliations—and you make no bones about advertising such prejudice.

You are a *chauvinist*.

6. fanatic

You have a one-track mind—and when you're riding a particular hobby, you ride it hard. You have such an excessive, all-inclusive zeal for one thing (and it may be your business, your profession, your husband or wife, your children, your stomach, your money, or whatever) that your obsession is almost absurd. You talk, eat, sleep that one thing—to the point where you bore everyone to distraction.

You are a *monomaniac*.

7. attacker

You are violently against established beliefs, revered traditions, cherished customs—such, you say, stand in the way of reform and progress and are always based on superstition and irrationality. Religion, family, marriage, ethics—you weren't there when these were started and you're not going to conform simply because most unthinking people do.

You are an *iconoclast*.

8. skeptic

There is no God—that's your position and you're not going to budge from it.

You are an *atheist*.

9. self-indulger

You are, as a male, lascivious, libidinous, lustful, lewd, wanton, amoral—but more important, you promiscuously attempt to satisfy (and are often successful in so doing) your sexual desires with any woman within your arm's reach.

You are a *lecher*.

10. worrier

You are always sick, though no doctor can find an organic cause for your ailments. You know you have ulcers, though medical tests show a healthy stomach. You have heart palpitations, but a cardiogram fails to show any abnormality. Your headaches are caused (you're sure of it) by a rapidly growing brain tumor—yet X rays show nothing wrong. These maladies are not imaginary, however; to you they are most real, non-existent as they may be in fact. And as you travel from doctor to doctor futilely seeking confirmation of your imminent death, you become more and more convinced that you're too weak to go on much longer. Organically, of course, there's nothing the matter with you. Perhaps tensions, insecurities, or a need for attention is taking the form of simulated bodily ills.

You are a *hypochondriac*.

USING THE WORDS

Can you pronounce the words?

1.	*martinet*	mahr-tə-NET'
2.	*sycophant*	SIK'-ə-fənt
3.	*dilettante*	dil'-ə-TAN'-tee
4.	*virago*	və-RAY'-gō
5.	*chauvinist*	SHŌ'-və-nist
6.	*monomaniac*	mon'-ə-MAY'-nee-ak
7.	*iconoclast*	ī-KON'-ə-klast'
8.	*atheist*	AY'-thee-ist
9.	*lecher*	LECH'-ər
10.	*hypochondriac*	hī'-pə-KON'-dree-ak

Can you work with the words?

WORDS	KEY IDEAS
1. martinet	a. superficiality
2. sycophant	b. patriotism
3. dilettante	c. godlessness
4. virago	d. single-mindedness
5. chauvinist	e. antitradition
6. monomaniac	f. sex
7. iconoclast	g. illness
8. atheist	h. discipline
9. lecher	i. turbulence
10. hypochondriac	j. flattery

KEY: 1–h, 2–j, 3–a, 4–i, 5–b, 6–d, 7–e, 8–c, 9–f, 10–g

Do you understand the words?

1. Does a *martinet* condone carelessness and neglect of duty?	YES	NO
2. Is a *sycophant* a sincere person?	YES	NO
3. Is a *dilettante* a hard worker?	YES	NO
4. Is a *virago* sweet and gentle?	YES	NO
5. Is a *chauvinist* modest and self-effacing?	YES	NO
6. Does a *monomaniac* have a one-track mind?	YES	NO
7. Does an *iconoclast* scoff at tradition?	YES	NO
8. Does an *atheist* believe in God?	YES	NO
9. Is a *lecher* misogynous?	YES	NO
0. Does a *hypochondriac* have a lively imagination?	YES	NO

EY: 1–no, 2–no, 3–no, 4–no, 5–no, 6–yes, 7–yes, 8–no, 9–no, 10–yes

Can you recall the words?

1. a person whose emotional disorder is reflected in non-organic or imaginary bodily ailments
   1. H_____
2. a strict disciplinarian
   2. M_____
3. a lewd and sexually aggressive male
   3. L_____
4. a toady to people of wealth or power
   4. S_____
5. a disbeliever in God
   5. A_____
6. a dabbler in the arts
   6. D_____
7. a shrewish, loud-mouthed female
   7. V_____
8. a scoffer at tradition
   8. I_____
9. person with a one-track mind
   9. M_____
10. a blatant superpatriot
    10. C_____

KEY: 1–hypochondriac, 2–martinet, 3–lecher, 4–sycophant, 5–atheist, 6–dilettante, 7–virago, 8–iconoclast, 9–monomaniac, 10–chauvinist

---

Can you use the words?

1. She scoffs at beliefs you have always held dear.
   1. _____
2. You know he's hale and hearty —but he constantly complains of his illness.
   2. _____
3. She insists her political affiliations are superior to yours.
   3. _____
4. She insists on her subordinates toeing the mark.
   4. _____

5. He makes sexual advances to
   everyone else's wife—and is
   too often successful.
6. He cultivates friends that can
   do him good—financially.
7. She dabbles with water colors.
8. She insists there is no Deity.
9. She's a shrew, a harridan, a
   scold, and a nag.
10. His only interest in life is his
    fish collection—and he is
    fanatically, almost
    psychotically, devoted to it.

5. _____

6. _____

7. _____

8. _____

9. _____

10. _____

KEY: 1–iconoclast, 2–hypochondriac, 3–chauvinist, 4–martinet,
      5–lecher, 6–sycophant, 7–dilettante, 8–atheist, 9–virago,
      10–monomaniac

(*End of Session 28*)

SESSION 29

ORIGINS AND RELATED WORDS

1. the French drillmaster

Jean Martinet was the Inspector General of Infantry during the
reign of King Louis XIV—and a stricter, more fanatic drillmaster
France had never seen. It was from this time that the French
Army's reputation for discipline dated, and it is from the name of
this Frenchman that we derive our English word *martinet*. The
word is always used in a derogatory sense and generally shows re-

sentment and anger on the part of the user. The secretary who calls his boss a *martinet,* the wife who applies the epithet to her husband, the worker who thus refers to the foreman—these speakers all show their contempt for the excessive, inhuman discipline to which they are asked to submit.

Since *martinet* comes from a man's name (in the Brief Intermission which follows we shall discover that a number of picturesque English words are similarly derived), there are no related forms built on the same root. There is an adjective *martinetish* (mahr-tə-NET'-ish) and another noun form, *martinetism,* but these are used only rarely.

2. a Greek "fig-shower"

Sycophant comes to us from the Greeks. According to Shipley's Dictionary of Word Origins:

> When a fellow wants to get a good mark, he may polish up an apple and place it on teacher's desk; his classmates call such a lad an apple-shiner. Less complimentary localities use the term bootlicker. The Greeks had a name for it: *fig-shower.* Sycophant is from Gr. *sykon,* fig, [and] *phanein,* to show. This was the fellow that informed the officers in charge when (1) the figs in the sacred groves were being taken, or (2) when the Smyrna fig-dealers were dodging the tariff.

Thus, a *sycophant* may appear to be a sort of "stool pigeon," since the latter curries the favor of police officials by "peaching" on his fellow criminals. *Sycophants* may use this means of ingratiating themselves with influential citizens of the community; or they may use flattery, servile attentions, or any other form of insinuating themselves into someone's good graces. A *sycophant* practices *sycophancy* (SIK'-ə-fən-see), and has a *sycophantic* (sik-ə-FAN'-tik) attitude. All three forms of the word are highly uncomplimentary—use them with care.

Material may be so delicate or fine in texture that anything behind it will show through. The Greek prefix *dia-* means *through;* and *phanein,* as you now know, means *to show*—hence such material is called *diaphanous* (dī-AF'-ə-nəs). Do not use the adjective in reference to all material that is transparent (for example, you would not call glass *diaphanous,* even though you can see right through it), but only material that is silky, gauzy, filmy, and, in addition, transparent or practically transparent. The word is often applied to female garments—nightgowns, negligees, etc.

3. just for one's own amusement

Dilettante is from the Italian verb *dilettare,* to delight. The *dilettante* paints, writes, composes, plays a musical instrument, or engages in scientific experiments purely for amusement—not to make money, become famous, or satisfy a deep creative urge (the latter, I presume, being the justifications for the time that professional artists, writers, composers, musicians, poets, and scientists spend at their chosen work). A *dilettantish* (dil-ǝ-TAN'-tish) attitude is superficial, unprofessional; *dilettantism* (dil-ǝ-TAN'-tiz-ǝm) is superficial, part-time dabbling in the type of activity that usually engages the full time and energy of the professional artist or scientist.

Do not confuse the *dilettante,* who has a certain amount of native talent or ability, with the *tyro* (TĪ'-rō), who is the inexperienced beginner in some art, but who may be full of ambition, drive, and energy. To call a person a *tyro* is to imply that he is just starting in some artistic, scientific, or professional field—he's not much good yet because he has not had time to develop his skill, if any. The *dilettante* usually has some skill but isn't doing much with it. On the other hand, anyone who has developed consummate skill in an artistic field, generally allied to music, is called a *virtuoso* (vur'-chōō-Ō'-sō)—like Heifetz or Menuhin on the violin, Horowitz or Rubinstein on the piano. Pluralize *virtuoso* in the normal way—*virtuosos;* or if you wish to sound more sophisticated, give it the continental form—*virtuosi* (vur'-chōō-Ō'-see). Similarly, the plural of *dilettante* is either *dilettantes* or *dilettanti* (dil-ǝ-TAN'-tee).

The *i* ending for a plural is the Italian form and is common in musical circles. For example, *libretto,* the story (or book) of an opera, may be pluralized to *libretti; concerto,* a form of musical composition, is pluralized *concerti.* However, the Anglicized *librettos* and *concertos* are perfectly correct also. *Libretto* is pronounced lǝ-BRET'-ō; *libretti* is lǝ-BRET'-ee; *concerto* is kǝn-

CHUR'-tō; and *concerti* is kən-CHUR'-tee. Suit your plural form, I would suggest, to the sophistication of your audience.

4. "masculine" women

Virago comes, oddly enough, from the Latin word for man, *vir.* Perhaps the derivation is not so odd after all; a *virago,* far from being stereotypically feminine (i.e., timid, delicate, low-spoken, etc.), is stereotypically masculine in personality—coarse, aggressive, loud-mouthed. *Termagant* (TUR'-mə-gənt) and *harridan* (HAIR'-ə-dən) are words with essentially the same uncomplimentary meaning as *virago.* To call a brawling woman a *virago,* a *termagant,* and a *harridan* is admittedly repetitious, but is successful in relieving one's feelings.

5. the old man

Nicolas Chauvin, soldier of the French Empire, so vociferously and unceasingly aired his veneration of Napoleon Bonaparte that he became the laughingstock of all Europe. Thereafter, an exaggerated and blatant patriot was known as a *chauvinist*—and still is today. *Chauvinism* (SHŌ'-və-niz-əm), by natural extension, applies to blatant veneration of, or boastfulness about, any other affiliation besides one's country.

To be *patriotic* is to be normally proud of, and devoted to, one's country—to be *chauvinistic* (shō'-və-NIS'-tik) is to exaggerate such pride and devotion to an obnoxious degree.

We might digress here to investigate an etymological side road down which the word *patriotic* beckons. *Patriotic* is built on the Latin word *pater, patris,* father—one's country is, in a sense, one's fatherland.

Let us see what other interesting words are built on this same root.

1. *patrimony* (PAT'-rə-mō-nee)—an inheritance from one's father. The *-mony* comes from the same root that gives us *money,* namely *Juno Moneta,* the Roman goddess who guarded the temples of finance. The adjective is *patrimonial* (pat'-rə-MŌ'-nee-əl).

2. *patronymic* (pat'-rə-NIM'-ik)—a name formed on the father's name, like *Johnson* (son of John), *Martinson, Aaronson,* etc. The word combines *pater, patris* with Greek *onyma,* name. *Onyma* plus the Greek prefix *syn-,* with or together, forms *synonym* (SIN'-ə-nim), a word of the same name (or meaning), etymologically "a together name." *Onyma* plus the prefix *anti-* against, forms *antonym* (AN'-tə-nim), a word of opposite meaning, etymologically "an against name." *Onyma* plus Greek *homos,* the same, forms *homonym* (HOM'-ə-nim), a word that sounds like another but has a different meaning and spelling, like *bare—bear, way—weigh, to—too—two,* etc., etymologically "a same name." A *homonym* is more accurately called a *homophone* (HOM'-ə-fōn'), a combination of *homos,* the same, and *phone,* sound. The adjective form of *synonym* is *synonymous* (sə-NON'-ə-məs). Can you write, and pronounce, the adjective derived from:

antonym?   _____
homonym?   _____
homophone? _____

3. *paternity* (pə-TUR'-nə-tee)—fatherhood, as to question someone's *paternity,* to file a *paternity* suit in order to collect child support from the assumed, accused, or self-acknowledged father. The adjective is *paternal* (pə-TUR'-nəl), fatherly. *Paternalism* (pə-TUR'-nə-liz-əm) is the philosophy or system of governing a country, or of managing a business or institution, so that the citizens, employees, or staff are treated in a manner suggesting a father-children relationship. (Such a system sounds, and often is, benign and protective, but plays havoc with the initiative, independence, and creativity of those in subordinate roles.) The adjective is *paternalistic* (pə-turn'-ə-LIS'-tik).

4. *patriarch* (PAY'-tree-ark')—a venerable, fatherlike old man; an old man in a ruling, fatherlike position. Here *pater, patris* is combined with the Greek root *archein,* to rule. The adjective is *patriarchal* (pay'-tree-AHR'-kəl), the system is a *patriarchy* (PAY'-tree-ahr'-kee).

5. *patricide* (PAT'-rə-sīd')—the killing of one's father. *Pater, patris* combines with *-cide,* a suffix derived from the Latin verb *caedo,* to kill. The adjective is *patricidal* (pat-rə-SĪ'-dəl).

This list does not exhaust the number of words built on *pater*, father, but is sufficient to give you an idea of how closely related many English words are. In your reading you will come across other words containing the letters *pater* or *patr*—you will be able to figure them out once you realize that the base is the word *father*. You might, if you feel ambitious, puzzle out the relationship to the "father idea" in the following words, checking with a dictionary to see how good your linguistic intuition is:

1. patrician
2. patron
3. patronize
4. patronizing (*adj.*)
5. paterfamilias
6. padre

6. the old lady

Pater, patris is *father. Mater, matris* is *mother.*
For example:

1. *matriarch* (MAY'-tree-ahrk')—the mother-ruler; the "mother person" that controls a large household, tribe, or country. This word, like *patriarch*, is built on the root *archein*, to rule. During the reign of Queen Elizabeth or Queen Victoria, England was a *matriarchy* (MAY'-tree-ahr'-kee). Can you figure out the adjective form? _____

2. *maternity* (mə-TUR'-nə-tee)—motherhood

3. *maternal* (mə-TURN'-əl)—motherly

4. *matron* (MAY'-trən)—an older woman, one sufficiently mature to be a mother. The adjective *matronly* (MAY'-trən-lee) conjures up for many people a picture of a woman no longer in the glow of youth and possibly with a bit of added weight in the wrong places, so this word should be used with caution; it may be hazardous to your health if the lady you are so describing is of a tempestous nature, or is a *virago*.

5. *alma mater* (AL'-mə MAY'-tər or AHL'-mə MAH'-tər)—etymologically, "soul mother"; actually, the school or college from which one has graduated, and which in a sense is one's intellectual mother.

6. *matrimony* (MAT'-rə-mō'-nee)—marriage. Though this word is similar to *patrimony* in spelling, it does not refer to *money*, as *patrimony* does; unless, that is, you are cynical enough to believe that people marry for money. As the language was growing, marriage and children went hand in hand—it is therefore not surprising that the word for *marriage* should be built on the Latin root for *mother*. Of course, times have changed, but the sexist nature of the English language has not. The noun suffix *-mony* indicates state, condition, or result, as in *sanctimony, parsimony,* etc. The adjective is *matrimonial* (mat'-rə-MŌ'-nee-əl).

7. *matricide* (MAT'-rə-sīd')—the killing of one's mother. The adjective? _____.

7. murder most foul . . .

Murder unfortunately is an integral part of human life, so there is a word for almost every kind of killing you can think of. Let's look at some of them.

1. *suicide* (SŌŌ'-ə-sīd')—killing oneself (intentionally); *-cide* plus *sui*, of oneself. This is both the act and the person who has been completely successful in performing the act (*partially* doesn't count); also, in colloquial usage, *suicide* is a verb. The adjective?

_____.

2. *fratricide* (FRAT'-rə-sīd')—the killing of one's brother; *-cide* plus *frater, fratris,* brother. The adjective? _____

3. *sororicide* (sə-RAWR'-ə-sīd')—the killing of one's sister; *-cide* plus *soror*, sister. The adjective? _____

4. *homicide* (HOM'-ə-sīd')—the killing of a human being; *-cide* plus *homo*, person. In law, *homicide* is the general term for any slaying. If intent and premeditation can be proved, the act is *murder* and punishable as such. If no such intent is present, the act is called *manslaughter* and receives a lighter punishment. Thus, if your mate/lover/spouse makes your life unbearable and you slip some arsenic into his/her coffee one bright morning, you are committing murder—that is, if he/she succumbs. On the other hand, if you run your victim down—quite accidentally—with

your car, bicycle, or wheelchair, with no intent to kill, you will be accused of *manslaughter*—that is, if death results and if you can prove you didn't really mean it. It's all rather delicate, however, and you might do best to put thoughts of justifiable *homicide* out of your mind. The adjective? _____

5. *regicide* (REJ′-ə-sīd′)—the killing of one's king, president, or other governing official. Booth committed *regicide* when he assassinated Abraham Lincoln. Adjective? _____. Derivation: Latin *rex, regis,* king, plus *-cide.*

6. *uxoricide* (uk-SAWR′-ə-sīd′)—the killing of one's wife. Adjective? _____. Derivation: Latin *uxor,* wife, plus *-cide.*

7. *mariticide* (mə-RIT′-ə-sīd′)—the killing of one's husband. Adjective? _____. Derivation: Latin *maritus,* husband, plus *-cide.*

8. *infanticide* (in-FAN′-tə-sīd′)—the killing of a newborn child. Adjective? _____ Derivation: Latin *infans, infantis,* baby, plus *-cide.*

9. *genocide* (JEN′-ə-sīd′)—the killing of a whole race or nation. This is a comparatively new word, coined in 1944 by a UN official named Raphael Lemkin, to refer to the mass murder of the Jews, Poles, etc. ordered by Hitler. Adjective? _____ _____. Derivation: Greek *genos,* race, kind, plus *-cide.*

10. *parricide* (PAIR′-ə-sīd′)—the killing of either or both parents. Adjective? _____.

Lizzie Borden was accused of, and tried for, *parricide* in the 1890s, but was not convicted. A bit of doggerel that was popular at the time, and, so I have been told, little girls jumped rope to, went somewhat as follows:

> Lizzie Borden took an ax
> And gave her mother forty whacks—
> And when she saw what she had done,
> She gave her father forty-one.

REVIEW OF ETYMOLOGY

PREFIX, ROOT, SUFFIX	MEANING	ENGLISH WORD
1. *sykon*	fig	_____
2. *phanein*	to show	_____
3. *dia-*	through	_____
4. *vir*	man (male)	_____
5. *pater, patris*	father	_____
6. *syn-*	with, together	_____
7. *onyma*	name	_____
8. *anti*	against	_____
9. *homos*	the same	_____
10. *phone*	sound	_____
11. *-ity*	noun suffix	_____
12. *-ism*	noun suffix	_____
13. *-al*	adjective suffix	_____
14. *-ic*	adjective suffix	_____
15. *archein*	to rule	_____
16. *-cide*	killing	_____
17. *mater, matris*	mother	_____
18. *alma*	soul	_____
19. *-mony*	noun suffix	_____
20. *sui*	of oneself	_____
21. *frater, fratris*	brother	_____
22. *soror*	sister	_____
23. *homo*	person, human	_____
24. *rex, regis*	king	_____
25. *uxor*	wife	_____
26. *maritus*	husband	_____
27. *infans, infantis*	baby	_____
28. *genos*	race, kind	_____

USING THE WORDS

Can you pronounce the words? (I)

1.	*martinetish*	mahr-tə-NET'-ish
2.	*sycophancy*	SIK'-ə-fən-see
3.	*sycophantic*	sik'-ə-FAN'-tik
4.	*diaphanous*	dī-AF'-ə-nəs
5.	*dilettanti*	dil'-ə-TAN'-tee
6.	*dilettantism*	dil-ə-TAN'-tiz-əm
7.	*dilettantish*	dil-ə-TAN'-tish
8.	*tyro*	TĪ'-rō
9.	*virtuoso*	vur'-chōō-Ō'-sō
10.	*virtuosi*	vur'-chōō-Ō'-see
11.	*termagant*	TUR'-mə-gənt
12.	*harridan*	HAIR'-ə-dən

Can you pronounce the words? (II)

1.	*chauvinism*	SHŌ'-və-niz-əm
2.	*chauvinistic*	shō-və-NIS'-tik
3.	*patrimony*	PAT'-rə-mō-nee
4.	*patronymic*	pat'-rə-NIM'-ik
5.	*synonym*	SIN'-ə-nim
6.	*synonymous*	sə-NON'-ə-məs
7.	*antonym*	AN'-tə-nim
8.	*antonymous*	an-TON'-ə-məs
9.	*homonym*	HOM'-ə-nim
10.	*homonymous*	hə-MON'-ə-məs
11.	*homophone*	HOM'-ə-fōn
12.	*homophonous*	hə-MOF'-ə-nəs

Can you pronounce the words? (III)

1.	*paternity*	pə-TUR'-nə-tee
2.	*paternal*	pə-TUR'-nəl

3. *paternalism*   pə-TUR'-nə-liz-əm
4. *paternalistic*   pə-turn'-ə-LIS'-tik
5. *patriarch*   PAY'-tree-ahrk'
6. *patriarchal*   pay'-tree-AHR'-kəl
7. *patriarchy*   PAY'-tree-ahr'-kee
8. *patricide*   PAT'-rə-sīd'
9. *patricidal*   pat'-rə-SĪ'-dəl

Can you pronounce the words? (IV)

1. *matriarch*   MAY'-tree-ahrk'
2. *matriarchy*   MAY'-tree-ahr'-kee
3. *matriarchal*   may'-tree-AHR'-kəl
4. *maternity*   mə-TUR'-nə-tee
5. *maternal*   mə-TURN'-əl
6. *matron*   MAY'-trən
7. *matronly*   MAY'-trən-lee
8. *alma mater*   AL'-mə MAY'-tər
                      or AHL'-mə MAH'-tər
9. *matrimony*   MAT'-rə-mō-nee
10. *matrimonial*   mat-rə-MŌ'-nee-əl
11. *matricide*   MAT'-rə-sīd'
12. *matricidal*   mat-rə-SĪ'-dəl

Can you pronounce the words? (V)

1. *suicide*   SOO'-ə-sīd'
2. *suicidal*   soo-ə-SĪ'-dəl
3. *fratricide*   FRAT'-rə-sīd'
4. *fratricidal*   frat-rə-SĪ'-dəl
5. *sororicide*   sə-RAWR'-ə-sīd'
6. *sororicidal*   sə-rawr'-ə-SĪ'-dəl
7. *homicide*   HOM'-ə-sīd'
8. *homicidal*   hom'-ə-SĪ'-dəl
9. *regicide*   REJ'-ə-sīd'
10. *regicidal*   rej'-ə-SĪ'-dəl

299

Can you pronounce the words? (VI)

1.	*uxoricide*	uk-SAWR'-ə-sīd'
2.	*uxoricidal*	uk-sawr'-ə-SĪ'-dəl
3.	*mariticide*	mə-RIT'-ə-sīd'
4.	*mariticidal*	mə-rit'-ə-SĪ'-dəl
5.	*infanticide*	in-FAN'-tə-sīd'
6.	*infanticidal*	in-fan'-tə-SĪ'-dəl
7.	*genocide*	JEN'-ə-sīd'
8.	*genocidal*	jen'-ə-SĪ'-dəl
9.	*parricide*	PAIR'-ə-sīd'
10.	*parricidal*	pair'-ə-SĪ'-dəl

Can you work with the words? (I)

1.	sycophancy	a.	murder of one's father
2.	dilettantism	b.	excessive patriotism
3.	chauvinism	c.	murder of one's ruler
4.	patrimony	d.	inheritance from one's father
5.	patricide	e.	murder of one's sister
6.	matricide	f.	murder of one's brother
7.	fratricide	g.	murder of a person
8.	sororicide	h.	toadying
9.	homicide	i.	murder of one's mother
10.	regicide	j.	dabbling

KEY: 1–h, 2–j, 3–b, 4–d, 5–a, 6–i, 7–f, 8–e, 9–g, 10–c

Can you work with the words? (II)

1.	uxoricide	a.	marriage
2.	infanticide	b.	killing of one's child
3.	genocide	c.	fatherhood
4.	matrimony	d.	mother-ruler
5.	matriarch	e.	killing of one's wife
6.	maternity	f.	older woman
7.	matron	g.	one's school or college

300

8. alma mater
9. paternity
10. patriarch

h. motherhood
i. old man in governing position
j. killing of whole groups of people

Can you work with the words? (III)

1. parricide

a. catering to people of power or position

2. patronymic
3. chauvinistic
4. sycophantic
5. diaphanous
6. dilettanti
7. tyro
8. virtuoso
9. termagant

b. name from father
c. dabblers
d. an accomplished musician
e. filmy, gauzy
f. blatantly overpatriotic
g. loud-mouthed woman
h. a beginner
i. killing of either or both parents

Can you work with the words? (IV)

1. synonyms

a. system in which those in power have a father-child relationship with subordinates

2. antonyms
3. homonyms
4. paternalism
5. suicide

b. like a strict disciplinarian
c. self-killing
d. fatherly
e. referring to or like, those who "play at" an art

6. mariticide

f. words that sound alike but are spelled differently and have unrelated meanings

7. martinetish	g. words of similar meaning
8. dilettantish	h. referring to, or like, an older woman
9. paternal	i. husband-killing
10. matronly	j. words of opposite meaning

KEY: 1–g, 2–j, 3–f, 4–a, 5–c, 6–i, 7–b, 8–e, 9–d, 10–h

Can you work with the words? (V)

1. harridan	a. motherly
2. homophones	b. similar in meaning
3. maternal	c. referring to a system in which older men are in power
4. matrimonial	d. the same in sound but not in spelling or meaning
5. synonymous	e. likely to kill; referring to the killing of a person
6. antonymous	f. referring to a system in which older women are in power
7. homonymous	g. virago
8. patriarchal	h. opposite in meaning
9. matriarchal	i. referring to marriage
10. homicidal	j. words that sound the same

KEY: 1–g, 2–j, 3–a, 4–i, 5–b, 6–h, 7–d, 8–c, 9–f, 10–e

Do you understand the words?

1. Does a *sycophantic* attitude show sincere admiration?	YES	NO
2. Is a *diaphanous* gown revealing?	YES	NO
3. Does *dilettantism* show firmness and tenacity?	YES	NO
4. Is a *tyro* particularly skillful?	YES	NO
5. Is a violin *virtuoso* an accomplished musician?	YES	NO

6. Is a *termagant* a pleasant person?	YES	NO
7. Does *chauvinism* show modesty?	YES	NO
8. Does a substantial *patrimony* obviate financial insecurity?	YES	NO
9. If you know a person's *patronymic* can you deduce his father's name?	YES	NO
10. Is a *patriarch* a male?	YES	NO
11. Does a *matriarch* have a good deal of power?	YES	NO
12. Does *fratricide* mean murder of one's sister?	YES	NO
13. Did the assassin of Abraham Lincoln commit *regicide*?	YES	NO
14. Do dictators and tyrants sometimes commit *genocide*?	YES	NO
15. Are an *uxoricidal* husband and his *mariticidal* wife likely to have a peaceful and affectionate marriage?	YES	NO

KEY: 1–no, 2–yes, 3–no, 4–no, 5–yes, 6–no, 7–no, 8–yes, 9–yes, 10–yes, 11–yes, 12–no, 13–yes, 14–yes, 15–no

---

Can you recall the words? (I)

1. father-killing (*noun*)	1. P	___
2. wife-killing (*noun*)	2. U	___
3. mature woman	3. M	___
4. toadying to people of influence (*adj.*)	4. S	___
5. skilled musician	5. V	___
6. exaggerated patriotism	6. C	___
7. turbulent female (three words)	7. T	___
	or H	___
	or V	___
8. name derived from father's name	8. P	___
9. powerful father figure in a ruling position	9. P	___

10. powerful mother figure in a ruling position
11. motherly
12. motherhood
13. marriage
14. one's school or college
15. attitude of catering to wealth or prestige (*noun*)
16. killing of a race or nation
17. dabbling in the fine arts (*noun*)
18. a beginner in a field
19. plural of *virtuoso* (Italian form)
20. having an attitude of excessive patriotism (*adj.*)
21. inheritance from father
22. sheer, transparent
23. mother-killing (*noun*)
24. brother-killing (*noun*)
25. sister-killing (*noun*)
26. killing of a human being
27. killing of one's ruler
28. killing of a baby
29. killing of one's husband
30. killing of either parent or of both parents

10. M_____
11. M_____
12. M_____
13. M_____
14. A_____
15. S_____
16. G_____
17. D_____
18. T_____
19. V_____
20. C_____
21. P_____
22. D_____
23. M_____
24. F_____
25. S_____
26. H_____
27. R_____
28. I_____
29. M_____
30. P_____

KEY: 1–patricide, 2–uxoricide, 3–matron, 4–sycophantic, 5–virtuoso, 6–chauvinism, 7–termagant, harridan, virago, 8–patronymic, 9–patriarch, 10–matriarch, 11–maternal, 12–maternity, 13–matrimony, 14–alma mater, 15–sycophancy, 16–genocide, 17–dilettantism, 18–tyro, 19–virtuosi, 20–chauvinistic, 21–patrimony, 22–diaphanous, 23–matricide, 24–fratricide, 25–sororicide, 26–homicide, 27–regicide, 28–infanticide, 29–mariticide, 30–parricide

---

Can you recall the words? (II)

1. words of similar meaning	1. S_____s
2. words of opposite meaning	2. A_____s
3. words of the same sound	3. H_____s
	or H_____s
4. fatherly	4. P_____
5. protective and fatherly toward one's subordinates (*adj.*)	5. P_____
6. older woman	6. M_____
7. self-destructive	7. S_____
8. meaning the same (*adj.*)	8. S_____
9. having opposite meanings (*adj.*)	9. A_____
10. sounding the same but spelled differently (*adj.*)	10. H_____
	or H_____

KEY: 1–synonyms, 2–antonyms, 3–homonyms *or* homophones, 4–paternal, 5–paternalistic, 6–matron, 7–suicidal, 8–synonymous, 9–antonymous, 10–homonymous *or* homophonous

---

(*End of Session 29*)

SESSION 30

ORIGINS AND RELATED WORDS

1. brothers and sisters, wives and husbands

Frater, brother; *soror,* sister; *uxor,* wife; and *maritus,* husband —these roots are the source of a number of additional English words:

1. to *fraternize* (FRAT'-ər-nīz')—etymologically, to have a brotherly relationship (with). This verb may be used to indicate social intercourse between people, irrespective of sex, as in, "Members of the faculty often *fraternized* after school hours."

Additionally, and perhaps more commonly, there may be the implication of having a social relationship with one's subordinates in an organization, or even with one's so-called inferiors, as in, "The president of the college was reluctant to *fraternize* with faculty members, preferring to keep all her contacts with them on an exclusively professional basis"; or as in, "The artist enjoyed *fraternizing* with thieves, drug addicts, prostitutes, and pimps, partly out of social perversity, partly to find interesting faces to put in his paintings."

The verb also gained a new meaning during and after World War II, when soldiers of occupying armies had sexual relations with the women of conquered countries, as in, "Military personnel were strictly forbidden to *fraternize* with the enemy." (How euphemistic can you get?)

Can you write the noun form of *fraternize?*_____
_____

2. *fraternal* (frə-TUR'-nəl)—brotherly. The word also designates *non-identical* (twins).

3. *fraternity* (frə-TUR'-nə-tee)—a men's organization in a high school or college, often labeled with Greek letters (the Gamma Delta Epsilon *Fraternity*); or any group of people of similar interests or profession (the medical *fraternity*, the financial *fraternity*).

4. *sorority* (sə-RAWR'-ə-tee)—a women's organization in high school or college, again usually Greek-lettered; or any women's social club.

5. *uxorious* (uk-SAWR'-ee-əs)—an adjective describing a man who excessively, even absurdly, caters to, dotes on, worships, and submits to the most outlandish or outrageous demands of, his wife. This word is *not* synonymous with *henpecked*, as the henpecked husband is dominated by his wife, perhaps because of his own fear or weakness, while the *uxorious* husband is dominated only by his neurosis, and quite likely the wife finds his *uxoriousness* (uk-SAWR'-ee-əs-nəs) comical or a pain in the neck. (There can, indeed, be too much of a good thing!)

6. *uxorial*—pertaining to, characteristic of, or befitting, a wife, as *uxorial* duties, privileges, attitudes, etc.

7. *marital* (MAIR'-ə-təl)—etymologically, pertaining or referring to, or characteristic of, a husband; but the meaning has changed to include the marriage relationship of both husband *and* wife (don't ever let anyone tell you that our language is not sexist!), as *marital* duties, obligations, privileges, arguments, etc. Hence *extramarital* is literally *outside the marriage,* as in *extramarital* affairs (hanky-panky with someone other than one's spouse). And *premarital* (Latin prefix *pre-,* before) describes events that occur before a planned marriage, as *premarital* sex, a *premarital* agreement as to the division of property, etc.

2. of cabbages and kings (without the cabbage)

Rex, regis is Latin for *king. Tyrannosaurus rex* was the king (i.e., the largest) of the dinosaurs (etymologically, "king of the tyrant lizards"). Dogs are often named *Rex* to fool them into thinking they are kings rather than slaves. And *regal* (REE'-gəl) is royal, or fit for a king, hence magnificent, stately, imperious, splendid, etc., as in *regal* bearing or manner, a *regal* mansion, a *regal* reception, etc. The noun is *regality* (rə-GAL'-ə-tee).

Regalia (rə-GAYL'-yə), a plural noun, designated the emblems or insignia or dress of a king, and now refers to any impressively formal clothes; or, more commonly, to the decorations, insignia, or uniform of a rank, position, office, social club, etc. "The Shriners were dressed in full *regalia,*" "The five-star general appeared in full *regalia,*" etc.

3. "madness" of all sorts

The *monomaniac* develops an abnormal obsession in respect to *one* particular thing (Greek *monos,* one), but is otherwise normal. The obsession itself, or the obsessiveness, is *monomania* (mon'-ə-MAY'-nee-ə), the adjective is *monomaniacal* (mon'-ə-mə-NĪ'-ə-kəl). *Monomaniacal,* like the adjective forms of various other manias, is tricky to pronounce—practice carefully to make sure you can say it correctly without stuttering.

307

Psychology recognizes other abnormal states, all designating obsessions, and built on Greek *mania,* madness.

1. *dipsomania* (dip′-sə-MAY′-nee-ə)—morbid compulsion to keep on absorbing alcoholic beverages (Greek *dipsa,* thirst). The *dipsomaniac* has been defined as the person for whom one drink is too many, a thousand not enough. Recent investigations suggest that *dipsomania,* or alcoholism, may not necessarily be caused by anxieties or frustrations, but possibly by a metabolic or physiological disorder.

Adjective: *dipsomaniacal* (dip′-sə-mə-NĪ′-ə-kəl).

2. *kleptomania* (klep′-tə-MAY′-nee-ə)—morbid compulsion to steal, not from any economic motive, but simply because the urge to take another's possessions is irresistible. The *kleptomaniac* (Greek *klepte,* thief) may be wealthy, and yet be an obsessive shoplifter. The *kleptomaniac,* for reasons that psychologists are still arguing about, is more often a female than a male, and may pinch her best friend's valueless trinket, or a cheap ashtray or salt shaker from a restaurant, not because she wants, let alone needs, the article, but because she apparently can't help herself; she gets carried away. (When she arrives home, she may toss it in a drawer with other loot, and never look at it again.)

Can you write (and *correctly* pronounce) the adjective?

---

3. *pyromania* (pī′-rə-MAY′-nee-ə)—morbid compulsion to set fires. *Pyromania* should not be confused with *incendiarism* (in-SEN′-dee-ə-riz-əm), which is the malicious and deliberate burning of another's property, and is *not* a compulsive need to see the flames and enjoy the thrill of the heat and the smoke. Some *pyromaniacs* join volunteer fire companies, often heroically putting out the very blazes they themselves have set. An *incendiary* (in-SEN′-dee-air-ee) is antisocial, and usually sets fires for revenge. Either of these two dangerous characters is called, colloquially, a "firebug."

In law, setting fire to another's, or to one's own, property for the purpose of economic gain (such as the collection of the proceeds of an insurance policy) is called *arson* (AHR′-sən) and is a felony. The *pyromaniac* sets fire for the thrill; the *incendiary* for revenge; the *arsonist* (AHR′-sə-nist) for money.

Pyromania is built on Greek *pyros,* fire; *incendiarism* on Latin *incendo, incensus,* to set fire; *arson* on Latin *ardo, arsus,* to burn.

Can you write, and pronounce, the adjective form of *pyromaniac?* _____.

4. *megalomania* (meg′-ə-lə-MAY′-nee-ə)—morbid delusions of grandeur, power, importance, godliness, etc. Jokes accusing the heads of governments of *megalomania* are common. Here's an old chestnut from the forties:

> Churchill, Roosevelt, and Stalin were talking about their dreams.
> Churchill: I dreamed last night that God had made me *Prime Minister* of the whole world.
> Roosevelt: I dreamed that God had made me *President* of the whole world.
> Stalin: How could you gentlemen have such dreams? *I* didn't dream of offering you those positions!

Hitler, Napoleon, and Alexander the Great have been called *megalomaniacs*—all three certainly had delusions about their invincibility.

Can you write (and pronounce correctly!) the adjective derived from *megalomaniac?* _____.

Megalomania is built on Greek *megas,* great, big, large, plus *mania.*

[Can you think of the word for what someone speaks through to make the *sound* (phone) of his voice *greater?* _____ _____.

5. *nymphomania* (nim′-fə-MAY′-nee-ə)—morbid, incessant, uncontrollable, and intense desire, on the part of a female, for sexual intercourse (from Greek *nymphe,* bride, plus *mania*).

The person?   _____
The adjective?   _____

6. *satyromania* (sə-teer′-ə-MAY′-nee-ə)—the same morbid, incessant, etc. desire on the part of a male (from Greek *satyros,* satyr, plus *mania*).

The person?   _____
The adjective?   _____

309

A *satyr* (SAY'-tər) was a mythological Greek god, notorious for lechery. He had horns, pointed ears, and the legs of a goat; the rest of him was in human form. *Satyromania* is also called *satyriasis* (sat'-ə-RĪ'-ə-sis).

4. and now phobias

So much for *maniacs*. There is another side to the coin. Just as personality disorders can cause morbid *attraction* toward certain things or acts (stealing, fire, power, sex, etc.), so also other emotional ills can cause violent or morbid *repulsions* to certain conditions, things, or situations. There are people who have irrational and deep-seated dread of cats, dogs, fire, the number thirteen, snakes, thunder or lightning, various colors, and so on almost without end:* Such morbid dread or fear is called, in the language of psychology, a *phobia*, and we might pause to investigate the three most common ones. These are:

1. *claustrophobia* (klaw'-strə-FŌ'-bee-ə)—morbid dread of being physically hemmed in, of enclosed spaces, of crowds, etc. From Latin *claustrum*, enclosed place, plus Greek *phobia*, morbid fear. The person: *claustrophobe* (KLAW'-strə-fōb'). Adjective: *claustrophobic* (klaw'-strə-FŌ'-bik).

2. *agoraphobia* (ag'-ə-rə-FŌ'-bee-ə)—morbid dread of open space, the reverse of *claustrophobia*. People suffering from *agoraphobia* prefer to stay shut in their homes as much as possible, and become panic-stricken in such places as open fields, large public buildings, airport terminals, etc. From Greek *agora*, market place, plus *phobia*.

The person? _____
The adjective? _____

3. *acrophobia* (ak'-rə-FŌ'-bee-ə)—morbid dread of high places. The victims of this fear will not climb ladders or trees, or stand on tops of furniture. They refuse to go onto the roof of a building or look out the window of one of the higher floors. From Greek *akros*, highest, plus *phobia*.

The person? _____
The adjective? _____

* For some of these esoteric phobias, see Appendix.

REVIEW OF ETYMOLOGY

PREFIX, ROOT, SUFFIX	MEANING	ENGLISH WORD
1. *frater, fratris*	brother	_____
2. *soror*	sister	_____
3. *uxor*	wife	_____
4. *maritus*	husband	_____
5. *rex, regis*	king	_____
6. *mania*	madness	_____
7. *monos*	one	_____
8. *-ac*	noun suffix, "one who"	_____
9. *-al*	adjective suffix	_____
10. *dipsa*	thirst	_____
11. *klepte*	thief	_____
12. *pyros*	fire	_____
13. *incendo, incensus*	to set fire	_____
14. *ardo, arsus*	to burn	_____
15. *mega*	great, large, big	_____
16. *phone*	sound	_____
17. *satyros*	satyr	_____
18. *nymphe*	bride	_____
19. *claustrum*	enclosed place	_____
20. *agora*	market place	_____
21. *akros*	highest	_____
22. *-ic*	adjective suffix	_____
23. *phobia*	morbid dread	_____
24. *pre-*	before	_____
25. *extra-*	outside	_____

USING THE WORDS

Can you pronounce the words? (I)

1. *fraternize*   FRAT'-ər-nīz'

2. *fraternization*   frat'-ər-nə-ZAY'-shən
3. *fraternal*   frə-TUR'-nəl
4. *fraternity*   frə-TUR'-nə-tee
5. *sorority*   sə-RAWR'-ə-tee
6. *uxorious*   uk-SAWR'-ee-əs
7. *uxorial*   uk-SAWR'-ee-əl
8. *marital*   MAIR'-ə-təl
9. *extramarital*   ek'-strə-MAIR'-ə-təl
10. *premarital*   pree-MAIR'-ə-təl
11. *regal*   REE'-gəl
12. *regality*   rə-GAL'-ə-tee
13. *regalia*   rə-GAYL'-yə

Can you work with the words? (I)

1. fraternize
2. fraternal
3. sorority
4. uxorious
5. uxorial
6. marital
7. extramarital
8. premarital
9. regal
10. regalia

a. pertaining to, characteristic of, or befitting, a wife
b. outside the marriage
c. kingly, royal; splendid, stately, magnificent, etc.
d. referring to marriage
e. before marriage
f. socialize
g. excessively indulgent to, or doting on, one's wife
h. brotherly
i. badges, insignia, dress, etc. of rank or office
j. sisterhood

KEY: 1–f, 2–h, 3–j, 4–g, 5–a, 6–d, 7–b, 8–e, 9–c, 10–i

Can you pronounce the words? (II)

1. *monomania*   mon'-ə-MAY'-nee-ə
2. *monomaniac*   mon'-ə-MAY'-nee-ak

3. *monomaniacal*	mon'-ə-mə-NĬ'-ə-kəl
4. *dipsomania*	dip'-sə-MAY'-nee-ə
5. *dipsomaniac*	dip'-sə-MAY'-nee-ak
6. *dipsomaniacal*	dip'-sə-mə-NĬ'-ə-kəl
7. *kleptomania*	klep'-tə-MAY'-nee-ə
8. *kleptomaniac*	klep'-tə-MAY'-nee-ak
9. *kleptomaniacal*	klep'-tə-mə-NĬ'-ə-kəl
10. *pyromania*	pĭ'-rə-MAY'-nee-ə
11. *pyromaniac*	pĭ'-rə-MAY'-nee-ak
12. *pyromaniacal*	pĭ'-rə-mə-NĬ'-ə-kəl

Can you work with the words? (II)

1. monomania		a.	obsession for alcohol
2. dipsomania		b.	obsession for setting fires
3. kleptomania		c.	obsession in one area
4. pyromania		d.	obsession for thievery

KEY: 1–c, 2–a, 3–d, 4–b

Can you pronounce the words? (III)

1. *incendiarism*	in-SEN'-dee-ə-riz-əm
2. *incendiary*	in-SEN'-dee-air-ee
3. *arson*	AHR'-sən
4. *arsonist*	AHR'-sə-nist
5. *megalomania*	meg'-ə-lə-MAY'-nee-ə
6. *megalomaniac*	meg'-ə-lə-MAY'-nee-ak
7. *megalomaniacal*	meg'-ə-lə-mə-NĬ'-ə-kəl
8. *nymphomania*	nim'-fə-MAY'-nee-ə
9. *nymphomaniac*	nim'-fə-MAY'-nee-ak
10. *nymphomaniacal*	nim'-fə-mə-NĬ'-ə-kəl
11. *satyromania*	sə-teer'-ə-MAY'-nee-ə
12. *satyromaniacal*	sə-teer'-ə-mə-NĬ'-ə-kəl
13. *satyriasis*	sat'-ə-RĬ'-ə-sis

313

Can you pronounce the words? (IV)

1. *claustrophobia*   klaw′-strə-FŌ′-bee-ə
2. *claustrophobe*   KLAW′-strə-fōb′
3. *claustrophobic*   klaw′-strə-FŌ′-bik
4. *agoraphobia*   ag′-ə-rə-FŌ′-bee-ə
5. *agoraphobe*   AG′-ə-rə-fōb′
6. *agoraphobic*   ag′-ə-rə-FŌ′-bik
7. *acrophobia*   ak′-rə-FŌ′-bee-ə
8. *acrophobe*   AK′-rə-fōb′
9. *acrophobic*   ak′-rə-FŌ′-bik

Can you work with the words? (III)

1. incendiarism   a. delusions of grandeur
2. arson   b. compulsive sexual needs on
                      the part of a male
3. megalomania   c. morbid dread of open spaces
4. nymphomania   d. morbid dread of enclosed
                      places
5. satyromania   e. malicious setting of fires, as
                      for revenge, etc.
6. claustrophobia f. morbid dread of heights
7. agoraphobia   g. compulsive sexual needs on
                      the part of a female
8. acrophobia   h. felony of setting fire for eco-
                      nomic gain

KEY: 1–e, 2–h, 3–a, 4–g, 5–b, 6–d, 7–c, 8–f

Can you work with the words? (IV)

1. incendiary   a. one who has delusions of
                   greatness or power
2. arsonist   b. male compulsion for sexual
                   intercourse

314

3. megalomaniac	c. one who fears shut-in or crowded places
4. nymphomaniac	d. one who sets fires out of malice
5. satyriasis	e. one who fears heights
6. claustrophobe	f. one who fears large or open spaces
7. agoraphobe	g. one who sets fires for economic and illegal profit
8. acrophobe	h. woman with compulsive, incessant sexual desire

---

KEY: 1–d, 2–g, 3–a, 4–h, 5–b, 6–c, 7–f, 8–e

Do you understand the words?

1.	Is a *sorority* a men's organization?	YES	NO
2.	Is an *uxorious* husband likely to be psychologically dependent on his wife?	YES	NO
3.	Are *extramarital* affairs adulterous?	YES	NO
4.	Do VIPs often receive *regal* treatment?	YES	NO
5.	Is an admiral of the fleet in *regalia* informally dressed?	YES	NO
6.	Do *monomaniacal* people have varied interests?	YES	NO
7.	Can a *dipsomaniac* safely indulge in social drinking?	YES	NO
8.	Do people of *pyromaniacal* tendencies fear fire?	YES	NO
9.	Is *incendiarism* an uncontrollable impulse?	YES	NO
10.	Does an *arsonist* expect a reward for his actions?	YES	NO
11.	Is it necessary to seduce a *nymphomaniac*?	YES	NO

315

12. Do *megalomaniacs* have low opinions of themselves?	YES	NO
13. Is a *satyromaniac* lecherous?	YES	NO
14. Are *satyriasis* and *asceticism* compatible conditions?	YES	NO
15. Does a *claustrophobe* enjoy cramped quarters?	YES	NO
16. Would an *agoraphobe* be comfortable in a small cell-like room?	YES	NO
17. Does an *acrophobe* enjoy mountain-climbing?	YES	NO

KEY: 1–no, 2–yes, 3–yes, 4–yes, 5–no, 6–no, 7–no, 8–no, 9–no, 10–yes, 11–no, 12–no, 13–yes, 14–no, 15–no, 16–yes, 17–no

---

Can you recall the words?

1. to socialize — 1. F_____
2. excessively indulgent to, and doting on, one's wife — 2. U_____
3. full dress, with ribbons, insignia, badges of office, etc. — 3. R_____
4. obsessed in one area or with one overriding interest (*adj.*) — 4. M_____
5. having a compulsion to set fires (*adj.*) — 5. P_____
6. having a psychological compulsion to steal (*adj.*) — 6. K_____
7. person who sets fires for revenge — 7. I_____
8. felony of putting the torch to property for economic profit — 8. A_____
9. obsessive need for sexual gratification by a male — 9. S_____ *or* S_____

316

10. morbidly dreading enclosed or cramped places (*adj.*)

10. C_____

11. morbidly dreading heights (*adj.*)

11. A_____

12. morbidly dreading wide-open spaces (*adj.*)

12. A_____

13. having delusions of grandeur or power (*adj.*)

13. M_____

14. referring to a female who obsessively needs sexual gratification (*adj.*)

14. N_____

15. alcoholism

15. D_____

16. stealing for thrills or out of psychological compulsion (*adj.*)

16. K_____

17. brotherly

17. F_____

18. characteristic of, or befitting, a wife

18. U_____

19. referring to, characteristic of, or involved in, the matrimonial relationship

19. M_____

20. kingly; royal; splendid; etc.

20. R_____

21. outside the marriage (*adj.*)

21. E_____

22. before marriage (*adj.*)

22. P_____

KEY: 1–fraternize, 2–uxorious, 3–regalia, 4–monomaniacal, 5–pyromaniacal, 6–kleptomaniacal, 7–incendiary, 8–arson, 9–satyromania *or* satyriasis, 10–claustrophobic, 11–acrophobic, 12–agoraphobic, 13–megalomaniacal, 14–nymphomaniacal, 15–dipsomania, 16–kleptomaniacal, 17–fraternal, 18–uxorial, 19–marital, 20–regal, 21–extramarital, 22–premarital

---

(*End of Session 30*)

317

SESSION 31

ORIGINS AND RELATED WORDS

1. no reverence

The *iconoclast* sneers at convention and tradition, attempts to expose our cherished beliefs, our revered traditions, or our stereotypical thinking as shams and myths. H. L. Mencken was the great *iconoclast* of the 1920s; Tom Wolfe (*The Kandy-Kolored Tangerine-Flake Streamline Baby*), of the 1960s.

Adolescence is that confused and rebellious time of life in which *iconoclasm* (ī-KON'-ə-klaz'-əm) is quite normal—indeed the adolescent who is not *iconoclastic* (ī-kon'-ə-KLAST'-ik) to some degree might be considered either immature or maladjusted. The words are from *eikon*, a religious image, plus *klaein*, to break. *Iconoclasm* is not of course restricted to religion.

2. is there a God?

Atheist combines the Greek negative prefix *a-* with *theos*, God. Do not confuse *atheism* (AY'-thee-iz-əm) with *agnosticism* (ag-NOS'-tə-siz-əm), the philosophy that claims that God is unknowable, that He may or may not exist, and that human beings can never come to a final conclusion about Him. The *agnostic* (ag-NOS'-tik) does not deny the existence of a deity, as does the *atheist*, but simply holds that no proof can be adduced one way or the other.

3. how to know

Agnostic (which is also an adjective) is built on the Greek root *gnostos*, known, and the negative prefix *a-*. An *agnostic* claims that all but material phenomena is unknown, and, indeed, unknowable.

A *diagnosis* (dī-əg-NŌ'-sis), constructed on the allied Greek root *gnosis*, knowledge, plus *dia-*, through, is a knowing through examination or testing. A *prognosis* (prog-NŌ′-sis), on the other hand, is etymologically a knowing beforehand, hence a prediction, generally, but not solely, as to the course of a disease. (The Greek prefix *pro-*, before, plus *gnosis*.)

Thus, you may say to a doctor: "What's the *diagnosis*, Doc?"

"Diabetes."

Then you say, "And what's the *prognosis?*"

"If you take insulin and watch your diet, you'll soon be as good as new."

The doctor's *prognosis*, then, is a forecast of the development or trend of a disease. The doctor knows beforehand, from previous similar cases, what to expect.

The verb form of *diagnosis* is *diagnose* (dĭ′-əg-NŌS′); the verb form of *prognosis* is *prognosticate* (prog-NOS′-tə-kayt′). To use the verb *prognosticate* correctly, be sure that your meaning involves the forecasting of developments from a consideration of symptoms or conditions—whether the problem is physical, mental, political, economic, psychological, or what have you.

In school, you doubtless recall taking *diagnostic* (dĭ′-əg-NOS′-tik) tests; these measured not what you were supposed to have learned during the semester, but your general knowledge in a field, so that your teachers would know what remedial steps to take, just as doctors rely on their *diagnosis* to decide what drugs or treatments to prescribe.

In a reading center, various *diagnostic* machines and tests are used—these tell the clinician what is wrong with a student's reading and what measures will probably increase such a student's reading efficiency.

The medical specialist in *diagnosis* is a *diagnostician* (dĭ′-əg-nos-TISH′-ən).

The noun form of the verb *prognosticate* is *prognostication* (prog-nos′-tə-KAY′-shən).

4. getting back to God

Theos, God, is also found in:

1. *Monotheism* (MON′-ə-thee-iz-əm)—belief in *one* God. (*Monos*, one, plus *theos*, God.)

319

Using *atheism, atheist,* and *atheistic* as a model, write the word for the person who believes in one God: _____.
The adjective? _____.

2. *Polytheism* (POL'-ee-thee-iz-əm)—belief in *many* gods, as in ancient Greece or Rome. (*Polys,* many, plus *theos.*)
The person with such a belief? _____
The adjective? _____.

3. *Pantheism* (PAN'-thee-iz-əm)—belief that God is not in man's image, but is a combination of all forces of the universe. (*Pan,* all, plus *theos.*) The person? _____.
The adjective? _____.

4. *Theology* (thee-OL'-ə-jee)—the study of God and religion. (*Theos* plus *logos,* science or study.)
The student is a *theologian* (thee'-ə-LŌ'-jən), the adjective is *theological* (thee'-ə-LOJ'-ə-kəl).

5. of sex and the tongue

A *lecher* practices lechery (LECH'-ər-ee). The derivation is Old French *lechier,* to lick. The adjective *lecherous* (LECH'-ə-rəs) has many close or not-so-close synonyms, most of them also, and significantly, starting with the letter *l,* a sound formed with the tongue, supposedly the seat of sensation.

1. *libidinous* (lə-BID'-ə-nəs)—from *libido,* pleasure.

2. *lascivious* (lə-SIV'-ee-əs)—from *lascivia,* wantonness.

3. lubricious (lŏŏ-BRISH'-əs)—from *lubricus,* slippery, the same root found in *lubricate.* The noun is *lubricity* (lŏŏ-BRIS'-ə-tee).

4. licentious (lī-SEN'-shəs)—from *licere,* to be permitted, the root from which we get *license,* etymologically, "permission," and *illicit,* etymologically, "not permitted."

5. lewd—the previous four words derive from Latin, but this one is from Anglo-Saxon *lewed,* vile.

6. lustful—from an Anglo-Saxon word meaning *pleasure, desire.* Noun: *lust.*

Libidinous, lascivious, lubricious, licentious, lewd, lecherous, lustful are seven adjectives that indicate sexual desire and/or activity. The implication of all seven words is more or less derogatory.

Each adjective becomes a noun with the addition of the noun suffix *-ness; lubricity* and *lust* are alternate noun forms of two of the adjectives.

6. of sex and the itch

Prurient (PROO'-ee-ənt), from Latin *prurio,* to itch, to long for, describes someone who is filled with great sexual curiosity, desire, longing, etc. Can you form the noun? _____.

Pruritis (proŏr-Ī'-tis), from the same root, is a medical condition in which the skin is very itchy, but without a rash or eruptions. (Scratch enough, of course, as you will be irresistibly tempted to do, and something like a rash will soon appear.) The adjective is *pruritic* (proŏr-IT'-ik).

7. under and over

Hypochondria (hĭ-pə-KON'-dree-ə) is built on two Greek roots: *hypos,* under, and *chondros,* the cartilage of the breastbone. This may sound farfetched until you realize that under the breastbone is the abdomen; the ancient Greeks believed that morbid anxiety about one's health arose in the abdomen—and no one is more mŏrbidly, unceasingly, and unhappily anxious about health than the *hypochondriac.*

Hypochondriac is also an adjective—an alternate and more commonly used adjective form is *hypochondriacal* (hĭ'-pə-kən-DRĪ'-ə-kəl).

Hypos, under, is a useful root to know. The *hypodermic* needle penetrates *under* the skin; a *hypothyroid* person has an *underworking* thyroid gland; *hypotension* is abnormally low blood pressure.

On the other hand, *hyper* is the Greek root meaning *over*. The *hypercritical* person is excessively fault-finding; *hyperthyroidism is* an overworking of the thyroid gland; *hypertension* is high blood pressure; and you can easily figure out the meanings of *hyperacidity, hyperactive, hypersensitive*, etc.

The adjective forms of *hypotension* and *hypertension* are *hypotensive* and *hypertensive*.

REVIEW OF ETYMOLOGY

PREFIX, ROOT, SUFFIX	MEANING	ENGLISH WORD
1. *eikon*	religious image	_____
2. *klaein*	to break	_____
3. *a-*	negative prefix	_____
4. *theos*	God	_____
5. *gnostos*	known	_____
6. *-ism*	noun suffix	_____
7. *-ic*	adjective suffix	_____
8. *gnosis*	knowledge	_____
9. *dia-*	through	_____
10. *pro-*	before	_____
11. *-ate*	verb suffix	_____
12. *-ion*	noun suffix for verbs ending in *-ate*	_____
13. *-ician*	one who; expert	_____
14. *monos*	one	_____
15. *polys*	many	_____
16. *pan*	all	_____
17. *logos*	science, study	_____
18. *-al*	adjective suffix	_____
19. *prurio*	to itch, to long for	_____
20. *hypos*	under	_____
21. *hyper*	over	_____
22. *-ive*	adjective suffix	_____

USING THE WORDS

Can you pronounce the words? (I)

1.	*iconoclasm*	Ī-KON'-ə-klaz-əm
2.	*iconoclastic*	ī-kon'-ə-KLAS'-tik
3.	*atheism*	AY'-thee-iz-əm
4.	*atheistic*	ay'-thee-IS'-tik
5.	*agnostic*	ag-NOS'-tik
6.	*agnosticism*	ag-NOS'-tə-siz-əm
7.	*diagnosis*	dī'-əg-NŌ'-sis
8.	*diagnose*	DĪ'-əg-nōs'
9.	*diagnostic*	dī'-əg-NOS'-tik
10.	*diagnostician*	dī'-əg-nos-TISH'-ən
11.	*prognosis*	prog-NŌ'-sis
12.	*prognostic*	prog-NOS'-tik
13.	*prognosticate*	prog-NOS'-tə-kayt'
14.	*prognostication*	prog-nos'-tə-KAY'-shən

Can you pronounce the words? (II)

1.	*monotheism*	MON'-ə-thee-iz-əm
2.	*monotheist*	MON'-ə-thee'-ist
3.	*monotheistic*	mon'-ə-thee-IS'-tik
4.	*polytheism*	POL'-ee-thee-iz-əm
5.	*polytheist*	POL'-ee-thee'-ist
6.	*polytheistic*	pol'-ee-thee-IS'-tik
7.	*pantheism*	PAN'-thee-iz-əm
8.	*pantheist*	PAN'-thee-ist
9.	*pantheistic*	pan'-thee-IS'-tik
10.	*theology*	thee-OL'-ə-jee
11.	*theologian*	thee'-ə-LŌ'-jən
12.	*theological*	thee-ə-LOJ'-ə-kəl

Can you pronounce the words? (III)

1. *lechery*	LECH'-ər-ee
2. *lecherous*	LECH'-ər-əs
3. *libidinous*	lə-BID'-ə-nəs
4. *lascivious*	lə-SIV'-ee-əs
5. *lubricious*	lōō-BRISH'-əs
6. *lubricity*	lōō-BRIS'-ə-tee
7. *licentious*	lī-SEN'-shəs
8. *lewd*	LŌŌD
9. *lustful*	LUST'-fəl
10. *lust*	LUST

Can you pronounce the words? (IV)

1. *prurient*	PRŌŌR'-ee-ənt
2. *prurience*	PRŌŌR'-ee-əns
3. *pruritis*	prŏŏr-Ī'-tis
4. *pruritic*	prŏŏr-IT'-ik
5. *hypochondria*	hī-pə-KON'-dree-ə
6. *hypochondriacal*	hī'-pə-kən-DRĪ'-ə-kəl
7. *hypotension*	hī'-pō-TEN'-shən
8. *hypertension*	hī'-pər-TEN'-shən
9. *hypotensive*	hī'-pō-TEN'-siv
10. *hypertensive*	hī'-pər-TEN'-siv

This has been a long chapter, and we have discussed, more or less in detail, over one hundred words. Just to keep everything straight in your mind now, see how successfully you can work out the following matching exercises, which will concern any of the words discussed in this chapter.

Can you work with the words? (I)

| 1. martinet | a. lack of seriousness in an art or profession |
| 2. sycophancy | b. harridan, shrew |

3. dilettantism	c. excessive patriotism
4. tyro	d. name from father
5. virtuoso	e. venerable and influential old man
6. termagant	f. beginner
7. chauvinism	g. brilliant performer
8. patrimony	h. bootlicking
9. patronymic	i. inheritance from father
10. patriarch	j. strict disciplinarian

KEY: 1–j, 2–h, 3–a, 4–f, 5–g, 6–b, 7–c, 8–i, 9–d, 10–e

Can you work with the words? (II)

1. patricide	a. mother-killing
2. alma mater	b. tending to fixate obsessively on one thing
3. matricide	c. wife-killing
4. fratricide	d. father-killing
5. uxoricide	e. tending to set fires
6. uxorious	f. alcoholic
7. monomaniacal	g. wife-doting
8. pyromaniacal	h. school or college from which one has graduated
9. megalomaniacal	i. tending to delusions of grandeur
10. dipsomaniacal	j. brother-killing

KEY: 1–d, 2–h, 3–a, 4–j, 5–c, 6–g, 7–b, 8–e, 9–i, 10–f

Can you work with the words? (III)

| 1. kleptomania | a. disbelief in God |
| 2. libidinous | b. belief in many gods |

3. atheism   c. lewd
4. agnosticism   d. belief that God is nature
5. polytheism   e. morbid anxiety about health
6. monotheism   f. belief in one God
7. theology   g. study of religion
8. pantheism   h. obsessive thievery
9. satyriasis   i. abnormal male sexual needs
10. hypochondria   j. skepticism about God

KEY: 1–h, 2–c, 3–a, 4–j, 5–b, 6–f, 7–g, 8–d, 9–i, 10–e

Can you work with the words? (IV)

1. hypotension   a. high blood pressure
2. lascivious   b. malicious fire-setting
3. hypertension   c. abnormally low blood pressure
4. agnostic   d. fire-setting for illegal gain
5. incendiarism   e. to forecast (probable developments)
6. arson   f. a determination through examination or testing of the nature, type, causes, etc. of a condition
7. iconoclasm   g. one who claims that ultimate reality is unknowable
8. prognosticate   h. sexually immoral
9. diagnosis   i. a foretelling of probable developments
10. prognosis   j. a scoffing at tradition

KEY: 1–c, 2–h, 3–a, 4–g, 5–b, 6–d, 7–j, 8–e, 9–f, 10–i

Can you work with the words? (V)

1. prurience
2. satyromania
3. agoraphobia
4. claustrophobia
5. acrophobia
6. theologian
7. lubricious

8. hypochondriacal
9. hypotensive

10. hypertensive
11. pruritis

a. abnormal need for sexual intercourse by a male
b. fear of enclosed places
c. student of religion
d. sexual longing or curiosity
e. fear of heights
f. fear of open spaces
g. having, or referring to, abnormally low blood pressure
h. itching
i. having, or referring to, high blood pressure
j. sexually immoral; lewd
k. beset by anxieties about one's health

KEY: 1–d, 2–a, 3–f, 4–b, 5–e, 6–c, 7–j, 8–k, 9–g, 10–i, 11–h

Can you recall the words? (I)

I. manias and phobias

1. single fixed obsession
2. irresistible compulsion to set fires
3. unceasing desire, on the part of a woman, for sexual intercourse
4. obsessive desire to steal
5. delusions of grandeur
6. alcoholism
7. compulsion for sexual intercourse by a male

1. M_____
2. P_____
3. N_____

4. K_____
5. M_____
6. D_____
7. S_____
or S_____

8. dread of heights	8. A_____
9. dread of open spaces	9. A_____
10. dread of cramped quarters	10. C_____

KEY: 1–monomania, 2–pyromania, 3–nymphomania, 4–kleptomania, 5–megalomania, 6–dipsomania, 7–satyromania *or*
satyriasis, 8–acrophobia, 9–agoraphobia, 10–claustrophobia

Can you recall the words? (II)

II. sex

Write seven adjectives; all starting with *L*, more or less meaning
"sexually immoral, desirous, etc."; write the adjective starting with
P meaning "sexually curious or longing."

1. L_____	5. L_____
2. L_____	6. L_____
3. L_____	7. L_____
4. L_____	8. P_____

KEY: (*1–7 in any order*) 1–lecherous, 2–libidinous, 3–lasciv-
ous, 4–lubricious, 5–licentious, 6–lewd, 7–lustful, 8–prurient

---

Can you recall the words? (III)

III. God

1. study of religion	1. T_____
2. belief that God is the sum total of natural forces	2. P_____
3. belief that there is no God	3. A_____
4. belief that God's existence is unknowable	4. A_____

5. belief in one God   5. M_____

6. belief in many gods   6. P_____

KEY: 1–theology,   2–pantheism,   3–atheism,   4–agnosticism, 5–monotheism, 6–polytheism

---

Can you recall the words? (IV)

1. morbid anxiety about one's health   1. H_____

2. high blood pressure   2. H_____

3. malicious fire-setting   3. I_____

4. the felony of setting fire for economic gain   4. A_____

5. sneering contempt for convention or tradition   5. I_____

6. a forecast of development (of a disease, etc.)   6. P_____

7. designed to discover causes or conditions (*adj.*)   7. D_____

8. abnormally low blood pressure   8. H_____

9. to forecast (probable future developments) by examining present conditions   9. P_____

10. to determine the nature of a disease, condition, or state by examination   10. D_____

11. the act of forecasting (probable future developments) by examining present conditions   11. P_____

12. doctor who is an expert at recognizing the nature of a disease or condition   12. D_____

13. possessed of, or referring to, high blood pressure   13. H_____

14. possessed of, or referring to,   14. H_____
    abnormally low blood pressure
15. one who studies religion   15. T_____

KEY: 1–hypochondria, 2–hypertension, 3–incendiarism, 4–arson,
5–iconoclasm, 6–prognosis, 7–diagnostic, 8–hypotension,
9–prognosticate, 10–diagnose, 11–prognostication, 12–diagnostician, 13–hypertensive, 14–hypotensive, 15–theologian

---

CHAPTER REVIEW

A. Do you recognize the words?

1. Disciplinarian:
    (a) martinet, (b) virago, (c) dilettante
2. Bootlicker:
    (a) chauvinist, (b) sycophant, (c) lecher
3. Scoffer at tradition:
    (a) monomaniac, (b) hypochondriac, (c) iconoclast
4. Disbeliever in God:
    (a) agnostic, (b) atheist, (c) chauvinist
5. Accomplished musician:
    (a) tyro, (b) dilettante, (c) virtuoso
6. Sheer, flimsy:
    (a) diaphanous, (b) uxorious, (c) paternal
7. Abusive woman:
    (a) termagant, (b) virtuoso, (c) matriarch
8. Murder of one's wife:
    (a) genocide, (b) uxoricide, (c) sororicide
9. Old man in ruling position:
    (a) matriarch, (b) patricide, (c) patriarch
10. Morbid compulsion to steal:
    (a) dipsomania, (b) nymphomania, (c) kleptomania
11. Delusions of grandeur:
    (a) megalomania, (b) egomania, (c) pyromania

12. Lewd, lustful:
    (a) prurient, (b) agnostic, (c) hypochondriac
13. Belief in many gods:
    (a) polytheism, (b) monotheism, (c) agnosticism
14. Setting fire for economic gain:
    (a) pyromania, (b) incendiarism, (c) arson
15. Morbid fear of heights:
    (a) agoraphobia, (b) acrophobia, (c) claustrophobia
16. High blood pressure:
    (a) hypotension, (b) hypertension, (c) hypochondria
17. Abnormal need for sexual intercourse by a male:
    (a) lechery, (b) lubricity, (c) satyriasis

KEY: 1–a, 2–b, 3–c, 4–b, 5–c, 6–a, 7–a, 8–b, 9–c, 10–c, 11–a,
     12–a, 13–a, 14–c, 15–b, 16–b, 17–c

B. Can you recognize roots?

ROOT	MEANING	EXAMPLE
1. *sykon*	_____	sycophant
2. *phanein*	_____	diaphanous
3. *vir*	_____	virago
4. *pater, patris*	_____	paternal
5. *onyma*	_____	synonym
6. *homos*	_____	homonym
7. *phone*	_____	homophone
8. *archein*	_____	matriarchy
9. *mater, matris*	_____	maternity
10. *alma*	_____	alma mater
11. *sui*	_____	suicide
12. *caedo (-cide)*	_____	parricide
13. *frater, fratris*	_____	fraternity
14. *soror*	_____	sorority
15. *homo*	_____	homicide
16. *rex, regis*	_____	regal
17. *uxor*	_____	uxorious
18. *maritus*	_____	marticide
19. *infans, infantis*	_____	infanticide

20. *genos*	_____	genocide
21. *mania*	_____	egomania
22. *monos*	_____	monomania
23. *dipsa*	_____	dipsomania
24. *klepte*	_____	kleptomania
25. *pyros*	_____	pyromania
26. *incendo, incensus*	_____	incendiarism
27. *ardo, arsus*	_____	arson
28. *mega*	_____	megalomaniac
29. *satyros*	_____	satyriasis
30. *nymphe*	_____	nymphomaniac
31. *claustrum*	_____	claustrophobia
32. *agora*	_____	agoraphobia
33. *akros*	_____	acrophobia
34. *phobia*	_____	zoophobia
35. *eikon*	_____	iconoclastic
36. *klaein*	_____	iconoclasm
37. *theos*	_____	monotheism
38. *gnostos*	_____	agnostic
39. *gnosis*	_____	prognosis
40. *polys*	_____	polytheism
41. *pan*	_____	pantheism
42. *logos*	_____	theology
43. *prurio*	_____	pruritis
44. *hypos*	_____	hypotension
45. *hyper*	_____	hypertension

KEY: 1–fig, 2–to show, 3–man (male), 4–father, 5–name, 6–the same, 7–sound, 8–to rule, 9–mother, 10–soul, 11–of oneself, 12–to kill, killing, 13–brother, 14–sister, 15–person, 16–king, 17–wife, 18–husband, 19–baby, 20–race, kind, 21–madness, 22–one, 23–thirst, 24–thief, 25–fire, 26–to set fire, 27–to burn, 28–great, large, 29–satyr, 30–bride, 31–enclosed place, 32–market place, 33–highest, 34–morbid dread, 35–religious image, 36–to break, 37–God, 38–known, 39–knowledge, 40–many, 41–all, 42–science, study, 43–to itch, 44–under, 45–over

---

1. If a *patronymic* is a name derived from the name of one's father, can you figure out the word for a name derived from one's *mother's* name? _____.

2. *Incendo, incensus,* to set on fire, is the origin of the adjective *incendiary,* the noun *incense,* and the verb to *incense.*

    (a) What is an *incendiary* statement or speech? _____
_____

    (b) Why do people use *incense,* and why is it called *incense?* _____
_____

    (c) If someone *incenses* you, or if you feel *incensed,* how does the meaning of the verb derive from the root? _____
_____

3. *Ardo, arsus,* to burn, is the source of *ardent* and *ardor.* Explain these two words in terms of the root.

    (a) ardent: _____.

    (b) ardor: _____.

4. What is used to make sound greater (use the roots for *great* and *sound*)? _____.

5. A *metropolis,* by etymology, is the mother city (Greek *meter,* mother, plus *polis,* city, state). Construct a word for a *great city* (think of *megalomania,* delusions of greatness): _____

6. *Polis,* city, state, is the origin of the word for the uniformed group guarding the city or state. The English word? _____. Can you think of the word from the same root for the art of governing the city or state? _____.

7. What is a *bibliokleptomaniac?* _____
_____

Coin a word for one who has an irresistible compulsion to steal *women:* _____. To steal *children* (use the Greek, not the Latin, root for *child*): _____. To steal *males* (use the Greek root): _____. To steal *people* (use the Greek root): _____.

8. What word can you coin for someone who has an obsession to reach the highest places? _____. To be in the market place, or in wide-open spaces? _____. To be in confined places? _____.

9. Coin a word for one who has a morbid dread of thieves: _____; of fire: _____; of women: _____; of males: _____; of people: _____.

10. Guess at the meaning, thinking of the roots you have learned, of *gnosiology:* _____.

11. Wolfgang Amadeus Theophilus Gottlieb Mozart was a famous eighteenth-century Austrian composer. You can recognize the roots in *Theophilus.* How are his other two middle names similar to *Theophilus?* _____

_____

12. Thinking of the root *phanein,* define *cellophane:* _____

13. Recognizing the root *hypos,* can you define *hypoglycemia?* _____

Construct a word that is the opposite of *hypoglycemia:* _____.

14. *Pan,* all, occurs in *Pantheon, pandemonium,* and *panorama.* Can you figure out the meanings?

    (a) Pantheon: _____

_____

    (b) pandemonium: _____

_____

(c) panorama: _____

15. Recognizing the roots in *monarchy,* define the word: _____

(*Answers in Chapter 18*)

MAGAZINES THAT WILL HELP YOU

When a pregnant woman takes calcium pills, she must make sure also that her diet is rich in vitamin D, since this vitamin makes the absorption of the calcium possible. In building your vocabulary by learning great quantities of new words, you too must take a certain vitamin, metaphorically speaking, to help you absorb, understand, and remember these words. This vitamin is reading—for it is in books and magazines that you will find the words that we have been discussing in these pages. To learn new words without seeing them applied in the context of your reading is to do only half the job and to run the risk of gradually forgetting the additions to your vocabulary. To combine your vocabulary-building with increased reading is to make assurance doubly sure.

You are now so alert to the words and roots we have discussed that you will find that most of your reading will be full of the new words you have learned—and every time you do see one of the words used in context in a book or magazine, you will understand it more fully and will be taking long steps toward using it yourself.

Among magazines, I would like particularly to recommend the following, which will act both to keep you mentally alert and to set the new words you are learning:

1. *Harper's Magazine*
2. *Atlantic Monthly*
3. *The New Yorker*
4. *Time*
5. *Newsweek*
6. *Esquire*

335

7. *Psychology Today*
8. *Saturday Review*
9. *Ms.*
10. *Mother Jones*
11. *Signs*
12. *National Geographic*
13. *Smithsonian*
14. *Human Nature*
15. *Scientific American*
16. *Natural History*

These periodicals are aimed at the alert, verbally sophisticated, educated reader; you will see in them, without fail, most of the words you have been studying in this book—not to mention hosts of other valuable words you will want to add to your vocabulary, many of which you will be able to figure out once you recognize their etymological structure.

(End of Session 31)

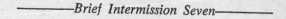

———————*Brief Intermission Seven*———————

SOME INTERESTING DERIVATIONS

PEOPLE WHO MADE OUR LANGUAGE

Bloomers

Mrs. Elizabeth Smith Miller invented them in 1849, and showed a working model to a famous women's rights advocate, *Amelia J. Bloomer*. Amelia was fascinated by the idea of garments that were both modest (they then reached right down to the ankles) and convenient—and promptly sponsored them. . . .

Boycott

Charles C. Boycott was an English land agent whose difficult duty it was to collect high rents from Irish farmers. In protest, the farmers ostracized him, not even allowing him to make purchases in town or hire workers to harvest his crops.

Marcel

Marcel was an ingenious Parisian hairdresser who felt he could improve on the button curls popular in 1875. He did, and made a fortune.

Silhouette

Finance Minister of France just before the Revolution, *Etienne de Silhouette* advocated the *simple* life, so that excess money could go into the treasury instead of into luxurious living. And the profile is the *simplest* form of portraiture, if you get the connection.

Derrick

A seventeenth-century English hangman, *Derrick* by name, hoisted to their death some of the most notorious criminals of the day.

Sadist

Because *Count de Sade*, an eighteenth-century Frenchman, found his greatest delight in torturing friends and mistresses, the term *sadist* was derived from his name. His works shocked his nation and the world by the alarming frankness with which he described his morbid and bloodthirsty cruelty.

Galvanism

Luigi Galvani, the Italian physiologist, found by accident that an electrically charged scalpel could send a frog's corpse into muscular convulsions. Experimenting further, he eventually discovered the principles of chemically produced electricity. His name is responsible not only for the technical expressions *galvanism, galvanized iron,* and *galvanometer,* but also for that highly graphic phrase, "*galvanized* into action."

Guppies

In 1868, *R. J. Lechmere Guppy*, president of the Scientific Association of Trinidad, sent some specimens of a tiny tropical fish to the British Museum. Ever since, fish of this species have been called *guppies*.

Nicotine

Four hundred years ago, *Jean Nicot,* a French ambassador, bought some tobacco seeds from a Flemish trader. Nicot's successful efforts to popularize the plant in Europe brought him linguistic immortality.

PLACES THAT MADE OUR LANGUAGE

Bayonne, France

Where first was manufactured the daggerlike weapon that fits over the muzzle end of a rifle—the *bayonet.*

Cantalupo, Italy

The first place in Europe to grow those luscious melons we now call *cantaloupes.*

Calicut, India

The city from which we first imported a kind of cotton cloth now known as *calico.*

Tuxedo Park, New York

In the country club of this exclusive and wealthy community, the short (no tails) dinner coat for men, or *tuxedo,* was popularized.

Egypt

It was once supposed that the colorful, fortunetelling wanderers, or *Gypsies,* hailed from this ancient land.

Damascus, Syria

Where an elaborately patterned silk, *damask,* was first made.

Tzu-t'ing, China

Once a great seaport in Fukien Province. Marco Polo called it *Zaitun,* and in time a silk fabric made there was called *satin.*

Frankfurt, Germany

Where the burghers once greatly enjoyed their smoked beef and pork sausages, which we now ask for in delicatessen stores and supermarkets by the name of *frankfurters, franks,* or *hot dogs.*

12

HOW TO FLATTER
YOUR FRIENDS

(Sessions 32–37)

_____

TEASER PREVIEW

What adjective aptly describes people who are:

- *friendly and easy to get along with?*
- *tireless?*
- *simple, frank, aboveboard?*
- *keen-minded?*
- *generous, noble, and forgiving?*
- *able to do many things skillfully?*
- *unflinching in the face of pain or disaster?*
- *brave, fearless?*
- *charming and witty?*
- *smooth, polished, cultured?*

_____

SESSION 32

Words are the symbols of emotions, as well as ideas. You can show your feeling by the tone you use ("You're silly" can be an insult, an accusation, or an endearment, depending on how you say it) or by the words you choose (you can label a quality either "childish" or "childlike," depending on whether you admire it or condemn it—it's the same quality, no matter what you call it).

In Chapter 11 we discussed ten basic words that you might use to show your disapproval. In this chapter we discuss ten adjectives that indicate wholehearted approval.

Consider the interesting types of people described in the following paragraphs, then note how accurately the adjective applies to each type.

IDEAS

1. put the kettle on, Polly

They are friendly, happy, extroverted, and gregarious—the sort of people who will invite you out for a drink, who like to transact business around the lunch table, who put the coffee to perking as soon as company drops in. They're sociable, genial, cordial, affable—and they like parties and all the eating and drinking that goes with them.

The adjective is: *convivial*

2. you can't tire them

Arnold Bennett once pointed out that we all have the same amount of time—twenty-four hours a day. Strictly speaking, that's as inconclusive an observation as Bennett ever made. It's not time that counts, but energy—and of that wonderful quality we all have very different amounts, from the persons who wake up tired, no matter how much sleep they've had, to lucky, well-adjusted mortals who hardly ever need to sleep.

Energy comes from a healthy body, of course; it also comes from a psychological balance, a lack of conflicts and insecurities.

Some people apparently have boundless, illimitable energy—they're on the go from morning to night, and often far into the night, working hard, playing hard, never tiring, never "pooped" or "bushed"—and getting twice as much done as any three other human beings.

The adjective is: *indefatigable*

3. no tricks, no secrets

They are pleasingly frank, utterly lacking in pretense or artificiality, in fact quite unable to hide their feelings or thoughts —and so honest and aboveboard that they can scarcely conceive of trickery, chicanery, or dissimulation in anyone. There is, then, about them the simple naturalness and unsophistication of a child.

The adjective is: *ingenuous*

4. sharp as a razor

They have minds like steel traps; their insight into problems that would confuse or mystify people of less keenness or discernment is just short of amazing.

The adjective is: *perspicacious*

5. no placating necessary

They are most generous about forgiving a slight, an insult, an injury. Never do they harbor resentment, store up petty grudges, or waste energy or thought on means of revenge or retaliation. How could they? They're much too big-hearted.

The adjective is: *magnanimous*

6. one-person orchestras

The range of their aptitudes is truly formidable. If they are writers, they have professional facility in poetry, fiction, biography, criticism, essays—you just mention it and they've done it, and very competently. If they are musicians, they can play the oboe, the bassoon, the French horn, the bass viol, the piano, the celesta, the xylophone, even the clavichord if you can dig one up. If they are artists, they use oils, water colors, *gouache,* charcoal, pen and ink—they can do anything! Or maybe the range of their abilities cuts across all fields, as in the case of Michelangelo, who was an expert sculptor, painter, poet, architect, and inventor. In case you're thinking "Jack of all trades . . . ," you're wrong— they're *masters* of all trades.

The adjective is: *versatile*

7. no grumbling

They bear their troubles bravely, never ask for sympathy, never yield to sorrow, never wince at pain. It sounds almost superhuman, but it's true.

The adjective is: *stoical*

8. no fear

There is not, as the hackneyed phrase has it, a cowardly bone in their bodies. They are strangers to fear, they're audacious, dauntless, contemptuous of danger and hardship.

The adjective is: *intrepid*

9. no dullness

They are witty, clever, delightful; and naturally, also, they are brilliant and entertaining conversationalists.

The adjective is: *scintillating*

344

10. city slickers

They are cultivated, poised, tactful, socially so experienced, sophisticated, and courteous that they're at home in any group, at ease under all circumstances of social intercourse. You cannot help admiring (perhaps envying) their smoothness and self-assurance, their tact and congeniality.

The adjective is: *urbane*

USING THE WORDS

Can you pronounce the words?

1.	*convivial*	kən-VIV′-ee-əl
2.	*indefatigable*	in′-də-FAT′-ə-gə-bəl
3.	*ingenuous*	in-JEN′-yōō-əs
4.	*perspicacious*	pur′-spə-KAY′-shəs
5.	*magnanimous*	məg-NAN′-ə-məs
6.	*versatile*	VUR′-sə-təl
7.	*stoical*	STŌ′-ə-kəl
8.	*intrepid*	in-TREP′-id
9.	*scintillating*	SIN′-tə-layt-ing
10.	*urbane*	ur-BAYN′

Can you work with the words?

1.	convivial	a. frank
2.	indefatigable	b. unflinching
3.	ingenuous	c. noble
4.	perspicacious	d. capable in many directions
5.	magnanimous	e. tireless
6.	versatile	f. fearless
7.	stoical	g. keen-minded

8. intrepid	h. witty
9. scintillating	i. friendly
10. urbane	j. polished, sophisticated

KEY: 1–i, 2–e, 3–a, 4–g, 5–c, 6–d, 7–b, 8–f, 9–h, 10–j

Do you understand the words? (I)

1.	*Convivial* people are unfriendly.	TRUE	FALSE
2.	Anyone who is *indefatigable* tires easily.	TRUE	FALSE
3.	An *ingenuous* person is artful and untrustworthy.	TRUE	FALSE
4.	A *perspicacious* person is hard to fool.	TRUE	FALSE
5.	A *magnanimous* person is easily insulted.	TRUE	FALSE
6.	A *versatile* person does many things well.	TRUE	FALSE
7.	A *stoical* person always complains of his hard lot.	TRUE	FALSE
8.	An *intrepid* explorer is not easily frightened.	TRUE	FALSE
9.	A *scintillating* speaker is interesting to listen to.	TRUE	FALSE
10.	Someone who is *urbane* is always making enemies.	TRUE	FALSE

KEY: 1–F, 2–F, 3–F, 4–T, 5–F, 6–T, 7–F, 8–T, 9–T, 10–F

Do you understand the words? (II)

1.	convivial—hostile	SAME	OPPOSITE
2.	indefatigable—enervated	SAME	OPPOSITE
3.	ingenuous—worldly	SAME	OPPOSITE

346

4. perspicacious—obtuse	SAME	OPPOSITE
5. magnanimous—petty	SAME	OPPOSITE
6. versatile—well-rounded	SAME	OPPOSITE
7. stoical—unemotional	SAME	OPPOSITE
8. intrepid—timid	SAME	OPPOSITE
9. scintillating—banal	SAME	OPPOSITE
10. urbane—crude	SAME	OPPOSITE

KEY: 1–O, 2–O, 3–O, 4–O, 5–O, 6–S, 7–S, 8–O, 9–O, 10–O

Can you recall the words?

1. witty	1. S_____
2. noble, forgiving	2. M_____
3. capable in many fields	3. V_____
4. keen-minded	4. P_____
5. uncomplaining	5. S_____
6. friendly	6. C_____
7. poised; polished	7. U_____
8. courageous	8. I_____
9. tireless	9. I_____
10. simple and honest; frank	10. I_____

KEY: 1–scintillating, 2–magnanimous, 3–versatile, 4–perspicacious, 5–stoical, 6–convivial, 7–urbane, 8–intrepid, 9–indefatigable, 10–ingenuous

(*End of Session 32*)

SESSION 33

ORIGINS AND RELATED WORDS

1. eat, drink, and be merry

The Latin verb *vivo*, to live, and the noun *vita*, life, are the source of a number of important English words.

Convivo is the Latin verb *to live together;* from this, in Latin, was formed the noun *convivium* (don't get impatient; we'll be back to English directly), which meant a *feast* or *banquet;* and from *convivium* we get our English word *convivial*, an adjective that describes the kind of person who likes to attend feasts and banquets, enjoying (and supplying) the jovial good fellowship characteristic of such gatherings.

Using the suffix *-ity* can you write the noun form of the adjective *convivial?* _____. (Can you pronounce it?)

2. living it up

Among many others, the following English words derive from Latin *vivo*, to live:

1. *vivacious* (vī-VAY′-shəs)—full of the joy of living; animated; peppy—a *vivacious* personality. Noun: *vivacity* (vī-VAS′-ə-tee). You can, as you know, also add *-ness* to any adjective to form a noun. Write the alternate noun form of *vivacious:*

_____

2. *vivid*—possessing the freshness of life; strong; sharp—a *vivid* imagination; a *vivid* color. Add *-ness* to form the noun:

_____

3. *revive* (rə-VĪV′)—bring back to life. In the 1960s, men's fashions of the twenties were *revived*. Noun: *revival* (rə-VĪ′-vəl).

4. *vivisection* (viv′-ə-SEK′-shən)—operating on a live animal.

348

Sect- is from a Latin verb meaning *to cut. Vivisection* is the process of experimenting on live animals to discover causes and cures of disease. *Antivivisectionists* object to the procedure, though many of our most important medical discoveries were made through *vivisection.*

5. *Viviparous* (vī-VIP′-ər-əs)—producing live babies. Human beings and most other mammals are *viviparous. Viviparous* is contrasted to *oviparous* (ō-VIP′-ər-əs), producing young from eggs. Most fish, fowl, and other lower forms of life are *oviparous.*

The combining root in both these adjectives is Latin *pareo,* to give birth (*parent* comes from the same root). In *oviparous,* the first two syllables derive from Latin *ovum,* egg.

Ovum, egg, is the source of *oval* and *ovoid,* egg-shaped; *ovulate* (Ō′-vyə-layt′), to release an egg from the *ovary: ovum* (Ō-vəm), the female germ cell which, when fertilized by a sperm, develops into an embryo, then into a *fetus* (FEE′-təs), and finally, in about 280 days in the case of humans, is born as an infant.

The adjective form of *ovary* is *ovarian* (ō-VAIR′-ee-ən); of *fetus, fetal* (FEE′-təl). Can you write the noun form of the verb *ovulate?* _____.

Love, you may or may not be surprised to hear, also comes from *ovum.*

No, not the kind of love you're thinking of. Latin *ovum* became *oeuf* in French, or with "the" preceding the noun (*the* egg), *l'oeuf,* pronounced something like LOOF. *Zero* (picture it for a moment) is shaped like an egg (0), so if your score in tennis is *fifteen,* and your opponent's is *zero,* you shout triumphantly, fifteen love! Let's go!"

3. more about life

Latin *vita,* life, is the origin of:

1. *vital* (VĪ′-təl)—essential to life; of crucial importance—a *vital* matter; also full of life, strength, vigor, etc. Add the suffix *-ity* to form the noun: _____. Add a verb suffix to construct the verb: _____ (meaning: *to give life to*). Finally, write the noun derived from the verb you have constructed: _____.

2. *Revitalize* (ree-VĪ'-tə-līz') is constructed from the prefix *re-*, again, back, the root *vita,* and the verb suffix. Meaning? _____. Can you write the noun formed from this verb? _____.

3. The prefix *de-* has a number of meanings, one of which is essentially negative, as in *defrost, decompose, declassify,* etc. Using this prefix, can you write a verb meaning *to rob of life, to take life from?* _____. Now write the noun form of this verb: _____.

4. *Vitamin*—one of the many nutritional elements on which life is dependent. Good eyesight requires vitamin A (found, for example, in carrots); strong bones need vitamin D (found in sunlight and cod-liver oil); etc.

Vitalize, revitalize, and *devitalize* are used figuratively—for example, a program or plan is *vitalized, revitalized,* or *devitalized,* according to how it's handled.

4. French life

Sometimes, instead of getting our English words directly from Latin, we work through one of the Latin-derived or Romance languages. (As you will recall, the Romance languages—French, Spanish, Italian, Portuguese, and Romanian—are so called because they were originally dialects of the old Roman tongue. English, by the way, is not a Romance language, but a Teutonic one. Our tongue is a development of a German dialect imposed on the natives of Britain by the Angles, Saxons, and Jutes of early English history. Though we have taken over into English more than 50 per cent of the Latin vocabulary and almost 30 per cent of the classical Greek vocabulary as roots and prefixes, our basic language is nevertheless German).

The French, using the same Latin root *vivo,* to live, formed two expressive phrases much used in English. French pronunciation is, of course, tricky, and if you are not at least superficially acquainted with that language, your pronunciation may sound a bit awkward to the sophisticated ear—but try it anyway. These phrases are:

1. *joie de vivre*—pronounced something like zhwahd′-VEEV′ (*zh* is identical in sound to the *s* of *pleasure*).

Literally *joy of living,* this phrase describes an immense delight in being alive, an effervescent keenness for all the daily activities that human beings indulge in. People who possess *joie de vivre* are never moody, depressed, bored, or apathetic—on the contrary, they are full of sparkle, eager to engage in all group activities, and, most important, always seem to be having a good time, no matter what they are doing. *Joie de vivre* is precisely the opposite of *ennui* (this is also a word of French origin, but is easy to pronounce: AHN′-wee), which is a feeling of boredom, discontent, or weariness resulting sometimes from having a jaded, oversophisticated appetite, sometimes from just finding all of life tedious and unappetizing, and sometimes implying in addition physical lassitude and general inactivity. Young children and simple people rarely experience *ennui*—to them life is always exciting, always new.

2. *bon vivant,* pronounced something like BŌNG′-vee-VAHNG′—the -NG a muted nasal sound similar to the -*ng* in *sing.*

A *bon vivant* is a person who lives luxuriously, especially in respect to rich food, good liquor, expensive theater parties, operas, and other accouterments of upper-class life. *Bon vivant* means, literally, a *good liver;* actually, a *high liver,* one who lives a luxurious life. When you think of a *bon vivant* (usually, language being sexist, a male), you get the picture of someone attired in top hat, "soup and fish" or tuxedo, raising his cane to call a taxi while a beautiful, evening-gowned and sophisticated-looking woman, sparkling in diamonds and furs, waits at his side. They're going to a champagne and partridge supper at an outrageously expensive restaurant, etc.—fill in your own details of the high life.

The *bon vivant* is of course a *convivial* person—and also likely to be a *gourmet* (gŏor-MAY′), another word from French.

5. food and how to enjoy it

The *gourmand* (GŌOR′-mənd) enjoys food with a sensual pleasure. To *gourmands* the high spots of the day are the times for breakfast, lunch, dinner, and midnight supper; in short, they like to eat, but the eating must be good. The verb form, *gormandize* (GAWR'-mən-dīz'), however, has suffered a degeneration in meaning—it signifies *to stuff oneself like a pig*.

A *gourmand* is significantly different from a *gourmet*, who has also a keen interest in food and liquor, but is much more fastidious, is more of a connoisseur, has a most discerning palate for delicate tastes, flavors, and differences; goes in for rare delicacies (like hummingbirds' tongues and other such absurdities); and approaches the whole business from a scientific, as well as a sensual, viewpoint. *Gourmet* is always a complimentary term, *gourmand* somewhat less so.

The person who eats voraciously, with no discernment whatever, but merely for the purpose of stuffing himself ("I know I haven't had enough to eat till I feel sick"), is called a *glutton* (GLUT'-ən)—obviously a highly derogatory term. The verb *gluttonize* is stronger than *gormandize;* the adjective *gluttonous* (GLUT'-ə-nəs) is about the strongest epithet you can apply to someone whose voracious eating habits you find repulsive. Someone who has a voracious, insatiable appetite for money, sex, punishment, etc. is also called a *glutton*.

REVIEW OF ETYMOLOGY

PREFIX, ROOT, SUFFIX	MEANING	ENGLISH WORDS
1. *vivo*	to live	_____
2. *-ous*	adjective suffix	_____
3. *re-*	again, back	_____
4. *sectus*	cut	_____
5. *anti-*	against	_____
6. *pareo*	egg	_____
7. *ovum*	to give birth, produce	_____
8. *vita*	life	_____
9. *-ize*	verb suffix	_____
10. *-ation*	noun suffix	_____
	added to verbs ending in *-ize*	_____

11. *de-* negative prefix   _____
12. *bon* good   _____
13. *-ate* verb suffix   _____

USING THE WORDS

Can you pronounce the words? (I)

1. *conviviality*   kən-viv′-ee-AL′-ə-tee
2. *vivacious*   vī-VAY′-shəs
3. *vivacity*   vī-VAS′-ə-tee
4. *vivid*   VIV′-id
5. *vividness*   VIV′-id-nəs
6. *revive*   rə-VĪV′
7. *revival*   rə-VĪV′-əl
8. *vivisection*   viv′-ə-SEK′-shən
9. *antivivisectionist*   an′-tee (or tī)-viv′-ə-SEK′-shən-ist
10. *viviparous*   vī-VIP′-ər-əs
11. *oviparous*   ō-VIP′-ər-əs
12. *oval*   Ō′-vəl
13. *ovoid*   Ō′-voyd′
14. *ovary*   Ō′-və-ree
15. *ovarian*   ō-VAIR′-ee-ən
16. *ovulate*   Ō-vyə-layt′
17. *ovulation*   ō-vyə-LAY′-shən

Can you pronounce the words? (II)

1. *vital*   VĪ′-təl
2. *vitality*   vī-TAL′-ə-tee
3. *vitalize*   VĪ′-tə-līz′
4. *vitalization*   vī′-tə-lə-ZAY′-shən
5. *revitalize*   ree-VĪ′-tə-līz′
6. *revitalization*   ree-vī′-tə-lə-ZAY′-shən
7. *devitalize*   dee-VĪ′-tə-līz′
8. *devitalization*   dee-vī′-tə-lə-ZAY′-shən

353

9. *joie de vivre*	zhwahd′-VEEV′
10. *ennui*	AHN′-wee
11. *bon vivant*	BŌNG′ vee-VAHNG′
12. *gourmand*	GŌŌR′-mənd
13. *gourmet*	gŏŏr-MAY′
14. *gormandize*	GAWR′-mən-dīz′
15. *glutton*	GLUT′-ən
16. *gluttonous*	GLUT′-ə-nəs
17. *gluttonize*	GLUT′-ə-nīz′
18. *vitamin*	VĪ′-tə-min

Can you work with the words? (I)

1.	oval, ovoid	a.	peppy
2.	revitalize	b.	bearing live young
3.	gluttonous	c.	strong, sharp
4.	vivacious	d.	piggish; greedy
5.	vivid	e.	egg-shaped
6.	viviparous	f.	bearing young in eggs
7.	oviparous	g.	give new life to

KEY: 1–e, 2–g, 3–d, 4–a, 5–c, 6–b, 7–f

Can you work with the words? (II)

1.	conviviality	a.	release of the egg
2.	vivisection	b.	a "high liver"
3.	antivivisectionist	c.	experimentation on live animals
4.	ovulation	d.	one who is a connoisseur of good food
5.	vitality	e.	effervescence; joy of living
6.	*joie de vivre*	f.	one who enjoys food
7.	ennui	g.	one who eats greedily; one who is greedy (as for punishment, etc.)

354

8. *bon vivant*
9. gourmand
10. gourmet
11. glutton

h. boredom
i. congeniality
j. strength, vigor
k. one who is against experimentation on live animals

KEY: 1–i, 2–c, 3–k, 4–a, 5–j, 6–e, 7–h, 8–b, 9–f, 10–d, 11–g

Can you work with the words? (III)

1. revive
2. vital

3. vitalize
4. devitalize
5. gluttonize
6. vitamin

a. rob of life or strength
b. nutritional element necessary for life
c. important, crucial
d. stuff oneself like a pig
e. breathe life into
f. bring back to life

KEY: 1–f, 2–c, 3–e, 4–a, 5–d, 6–b

Do you understand the words? (I)

1. conviviality—asceticism	SAME	OPPOSITE
2. vivacious—apathetic	SAME	OPPOSITE
3. vivid—dull	SAME	OPPOSITE
4. revive—kill	SAME	OPPOSITE
5. revitalize—rejuvenate	SAME	OPPOSITE
6. ennui—boredom	SAME	OPPOSITE
7. *bon vivant*—"man about town"	SAME	OPPOSITE
8. gormandize—starve	SAME	OPPOSITE
9. glutton—ascetic	SAME	OPPOSITE
10. *joie de vivre*—boredom	SAME	OPPOSITE

KEY: 1–O, 2–O, 3–O, 4–O, 5–S, 6–S, 7–S, 8–O, 9–O, 10–O

Do you understand the words? (II)

1. vivacity—liveliness	SAME	OPPOSITE
2. revival—renewal	SAME	OPPOSITE
3. vivisection—experimentation on corpses	SAME	OPPOSITE
4. ovulation—egg-releasing	SAME	OPPOSITE
5. devitalize—reinvigorate	SAME	OPPOSITE
6. vitality—fatigue	SAME	OPPOSITE
7. gluttonous—greedy	SAME	OPPOSITE
8. gourmand—ascetic	SAME	OPPOSITE
9. ovoid—egg-shaped	SAME	OPPOSITE

KEY: 1–S, 2–S, 3–O, 4–S, 5–O, 6–O, 7–S, 8–O, 9–S

Do you understand the words? (III)

1. Humans are *viviparous*.	TRUE	FALSE
2. Cows are *oviparous*.	TRUE	FALSE
3. *Ovulation* takes places in females only when they are married.	TRUE	FALSE
4. An *antivivisectionist* believes in experimenting on live animals.	TRUE	FALSE
5. *Vitamins* are essential to good health.	TRUE	FALSE
6. A *bon vivant* lives like a hermit.	TRUE	FALSE
7. A *gourmet* stuffs himself with food.	TRUE	FALSE
8. It is normal for young children to be overwhelmed with *ennui*.	TRUE	FALSE
9. People who are keenly alive possess *joie de vivre*.	TRUE	FALSE

KEY: 1–T, 2–F, 3–F, 4–F, 5–T, 6–F, 7–F, 8–F, 9–T

Can you recall the words?

1. bearing young by eggs (*adj.*)	1. O_____
2. bearing live young (*adj.*)	2. V_____

3. good-fellowship .... 3. C_____

4. operating on live animals .... 4. V_____

5. one who is opposed to such an ... 5. A_____
   activity

6. the process of releasing an egg .. 6. O_____
   from the ovary

7. to remove life or vigor from ...... 7. D_____

8. joy of living .... 8. J_____

9. one who eats like a pig .... 9. G_____

10. a "high liver" .... 10. B_____

11. one who is a connoisseur of ...... 11. G_____
    good food

12. one who gets a sensual .... 12. G_____
    enjoyment from good food

13. to stuff oneself like a pig; to .... 13. G_____
    eat greedily   *or* G_____

14. boredom; discontent; tedium ..... 14. E_____

15. liveliness, pep .... 15. V_____
                                      or V_____
                                      or V_____

16. egg-shaped .... 16. O_____
                                      or R_____

17. to bring renewed life or vigor ... 17. R_____
    to   *or* O_____

18. referring to the ovary (*adj.*) .... 18. O_____

19. essential to life; crucial; of ...... 19. V_____
    utmost importance

KEY: 1–oviparous, 2–viviparous, 3–conviviality, 4–vivisection, 5–antivivisectionist, 6–ovulation, 7–devitalize, 8–*joie de vivre,* 9–glutton, 10–*bon vivant,* 11–gourmet, 12–gourmand, 13–gluttonize *or* gormandize, 14–ennui, 15–vivacity, vivaciousness, *or* vitality, 16–oval *or* ovoid, 17–revitalize *or* revive, 18–ovarian, 19–vital

---

(*End of Session 33*)

SESSION 34

ORIGINS AND RELATED WORDS

1. no fatigue

Indefatigable is a derived form of *fatigue*—*in-* is a negative prefix, the suffix *-able* means *able to be;* hence, literally, *indefatigable* means *unable to be fatigued.* The noun is *indefatigability* (in'-də-fat'-ə-gə-BIL'-ə-tee).

2. how simple can one be?

Ingenuous is a complimentary term, though its synonyms *naïve, gullible,* and *credulous* are faintly derogatory.

To call people *ingenuous* implies that they are frank, open, artless—in other words, not likely to try to put anything over on you, nor apt to hide feelings or thoughts that more sophisticated persons would consider it wise, tactful, or expedient to conceal.

Ingenuous should not be confused with *ingenious* (in-JEEN'-yəs)—note the slight difference in spelling—which on the contrary means *shrewd, clever, inventive.*

The noun form of *ingenuous* is *ingenuousness;* of *ingenious, ingenuity* (in'-jə-NOO'-ə-tee) or ingeniousness.

To call people *naïve* (nah-EEV') is to imply that they have not learned the ways of the world, and are therefore idealistic and trusting beyond the point of safety; such idealism and trust have probably come from ignorance or inexperience. The noun is *naïveté* (nah-eev-TAY').

Credulous (KREJ'-ə-ləs) implies a willingness to believe almost anything, no matter how fantastic. *Credulity* (krə-JOO'-lə-tee), like *naïveté,* usually results, again, from ignorance or inexperience, or perhaps from an inability to believe that human beings are capable of lying.

Gullible (GUL'-ə-bəl) means *easily tricked, easily fooled, eas-*

358

ily imposed on. It is a stronger word than *credulous* and is more derogatory. *Gullibility* (gul'-ə-BIL'-ə-tee) results more from stupidity than from ignorance or inexperience.

These four synonyms, *ingenuous, naïve, credulous,* and *gullible,* are fairly close, but they contain areas of distinction worth remembering. Let's review them:

1. *ingenuous*—frank, not given to concealment
2. *naïve*—inexperienced, unsophisticated, trusting
3. *credulous*—willing to believe; not suspicious or skeptical
4. *gullible*—easily tricked

3. belief and disbelief

Credulous comes from Latin *credo,* to believe, the same root found in *credit* (if people *believe* in your honesty, they will extend *credit* to you; they will *credit* what you say). *-Ous* is an adjective suffix that usually signifies *full of.* So, strictly, *credulous* means *full of believingness.*

Do not confuse *credulous* with *credible.* (KRED'-ə-bəl). In the latter word we see combined the root *credo,* believe, with *-ible,* a suffix meaning *can be.* Something *credible* can be believed.

Let's chart some differences:

Credulous listeners—those who fully believe what they hear

A *credible* story—one that can be believed

An *incredulous* (in-KREJ'-ə-ləs) attitude—an attitude of skepticism, of non-belief

An *incredible* (in-KRED'-ə-bəl) story—one that cannot be believed

Incredible characters—persons who are so unique that you can scarcely believe they exist.

Nouns are formed as follows:

credulous—credulity (krə-JŌŌ'-lə-tee)
incredulous—incredulity (in-krə-JŌŌ'-lə-tee)
credible—credibility (kred'-ə-BIL'-ə-tee)
incredible—incredibility (in-kred'-ə-BIL'-ə-tee)

To check your understanding of these distinctions, try the next test.

Can you use these words correctly?

Use *credulous, credible,* or corresponding negative or noun forms in the following sentences:

1. She listened _____ly to her husband's confession of his frequent infidelity, for she had always considered him a paragon of moral uprightness.
2. He told his audience an _____ and fantastic story of his narrow escapes.
3. He'll believe you—he's very _____.
4. Make your characters more _____ if you want your readers to believe in them.
5. We listened dumb-struck, full of _____, to the shocking details of corruption and vice.
6. He has the most _____ good luck.
7. The _____ of it! How can such things happen?
8. Naïve people accept with complete _____, whatever anyone tells them.
9. "Do you believe me?" "Sure—your story is _____ enough."
10. I'm not objecting to the total _____ of your story, but only to your thinking that I'm _____enough to believe it!

KEY: 1–incredulously, 2–incredible, 3–credulous, 4–credible, 5–incredulity, 6–incredible, 7–incredibility, 8–credulity, 9–credible, 10–incredibility, credulous

---

4. what people believe in

Credo, to believe, is the origin of four other useful English words.

1. *Credo* (KREE'-do)—personal belief, code of ethics; the principles by which people guide their actions.

2. *Creed*—a close synonym of *credo;* in addition, a religious belief, such as Catholicism, Judaism, Protestantism, Hinduism, etc.

3. *Credence* (KREE'-dəns)—belief, as in, "I place no *credence* in his stories." or "Why should I give any *credence* to what you say?"

4. *Credentials* (krə-DEN'-shəls)—a document or documents proving a person's right to a title or privilege (i.e., a right to be believed), as in, "The new ambassador presented his *credentials* to the State Department."

5. heads and tails

We can hardly close our book on the words suggested by *ingenuous* without looking at the other side of the coin. If *ingenuous* means *frank, open,* then *disingenuous* (dis-in-JEN'-yōō-əs) should mean *not frank or open.* But *disingenuous* people are far more than simply *not ingenuous.* They are crafty, cunning, dishonest, artful, insincere, untrustworthy—and they are all of these while making a pretense of being simple, frank, and aboveboard. You are thinking of a wolf in sheep's clothing? It's a good analogy.

Similarly, a remark may be *disingenuous,* as may also a statement, an attitude, a confession, etc.

Add *-ness* to form the noun derived from *disingenuous:*

_____.

REVIEW OF ETYMOLOGY

PREFIX, ROOT, SUFFIX	MEANING	ENGLISH WORD
1. *in-*	negative prefix	_____
2. *-ness*	noun suffix	_____
3. *credo*	to believe	_____
4. *-ous*	adjective suffix	_____

5.	-ible	can be; able to be	_____
6.	-ity	noun suffix	_____
7.	-ence	noun suffix	_____
8.	dis-	negative prefix	_____

USING THE WORDS

Can you pronounce the words?

1.	*indefatigability*	in'-də-fat'-ə-gə-BIL'-ə-tee
2.	*ingenuousness*	in-JEN'-yo͞o-əs-ness
3.	*ingenious*	in-JEEN'-yəs
4.	*ingenuity*	in'-jə-NO͞O'-ə-tee
5.	*naïve*	nah-EEV'
6.	*naïveté*	nah-eev-TAY'
7.	*credulous*	KREJ'-ə-ləs
8.	*incredulous*	in-KREJ'-ə-ləs
9.	*gullible*	GUL'-ə-bəl
10.	*gullibility*	gul'-ə-BIL'-ə-tee
11.	*credible*	KRED'-ə-bəl
12.	*incredible*	in-KRED'-ə-bəl
13.	*credulity*	krə-JO͞O'-lə-tee
14.	*incredulity*	in'-krə-JO͞O'-lə-tee
15.	*credibility*	kred'-ə-BIL'-ə-tee
16.	*incredibility*	in-kred'-ə-BIL'-ə-tee
17.	*credo*	KREE'-dō
18.	*creed*	KREED
19.	*credence*	KREE'-dəns
20.	*credentials*	krə-DEN'-shəlz
21.	*disingenuous*	dis'-in-JEN'-yo͞o-əs
22.	*disingenuousness*	dis'-in-JEN'-yo͞o-əs-nəs

Can you work with the words? (I)

WORDS	DEFINITIONS
1. indefatigability	a. cunning
2. ingenuousness	b. skepticism

3. disingenuousness	c. personal code of ethics
4. naïveté	d. frankness
5. credibility	e. belief, trust
6. incredulity	f. tirelessness
7. credence	g. believability
8. credo	h. inexperience; unworldliness

KEY: 1–f, 2–d, 3–a, 4–h, 5–g, 6–b, 7–e, 8–c

Can you work with the words? (II)

1. ingenious	a. easily tricked
2. credulous	b. religious belief
3. gullible	c. inexperienced; unworldly
4. incredible	d. document proving privileges, identity, etc.
5. creed	e. unbelievable
6. credentials	f. shrewdness; cleverness
7. ingenuity	g. clever; inventive; shrewd
8. naïve	h. willing to believe

KEY: 1–g, 2–h, 3–a, 4–e, 5–b, 6–d, 7–f, 8–c

Do you understand the words?

1. Is *indefatigability* a sign of physical and emotional health?	YES	NO
2. Is *ingenuousness* a normal quality of young childhood?	YES	NO
3. Is *ingenuity* a characteristic of inventors?	YES	NO
4. Are some adolescents *naïve?*	YES	NO
5. Are unintelligent people often *gullible?*	YES	NO
6. Is *incredulity* the mark of the agnostic?	YES	NO
7. Does an *incredible* story invite belief?	YES	NO

8. Do people generally live by a *credo?* YES NO
9. Does our Constitution guarantee certain YES NO
   rights to Americans irrespective of their
   creed?
10. Are *ingenious* people sometimes YES NO
    disingenuous?
11. Do we generally give *credence* to YES NO
    incredible statements?

Can you recall the words?

1. inexperience; unsophistication	1. N_____
2. believing (*adj.*)	2. C_____
3. religious belief	3. C_____
4. believable	4. C_____
5. great reservoir of energy	5. I_____
6. frankness	6. I_____
7. crafty; dishonest	7. D_____
8. inventive; clever	8. I_____
9. easily tricked	9. G_____
10. skeptical	10. I_____
11. unbelievable	11. I_____
12. personal code	12. C_____

(*End of Session 34*)

SESSION 35

ORIGINS AND RELATED WORDS

1. how to look

The Latin root *specto,* to look, is the source of a host of common English words: *spectacle, spectator, inspect, retrospect* (a looking back), *prospect* (a looking ahead), etc. In a variant spelling, *spic-,* the root is found in *conspicuous* (easily seen or looked at), *perspicacious,* and *perspicuous.*

A *perspicacious* (pur'-spə-KAY'-shəs) person is keen-minded, mentally sharp, astute. *Per-* is a prefix meaning *through;* so the word etymologically means *looking through* (matters, etc.) keenly, intelligently. The noun: *perspicacity* (pur'-spə-KAS'-ə-tee). Write an alternate noun ending in *-ness:*

Perspicacity is a synonym of *acumen* (ə-KYŌŌ'-mən), mental keenness, sharpness, quickness; keen insight. The root is Latin *acuo,* to sharpen.

2. sharpness

From *acuo,* to sharpen, come such words as *acute,* sharp, sudden, as *acute pain,* an *acute* attack of appendicitis, *acute* reasoning, etc; and *acupuncture* (AK'-yŏŏ-punk'-chər), the insertion of a (sharp) needle into the body for medical purposes. The noun form of *acute,* referring to the mind or thinking, is *acuteness* or *acuity* (ə-KYŌŌ-ə-tee); in other contexts, *acuteness* only.

Acupuncture combines *acuo,* to sharpen, with *punctus,* point. When you *punctuate* a sentence, you put various *points* (periods, commas, etc.) where needed; when lightning *punctuates* the storm, or when the silence is *punctuated* by the wailing of police sirens, again *points,* etymologically speaking, interrupt the atmosphere, the quiet, etc.

If you are *punctual,* you're right on the point of time (noun: *punctuality*); if you're *punctilious* (punk-TIL'-ee-əs), you are exact, scrupulous, very careful to observe the proper *points* of behavior, procedure, etc. (noun: *punctiliousness*). And to *puncture* something, of course, is to make a hole in it with a sharp *point*—as to *puncture* someone's tire, or figuratively, illusions, fantasies, or ego. *Pungent* (PUN'-jənt) comes from another form of the root *punctus* (*pungo,* to pierce sharply), so a *pungent* smell or taste is sharp, spicy, pricking the nose or taste buds, so to speak; and a *pungent* wit sharply pierces one's sense of humor. Can you write the noun forms of this adjective? _____ or _____.

3. some more looking

Perspicacious should not be confused with *perspicuous* (pər-SPIK'-yōō-əs). Here is the important distinction:

Perspicacious means *smart, sharp, able to look through and understand quickly.* This adjective applies to persons, their reasoning, minds, etc.

Perspicuous is the obverse side of the coin—it means *easily understood from one look,* and applies to writing, style, books, and like things that have to be understood. Hence it is a synonym of *clear, simple, lucid.* If you write with *perspicuous* style, your language is clear, easy to understand. If you are *perspicacious,* you understand quickly, easily.

The noun form of *perspicuous* is *perspicuity* (pur'-spə-KYŌŌ'-ə-tee), or, of course, *perspicuousness.*

A *spectacle* is something to *look at; spectacles* (eyeglasses) are the means by which you get a comfortable and accurate *look* at the world. Anything *spectacular* is, etymologically, worth *looking* at.

A *spectator* is one who *looks at* what's happening.

To *inspect* is to *look into* something.

Retrospect (RET'-rə-spekt') is a backward *look*—generally the word is preceded by the preposition *in,* for instance, "His life *in retrospect* seemed dreary and dull," or "Most experiences seem more enjoyable *in retrospect* than in actuality" (*retro-*, backward).

Prospect (PROS'-pekt') is a forward *look; prospective* (prə-SPEK'-tiv) is the adjective. What's the *prospect* for inflation, for world peace, for the domestic energy supply? Your *prospective* mother-in-law is the one you can look forward to if you marry a certain person; similarly, your *prospective* bride, groom, child, job, vacation, etc. is the person, thing, or activity in the future that you look forward to. (The prefix is *pro-*, forward, ahead, before.)

If you enjoy looking at yourself, figuratively speaking, then you like to examine your mental processes and emotional reactions, in the intense way characteristic of the *introvert* (see Chapter 3). Your mind's eye turns inward, and you spend a good deal of time analyzing yourself, your character, your personality, your actions. Hence, since you look *inward,* you are *introspective* (in'-trə-SPEK'-tiv)—the prefix is *intro-,* inside, within. If you *introspect* (in'-trə-SPEKT'), you look inward and examine your inner reactions. Too much *introspection* (in'-trə-SPEK'-shən) or *introspectiveness* may lead to unhappiness or to depressing thoughts or feelings of anxiety—few people have the courage to see themselves as they really are.

There are times when you have to look *around* most carefully; you must then be *circumspect* (SUR'-kəm-spekt')—watchful, cautious, alert (*circum-*, around).

The noun is *circumspection* (sur'-kem-SPEK'-shən) or *circumspectness*.

If something looks good or sensible, but actually is not, we call it *specious* (SPEE'-shəs). A *specious* argument sounds plausible, but in reality is based on an error, a fallacy, or an untruth. The noun is *speciousness*.

REVIEW OF ETYMOLOGY

PREFIX, ROOT, SUFFIX	MEANING	ENGLISH WORD
1. *specto*	to look	_____
2. *per-*	through	_____

3. *acuo*	to sharpen	_____
4. *punctus*	point	_____
5. *-ate*	verb suffix	_____
6. *-al*	adjective suffix	_____
7. *pungo*	to pierce sharply	_____
8. *-ent*	adjective suffix	_____
9. *-ence, -ency*	noun suffixes	_____
10. *-ness*	noun suffix	_____
11. *-ity*	noun suffix	_____
12. *retro-*	backward	_____
13. *pro-*	forward, ahead, before	_____
14. *intro-*	inside, within	_____
15. *-ion*	noun suffix	_____
16. *-ive*	adjective suffix	_____
17. *circum-*	around	_____

USING THE WORDS

Can you pronounce the words? (I)

1. *perspicacious*	pur′-spə-KAY′-shəs
2. *perspicacity*	pur′-spə-KAS′-ə-tee
3. *acumen*	ə-KYOO′-mən
4. *acute*	ə-KYOOT′
5. *acuity*	ə-KYOO′-ə-tee
6. *acupuncture*	AK′-yoo-punk′-chər
7. *punctuate*	PUNK′-choo-ayt′
8. *punctilious*	punk-TIL′-ee-əs
9. *puncture*	PUNK′-chər
10. *pungent*	PUN′-jənt
11. *pungence*	PUN′-jəns
12. *pungency*	PUN′-jən-see

Can you pronounce the words? (II)

| 1. *perspicuous* | pər-SPIK′-yoo-əs |
| 2. *perspicuity* | pur′-spə-KYOO′-ə-tee |

368

3. *retrospect*	RET'-rə-spekt'
4. *prospect*	PROS'-pekt'
5. *prospective*	prə-SPEK'-tiv
6. *introspective*	in'-trə-SPEK'-tiv
7. *introspect*	in'-trə-SPEKT'
8. *introspection*	in'-trə-SPEK'-shən
9. *circumspect*	SUR'-kəm-spekt'
10. *circumspection*	sur'-kəm-SPEK'-shən
11. *specious*	SPEE'-shəs

Can you work with the words? (I)

1. perspicacious	a.	extremely careful, exact, or proper in procedure
2. acumen	b.	clear; easy to understand
3. acupuncture	c.	a forward look
4. punctilious	d.	looking inside, or examining or analyzing, oneself
5. pungent	e.	keen-minded
6. perspicuous	f.	sharp; spicy; piercing
7. retrospect	g.	careful, watchful, wary, cautious; "looking around"
8. prospect	h.	sharpness of mind or thinking
9. introspective	i.	a backward look
10. circumspect	j.	medical insertion of needles

KEY: 1–e, 2–h, 3–j, 4–a, 5–f, 6–b, 7–i, 8–c, 9–d, 10–g

Can you work with the words? (II)

1. acute	a.	pierce; make a hole in; (noun) a small hole
2. acuity	b.	clarity; lucidity; ability to be understood quickly and easily

369

3. punctuate   c. sounding plausible, or looking right, but actually false or untrue

4. puncture   d. in the future; describing that which, or one who, can be looked forward to

5. pungence, pungency   e. care; watchfulness; caution

6. perspicuity   f. sharp; sudden; keen-minded

7. prospective   g. tending to examine and to think about one's motives, feelings, etc.

8. introspective   h. interrupt sharply or suddenly

9. circumspection   i. sharpness or spiciness of taste, smell, wit, etc.

10. specious   j. keeness of mind, thinking, or intellect

KEY: 1–f, 2–j, 3–h, 4–a, 5–i, 6–b, 7–d, 8–g, 9–e, 10–c

Do you understand the words?

1.	perspicacious—dull-witted	SAME	OPPOSITE
2.	acumen—stupidity	SAME	OPPOSITE
3.	acute—sharp	SAME	OPPOSITE
4.	acuity—perspicacity	SAME	OPPOSITE
5.	punctilious—casual	SAME	OPPOSITE
6.	pungent—flat, dull	SAME	OPPOSITE
7.	perspicuous—clear	SAME	OPPOSITE
8.	retrospect—backward look	SAME	OPPOSITE
9.	prospect—expectation	SAME	OPPOSITE
10.	introspective—extroverted	SAME	OPPOSITE
11.	prospective—in the past	SAME	OPPOSITE
12.	circumspect—careless	SAME	OPPOSITE
13.	specious—true	SAME	OPPOSITE

KEY: 1–O, 2–O, 3–S, 4–S, 5–O, 6–O, 7–S, 8–S, 9–S, 10–O, 11–O, 12–O, 13–O

Can you recall the words? (I)

1. plausible, but false or incorrect   1. S_____
2. spiciness, sharpness; piercing   2. P_____
   quality   *or* P_____
3. clear; easily understood   3. P_____
4. sharpness of mind or of   4. A_____
   intelligence   *or* A_____
       or A_____
5. care and caution; wariness   5. C_____
       or C_____
6. piercing of the skin with   6. A_____
   needles for medical purposes
7. tending to examine one's   7. I_____
   motives, etc.; loooking inward
   (*adj.*)
8. exact in the observance of   8. P_____
   proper procedure
9. to pierce and make a small   9. P_____
   hole in
10. a backward look or view   10. R_____

KEY: 1–specious, 2–pungence *or* pungency, 3–perspicuous,
4–acumen *or* acuteness *or* acuity, 5–circumspection *or*
circumspectness, 6–acupuncture, 7–introspective, 8–punctilious, 9–puncture, 10–retrospect

---

Can you recall the words? (II)

1. keenness of mind   1. P_____
       or P_____
2. sharp; sudden; keen-minded   2. A_____
3. to interrupt suddenly   3. P_____
4. spicy; piercing in taste, smell,   4. P_____
   wit, etc.
5. clarity; clearness of style or   5. P_____
   language   *or* P_____

371

6. keen-minded; perceptive 6. P_____
7. a look forward 7. P_____
8. act or process of looking 8. I_____
   inward
9. carefully looking around; 9. C_____
   cautious; wary
10. anticipated; "to be"; looked 10. P_____
    forward to (*adj.*)

KEY: 1–perspicacity *or* perspicaciousness, 2–acute, 3–punctuate,
     4–pungent, 5–perspicuity *or* perspicuousness, 6–perspi-
     cacious, 7–prospect, 8–introspection, 9–circumspect,
     10–prospective

(*End of Session 35*)

SESSION 36

ORIGINS AND RELATED WORDS

1. the great and the small

You are familiar with Latin *animus,* mind. *Animus* and a related root, *anima,* life principle, soul, spirit (in a sense, these
meanings are all very similar), are the source of such words as *animal, animate* and *inanimate, animated,* and *animation;* knowing
the meaning of the roots, you have a better understanding of any
word built on them.

Magnanimous contains, in addition to *animus,* mind, the root
magnus, large, great, which you recall from *magniloquent. Magnanimous* people have such great, noble minds or souls that they
are beyond seeking petty revenge.

The noun is *magnanimity* (mag'-nə-NIM'-ə-tee).

On the other hand, people who have tiny, tiny minds or souls are *pusillanimous* (pyōō′-sə-LAN′-ə-mes)—Latin *pusillus,* tiny. Hence, they are contemptibly petty and mean. The noun is *pusillanimity* (pyōō′-sə-lə-NIM′-ə-tee).

Other words built on *animus,* mind:

1. *unanimous* (yōō-NAN′-ə-məs)—of one *mind.* If the Supreme Court hands down a *unanimous* opinion, all the judges are of *one* mind (Latin *unus,* one). The noun is *unanimity* (yōō′-nə-NIM′-ə-tee).

2. *equanimity* (ee′-kwə-NIM′-ə-tee *or* ek′-wə-NIM′-ə-tee)—etymologically, "equal (or balanced) mind." Hence, evenness or calmness of mind; composure. If you preserve your *equanimity* under trying circumstances, you keep your temper, you do not get confused, you remain calm (Latin *aequus,* equal).

3. *animus* (AN′-ə-məs)—hostility, ill will, malevolence. Etymologically, *animus* is simply *mind,* but has degenerated, as words often do, to mean *unfriendly mind.* The word is most often used in a pattern like, "I bear you no *animus,* even though you have tried to destroy me." (Such a statement shows real *magnanimity!*)

4. *animosity* (an′-ə-MOS′-ə-tee)—ill will, hostility. An exact synonym of *animus,* and a more common word. It is used in patterns like, "You feel a good deal of *animosity,* don't you?", "There is real *animosity* between Bill and Ernie," "If you bear me no *animosity,* why do you treat me so badly?"

2. turning

Versatile comes from *verto, versus,* to turn—*versatile* people can turn their hand to many things successfully. The noun is *versatility* (vur′-sə-TIL′-ə-tee).

3. Zeno and the front porch

Centuries ago, in ancient Greece, the philosopher Zeno lectured on a topic that still piques the human mind, to wit: "How to Live a Happy Life." Zeno would stand on a porch (the Greek word for which is *stoa*) and hold forth somewhat as follows: people should free themselves from intense emotion, be unmoved by both joy and sorrow, and submit without complaint to unavoidable necessity.

Today, psychologists suggest pretty much the exact opposite—let your emotions flow freely, express your love or animosity, don't bottle up your feelings. But in the fourth century B.C., when Zeno was expounding his credo, his philosophy of control of the passions fell on receptive ears. His followers were called *Stoics,* after the *stoa,* or porch, from which the master lectured.

If we call people *stoical,* we mean that they bear their pain or sorrow without complaint, they meet adversity with unflinching fortitude. This sounds very noble, you will admit—actually, according to modern psychological belief, it is healthier not to be so *stoical. Stoicism* (STŌ'-ə-siz-əm) may be an admirable virtue (mainly because we do not then have to listen to the *stoic's* troubles), but it can be overdone.

4. fear and trembling

Intrepid is from Latin *trepido,* to tremble. *Intrepid p*eople exhibit courage and fearlessness (and not a single tremble!) when confronted by dangers from which you and I would run like the cowards we are. (You recognize the negative prefix *in-.*)

The noun: *intrepidity* (in'-trə-PID'-ə-tee), or, of course, *intrepidness.*

Trepido is the source also of *trepidation* (trep'-ə-DAY'-shən) —great fear, trembling, or alarm.

5. quick flash

Scintilla, in Latin, is a quick, bright spark; in English the word *scintilla* (sin-TIL'-ə) may also mean *a spark,* but more commonly refers to a very small particle (which, in a sense, a spark is), as in, "There was not a *scintilla* of evidence against him."

In the verb *scintillate* (SIN'-tə-layt'), the idea of the spark remains; someone who *scintillates* sparkles with charm and wit, flashes brightly with humor. The noun is *scintillation* (sin'-tə LAY'-shən).

6. city and country

People who live in the big city go to theaters, attend the opera, visit museums and picture galleries, browse in bookstores, and shop at Robinson's, Bloomingdale's, Marshall Field, or other large department stores.

These activities fill them with culture and sophistication.

Also, they crowd into jammed subway trains or buses, squeeze into packed elevators, cross the street in competition with high-powered motorcars, patiently stand in line outside of movie houses, and then wait again in the lobby for seats to be vacated.

Also, they have the privilege of spending two hours a day going to and coming from work.

As a result, city-dwellers are refined, polished, courteous—or so the etymology of *urbane* (from Latin *urbs,* city) tells us. (And you must be absurdly credulous, if not downright gullible, to believe it.) The noun is *urbanity* (ur-BAN'-ə-tee).

So *urbane* people are gracious, affable, cultivated, suave, tactful—add any similar adjectives you can think of.

Urban (UR'-bən) as an adjective simply refers to cities—*urban* affairs, *urban* areas, *urban* populations, *urban* life, *urban* development, etc.

Consider some prefixes: *sub-,* near; *inter-,* between; *intra-,* inside, within; *ex-,* out.

Add each prefix to the root *urbs,* using the adjective suffix *-an:*

> sub_____: near the city
> (*Sub-* has a number of meanings: *under, near, close to,* etc.)
> inter_____: between cities
> intra_____: within a city
> ex_____: out of the city

The *suburbs* are residential sections, or small communities, close to a large city; Larchmont is a *suburb* of New York City, Whittier a *suburb* of Los Angeles.

Suburbia (sə-BUR'-bee-ə) may designate *suburbs* as a group; *suburban* residents, or *suburbanites* (sə-BUR'-bə-nīts'), as a group; or the typical manners, modes of living, customs, etc. of suburban residents.

An *interurban* bus travels *between* cities, an *intraurban* bus *within* a single city.

An *exurb* (EKS'-urb) lies well beyond, way outside, a large city, and generally refers to a region inhabited by well-to-do families. *Exurb* has derived forms corresponding to those of *suburb*. Can you construct them?

Plural noun: _____

Adjective: _____

Resident: _____

As a group; manners, customs, etc.: _____

Urbs is the city; Latin *rus, ruris* is the country, i.e., farmland, fields, etc. So *rural* (ROOR'-əl) refers to country or farm regions, agriculture, etc.—a wealthy *rural* area.

Rustic (RUS'-tik) as an adjective may describe furniture or dwellings made of roughhewn wood, or furnishings suitable to a farmhouse; or, when applied to a person, is an antonym of *urbane* —unsophisticated, boorish, lacking in social graces, uncultured. Noun: *rusticity* (rus-TIS'-ə-tee). *Rustic* is also a noun designating a person with such characteristics, as in, "He was considered a *rustic* by his classmates, all of whom came from cultured and wealthy backgrounds."

Urbane and *rustic,* when applied to people, are emotionally charged words. *Urbane* is complimentary, *rustic* derogatory.*

To *rusticate* (RUS'-tə-kayt') is to spend time in the country, away from the turmoil and tensions of big-city life. Can you construct the noun? _____.

---

* Incidentally, a word used with a derogatory connotation (*bitch, piggish, glutton, idiot,* etc.) is called a *pejorative* (pe-JAWR'-ə-tiv). *Pejorative* is also an adjective, as in, "She spoke in *pejorative* terms about her ex-husband." The derivation is Latin *pejor,* worse.

REVIEW OF ETYMOLOGY

PREFIX, ROOT, SUFFIX	MEANING	ENGLISH WORD
1. *animus*	mind	_____
2. *anima*	soul, spirit, life principle	_____
3. *magnus*	large, great	_____
4. *pusillus*	tiny	_____
5. *unus*	one	_____
6. *aequus (equ-)*	equal	_____
7. *verto, versus*	to turn	_____
8. *stoa*	porch	_____
9. *in-*	negative prefix	_____
10. *trepido*	to tremble	_____
11. *scintilla*	a spark	_____
12. *urbs*	city	_____
13. *sub-*	near, close to, under	_____
14. *inter-*	between	_____
15. *intra-*	within, inside	_____
16. *ex-*	out	_____
17. *rus, ruris*	country, farmlands	_____
18. *-ate*	verb suffix	_____
19. *-ion*	noun suffix aded to *-ate* verbs	_____

USING THE WORDS

Can you pronounce the words? (I)

1. *magnanimity*   mag′-nə-NIM′-ə-tee
2. *pusillanimous*   pyōō′-sə-LAN′-ə-məs
3. *pusillanimity*   pyōō′-sə-lə-NIM′-ə-tee
4. *unanimous*   yōō-NAN′-ə-məs

5. *unanimity*   yōō-nə-NIM'-ə-tee
6. *equanimity*   eek' (*or* ek')-wə-NIM'-ə-tee
7. *animus*   AN'-ə-məs
8. *animosity*   an'-ə-MOS'-ə-tee
9. *versatility*   vur'-sə-TIL'-ə-tee
10. *stoic*   STŌ'-ik
11. *stoicism*   STŌ'-ə-siz-əm

Can you pronounce the words? (II)

1. *intrepidity*   in'-trə-PID'-ə-tee
2. *trepidation*   trep'-ə-DAY'-shən
3. *scintilla*   sin-TIL'-ə
4. *scintillate*   SIN'-tə-layt'
5. *scintillation*   sin'-tə-LAY'-shən
6. *urbanity*   ur-BAN'-ə-tee
7. *suburbia*   sə-BUR'-bee-ə
8. *interurban*   in'-tər-UR'-bən
9. *intraurban*   in'-trə-UR'-bən
10. *exurbs*   EKS'-urbz
11. *exurban*   eks-UR'-bən
12. *exurbanite*   eks-UR'-bən-īt'
13. *exurbia*   eks-UR'-bee-ə

Can you pronounce the words? (III)

1. *rural*   RŌŌR'-əl
2. *rustic*   RUS'-tik
3. *rusticity*   rus-TIS'-ə-tee
4. *rusticate*   RUS'-tə-kayt'
5. *rustication*   rus'-tə-KAY'-shən
6. *pejorative*   pə-JAWR'-ə-tiv

Can you work with the words? (I)

1. magnanimity   a. calmness, composure
2. pusillanimity   b. ability either to do many different things well, or to func-

tion successfully in many areas

3. unanimity
c. fearlessness; great courage

4. equanimity
d. unemotionality; bearing of pain, etc. without complaint

5. animosity
e. big-heartedness; generosity; quality of forgiving easily

6. versatility
f. a sparkling with wit or cleverness

7. stoicism
g. fear and trembling; alarm

8. intrepidity
h. complete agreement, all being of one mind

9. trepidation
i. petty-mindedness

10. scintillation
j. anger, hostility, resentment, hatred

KEY: 1–e, 2–i, 3–h, 4–a, 5–j, 6–b, 7–d, 8–c, 9–g, 10–f

Can you work with the words? (II)

1. urbanity
a. referring to the countryside

2. suburbia
b. word with negative or derogatory connotation; describing such a word or words

3. exurbia
c. to spend time in the country

4. animus
d. residential areas near big cities; customs, etc. of the inhabitants of such areas

5. interurban
e. residential areas far from big cities; customs, etc. of the inhabitants of such areas

6. intraurban
f. between cities

7. rural
g. roughhewn, farmlike; unsophisticated, uncultured

8. rustic
h. sophistication, courtesy, polish, etc.

9. rusticate
10. pejorative

i. anger, hatred, hostility
j. within one city

KEY: 1–h, 2–d, 3–e, 4–i, 5–f, 6–j, 7–a, 8–g, 9–c, 10–b

(End of Session 36)

SESSION 37

READY FOR A STRONG REVIEW?

Drill, drill, drill! This is the important secret of learning words thoroughly.

Review, review, review! This is the secret of remembering, assimilating, digesting, and keeping as permanent acquisitions all the new words you have learned.

So pitch in with enthusiasm to the rest of this chapter, made up of a series of valuable tests on all the chapter words. Ready?

Can you work with the words? (I)

1. retrospect
2. acumen
3. magnanimity
4. pusillanimity
5. unanimity
6. equanimity
7. animosity
8. versatility

a. complete agreement
b. pettiness
c. malevolence
d. backward look
e. calmness
f. ability in many fields
g. mental keenness
h. generosity

KEY: 1–d, 2–g, 3–h, 4–b, 5–a, 6–e, 7–c, 8–f

Can you work with the words? (II)

1. stoicism
2. intrepidity
3. trepidation
4. scintillation

a. fearlessness
b. sparkle
c. inward look
d. uncomplaining attitude to pain or trouble

5. urbanity
6. introspection
7. circumspection
8. speciousness

e. falsity
f. polish, cultivation
g. care, cautiousness
h. fear

KEY: 1–d, 2–a, 3–h, 4–b, 5–f, 6–c, 7–g, 8–e

Can you work with the words? (III)

1. exurbs
2. pusillanimous
3. unanimous
4. animus
5. rustic
6. urban
7. introspective
8. circumspect
9. specious

a. of one mind
b. ill will
c. pertaining to the city
d. petty
e. self-analytical
f. regions far from the city
g. cautious
h. false, though plausible
i. countrified

KEY: 1–f, 2–d, 3–a, 4–b, 5–i, 6–c, 7–e, 8–g, 9–h

Can you work with the words? (IV)

1. perspicacity
2. perspicuity
3. stoic
4. scintilla

a. clearness
b. to be witty
c. spend time in the country
d. one who controls his emotions

5. scintillate e. to look inward
6. rural f. a very small amount
7. rusticate g. keen intelligence
8. introspect h. clear, understandable
9. perspicuous i. keen-minded
10. perspicacious j. pertaining to the country.

KEY: 1–g, 2–a, 3–d, 4–f, 5–b, 6–j, 7–c, 8–e, 9–h, 10–i

Do you understand the words? (I)

1. Does life often seem pleasanter in *retrospect?*	YES	NO
2. Are people of *acuity* gullible?	YES	NO
3. Is *perspicacity* a common characteristic?	YES	NO
4. Is a person of *acumen* likely to be naïve?	YES	NO
5. Is a *perspicuous* style of writing easy to read?	YES	NO
6. Should all writers aim at *perspicuity?*	YES	NO
7. Is *magnanimity* a characteristic of small-minded people?	YES	NO
8. Does a person of *pusillanimous* mind often think of petty revenge?	YES	NO
9. Is a *unanimous* opinion one in which all concur?	YES	NO

KEY: 1–yes, 2–no, 3–no, 4–no, 5–yes, 6–yes, 7–no, 8–yes, 9–yes

---

Do you understand the words? (II)

1. Is it easy to preserve one's *equanimity* under trying circumstances?	YES	NO
2. Do we bear *animus* toward our enemies?	YES	NO
3. Do we usually feel great *animosity* toward our friends?	YES	NO
4. Do we admire *versatility?*	YES	NO

5. Does a *stoic* usually complain?   YES   NO
6. Is *stoicism* a mark of an uninhibited   YES   NO
   personality?
7. Do cowards show *intrepidity* in the face   YES   NO
   of danger?
8. Do cowards often feel a certain amount   YES   NO
   of *trepidation*?
9. Is a *scintilla* of evidence a great   YES   NO
   amount?
10. Do dull people *scintillate*?   YES   NO
11. Is *urbanity* a characteristic of boorish   YES   NO
    people?

KEY: 1–no, 2–yes, 3–no, 4–yes, 5–no, 6–no, 7–no, 8–yes, 9–no,
      10–no, 11–no

Do you understand the words? (III)

1. Is New York City a *rural* community?   YES   NO
2. Is a village an *urban* community?   YES   NO
3. Do you *rusticate* in the city?.   YES   NO
4. Are extroverts very *introspective*?   YES   NO
5. Does an introvert spend a good deal of   YES   NO
   time in *introspection*?
6. In dangerous circumstances, is it wise to   YES   NO
   be *circumspect*?
7. Do *specious* arguments often sound   YES   NO
   convincing?

KEY: 1–no, 2–no, 3–no, 4–no, 5–yes, 6–yes, 7–yes

Do you understand the words? (IV)

1. retrospect—prospect   SAME   OPPOSITE
2. acute—perspicacious   SAME   OPPOSITE
3. acumen—stupidity   SAME   OPPOSITE
4. perspicuous—confused   SAME   OPPOSITE

383

5. magnanimous—noble	SAME	OPPOSITE
6. pusillanimous—petty	SAME	OPPOSITE
7. unanimous—divided	SAME	OPPOSITE
8. equanimity—nervousness	SAME	OPPOSITE
9. animosity—hostility	SAME	OPPOSITE
10. animus—friendliness	SAME	OPPOSITE
11. versatility—monomania	SAME	OPPOSITE
12. stoicism—cowardice	SAME	OPPOSITE
13. intrepidity—fear	SAME	OPPOSITE
14. trepidation—courage	SAME	OPPOSITE
15. scintilla—slight amount	SAME	OPPOSITE
16. urbanity—refinement	SAME	OPPOSITE
17. rustic—crude	SAME	OPPOSITE
18. rural—urban	SAME	OPPOSITE
19. introspective—self-analytic	SAME	OPPOSITE
20. circumspect—careless	SAME	OPPOSITE
21. specious—true	SAME	OPPOSITE

KEY: 1–O, 2–S, 3–O, 4–O, 5–S, 6–S, 7–O, 8–O, 9–S, 10–O, 11–O, 12–O, 13–O, 14–O, 15–S, 16–S, 17–S, 18–O, 19–S, 20–O, 21–O

Can you recall the words? (I)

1. ability in many fields	1. V_____
2. pertaining to the city (*adj.*)	2. U_____
3. to spend time in the country	3. R_____
4. merest spark; small amount	4. S_____
5. courage	5. I_____

KEY: 1–versatility, 2–urban, 3–rusticate, 4–scintilla, 5–intrepidity

Can you recall the words? (II)

1. unflinching fortitude	1. S_____
2. countrified; unpolished	2. R_____

384

3. pertaining to the countryside
   (*adj.*)
   3. R_____
4. a looking back to the past
   4. R_____
5. nobleness of mind or spirit
   5. M_____

KEY: 1–stoicism, 2–rustic, 3–rural, 4–retrospect, 5–magnanimity

---

Can you recall the words? (III)

1. keen-mindedness   1. A_____
2. clear, lucid   2. P_____
3. petty, mean   3. P_____
4. all of one mind or opinion   4. U_____
5. ill will   5. A_____
   or A_____

KEY: 1–acuity, 2–perspicuous, 3–pusillanimous, 4–unanimous,
     5–animus *or* animosity

Can you recall the words? (IV)

1–4. keenness of mind   1. P_____
   or P_____
   2. A_____
   3. A_____
   4. A_____
5. clearness of style or language   5. P_____
6. one who keeps his emotions,   6. S_____
    during times of trouble,
    hidden
7. sophistication, courtesy,   7. U_____
    refinement

KEY: 1–perspicacity *or* perspicaciousness, 2–acumen, 3–acuity,
     4–acuteness (2–4 in any order), 5–perspicuity, 6–stoic,
     7–urbanity

Can you recall the words? (V)

1. pettiness of character	1. P_____
2. noun form of *unanimous*	2. U_____
3. mental calmness, balance	3. E_____
4. fear and trembling	4. T_____
5. to sparkle with wit and humor	5. S_____

KEY: 1–pusillanimity, 2–unanimity, 3–equanimity, 4–trepidation, 5–scintillate

Can you recall the words? (VI)

1. a looking inward; an examining of one's mental processes or emotional reactions	1. I_____
2. cautious	2. C_____
3. seemingly true, actually false	3. S_____
4. to think of one's mental processes	4. I_____
5. care, watchfulness	5. C_____

KEY: 1–introspective, 2–circumspect, 3–specious, 4–introspect, 5–circumspection

THREE FURTHER TESTS

I. matching

WORD	MEANING
1. convivial	a. frank
2. indefatigable	b. noble, forgiving
3. ingenuous	c. unflinching; unemotional

386

4. perspicacious
5. magnanimous
6. versatile
7. stoical
8. intrepid
9. scintillating
10. urbane

d. courteous; polished; suave
e. companionable, gregarious
f. witty
g. capable in many directions
h. brave
i. keen-minded
j. tireless

KEY: 1–e, 2–j, 3–a, 4–i, 5–b, 6–g, 7–c, 8–h, 9–f, 10–d

II. same or opposite?

1. vivacious—sluggish	SAME	OPPOSITE
2. vital—crucial	SAME	OPPOSITE
3. ennui—boredom	SAME	OPPOSITE
4. *bon vivant*—gourmand	SAME	OPPOSITE
5. gourmet—ascetic	SAME	OPPOSITE
6. ingenuous—crafty	SAME	OPPOSITE
7. naïve—sophisticated	SAME	OPPOSITE
8. credulous—skeptical	SAME	OPPOSITE
9. disingenuous—insincere	SAME	OPPOSITE
10. credo—belief	SAME	OPPOSITE

KEY: 1–O, 2–S, 3–S, 4–S, 5–O, 6–O, 7–O, 8–O, 9–S, 10–S

III. changing parts of speech

Change these adjectives to nouns *not* ending in *-ness*.

1. indefatigable   1. _____
2. perspicacious   2. _____
3. stoical   3. _____
4. urbane   4. _____
5. naïve   5. _____
6. incredulous   6. _____
7. incredible   7. _____
8. perspicuous   8. _____

9. magnanimous   9. —————
10. pusillanimous   10. —————

KEY: 1–indefatigability, 2–perspicacity, 3–stoicism, 4–urbanity, 5–naïveté, 6–incredulity, 7–incredibility, 8–perspicuity, 9–magnanimity, 10–pusillanimity

CHAPTER REVIEW

A. Do you recognize the words?

1. Tireless:
    (a) convivial, (b) indefatigable, (c) versatile
2. Frank, unsophisticated:
    (a) ingenuous, (b) ingenious, (c) intrepid
3. Unflinching, uncomplaining:
    (a) perspicacious, (b) urbane, (c) stoical
4. Noble, forgiving, generous:
    (a) pusillanimous, (b) unanimous, (c) magnanimous
5. Between cities:
    (a) interurban, (b) intraurban, (c) exurban
6. Giving birth to live young:
    (a) oviparous, (b) ovulation, (c) viviparous
7. Tedium, boredom:
    (a) ennui, (b) *joie de vivre*, (c) vitality
8. Connoisseur of choice food:
    (a) gourmet, (b) gourmand, (c) glutton
9. Inexperienced in the ways of the world:
    (a) credulous, (b) naïve, (c) credible
10. Easily tricked:
    (a) gullible, (b) incredulous, (c) ingenious
11. Backward look:
    (a) prospect, (b) retrospect, (c) introspection
12. Clearness:
    (a) perspicacity, (b) perspicuity, (c) intrepidity
13. Resentment:
    (a) animosity, (b) stoicism, (c) urbanity

14. Countrified:
    (a) rustic, (b) specious, (c) circumspect

KEY: 1–b, 2–a, 3–c, 4–c, 5–a, 6–c, 7–a, 8–a, 9–b, 10–a, 11–b, 12–b, 13–a, 14–a

---

B. Can you recognize roots?

ROOT	EXAMPLE	MEANING
1. *vivo*	_____	vivacious
2. *sectus*	_____	vivisection
3. *pareo*	_____	viviparous
4. *ovum*	_____	oviparous
5. *vita*	_____	vital
6. *bon*	_____	*bon vivant*
7. *credo*	_____	credible
8. *specto*	_____	spectator
9. *acuo*	_____	acupuncture
10. *punctus*	_____	punctuate
11. *pungo*	_____	pungent
12. *animus*	_____	animosity
13. *pusillus*	_____	pusillanimous
14. *magnus*	_____	magnanimous
15. *unus*	_____	unanimous
16. *aequus (equ-)*	_____	equanimity
17. *verto, versus*	_____	versatile
18. *stoa*	_____	stoical
19. *trepido*	_____	trepidation
20. *scintilla*	_____	scintillate
21. *urbs*	_____	urban
22. *rus, ruris*	_____	rural, rustic

KEY: 1–to live, 2–cut, 3–to give birth, produce, 4–egg, 5–life, 6–good, 7–to believe, 8–to look, 9–to sharpen, 10–point, 11–to pierce sharply, 12–mind, 13–tiny, 14–big, great, large, 15–one, 16–equal, 17–to turn, 18–porch, 19–to tremble, 20–spark, 21–city, 22–country, countryside

---

TEASER QUESTIONS FOR THE AMATEUR ETYMOLOGIST

1. Recalling the root *vivo,* to live, can you think of the verb that means *to live on?* _____.
Can you write the noun form? _____.

2. How would you explain a *vivarium?* _____ _____.

3. Recalling the meanings of Latin *vita,* what would you understand if someone asked you for your *vita* before you appeared for an interview for a professional position? _____ _____.

4. *Unus* is Latin for *one.* Can you use this root to construct words meaning:

    (a) animal with *one* horn: _____

    (b) of *one* form: _____

    (c) to make *one:* _____

    (d) *one*ness: _____

    (e) *one*-wheeled vehicle: _____

5. *Annus* is Latin for *year; verto, versus,* as you know, means *to turn.* Can you, then, explain the word *anniversary* in terms of its roots? _____ _____.

6. How about *universe* and *university* in terms of their roots (*unus,* one; *verto, versus,* to turn)?

    (a) universe: _____

    (b) university: _____

7. Use *inter-,* between, to form words of the following meanings:

    (a) *between* states (*adj.*): _____

    (b) *between* nations (*adj.*): _____

    (c) in the middle *between* elementary and advanced (*adj.*): _____

    (d) to break in (*between* people conversing): _____

    (e) *between* persons (*adj.*): _____

8. Use *intra-*, within, to form words with the following meanings (all *adjectives*):

   (a) *within* one state: _____

   (b) *within* one nation: _____

   (c) *within* one's own person or mind: _____

   (d) *within* the muscles: _____

(*Answers in Chapter 18*)

WORDS INFLUENCE YOUR THINKING

By now, you have thoroughly explored hundreds upon hundreds of valuable words and scores upon scores of important Greek and Latin roots.

As you went along you stopped at frequent intervals to say aloud, think about, work with, and recall the words you were adding to your vocabulary.

By now, therefore, the words you have been learning are probably old friends of yours; they have started to influence your thinking, have perhaps begun to appear in your conversation, and have certainly become conspicuous in your reading. In short, they have been effective in making changes in your intellectual climate.

Let us pause now for another checkup of the success of your study. In the next chapter, you will find a second Comprehensive Test. Take the test cold if you feel that all the material is at your fingertips; or spend a little time reviewing Chapters 9, 10, 11, and 12 if you believe such review is necessary.

(*End of Session 37*)

13

HOW TO CHECK
YOUR PROGRESS

Comprehensive Test II

SESSION 38

I—etymology

ROOT	MEANING	EXAMPLE
1. *scribo, scriptus*	_____	proscribe
2. *aequus (equ-)*	_____	equivocal
3. *malus*	_____	malign
4. *dico, dictus*	_____	malediction
5. *volo*	_____	malevolent
6. *facio*	_____	malefactor
7. *bonus, bene*	_____	benevolent
8. *fides*	_____	infidelity
9. *dono*	_____	condone
10. *nox, noctis*	_____	equinox
11. *equus*	_____	equestrian
12. *libra*	_____	equilibrium
13. *taceo*	_____	taciturn

14. *loquor*	————————	loquacious
15. *solus*	————————	soliloquy
16. *venter, ventris*	————————	ventral
17. *magnus*	————————	magniloquence
18. *verbum*	————————	verbatim
19. *volvo, volutus*	————————	voluble
20. *animus*	————————	pusillanimous
21. *dorsum*	————————	endorse
22. *vox, vocis*	————————	vocal
23. *fero*	————————	vociferous
24. *ambulo*	————————	somnambulist
25. *somnus*	————————	somnolent

II—more etymology

ROOT	MEANING	EXAMPLE
1. *phanein*	————————	sycophant
2. *vir*	————————	virago
3. *pater, patris*	————————	patricide
4. *onyma*	————————	synonym
5. *homos*	————————	homonym
6. *phone*	————————	homophone
7. *archein*	————————	matriarch
8. *mater, matris*	————————	matron
9. *caedo (-cide)*	————————	suicide
10. *homo*	————————	homicide
11. *uxor*	————————	uxorious
12. *maritus*	————————	mariticide
13. *pyros*	————————	pyromania
14. *theos*	————————	atheist
15. *vivo*	————————	viviparous
16. *credo*	————————	credulous
17. *pungo*	————————	pungency
18. *unus*	————————	unanimous
19. *trepido*	————————	intrepid
20. *scintilla*	————————	scintillate
21. *urbs*	————————	urbanity
22. *rus, ruris*	————————	rural, rustic

23. *gnosis*	_____	prognosis
24. *pan*	_____	pantheism
25. *omnis*	_____	omniscient

III—same or opposite?

		S	O
1. disparage—praise		S	O
2. proscribe—prohibit		S	O
3. placate—irritate		S	O
4. taciturn—talkative		S	O
5. cogent—brilliant		S	O
6. atheistic—religious		S	O
7. convivial—unfriendly		S	O
8. ingenuous—naïve		S	O
9. perspicacious—keen-minded		S	O
10. intrepid—fearful		S	O
11. malign—praise		S	O
12. inarticulate—verbal		S	O
13. verbose—laconic		S	O
14. tyro—virtuoso		S	O
15. megalomania—modesty		S	O
16. satyriasis—nymphomania		S	O
17. claustrophobia—agoraphobia		S	O
18. indefatigability—tirelessness		S	O
19. credulous—skeptical		S	O
20. animosity—hostility		S	O

IV—matching

1. is lewd and lustful	a. chauvinist
2. caters to the rich	b. sycophant
3. is an accomplished musician	c. dilettante
4. sneers at traditions	d. iconoclast
5. is the mother-ruler of a family tribe, or nation	e. lecher
6. has an irresistable urge to steal	f. tyro

7. is excessively patriotic
8. is a loud-mouthed woman
9. is a beginner
10. is a dabbler

g. virtuoso
h. termagant
i. matriarch
j. kleptomaniac

V—more matching

1. does not know whether or not God exists
2. is a criminal
3. is a connoisseur of good food
4. sets fires for revenge
5. meets adversity or pain without flinching
6. walks in his sleep
7. is obsessively addicted to drink
8. has imaginary ailments
9. compulsively sets fires
10. is a woman who is sexually insatiable

a. dipsomaniac
b. pyromaniac
c. agnostic
d. hypochondriac
e. gourmet
f. stoic
g. malefactor
h. somnambulist
i. nymphomaniac
j. incendiary

VI—recall a word

1. to make unnecessary
2. to flatter fulsomely
3. to spread slander about
4. economical in speech
5. trite and hackneyed
6. word for word
7. killing of masses of people
8. inheritance from one's father
9. belief in many gods
10. a person aggressively fighting for a cause
11. sincere; valid; in good faith

1. O_____
2. A_____
3. M_____
4. L_____
5. B_____
6. V_____
7. G_____
8. P_____
9. P_____
10. M_____

11. B_____
F_____

12. babbling ceaselessly about trivia (*adj.*)

13. to speak to oneself, as in a play

14. masterpiece

15. unselfish; not revengeful

16. able to walk after being bedridden

17. inability to fall asleep

18. morbid fear of heights

19. the killing of one's brother

20. opposite in meaning (*adj.*)

21. "joy of life"

22. to rob of life or vigor

23. inexperience, unsophistication

24. scrupulously careful in the observance of proper procedure

25. clear, understandable (of style or language)

26. wary, cautious, watchful

27. a backward look

28. all of one mind (*adj.*)

29. uncomplaining in face of pain, misfortune, or emotional difficulties (*adj.*)

30. between cities (*adj.*)

12. G_____

13. S_____

14. M_____
O_____

15. M_____

16. A_____

17. L_____

18. A_____

19. F_____

20. A_____

21. J_____D_____
V_____

22. D_____

23. N_____

24. P_____

25. P_____

26. C_____

27. R_____

28. U_____

29. S_____

30. L_____

KEY: A correct answer counts one point. Score your points for each part of the test, then add for a total.

I

1–to write, 2–equal, 3–bad, evil, 4–to say or tell, 5–to wish, 6–to do or make, 7–good, well, 8–faith, 9–to give, 10–night, 11–horse, 12–balance, pound, 13–to be silent, 14–to speak, 15–alone, 16–belly, 17–big, large, great, 18–word, 19–to roll, 20–mind, 21–back, 22–voice, 23–to bear or carry, 24–to walk, 25–sleep

Your score: _____

II

1–to show, 2–man, male, 3–father, 4–name, 5–the same, 6–sound, 7–to rule, 8–mother, 9–to kill, killing, 10–person, 11–wife, 12–husband, 13–fire, 14–God, 15–to live, 16–to believe, 17–to pierce sharply, 18–one, 19–to tremble, 20–spark, 21–city, 22–country (countryside), 23–knowledge, 24–all, 25–all

Your score: _____

III

1–O, 2–S, 3–O, 4–O, 5–S, 6–O, 7–O, 8–S, 9–S, 10–O, 11–O, 12–O, 13–O, 14–O, 15–O, 16–O, 17–O, 18–S, 19–O, 20–S

Your score: _____

IV

1–e, 2–b, 3–g, 4–d, 5–i, 6–j, 7–a, 8–h, 9–f, 10–c

Your score : _____

V

1–c, 2–g, 3–e, 4–j, 5–f, 6–h, 7–a, 8–d, 9–b, 10–i

Your score : _____

VI

1–obviate, 2–adulate, 3–malign, 4–laconic, 5–banal, 6–verbatim, 7–genocide, 8–patrimony, 9–polytheism, 10–militant, 11–bona fide, 12–garrulous, 13–soliloquize, 14–magnum opus, 15–magnanimous, 16–ambulatory, 17–insomnia, 18–acrophobia, 19–fratricide, 20–antonymous, 21–*joie de vivre*, 22–devitalize, 23–naïveté, 24–punctilious, 25–perspicuous, 26–circumspect, 27–retrospect, 28–unanimous, 29–stoical, 30–interurban

Your score: _____

Your total score: _____

Significance of Your Total Score:

100–120: Masterly work; you are ready to move right along.
 80– 99: Good work; this review was useful to you.

65– 79: Average work; you're getting a good deal out of your study, but perhaps you should review thoroughly after each session.

50– 64: Barely acceptable; work harder.

35– 49: Poor; further review is suggested before you go on.

 0– 34: You can do much better if you really try.

You might turn back for a moment to Chapter 8, in which you recorded your score on the first Comprehensive Test. Did you do better this time? Let's make a record of both scores at this point for the sake of comparison and to give you a mark to shoot at in the Comprehensive Test you will take in Chapter 17.

SCORES

Test I (Chapter 8): ＿＿＿＿＿＿ out of 120
Test II (Chapter 13): ＿＿＿＿＿＿ out of 120

(End of Session 38)

PART THREE

FINISHING WITH A FEELING OF COMPLETE SUCCESS

14

HOW TO TALK ABOUT COMMON PHENOMENA AND OCCURRENCES

(Sessions 39–41)

TEASER PREVIEW

What word aptly describes:

- *dire poverty?*
- *emotion experienced without direct participation?*
- *something which lasts a very short time?*
- *an inoffensive word for an unpleasant idea?*
- *light and easy banter?*
- *someone who is cowlike in his stolidity?*
- *homesickness?*
- *harsh sound?*
- *a meat-eating animal?*
- *something kept secret?*

SESSION 39

This world, Robert Louis Stevenson once claimed—with, I think, questionable logic—is so full of a number of things that we should all be as happy as kings.

I doubt very strongly that happiness comes from the outside, or that kings are necessarily happy. But I will go this far (and no further) with Stevenson: the world is certainly full of a number of things. For instance, poverty and misery, hospitals and insane asylums, slums and racial restrictions, cut-down forests and once fertile lands becoming progressively more arid, war and death and taxes and bumbling diplomats. I know that Stevenson had a different sort of thing in mind, for romantic poets tend to view the world through rose-tinted spectacles, but it is often necessary to counter one extreme with another—and I simply wish to set the record straight.

In this chapter we are going to discuss a number of things to be found in the world and in the minds of its inhabitants—poverty and wealth; secondhand emotions; the relativity of time; praise of various sorts; small talk and how to indulge in it; animals; longings for the past; sounds; eating habits; and many kinds and conditions of secrecy.

As you see, when you start exploring ideas, as we constantly do in these chapters, you never know what will turn up.

IDEAS

1. for want of the green stuff

There are those people who are forced (often through no fault of their own) to pursue an existence not only devoid of such luxuries as radios, television sets, sunken bathtubs, electric orange-juice squeezers, automobiles, Jacuzzis, private swimming pools, etc., but lacking also in many of the pure necessities of living—sufficient food, heated homes, hot water, vermin- and rodent-free surroundings, decent clothing, etc.

Such people live:

in *penury*

2. at least watch it

All normal people want and need love and at least a modicum of excitement in their lives—so say the psychologists. If no one loves them, and if they can find no one on whom to lavish their own love, they may often satisfy their emotional longings and needs by getting their feelings secondhand—through reading love stories, attending motion pictures, watching soap operas, etc.

These are:

vicarious feelings

3. time is fleeting

During the late winter and early spring of 1948–49, great numbers of people went practically berserk joining and forming "pyramid clubs." If you have not heard of this amazing phenomenon, I won't attempt to describe it in any of its multifarious ramifications, but the main point was that you paid two dollars, treated some people to coffee and doughnuts, and shortly thereafter (if you were gullible enough to fall for this get-rich-quick scheme) supposedly received a return of some fantastic amount like $2,064 for your investment.

For a short time, pyramid clubs were a rage—soon they had vanished from the American scene.

Anything that lasts for but a short time and leaves no trace is:

ephemeral

4. how not to call a spade . . .

Words are only *symbols* of things—they are not the things themselves. (This, by the way, is one of the basic tenets of seman-

403

tics.) But many people identify the word and the thing so closely that they fear to use certain words that symbolize things that are unpleasant to them.

I know that this is confusing, so let me illustrate.

Words having to do with death, sex, certain portions of the anatomy, excretion, etc. are avoided by certain people.

These people prefer circumlocutions—words that "talk around" an idea or that mean or imply something but don't come right out and say so directly.

For example:

WORD	CIRCUMLOCUTION
die	expire; depart this life; pass away; leave this vale of tears
sexual intercourse	(intimate) relations; "playing house"; "shacking up"
prostitute	lady of the evening; *fille de joie;* painted woman; lady of easy virtue; *fille de nuit;* streetwalker; hooker
house of prostitution	house of ill-fame; bawdyhouse; house of ill-repute; bagnio; brothel; bordello; "house"; "massage parlor"
buttocks, behind	derrière; rear end; butt; tail
breasts	bosom; bust; curves
toilet	powder room; little girl's room; facilities; washroom; lavatory; head

The left-hand column is the direct, non-pussyfooting word. The right-hand column is made up of:

euphemisms

5. small talk

"Whenever I'm in the dumps, I get a new suit."
"Oh, so that's where you get them!"
"Lend me a dime—I want to phone one of my friends."
"Here's a quarter—call them all."
"The doctor says I have snoo in my blood!"

404

"Snoo? What's snoo?"
"Not a darn! What's new with you?"
"What are twins?"
"Okay, what are twins?"
"Womb mates!"
"I took a twip yesterday."
"A twip?"
"Yes, I took a twip on a twain!"

These are examples of:

badinage

6. everything but give milk

You've seen a cow contentedly munching its cud. Nothing seems capable of disturbing this animal—and the animal seems to want nothing more out of life than to lead a simple, vegetable existence.

Some people are like a cow—calm, patient, placid, phlegmatic, vegetable-like. They are:

*bovine**

7. good old days

Do you sometimes experience a keen, almost physical, longing for associations or places of the past?

When you pass the neighborhood in which you were born and where you spent your early years, do you have a sharp, strange reaction, almost akin to mild nausea?

When you are away from home and friends and family, do pleasant remembrances crowd in on your mind to the point where your present loneliness becomes almost unbearable, and you actually feel a little sick?

This common feeling is called:

nostalgia

* Remember Ogden Nash's delightful definition?
> The cow is of the bovine ilk,
> One end moo, the other end milk.

8. sounds that grate

Some sounds are so harsh, grating, and discordant that they offend the ear. They lack all sweetness, harmony, pleasantness. Traffic noises of a big city, electronic rock music, chalk squeaking on a blackboard. . . .

Such blaring, ear-splitting, or spine-tingling sounds are called:

cacophonous

9. eating habits

Lions, tigers, wolves, and some other mammals subsist entirely on flesh. No spinach, salad greens, whole-wheat cereals, sugar, or spices—just good, red meat.

These mammals are:

carnivorous

10. private and public

There are certain things most of us do in private, like taking a bath. Some people like to engage in other activities in complete privacy—eating, reading, watching TV, sleeping, for example.

The point is that, while these activities may be conducted in privacy, there is never any reason for keeping them secret.

But there are other activities that are kept not only private, but well-shrouded in secrecy and concealed from public knowledge. These activities are unethical, illegal, or unsafe—like having an affair with someone whose spouse is your best friend, betraying military secrets to the enemy, trading in narcotics, bribing public officials, etc.

Arrangements, activities, or meetings that fall under this category are called:

clandestine

USING THE WORDS

Can you pronounce the words?

1.	*penury*	PEN'-yə-ree
2.	*vicarious*	vī-KAIR'-ee-əs
3.	*ephemeral*	ə-FEM'-ə-rəl
4.	*euphemism*	YOO'-fə-miz-əm
5.	*badinage*	BAD'-ə-nəj
6.	*bovine*	BŌ'-vīn'
7.	*nostalgia*	nə-STAL'-jə
8.	*cacophony*	kə-KOF'-ə-nee
9.	*carnivorous*	kahr-NIV'-ər-əs
10.	*clandestine*	klan-DES'-tin

Can you work with the words?

1.	penury	a.	impermanent
2.	vicarious	b.	banter
3.	ephemeral	c.	homesickness
4.	euphemism	d.	meat-eating
5.	badinage	e.	circumlocution
6.	bovine	f.	harsh noise
7.	nostalgia	g.	poverty
8.	cacophony	h.	secret
9.	carnivorous	i.	placid; stolid; cowlike
10.	clandestine	j.	secondhand

KEY: 1–g, 2–j, 3–a, 4–e, 5–b, 6–i, 7–c, 8–f, 9–d, 10–h

Do you understand the words? (I)

1. Do wealthy people normally live in
   penury?   YES   NO

407

2. Is a *vicarious* thrill one that comes from direct participation?   YES   NO

3. Do *ephemeral* things last a very short time?   YES   NO

4. Is a *euphemism* the substitution of an inoffensive term for another of the same meaning that may sound offensive, vulgar, or indelicate?   YES   NO

5. Does *badinage* show lighthearted frivolity?   YES   NO

6. Are *bovine* people high-strung and nervous?   YES   NO

7. Does one get a feeling of *nostalgia* for past occurrences and relationships?   YES   NO

8. Is *cacophony* pleasant and musical?   YES   NO

9. Do *carnivorous* animals eat meat?   YES   NO

10. Is a *clandestine* meeting conducted in secrecy?   YES   NO

KEY: 1–no, 2–no, 3–yes, 4–yes, 5–yes, 6–no, 7–yes, 8–no, 9–yes, 10–yes

---

Do you understand the words? (II)

1. penury—affluence   SAME   OPPOSITE
2. vicarious—actual   SAME   OPPOSITE
3. ephemeral—eternal   SAME   OPPOSITE
4. euphemism—less offensive word   SAME   OPPOSITE
5. badinage—light, teasing talk   SAME   OPPOSITE
6. bovine—high-strung   SAME   OPPOSITE
7. nostalgia—longing for the past   SAME   OPPOSITE
8. cacophony—euphony   SAME   OPPOSITE
9. carnivorous—herbivorous   SAME   OPPOSITE
10. clandestine—hidden   SAME   OPPOSITE

KEY: 1–O, 2–O, 3–O, 4–S, 5–S, 6–O, 7–O, 8–O, 9–O, 10–S

(The new words used in this test will be discussed in later sections of this chapter.)

Can you recall the words?

1. harsh sound   1. C_____
2. having a short life   2. E_____
3. dire poverty   3. P_____
4. substitution of an indirect or pleasant word or phrase for a possibly offensive one of the same meaning   4. E_____
5. experienced as a spectator, rather than as a participant   5. V_____
6. acute feeling of homesickness   6. N_____
7. light, half-teasing banter   7. B_____
8. subsisting solely on meat   8. C_____
9. cowlike; stolid   9. B_____
10. secret; concealed   10. C_____

KEY: 1–cacophony, 2–ephemeral, 3–penury, 4–euphemism, 5–vicarious, 6–nostalgia, 7–badinage, 8–carnivorous, 9–bovine, 10–clandestine

---

(End of Session 39)

SESSION 40

ORIGINS AND RELATED WORDS

1. money, and what it will buy

The modern world operates largely by means of a price structure—wealth and poverty are therefore words that indicate the possession, on the one hand, or the lack, on the other, of money. *Penury,* from Latin *penuria,* need, neediness, is dire, abject poverty, complete lack of financial resources. It is one of the two strongest English words there are to denote absence of money. The adjective form, *penurious* (pə-NYŌŌr′-ee-əs *or* pə-NŌŌR′ ēe-əs), strangely enough, *may* mean *poverty-stricken,* but more commonly signifies *stingy, close-fisted, niggardly;* so sparing in the use of money as to give the appearance of *penury.*

Penurious is a synonym of *parsimonious* (pahr′-sə-MŌ′-nee-əs), but is much stronger in implication. A *parsimonious* person is stingy; a *penurious* person is twice as stingy. *Penury,* then, is poverty; *penuriousness* is stinginess, excessive frugality. The noun form of *parsimonious* is *parsimony* (PAHR′-sə-mō′-nee).

A somewhat milder word than *penury* for poverty (if you can imagine a mild degree of poverty) is *indigence* (IN′-də-jəns). *Indigent* (IN′-də-jənt) people are not absolutely penniless—they are simply living in reduced circumstances, forgoing many creature comforts, forced to undergo the type of hardships that may accompany a lack of sufficient funds.

On the other hand, a close synonym of *penury,* and one of equal strength, is *destitution* (des′-tə-TŌŌ′-shən). *Destitute* (DES′-tə-tōōt) people do not even have the means for mere subsistence—as such, they are perhaps on the verge of starvation. *Penury* and *destitution* are not merely straitened circumstances—they are downright desperate circumstances.

To turn now to the brighter side of the picture, the possession of money, especially in increasing amounts, is expressed by *affluence* (AF′-lōō-əns). *Affluent* (AF′-lōō-ənt) people, people of *affluence,* or those living in *affluent* circumstances, are more than comfortable; in addition, there is the implication that their wealth is increasing. People who live in *affluence* probably own large and costly homes, run big, new cars, belong to expensive golf or country clubs, etc.

A much stronger term is *opulence* (OP′-yə-ləns), which not only implies much greater wealth than *affluence,* but in addition suggests lavish expenditures and ostentatiously luxurious surroundings. People of *opulence* own estates; drive only outrageously expensive and specially equipped cars (Rolls-Royces, Mercedes-Benzes, Porsches, etc.); have a corps of servants, including a major-domo; belong to golf and yacht and country clubs, etc., etc. Embroider the fantasy as much as you wish to. *Opulent* (OP′-yə-lənt) may describe people, surroundings, styles of life, or the like.

Affluent is a combination of the prefix *ad-*, to, toward (changing to *af-* before a root beginning with *f*), plus the Latin verb *fluo*, to flow—*affluence* is that delightful condition in which money keeps flowing to us, and no one ever turns off the spigot. Other words from the same root, *fluo*, to flow, are *fluid, influence, confluence* (a "flowing together"), *fluent* (the words flow smoothly), etc.

Opulent is from Latin *opulentus*, wealthy. No other English words derive from this root.

2. doing and feeling

If you watch a furious athletic event, and *you* get tired, though the athletes expend all the energy—that's *vicarious* fatigue.

If your friend goes on a bender, and as you watch him absorb one drink after another, *you* begin to feel giddy and stimulated, that's *vicarious* intoxication.

If you watch a mother in a motion picture or dramatic play suffer horribly at the death of her child, and *you* go through the same agony, that's *vicarious* torment.

You can experience an emotion, then, in two ways: firsthand, through actual participation; or *vicariously*, by becoming empathetically involved in another person's feelings.

Some people, for example, lead essentially dull and colorless lives. Through their children, through reading or attending the theater, however, they can experience all the emotions felt by others whose lives move along at a swift, exciting pace. These people live at second hand; they live *vicariously*.

3. time is relative

Elephants and turtles live almost forever; human beings in the United States have a life expectancy in general of sixty-eight to seventy-six years (though the gradual conquest of disease is constantly lengthening our span);† dogs live from seven to ten years; and some insects exist for only a few hours or days.

One such short-lived creature is the dayfly, which in Greek was called *ephemera*. Hence anything so short-lived, so unenduring that it scarcely seems to outlast the day, may be called *ephemeral*.

A synonym of *ephemeral* is *evanescent* (ev-ə-NES′-ənt), fleeting, staying for a remarkably short time, vanishing. Something intangible, like a feeling, may be called *evanescent;* it's here, and before you can quite comprehend it, it's gone—vanished.

The noun is *evanescence* (ev′-ə-NES′-əns); the verb is to *evanesce* (ev-ə-NES′).

Evanescent is built on the prefix *e-* (*ex-*), out, the root *vanesco,* to vanish, and the adjective suffix *-ent.*

The suffix *-esce* often, but not always, means *begin to. -Escent* may mean *becoming* or *beginning to.* Thus:

> *adolescent*—beginning to grow up;
> beginning to become an adult
> *evanesce*—begin to vanish
> *convalesce*—begin to get well after illness
> *putrescent*—beginning to rot;
> beginning to become putrid
> *obsolescent*—becoming obsolete

4. an exploration of various good things

A *euphemism* is a word or expression that has been substituted for another that is likely to offend—it is built on the Greek prefix *eu-,* good, the root *pheme,* voice, and the noun suffix *-ism.* (Etymologically, "something said in a good voice!") Adjective: *euphemistic* (yōō′-fə-MIS′-tik)

Other English words constructed from the prefix *eu-:*

1. *euphony* (YOO′-fə-nee)—good sound; pleasant lilt or rhythm (*phone,* sound)

Adjective: *euphonic* (yōō-FON′-ik) or *euphonious* (yōō-FŌ′-nee-əs)

† Latest figures, 1978, for the United States: males, 68.5 years; females, 76.4 years.

412

2. *eulogy* (Y$\overline{OO}$′-lə-jee)—etymologically, "good speech"; a formal speech of praise, usually delivered as a funeral oration. *Logos* in this term means *word* or *speech,* as it did in *philology* (Chapter 6). *Logos* more commonly means *science* or *study,* but has the alternate meaning in *eulogy, philology, monologue, dialogue, epilogue* (words upon the other words, or "after-words"), and *prologue* (words before the main part, "before-words," or introduction).

Adjective: *eulogistic* (yoo-lə-JIS′-tik); verb: *eulogize* (Y$\overline{OO}$-lə-jīz′); person who delivers a *eulogy: eulogist* (Y$\overline{OO}$-lə-jist)

3. *euphoria* (yoo-FAWR′-ee-ə)—good feeling, a sense of mental buoyancy and physical well-being

Adjective: *euphoric* (yoo-FAWR′-ik)

4. *euthanasia* (yoo′-thə-NAY′-zhə)—etymologically, "good death"; method of painless death inflicted on people suffering from incurable diseases—not legal at the present time, but advocated by many people. The word derives from *eu-* plus Greek *thanatos,* death.

5. exploration of modes of expression

Badinage is a half-teasing, non-malicious, frivolous banter, intended to amuse rather than wound. *Badinage* has a close synonym, *persiflage* (PUR′-sə-flahzh′), which is a little more derisive, a trifle more indicative of contempt or mockery—but still totally unmalicious.

In line with *badinage* and *persiflage,* there are four other forms of expression you should be familiar with: *cliché* (klee-SHAY′), *bromide* (BR$\overline{O}$′-mīd′), *platitude* (PLAT′-ə-t$\overline{oo}$d), and *anodyne* (AN′-ə-dīn′).

A *cliché* is a pattern of words which was once new and fresh, but which now is so old, worn, and threadbare that only banal, unimaginative speakers and writers ever use it. Examples are: *fast and furious; unsung heroes; by leaps and bounds; conspicuous by its absence; green with envy;* etc. The most devastating criticism you can make of a piece of writing is to say, "It is full of *clichés";* the most pointed insult to a person's way of talking is, "You speak in *clichés."*

413

A *bromide* is any trite, dull, and probably fallacious remark that shows little evidence of original thinking, and that therefore convinces a listener of the total absence of perspicacity on the part of the speaker.

For instance, some cautious, dull-minded individual might warn you not to take a chance in these words: "Remember it's better to be safe than sorry!"

Your sneering response might be: "Oh, that old *bromide!*"

A *platitude* is similar to a *cliché* or *bromide,* in that it is a dull, trite, hackneyed, unimaginative pattern of words—but, to add insult to injury (*cliché*), the speaker uses it with an air of novelty—as if he just made it up, and isn't he the brilliant fellow!

An *anodyne,* in the medical sense, is a drug that allays pain without curing an illness, like aspirin or morphine. Figuratively, an *anodyne* is a statement made to allay someone's fears or anxieties, not believed by the speaker, but intended to be believed by the listener. "Prosperity is just around the corner" was a popular *anodyne* of the 1930s.

A *bromide* is also a drug, formerly used as a sedative. Sedatives dull the senses—the statement labeled a *bromide* comes from a speaker of dull wit and has a sedative effect on the listener. The adjective is *bromidic* (brō-MID′-ik), as in "his *bromidic* way of expressing himself."

Platitude derives from Greek *platys,* broad or flat, plus the noun suffix *-tude.* Words like *plateau* (flat land), *plate* and *platter* (flat dishes), and *platypus* (flat foot) all derive from the same root as *platitude,* a flat statement, i.e., one that falls flat, despite the speaker's high hopes for it. The adjective is *platitudinous* (plat′-ə-TŌO-də-nəs), as in, "What a *platitudinous* remark."

Anodyne is a combination of the negative prefix *an-* with Greek *odyne,* pain. *Anodynes,* as drugs, lessen pain; as statements, they are intended to reduce or eliminate emotional pain or anxiety.

REVIEW OF ETYMOLOGY

PREFIX, ROOT, SUFFIX	MEANING	ENGLISH WORD
1. *penuria*	need, neediness	_____
2. *ad-* (*af-*)	to, toward	_____
3. *fluo*	to flow	_____

414

4. *opulentus*	wealthy	_____
5. *ephemera*	dayfly	_____
6. *e-, ex-*	out	_____
7. *vanesco*	to vanish	_____
8. *-esce*	begin to	_____
9. *-ent*	adjective suffix	_____
10. *-ence*	noun suffix	_____
11. *eu-*	good	_____
12. *pheme*	voice	_____
13. *-ism*	noun suffix	_____
14. *phone*	sound	_____
15. *-ic*	adjective suffix	_____
16. *-ous*	adjective suffix	_____
17. *logos*	word, speech	_____
18. *-ize*	verb suffix	_____
19. *thanatos*	death	_____
20. *platys*	broad or flat	_____
21. *an-*	negative prefix	_____
22. *odyne*	pain	_____

USING THE WORDS

Can you pronounce the words? (I)

1. *penurious*	pə-NYŌŌ′-ee-əs *or*
2. *penuriousness*	pə-NYŌŌR′-ee-əs-nəs *or*
	pə-NŌŌR′-ee-əs-nəs
3. *parsimonious*	pahr′-sə-MŌ′-nee-əs
4. *parsimony*	PAHR′-sə-mō′-nee
5. *indigence*	IN′-də-jəns
6. *indigent*	IN′-də-jənt
7. *destitution*	des′-tə-TŌŌ′-shən
8. *destitute*	DES′-tə-tōōt
9. *affluence*	AF′-lōō-əns
10. *affluent*	AF′-lōō-ənt
11. *opulence*	OP′-yə-ləns
12. *opulent*	OP′-yə-lənt

415

Can you pronounce the words? (II)

1. *evanescent* — ev'-ə-NES'-ənt
2. *evanescence* — ev'-ə-NES'-əns
3. *evanesce* — ev'-ə-NES'
4. *euphemistic* — yōō-fə-MIS'-tik
5. *euphony* — YŌō'-fə-nee
6. *euphonic* — yōō-FON'-ik
7. *euphonious* — yōō-FŌ'-nee-əs
8. *eulogy* — YŌō'-lə-jee
9. *eulogistic* — yōō'-lə-JIS'-tik
10. *eulogize* — YŌō'-lə-jīz'

Can you pronounce the words? (III)

1. *euphoria* — yōō-FAWR'-ee-ə
2. *euphoric* — yōō-FAWR'-ik
3. *euthanasia* — yōō'-thə-NAY'-zha
4. *persiflage* — PUR'-sə-flahzh'
5. *cliché* — klee-SHAY'
6. *bromide* — BRŌ'-mīd'
7. *bromidic* — brō-MID'-ik
8. *platitude* — PLAT'-ə-tōōd
9. *platitudinous* — plat'-ə-TOO'-də-nəs
10. *anodyne* — AN'-ə-dīn'

Can you work with the words? (I)

1. penurious	a. poor; of limited means
2. indigent	b. inoffensive
3. affluent	c. flat, trite
4. evanescent	d. feeling tiptop
5. euphemistic	e. wealthy
6. euphonious	f. pleasant in sound
7. euphoric	g. stingy; tight-fisted
8. platitudinous	h. fleeting

KEY: 1–g, 2–a, 3–e, 4–h, 5–b, 6–f, 7–d, 8–c

Can you work with the words? (II)

1. parsimony
2. destitution
3. opulence
4. evanescence
5. euphony
6. euphoria
7. euthanasia
8. platitude

a. lavish luxury
b. painless death
c. pleasant sound
d. trite remark
e. impermanence
f. feeling of well-being
g. stinginess
h. poverty

KEY: 1–g, 2–h, 3–a, 4–e, 5–c, 6–f, 7–b, 8–d

Can you work with the words? (III)

1. anodyne
2. bromide
3. persiflage

4. eulogy
5. penuriousness
6. indigence
7. affluence

a. light, teasing banter
b. tightfistedness
c. statement intended to allay anxiety
d. poverty, want
e. high, formal praise
f. wealth
g. trite statement

KEY: 1–c, 2–g, 3–a, 4–e, 5–b, 6–d, 7–f

Can you work with the words? (IV)

1. parsimonious
2. destitute
3. opulent
4. vicarious
5. euphonic
6. eulogistic
7. evanesce
8. eulogize

a. begin to vanish
b. stingy, frugal
c. highly praising
d. hackneyed phrase
e. ostentatiously wealthy
f. stilted in expression
g. pleasant-sounding
h. in want

417

9. bromidic   **i.** secondhand
10. cliché   **j.** praise

KEY: 1–b, 2–h, 3–e, 4–i, 5–g, 6–c, 7–a, 8–j, 9–f, 10–d

Do you understand the words? (I)

1. Do *penurious* people satisfy their extravagant desires?   YES   NO
2. Is *penuriousness* the characteristic of a miser?   YES   NO
3. If you are *parsimonious* with praise, do you lavish it on others?   YES   NO
4. Are people with extremely low incomes forced to live a life of *parsimony?*   YES   NO
5. Is *indigence* a sign of wealth?   YES   NO
6. Are *indigent* people often aided by state welfare?   YES   NO
7. If you live in a state of *destitution,* do you have all the money you need?   YES   NO
8. Is a completely *destitute* person likely to have to live in want?   YES   NO
9. Does a person of *affluence* generally have petty money worries?   YES   NO
10. Are *opulent* surroundings indicative of great wealth?   YES   NO

KEY: 1–no, 2–yes, 3–no, 4–yes, 5–no, 6–yes, 7–no, 8–yes, 9–no, 10–yes

---

Do you understand the words? (II)

1. Can you engage in *vicarious* exploits by reading spy novels?   YES   NO
2. Does an *evanescent* feeling remain for a considerable time?   YES   NO

3. Do parents generally indulge in *euphemisms* in front of young children? YES NO
4. Is poetry generally *euphonious*? YES NO
5. Does a sincere *eulogy* indicate one's feeling of admiration? YES NO
6. Is *euphoria* a feeling of malaise? YES NO
7. Is *euthanasia* practiced on animals? YES NO
8. Is *persiflage* an indication of seriousness? YES NO
9. Does a liberal use of *clichés* show original thinking? YES NO
10. Is an *anodyne* intended to relieve fears? YES NO

KEY: 1–yes, 2–no, 3–yes, 4–yes, 5–yes, 6–no, 7–yes, 8–no, 9–no, 10–yes

Do you understand the words? (III)

1. Is a *platitude* flat and dull? YES NO
2. If a person uses *bromides,* is he likely to be an interesting conversationalist? YES NO
3. If you indulge in *persiflage,* are you being facetious? YES NO
4. Are the works of Beethoven considered *euphonious*? YES NO
5. Can parents receive a *vicarious* thrill from their children's triumphs? YES NO

KEY: 1–yes, 2–no, 3–yes, 4–yes, 5–yes

Can you recall the words?

1. a statement, usually untrue, meant to alleviate fear
2. light banter
3. a hackneyed phrase

1. A_____
2. P_____
3. C_____

4. fleeting—lasting a very short time (*adj.*) 4. E_____

5. laudatory—delivered in tones of formal praise (*adj.*) 5. E_____

6. process of painlessly putting to death a victim of an incurable disease 6. E_____

7. stingy (*adj.*) 7. P_____
or P_____

8. in want (*adj.*) 8. D_____

9. wealth 9. A_____

10. immense wealth 10. O_____

11. adverb describing the manner of responding empathetically to another's acts 11. V_____

12. stinginess (*noun*) 12. P_____
or P_____

13–14. poverty 13. I_____
14. D_____

15. impermanence 15. E_____

16. pleasing sound 16. E_____

17. substituting inoffensive words (*adj.*) 17. E_____

18. sense of well-being 18. E_____

19. trite remark 19. B_____

20. banal remark 20. P_____

21. begin to vanish (*v.*) 21. E_____

22. poverty-stricken (*adj.*) 22. I_____

23–24. wealthy (two *adjs.*) 23. A_____
24. O_____

25. feeling tiptop (*adj.*) 25. E_____

26. pleasant in sound (*adj.*) 26. E_____
or E_____

27. formal praise 27. E_____

28. trite (*adj.*) 28. B_____

29. flat, dull (*adj.*) 29. P_____

30. to praise 30. E_____

KEY: 1–anodyne, 2–persiflage, 3–cliché, 4–evanescent, 5–eulogistic, 6–euthanasia, 7–parsimonious *or* penurious,

8–destitute, 9–affluence, 10–opulence, 11–vicariously,
12–parsimony or penuriousness, 13–indigence, 14–destitution, 15–evanescence, 16–euphony, 17–euphemistic,
18–euphoria, 19–bromide, 20–platitude, 21–evanesce,
22–indigent, 23–affluent, 24–opulent, 25–euphoric,
26–euphonic or euphonious, 27–eulogy, 28–bromidic,
29–platitudinous, 30–eulogize

(End of Session 40)

SESSION 41

ORIGINS AND RELATED WORDS

1. people are the craziest animals

Bovine, placid like a cow, stolid, patient, unexcitable, is built on
the Latin word for *ox* or *cow, bovis,* plus the suffix *-ine,* like, similar to, or characteristic of. To call someone *bovine* is of course far
from complimentary, for this adjective is considerably stronger
than *phlegmatic,* and implies a certain mild contempt on the part
of the speaker. A *bovine* person is somewhat like a vegetable: eats
and grows and lives, but apparently is lacking in any strong feelings.

Humans are sometimes compared to animals, as in the following adjectives:

1. *leonine* (LEE′-ə-nīn′)—like a lion in appearance or temperament.

2. *canine* (KAY′-nīn′)—like a dog. As a noun, the word refers
to the species to which dogs belong. Our *canine* teeth are similar
to those of a dog.

3. *feline* (FEE'-līn')—catlike. We may speak of *feline* grace; or (insultingly) of *feline* temperament when we mean that a person is "catty."

4. *porcine* (PAWR'-sīn')—piglike.

5. *vulpine* (VUL'-pīn')—foxlike in appearance or temperament. When applied to people, this adjective usually indicates the shrewdness of a fox.

6. *ursine* (UR'-sīn')—bearlike.

7. *lupine* (LOO'-pīn)—wolflike.

8. *equine* (EE'-kwīn')—horselike; "horsy."

9. *piscine* (PIS'-īn')—fishlike.

All these adjectives come from the corresponding Latin words for the animals; and, of course, each adjective also describes, or refers to, the specific animal as well as to the person likened to the animal.

1.	*leo*	lion
2.	*canis*	dog
3.	*felis*	cat
4.	*porcus*	pig
5.	*vulpus*	fox
6.	*ursus*	bear
7.	*lupus*	wolf
8.	*equus*	horse
9.	*piscis*	fish

The word for meat from a pig—*pork*—derives, obviously, from *porcus*. *Ursa Major* and *Ursa Minor*, the *Great Bear* and the *Little Bear*, the two conspicuous groups of stars in the northern sky (conspicuous, of course, only on a clear night), are so labeled because in formation they resemble the outlines of bears. The feminine name *Ursula* is, by etymology, "a little bear," which, perhaps, is a strange name to burden a child with. The skin disease *lupus* was so named because it eats into the flesh, as a wolf might.

2. you can't go home again

Nostalgia, built on two Greek roots, *nostos,* a return, and *algos,* pain (as in *neuralgia, cardialgia,* etc.), is a feeling you can't ever understand until you've experienced it—and you have probably experienced it whenever some external stimulus has crowded your mind with scenes from an earlier day.

You know how life often seems much pleasanter in retrospect? Your conscious memory tends to store up the pleasant experiences of the past (the trauma and unpleasant experiences may get buried in the unconscious), and when you are lonely or unhappy you may begin to relive these pleasant occurrences. It is then that you feel the emotional pain and longing that we call *nostalgia*.

The adjective is *nostalgic* (nos-TAL′-jik), as in "motion pictures that are *nostalgic* of the fifties," or as in, "He feels *nostalgic* whenever he passes 138th Street and sees the house in which he grew up."

3. soundings

Cacophony is itself a harsh-sounding word—and is the only one that exactly describes the unmusical, grating, ear-offending noises you are likely to hear in man-made surroundings: the New York subway trains thundering through their tunnels (they are also, these days in the late 1970s, eye-offending, for which we might coin the term *cacopsis*, noun, and *cacoptic*, adjective), the traffic bedlam of rush hours in a big city, a steel mill, an automobile factory, a blast furnace, etc. Adjective: *cacophonous* (kə-KOF′-ə-nəs).

These words are built on the Greek roots *kakos,* bad, harsh, or ugly, and *phone,* sound.

Phone, sound, is found also in:

1. *telephone*—etymologically, "sound from afar"

2. *euphony*—pleasant sound

3. *phonograph*—etymologically, "writer of sound"

4. *saxophone*—a musical instrument (hence *sound*) invented by Adolphe Sax

5. *xylophone*—a musical instrument; etymologically, "sounds through wood" (Greek *xylon,* wood)

6. *phonetics* (fə-NET′-iks)—the science of the sounds of language; the adjective is *phonetic* (fə-NET′-ik), the expert a *phonetician* (fō′-nə-TISH′-ən)

7. *phonics*—the science of sound; also the method of teaching reading by drilling the sounds of letters and syllables

4. the flesh and all

Carnivorous combines *carnis,* flesh, and *voro,* to devour. A *carnivorous* animal, or *carnivore* (KAHR'-nə-vawr'), is one whose main diet is meat.

Voro, to devour, is the origin of other words referring to eating habits:

1. *herbivorous* (hur-BIV'-ər-əs)—subsisting on grains, grasses, and other vegetation, as cows, deer, horses, etc. The animal is a *herbivore* (HUR'-bə-vawr'). Derivation: Latin *herba,* herb, plus *voro,* to devour

2. *omnivorous* (om-NIV'-ər-əs)—eating everything: meat, grains, grasses, fish, insects, and anything else digestible. The only species so indiscriminate in their diet are humans and rats, plus, of course, some cats and dogs that live with people (in contrast to *felines* and *canines*—lions, tigers, bobcats, wolves, etc.—that are not domesticated). *Omnivorous* (combining Latin *omnis,* all, with *voro,* plus the adjective suffix *-ous*) refers not only to food. An *omnivorous* reader reads everything in great quantities (that is, devours *all* kinds of reading matter).

3. *voracious* (vaw-RAY'-shəs)—*devouring;* hence, greedy or gluttonous; may refer either to food or to any other habits. One may be a *voracious* eater, *voracious* reader, *voracious* in one's pursuit of money, pleasure, etc. Think of the two noun forms of *loquacious.* Can you write two nouns derived from *voracious*? (1) _____, (2) _____.

5. "allness"

Latin *omnis,* all, is the origin of:

1. *omnipotent* (om-NIP'-ə-tənt)—all-powerful, an adjective usually applied to God; also, to any ruler whose governing powers are unlimited, which allows for some exaggeration, as King Canute the Great proved to his sycophantic courtiers when he or-

dered the tide to come so far up the beach and no further. He got soaking wet! (*Omnis* plus Latin *potens, potentis,* powerful, as in *potentate,* a powerful ruler; *impotent* (IM'-pə-tənt), powerless; *potent,* powerful; and *potential,* possessing power or ability not yet exercised). Can you write the noun form of *omnipotent?*

_____.

2. *omniscient* (om-NISH'-ənt)—all-knowing: hence, infinitely wise. (*Omnis* plus *sciens,* knowing.) We have discussed this adjective in a previous chapter, so you will have no problem writing the noun: _____.

3. *omnipresent* (om'-nə-PREZ'-ənt)—present in all places at once. Fear was *omnipresent* in Europe during 1939 just before World War II. A synonym of *omnipresent* is *ubiquitous* (yōō-BIK'-wə-təs), from Latin *ubique,* everywhere. The *ubiquitous* ice cream vendor seems to be *everywhere* at the same time, tinkling those little bells, once spring arrives. The *ubiquitous* little red wagon rides around *everywhere* in airports to refuel departing planes. "*Ubiquitous* laughter greeted the press secretary's remark," i.e., laughter was heard *everywhere* in the room. The noun forms are *ubiquity* (yōō-BIK'-wə-tee) or _____. (Can you think of the alternate form?)

4. *omnibus* (OM'-nə-bəs)—etymologically, "for all, including all." In the shortened form *bus* we have a public vehicle for *all* who can pay; in a John Galsworthy *omnibus* we have a book containing *all* of Galsworthy's works; in an *omnibus* legislative bill we have a bill containing *all* the miscellaneous provisions and appropriations left out of other bills.

6. more flesh

Note how *carnis,* flesh, is the building block of:

1. *carnelian* (kahr-NEEL'-yən)—a reddish color, the color of red *flesh.*

2. *carnival* (KAHR'-nə-vəl)—originally the season of merrymaking just before Lent, when people took a last fling before saying "*Carne vale!*" "Oh *flesh,* farewell!" (Latin *vale,* farewell, goodbye). Today a *carnival* is a kind of outdoor entertainment

with games, rides, side shows, and, of course, lots of food—also any exuberant or riotous merrymaking or festivities.

3. *carnal* (KAHR'-nəl)—most often found in phrases like "*carnal* pleasures" or "*carnal* appetites," and signifying pleasures or appetites of the *flesh* rather than of the spirit—hence, sensual, lecherous, lascivious, lubricious, etc. The noun is *carnality* (kahr-NAL'-ə-tee).

4. *carnage* (KAHR'-nəj)—great destruction of life (that is, of human *flesh*), as in war or mass murders.

5. *reincarnation* (ree'-in-kahr-NAY'-shən)—a rebirth or reappearance. Believers in *reincarnation* maintain that one's soul persists after it has fled the *flesh,* and eventually reappears in the body of a newborn infant or animal, or in another form. Some of us, according to this interesting philosophy, were once Napoleon, Alexander the Great, Cleopatra, etc. The verb is to *reincarnate* (ree-in-KAHR'-nayt), to bring (a soul) back in another bodily form.

6. *incarnate* (in-KAHR'-nət)—in the *flesh.* If we use this adjective to call someone "the devil *incarnate,*" we mean that here is the devil in the *flesh.* Or we may say that someone is evil *incarnate,* that is, the personification of evil, evil invested with human or bodily form. The verb to *incarnate* (in-KAHR'-nayt) is to embody, give bodily form to, or make real.

7. dark secrets

Clandestine comes from Latin *clam,* secretly, and implies secrecy or concealment in the working out of a plan that is dangerous or illegal. *Clandestine* is a close synonym of *surreptitious* (sur'-əp-TISH'-əs), which means stealthy, sneaky, furtive, generally because of fear of detection.

The two words cannot always, however, be used interchangeably. We may speak of either *clandestine* or *surreptitious* meetings or arrangements; but usually only of *clandestine* plans and only of *surreptitious* movements or actions. Can you write the noun form of *surreptitious?* _____

REVIEW OF ETYMOLOGY

PREFIX, ROOT, SUFFIX	MEANING	ENGLISH WORD
1. *-ine*	like, similar to, characteristic of	_____
2. *leo*	lion	_____
3. *felis*	cat	_____
4. *porcus*	pig	_____
5. *canis*	dog	_____
6. *vulpus*	fox	_____
7. *ursus*	bear	_____
8. *lupus*	wolf	_____
9. *equus*	horse	_____
10. *piscis*	fish	_____
11. *nostos*	a return	_____
12. *algos*	pain	_____
13. *-ic*	adjective suffix	_____
14. *kakos*	bad, harsh, ugly	_____
15. *phone*	sound	_____
16. *xylon*	wood	_____
17. *carnis*	flesh	_____
18. *voro*	to devour	_____
19. *herba*	herb	_____
20. *omnis*	all	_____
21. *-ous*	adjective suffix	_____
22. *potens, potentis*	powerful	_____
23. *sciens*	knowing	_____
24. *ubique*	everywhere	_____
25. *-ity*	noun suffix	_____
26. *vale*	farewell	_____
27. *-al*	adjective suffix	_____
28. *re-*	again, back	_____
29. *-ate*	verb suffix	_____
30. *in-*	in	_____

31. *clam*	secretly	————————
32. *-ent*	adjective suffix	————————
33. *-ence*	noun suffix	————————

USING THE WORDS

Can you pronounce the words? (I)

1. *leonine*	LEE'-ə-nīn'
2. *canine*	KAY'-nīn'
3. *feline*	FEE'-līn'
4. *porcine*	PAWR'-sīn'
5. *vulpine*	VUL'-pīn'
6. *ursine*	UR'-sīn'
7. *lupine*	LOO'-pīn'
8. *equine*	EE'-kwīn'
9. *piscine*	PIS'-īn'
10. *nostalgic*	nos-TAL'-jik

Can you pronounce the words? (II)

1. *cacophonous*	kə-KOF'-ə-nəs
2. *phonetics*	fə-NET'-iks
3. *phonetic*	fə-NET'-ik
4. *phonetician*	fō-nə-TISH'-ən
5. *carnivore*	KAHR'-nə-vawr'
6. *herbivore*	HUR'-bə-vawr'
7. *herbivorous*	hur-BIV'-ər-əs
8. *omnivorous*	om-NIV'-ər-əs
9. *voracious*	vaw-RAY'-shəs
10. *voracity*	vaw-RAS'-ə-tee
11. *omnipotent*	om-NIP'-ə-tənt
12. *impotent*	IM'-pə-tənt
13. *impotence*	IM'-pə-təns
14. *omnipotence*	om-NIP'-ə-təns

Can you pronounce the words? (III)

1. *omniscient*   om-NISH'-ənt
2. *omniscience*   om-NISH'-əns
3. *omnipresent*   om'-nə-PREZ'-ənt
4. *omnipresence*   om'-nə-PREZ'-əns
5. *ubiquitous*   yŏŏ-BIK'-wə-təs
6. *ubiquity*   yŏŏ-BIK'-wə-tee
7. *ubiquitousness*   yŏŏ-BIK'-wə-təs-nəs
8. *omnibus*   OM'-nə-bəs

Can you pronounce the words? (IV)

1. *carnelian*   kahr-NEEL'-yən
2. *carnal*   KAHR'-nəl
3. *carnality*   kahr-NAL'-ə-tee
4. *carnage*   KAHR'-nəj
5. *reincarnation*   ree'-in-kahr-NAY'-shən
6. *reincarnate (v.)*   ree'-in-KAHR'-nayt
7. *incarnate (adj.)*   in-KAHR'-nət
8. *incarnate (v.)*   in-KAHR'-nayt
9. *surreptitious*   sur'-əp-TISH'-əs
10. *surreptitiousness*   sur'-əp-TISH'-əs-nəs

Can you work with the words? (I)

1. leonine   a. doglike
2. canine   b. greedy, devouring
3. feline   c. foxlike
4. porcine   d. all-powerful
5. vulpine   e. stealthy, clandestine
6. ursine   f. lionlike
7. voracious   g. all-knowing
8. omnipotent   h. bearlike
9. omniscient   i. catlike
10. surreptitious   j. piglike

KEY: 1–f, 2–a, 3–i, 4–j, 5–c, 6–h, 7–b, 8–d, 9–g, 10–e

Can you work with the words? (II)

1. nostalgic
2. cacophonous
3. herbivorous
4. omnivorous
5. ubiquitous
6. carnal
7. incarnate

a. harsh-sounding
b. eating everything
c. lewd, lecherous, lubricious
d. found everywhere
e. homesick
f. grass-eating
g. in the flesh

KEY: 1–e, 2–a, 3–f, 4–b, 5–d, 6–c, 7–g

Can you work with the words? (III)

1. phonetics
2. carnivore
3. voracity
4. omnipotence
5. omniscience
6. omnipresence
7. omnibus
8. carnelian
9. carnality
10. carnage
11. surreptitiousness
12. reincarnation

a. universality
b. a color
c. infinite power
d. furtiveness; stealth; sneakiness
e. lechery, lasciviousness, lubricity
f. infinite wisdom
g. science of speech sounds
h. slaughter
i. a collection of all things
j. greediness
k. meat-eater
l. a return to life in a new body or form

KEY: 1–g, 2–k, 3–j, 4–c, 5–f, 6–a, 7–i, 8–b, 9–e, 10–h, 11–d, 12–l

Can you work with the words? (IV)

1. lupine
2. equine
3. piscine
4. phonetician

5. impotent

6. ubiquity
7. reincarnate (*v.*)
8. incarnate (*v.*)

a. fishlike
b. powerless
c. wolflike
d. bring back into a new body or form
e. occurrence, or existence, everywhere
f. horselike
g. expert in speech sounds
h. embody; make real; put into bodily form

KEY: 1–c, 2–f, 3–a, 4–g, 5–b, 6–e, 7–d, 8–h

Do you understand the words? (I)

1. A person of *leonine* appearance looks like a tiger.	TRUE	FALSE
2. *Canine* habits refers to the habits of dogs.	TRUE	FALSE
3. *Feline* grace means catlike grace.	TRUE	FALSE
4. *Porcine* appearance means wolflike appearance.	TRUE	FALSE
5. *Vulpine* craftiness means foxlike craftiness.	TRUE	FALSE
6. *Ursine* means bearlike.	TRUE	FALSE
7. *Nostalgic* feelings refer to a longing for past experiences.	TRUE	FALSE
8. *Cacophonous* music is pleasant and sweet.	TRUE	FALSE
9. An elephant is a *carnivore*.	TRUE	FALSE
10. Deer are *herbivorous*.	TRUE	FALSE

KEY: 1–F, 2–T, 3–T, 4–F, 5–T, 6–T, 7–T, 8–F, 9–F, 10–T

Do you understand the words? (II)

1.	An *omnivorous* reader does very little reading.	TRUE	FALSE
2.	A *voracious* eater is gluttonous.	TRUE	FALSE
3.	True *omnipotence* is unattainable by human beings.	TRUE	FALSE
4.	No one is *omniscient*.	TRUE	FALSE
5.	Fear of economic ruin was practically *omnipresent* in the early nineteen-thirties.	TRUE	FALSE
6.	When an airplane lands for refueling, the *ubiquitous* little red gasoline wagon comes rolling up.	TRUE	FALSE
7.	An author's *omnibus* contains all his published writings.	TRUE	FALSE
8.	*Carnelian* is a deep blue color.	TRUE	FALSE
9.	*Carnality* is much respected in a puritanical society.	TRUE	FALSE
10.	There is considerable *carnage* in war.	TRUE	FALSE
11.	A *surreptitious* glance is meant to be conspicuous.	TRUE	FALSE
12.	A person who is evil *incarnate* is a vicious character.	TRUE	FALSE

KEY: 1–F, 2–T, 3–T, 4–T, 5–T, 6–T, 7–T, 8–F, 9–F, 10–T, 11–F, 12–T

Can you recall the words?

I—adverbs

1–2. secretly (two forms)	1.	C_____
	2.	S_____
3. in a harsh and noisy manner	3.	C_____

432

4. in a homesick manner   4. N_____
5. in a greedy, devouring manner   5. V_____

KEY: 1–clandestinely, 2–surreptitiously, 3–cacophonously, 4–nostalgically, 5–voraciously

---

II—nouns

1. greediness   1. V_____
2. unlimited power   2. O_____
3. infinite knowledge   3. O_____
4. a gathering of all things   4. O_____
5. lechery; indulgence in fleshly pleasures   5. C_____
6. slaughter   6. C_____
7. stealthiness; secretiveness   7. S_____
8. harsh sound   8. C_____
9. science of speech sounds   9. P_____
10. a return to life in new form   10. R_____

KEY: 1–voracity, 2–omnipotence, 3–omniscience, 4–omnibus, 5–carnality, 6–carnage, 7–surreptitiousness, 8–cacophony, 9–phonetics, 10–reincarnation

---

III—adjectives

1. lionlike   1. L_____
2. doglike   2. C_____
3. catlike   3. F_____
4. cowlike   4. B_____
5. foxlike   5. V_____
6. bearlike   6. U_____
7. homesick   7. N_____
8. grating in sound   8. C_____
9. meat-eating   9. C_____
10. grass-eating   10. H_____

11. all-eating; indiscriminate   11. O_____
12. devouring; greedy   12. V_____
13. in the flesh   13. L_____

KEY: 1–leonine, 2–canine, 3–feline, 4–bovine, 5–vulpine, 6–ursine, 7–nostalgic, 8–cacophonous, 9–carnivorous, 10–herbivorous, 11–omnivorous, 12–voracious, 13–incarnate

IV. more adjectives

1. all-powerful   1. O_____
2. all-knowing   2. O_____
3. present or existing everywhere   3. O_____
4. found everywhere   4. U_____
5. lewd, lascivious, lecherous   5. C_____
6. secret   6. C_____

KEY: 1–omnipotent, 2–omniscient, 3–omnipresent, 4–ubiquitous, 5–carnal, 6–clandestine

V. final mop-up

1. wolflike   1. L_____
2. horselike   2. E_____
3. fishlike   3. P_____
4. referring to speech sounds   4. P_____
5. expert in speech sounds   5. P_____
6. powerless   6. I_____
7–8. existence everywhere   7. U_____
     or U_____
     8. O_____
9. to bring back into another   9. R_____
     body or form

434

10. to embody, make real, or put   10. I_____
    into bodily form

CHAPTER REVIEW

A. Do you recognize the words?

1. Utter want:
   (a) affluence, (b) opulence, (c) penury
2. Experienced secondhand:
   (a) ephemeral, (b) vicarious, (c) evanescent
3. Inoffensive circumlocution:
   (a) badinage, (b) persiflage, (c) euphemism
4. Homesick:
   (a) nostalgic, (b) bromide, (c) clandestine
5. Meat-eating:
   (a) herbivorous, (b) voracious, (c) carnivorous
6. Stingy:
   (a) indigent, (b) parsimonious, (c) opulent
7. Extreme financial need:
   (a) destitution, (b) affluence, (c) parsimony
8. Great and increasing wealth:
   (a) penuriousness, (b) affluence, (c) omnipresence
9. Remaining for a short time:
   (a) euphemistic, (b) evanescent, (c) eulogistic
10. Sweet-sounding:
    (a) euphonious, (b) cacophonous, (c) euphoric
11. Praise glowingly:
    (a) evanesce, (b) eulogize, (c) reincarnate
12. Sense of physical well-being:
    (a) euthanasia, (b) euphoria, (c) persiflage

13. Hackneyed expression:
     (a) anodyne, (b) badinage, (c) cliché
14. catlike:
     (a) leonine, (b) feline, (c) canine
15. Bearlike:
     (a) vulpine, (b) ursine, (c) porcine
16. All-knowing:
     (a) omnipotent, (b) omniscient, (c) omnipresent
17. Found everywhere:
     (a) ubiquitous, (b) omnivorous, (c) omnibus
18. Destruction:
     (a) carnage, (b) carnality, (c) reincarnation
19. Stealthy:
     (a) voracious, (b) surreptitious, (c) incarnate

KEY: 1–c, 2–b, 3–c, 4–a, 5–c, 6–b, 7–a, 8–b, 9–b, 10–a, 11–b,
     12–b, 13–c, 14–b, 15–b, 16–b, 17–a, 18–a, 19–b

B. Can you recognize roots?

ROOT	MEANING	EXAMPLE
1. *penuria*	_____	penury
2. *fluo*	_____	affluent
3. *opulentus*	_____	wealthy
4. *ephemera*	_____	ephemeral
5. *vanesco*	_____	evanescent
6. *pheme*	_____	euphemism
7. *phone*	_____	phonetics
8. *logos*	_____	eulogy
9. *thanatos*	_____	euthanasia
10. *platys*	_____	platitude, platypus
11. *odyne*	_____	anodyne
12. *leo*	_____	leonine
13. *felis*	_____	feline
14. *porcus*	_____	porcine
15. *canis*	_____	canine
16. *vulpus*	_____	vulpine

436

17. *lupus*	_____	lupine
18. *equus*	_____	equine
19. *piscis*	_____	piscine
20. *nostos*	_____	nostalgia
21. *algos*	_____	nostalgic
22. *kakos*	_____	cacophonous
23. *xylon*	_____	xylophone
24. *carnis*	_____	carnivorous
25. *voro*	_____	omnivorous
26. *herba*	_____	herbivorous
27. *omnis*	_____	omnipotent
28. *potens, potentis*	_____	impotent
29. *sciens*	_____	omniscience
30. *ubique*	_____	ubiquitous
31. *vale!*	_____	carnival
32. *clam*	_____	clandestine

KEY: 1–want, neediness, 2–to flow, 3–wealthy, 4–dayfly, 5–to vanish, 6–voice, 7–sound, 8- word, speech, 9–death, 10–flat, broad, 11–pain, 12–lion, 13–cat, 14–pig, 15–dog, 16–fox, 17–wolf, 18–horse, 19–fish, 20–a return, 21–pain, 22–bad, harsh, ugly, 23–wood, 24–flesh, 25–to devour, 26–herb, 27–all, 28–pow .ful, 29–knowing, 30–everywhere, 31–farewell!, 32–secretly

TEASER QUESTIONS FOR THE AMATEUR ETYMOLOGIST

1. American poet William Cullen Bryant wrote a poem in 1811 called *Thanatopsis*. You are familiar with both roots in the word. Can you figure out the meaning? _____

2. If you wanted to coin a word for the study or science of death and dying, what would you come up with?

_____.

3. *Pheme,* as you know from *euphemism,* means *voice.* This root derives from a Greek verb *phanai,* to speak, which, as it trav-

eled through Latin, Old French, and Middle English, finally took on the spelling *phet-*, *phec-*, or *phes-*. And you recall that the Greek prefix *pro-* means *beforehand* or *ahead* (as in *prognosis*, *prologue*, etc.). Can you now combine elements to form a word meaning:

> (a) to say beforehand; to foretell (an occurrence before it actually happens)? _____.
> (b) the foretelling of such an occurrence? _____
> _____.
> (c) the person who foretells? _____.

4. Can you combine a *Latin* prefix and root to form words of the same meaning?

> (a) to foretell: _____.
> (b) the act of foretelling: _____.

5. An eminent psychoanalyst, Richard Karpe of Connecticut, has coined the term *nostopathy* (nos-TOP′-ə-thee) for an emotional disorder he diagnosed among a number of his patients who were returning veterans of World War II and of the Korean and Vietnam wars. You know both roots in the word. Can you figure out the meaning? _____
_____
_____.

6. Coin a word that means:

> (a) the killing of foxes: _____,
> (b) the killing of wolves: _____,
> (c) the killing of lions, tigers, and other cats: _____,
> (d) the killing of bears: _____.

7. Figure out an adjective that means:

> (a) fish-eating: _____,
> (b) insect-eating: _____.

8. Have you ever wondered whether the Canary Islands were named after the Latin root *canis*, dog? They were. Large, wild dogs inhabited the area. Pretty songbirds also abounded there. What were these birds called? _____.

9. A new verb was coined some years ago, based on the Latin root *potens, potentis,* meaning (of a drug) *to make more effective*

438

or powerful; to augment the effect of another drug. Can you figure out what this verb would be? _____

(*Answers in Chapter 18*)

GETTING USED TO NEW WORDS

Reference has been made, in previous chapters, to the intimate relationship between reading and vocabulary building. Good books and the better magazines will not only acquaint you with a host of new ideas (and, therefore, new words, since every word is the verbalization of an idea), but also will help you gain a more complete and a richer understanding of the hundreds of words you are learning through your work in this book. If you have been doing a sufficient amount of stimulating reading—and that means, at minimum, several magazines a week and at least three books of non-fiction a month—you have been meeting, constantly, over and over again, the new words you have been learning in these pages. Every such encounter is like seeing an old friend in a new place. You know how much better you understand your friends when you have a chance to see them react to new situations; similarly, you will gain a much deeper understanding of the friends you have been making among words as you see them in different contexts and in different places.

My recommendations in the past have been of non-fiction titles, but novels too are a rich source of additions to your vocabulary—provided you stay alert to the new words you will inevitably meet in reading novels.

The natural temptation, when you encounter a brand-new word in a novel, is to ignore it—the lines of the plot are perfectly clear even if many of the author's words are not.

I want to counsel strongly that you resist the temptation to ignore the unfamiliar words you may meet in your novel reading: resist it with every ounce of your energy, for only by such resistance can you keep building your vocabulary as you read.

What should you do? Don't rush to a dictionary, don't bother underlining the word, don't keep long lists of words that you will eventually look up *en masse*—these activities are likely to become

439

painful and you will not continue them for any great length of time.

Instead, do something quite simple—and very effective.

When you meet a new word, underline it with a *mental* pencil. That is, pause for a second and attempt to figure out its meaning from its use in the sentence or from its etymological root or prefix, if it contains one you have studied. Make a mental note of it, say it aloud once or twice—and then go on reading.

That's all there is to it. What you are doing, of course, is developing the same type of mind-set toward the new word that you have developed toward the words you have studied in this book. And the results, of course, will be the same—you will begin to notice the word occurring again and again in other reading you do, and finally, having seen it in a number of varying contexts, you will begin to get enough of its connotation and flavor to come to a fairly accurate understanding of its meaning. In this way you will be developing alertness not only to the words you have studied in this book, but to all expressive and meaningful words. And your vocabulary will keep growing.

But of course that will happen only if you keep reading.

I do not wish to recommend any particular novels or novelists, since the type of fiction one enjoys is a very personal matter. You doubtless know the kind of story you like—mystery, science fiction, spy, adventure, historical, political, romantic, Western, biographical, one or all of the above. Or you may be entranced by novels of ideas, of sexual prowess, of fantasy, of life in different segments of society from your own. No matter. Find the kind of novel or novelist *you* enjoy by browsing in the public library or among the thousands of titles in bookstores that have a rich assortment of paperbacks as well as hardbacks.

And then read! And keep on the alert for new words! You will find them by the hundreds and thousands. Bear in mind: *people with rich vocabularies have been reading omnivorously, voraciously, since childhood*—including the ingredients listed in small print on bread wrappers and cereal boxes.

(*End of Session 41*)

HOW TO SPELL A WORD

The spelling of English words is archaic, it's confusing, it's needlessly complicated, and, if you have a sense of humor, it's downright comical. In fact, any insulting epithet you might wish to level against our weird methods of putting letters together to form words would probably be justified—but it's our spelling, and we're stuck with it.

How completely stuck we are is illustrated by a somewhat ludicrous event that goes back to 1906, and that cost philanthropist Andrew Carnegie $75,000.

Working under a five-year grant of funds from Carnegie, and headed by the esteemed scholar Brander Matthews, the Simplified Spelling Board published in that year a number of recommendations for bringing some small semblance of order out of the great chaos of English spelling. Their suggestions affected a mere three hundred words out of the half million then in the language. Here are a few examples, to give you a general idea:

SPELLING THEN CURRENT	SIMPLIFIED SPELLING
mediaeval	*medieval*
doubt	*dout*
debtor	*dettor*
head	*hed*
though	*tho*

through	thru
laugh	laf
tough	tuf
knife	nife
theatre	theater
centre	center
phantom	fantom

These revisions seemed eminently sensible to no less a personage than the then President of the United States, Theodore Roosevelt. So delighted was he with the new garb in which these three hundred words could be clothed that he immediately ordered that all government documents be printed in simplified spelling. And the result? Such a howl went up from the good citizens of the republic, from the nation's editors and schoolteachers and businessmen, that the issue was finally debated in the halls of Congress. Almost to a man, senators and representatives stood opposed to the plan. Teddy Roosevelt, as you have doubtless heard, was a stubborn fellow—but when Congress threatened to hold up the White House stationery appropriation unless the President backed down, Teddy rescinded the order. Roosevelt ran for re-election some time later, and lost. That his attitude toward spelling contributed to his defeat is of course highly doubtful—nevertheless an opposition New York newspaper, the day the returns were in, maliciously commented on the outgoing incumbent in a one-word simplified-spelling editorial: "THRU!"

Roosevelt was not the first President to be justifiably outraged by our ridiculous orthography. Over a hundred years ago, when Andrew Jackson was twitted on his poor spelling, he is supposed to have made this characteristic reply, "Well, sir, it is a damned poor mind that cannot think of more than one way to spell a word!" And according to one apocryphal version, it was Jackson's odd spelling that gave birth to the expression "okay." Jackson thought, so goes the story, that "all correct" was spelled "orl korrect," and he used O.K. as the abbreviation for these words when he approved state papers.

Many years ago, the British playwright George Bernard Shaw offered a dramatic proposal for reducing England's taxes. Just

442

eliminate unnecessary letters from our unwieldy spelling, he said, and you'll save enough money in paper and printing to cut everyone's tax rate in half. Maybe it would work, but it's never been put to the test—and the way things look now, it never will be. Current practice more and more holds spelling exactly where it is, bad though it may be. It is a scientific law of language that if enough people make a "mistake," the "mistake" becomes acceptable usage. That law applies to pronunciation, to grammar, to word meanings, but not to spelling. Maybe it's because of our misbegotten faith in, and worship of, the printed word—maybe it's because written language tends to be static, while spoken language constantly changes. Whatever the cause, spelling today successfully resists every logical effort at reform. "English spelling," said Thorstein Veblen, "satisfies all the requirements of the canons of reputability under the law of conspicuous waste. It is archaic, cumbrous, and ineffective." Perfectly true. Notwithstanding, it's here to stay.

Your most erudite friend doubtless misspells the name of the Hawaiian guitar. I asked half a dozen members of the English department of a large college to spell the word—without exception they responded with *ukelele*. Yet the only accepted form is *ukulele*.

Judging from my experience with my classes at Rio Hondo College, half the population of the country must think the word is spelled *alright*. Seventy-five per cent of the members of my classes can't spell *embarrassing* or *coolly*. People will go on misspelling these four words, but the authorized spellings will remain impervious to change.

Well, you know the one about Mohammed and the mountain. Though it's true that we have modernized spelling to a microscopic extent in the last eighty years (*traveler, center, theater, medieval, labor,* and *honor,* for example, have pretty much replaced *traveller, centre, theatre, mediaeval, labour,* and *honour*), still the resistance to change has not observably weakened. If spelling won't change, as it probably won't, those of us who consider ourselves poor spellers will have to. We'll just have to get up and go to the mountain.

Is it hard to become a good speller? I have demonstrated over and over again in my classes that anyone of normal intelligence and average educational background can become a good speller in very little time.

What makes the task so easy?

First—investigations have proved that 95 per cent of the spelling errors that educated people make occur in just one hundred words. Not only do we all misspell the same words—but we misspell them in about the same way.

Second—correct spelling relies exclusively on memory, and the most effective way to train memory is by means of association or, to use the technical term, mnemonics.

If you fancy yourself an imperfect or even a terrible speller, the chances are very great that you've developed a complex solely because you misspell some or all of the hundred words with which this Intermission deals. When you have conquered this single list, and I shall immediately proceed to demonstrate how easy it is, by means of mnemonics, to do so, 95 per cent of your spelling difficulties will in all likelihood vanish.

Let us start with twenty-five words from the list. In the first column you will find the correct spelling of each, and in the second column the simple mnemonic that will forevermore fix that correct spelling in your memory.

CORRECT SPELLING	MNEMONIC
1. all right	Two words, no matter what it means. Keep in mind that it's the opposite of *all wrong*.
2. coolly	Of course you can spell *cool*—simply add the adverbial ending -ly.
3. supersede	This is the only word in the language ending in -*sede* (the only one, mind you—there isn't a single other one so spelled).
4. succeed	The only three words in the entire
5. proceed	language ending in -*ceed*. When you
6. exceed	think of the three words in the order given here, the initial letters form the beginning of SPEED.

7. cede, precede, recede, etc.	All other words with a similar-sounding final syllable end in *-cede*.
8. procedure	One of the double *e*'s of *proceed* moves to the end in the noun form, *procedure*.
9. stationery	This is the word that means paper, and notice the *-er* in *paper*.
10. stationary	In this spelling, the words means standing, and notice the *-a* in *stand*.
11. recommend	*Commend,* which we all spell correctly, plus the prefix *re-*.
12. separate 13. comparative	Look for *a rat* in both words.
14. ecstasy	to *sy* (sigh) with ecstasy
15. analyze 16. paralyze	The only two non-technical words in the whole language ending in *-yze*.
17. repetition	First four letters identical with those in the allied form *repeat*.
18. irritable 19. inimitable	Think of allied forms *irritate* and *imitate*.
20. absence	Think of the allied form *absent,* and you will not be tempted to misspell it *abscence*.
21. superintendent	The superintend*ent* in an apartm*ent* house collects the *rent*—thus you avoid *superintendant*.
22. conscience	*Science* plus prefix *con-*.
23. anoint	Think of *an ointment,* hence no double *n*.
24. ridiculous	Think of the allied form *ridicule,* which we usually spell correctly, thus avoiding *rediculous*.
25. despair	Again, think of another form— *des*perate—and so avoid *dis*pair.

Whether or not you have much faith in your spelling ability, you will need very little time to conquer the preceding twenty-five

445

demons. Spend a few minutes, now, on each of those words in the list that you're doubtful of, and then test your success by means of the exercise below. Perhaps to your astonishment, you will find it easy to make a high score.

A test of your learning

Instructions: After studying the preceding list of words, fill in the missing letters correctly.

1. a_____right
2. coo_____y
3. super_____
4. suc_____
5. pro_____
6. ex_____
7. pre_____
8. proc_____dure
9. station_____ry (paper)
10. station_____ry (still)
11. sep_____rate
12. compar_____tive
13. re_____o_____end

14. ecsta_____y
15. anal_____e
16. paral_____e
17. rep_____tition
18. irrit_____ble
19. inimit_____ble
20. ab_____ence
21. superintend_____nt
22. con_____nce
23. a_____oint
24. r_____diculous
25. d_____spair

Mere repetitious drill is of no value in learning to spell a word correctly. You've probably heard the one about the youngster who was kept after school because he was in the habit of using the ungrammatical expression "I have went." Miss X was going to cure her pupil, even if it required drastic measures. So she ordered him to write "I have gone" one thousand times. "Just leave your work on my desk before you go home," she said, "and I'll find it when I come in tomorrow morning." Well, there were twenty pages of neat script on her desk next morning, one thousand lines of "I have gone's," and on the last sheet was a note from the child. "Dear Teacher," it read, "I have done the work and I have went home." If this didn't actually happen, it logically could have, for in any drill, if the mind is not actively engaged, no learning will result. If you drive a car, or sew, or do any familiar and repetitious manual work, you know how your hands can carry on an accustomed task while your mind is far away. And if you hope to learn to spell by filling pages with a word, stop wasting your time. All you'll get for your trouble is writer's cramp.

The only way to learn to spell those words that now plague you is to devise a mnemonic for each one.

If you are never quite sure whether it's *indispensible* or *indispensable,* you can spell it out one hundred, one thousand, or one million times—and the next time you have occasion to write it in a sentence, you'll still wonder whether to end it with *-ible* or *-able.* But if you say to yourself *just once* that *able* people are generally *indispensable,* that thought will come to you whenever you need to spell the word; in a few seconds you've conquered another spelling demon. By engineering your own mnemonic through a study of the architecture of a troublesome word, you will become so quickly and completely involved with the correct spelling of that word that it will be impossible for you ever to be stumped again.

Let us start at once. Below you will find another twenty-five words from the list of one hundred demons, each offered to you in both the correct form and in the popular misspelling. Go through the test quickly, checking off what you consider a proper choice in each case. In that way you will discover which of the twenty-five you would be likely to get caught on. Then devise a personal mnemonic for each word you flunked, writing your ingenious result out in the margin of the page. And don't be alarmed if some of your mnemonics turn out kind of silly—the sillier they are the more likely you are to recall them in an emergency. One of my pupils, who could not remember how many *l*'s to put into *tranquillity* (or is it *tranquility?*), shifted his mind into high gear and came up with this: "In the old days life was more *tranquil* than today, and people wrote with *quills* instead of fountain pens. Hence—*tranquillity!*" Another pupil, a girl who always chewed her nails over *irresistible* before she could decide whether to end it with *-ible* or *-able,* suddenly realized that a certain brand of *lipstick* was called *irresistible,* the point being of course that the only vowel in *lipstick* is *i*—hence, *-ible!* Silly, aren't they? But they work. Go ahead to the test now; and see how clever—or silly—you can be.

SPELLING TEST

1. a. supprise
   b. surprise
2. a. inoculate
   b. innoculate
3. a. definitely
   b. definately
4. a. priviledge
   b. privilege
5. a. incidently
   b. incidentally
6. a. predictible
   b. predictable
7. a. dissipate
   b. disippate
8. a. descriminate
   b. discriminate
9. a. description
   b. discription
10. a. baloon
    b. balloon
11. a. occurence
    b. occurrence
12. a. truely
    b. truly
13. a. arguement
    b. argument
14. a. assistant
    b. asisstant
15. a. grammer
    b. grammar
16. a. parallel
    b. paralell
17. a. drunkeness
    b. drunkenness
18. a. suddeness
    b. suddenness
19. a. embarassment
    b. embarrassment
20. a. weird
    b. wierd
21. a. pronounciation
    b. pronunciation
22. a. noticeable
    b. noticable
23. a. developement
    b. development
24. a. vicious
    b. viscious
25. a. insistent
    b. insistant

KEY: 1–b, 2–a, 3–a, 4–b, 5–b, 6–b, 7–a, 8–b, 9–a, 10–b, 11–b,
     12–b, 13–b, 14–a, 15–b, 16–a, 17–b, 18–b, 19–b, 20–a,
     21–b, 22–a, 23–b, 24–a, 25–a

By now you're well on the way toward developing a definite superiority complex about your spelling—which isn't a half-bad thing, for I've learned, working with my students, that many peo-

ple think they're awful spellers, and have completely lost faith in
their ability, solely because they get befuddled over no more than
two dozen or so common words that they use over and over again
and always misspell. Every other word they spell perfectly, but
they still think they're prize boobs in spelling until their self-
confidence is restored. So if you're beginning to gain more assurance, you're on the right track. The conquest of the one hundred
common words most frequently misspelled is not going to assure
you that you will always come out top man in a spelling bee, but
it's certain to clean up your writing and bolster your ego.

So far you have worked with fifty of the one hundred spelling
demons. Here, now, is the remainder of the list. Test yourself, or
have someone who can keep a secret test you, and discover which
ones are your Waterloo. Study each one you miss as if it were a
problem in engineering. Observe how it's put together and devise
whatever association pattern will fix the correct form in your
mind.

Happy spelling!

SPELLING DEMONS

These fifty words complete the list of one hundred words that
most frequently stump the inexpert spellers:

1. embarrassing
2. judgment
3. indispensable
4. disappear
5. disappoint
6. corroborate
7. sacrilegious
8. tranquillity
9. exhilaration
10. newsstand
11. license
12. irresistible
13. persistent
14. dilemma
15. perseverance
16. until (but till)
17. tyrannize
18. vacillate
19. oscillate
20. accommodate
21. dilettante
22. changeable
23. accessible
24. forty
25. desirable
26. panicky

27. seize
28. leisure
29. receive
30. achieve
31. holiday
32. existence
33. pursue
34. pastime
35. possesses
36. professor
37. category
38. rhythmical

39. vacuum
40. benefited
41. committee
42. grievous
43. conscious
44. plebeian
45. tariff
46. sheriff
47. connoisseur
48. necessary
49. sergeant
50. misspelling

15

HOW TO TALK
ABOUT WHAT GOES ON

(Sessions 42–44)

TEASER PREVIEW

What verb, ending in -ate, means:

- *to exhaust?*
- *to scold severely?*
- *to deny oneself?*
- *to repeat the main points?*
- *to be a victim of mental or intellectual stagnation?*
- *to pretend?*
- *to hint?*
- *to make (something) easier to bear?*
- *to show sympathy?*
- *to waver indecisively?*

451

SESSION 42

WORDS are symbols of ideas—and we have been learning, discussing, and working with words as they revolve around certain basic concepts.

Starting with an idea (personality types, doctors, occupations, science, lying, actions, speech, insults, compliments, etc.), we have explored the meanings and uses of ten basic words; then, working from each word, we have wandered off toward any ideas and additional words that a basic word might suggest, or toward any *other* words built on the same Latin or Greek roots.

By this natural and logical method, you have been able to make meaningful and lasting contact with fifty to a hundred or more words in each chapter. And you have discovered, I think, that while five *isolated* words may be difficult to learn in one day, fifty to a hundred or more *related* words are easy to learn in a few sessions.

In this session we learn words that tell what's going on, what's happening, what people do to each other or to themselves, or what others do to *them*.

IDEAS

1. complete exhaustion

You have stayed up all night. And what were you doing? Playing poker, a very pleasant way of whiling away time? No. Engaging in some creative activity, like writing a short story, planning a political campaign, discussing fascinating questions with friends? No.

The examples I have offered are exciting or stimulating—as psychologists have discovered, it is not work or effort that causes fatigue, but boredom, frustration, or a similar feeling.

You have stayed up all night with a very sick husband, wife, child, or dear friend. And despite all your ministrations, the patient is sinking. You can see how this long vigil contains all the elements of frustration that contribute to mental, physical, and nervous fatigue.

And so you are bushed—but completely bushed. Your exhaustion is mental, it is physiological, it is emotional.

What verb expresses the effect of the night's frustrations on you?

to enervate

2. tongue-lashing

You suddenly see the flashing red light as you glance in your rear-view mirror. It's the middle of the night, yet the police flasher is clear as day—and then you hear the low growl of the siren. So you pull over, knowing you were speeding along at 70 on the 55-mile-an-hour-limit freeway—after all, there was not another car in sight on the deserted stretch of road you were traveling.

The cop is pleasant, courteous, smiling; merely asks for your driver's license and registration; even says "Please."

Feeling guilty and stupid, you become irritated. So what do you do?

You lash out at the officer with all the verbal vituperation welling up in you from your self-anger. You scold him harshly for not spending his time looking for violent criminals instead of harassing innocent motorists; you call into question his honesty, his ambition, his fairness, even his ancestry. To no avail, of course—you stare at the traffic ticket morosely as the police cruiser pulls away.

What verb describes how you reacted?

to castigate

3. altruistic

Phyllis is selfless and self-sacrificing. Her husband's needs and desires come first—even when they conflict with her own. Clothes for her two daughters are her main concern—even if she has to wear a seven-year-old coat and outmoded dresses so that Paula and Evelyn can look smart and trim. At the dinner table, she heaps everyone's plate—while she herself often goes without. Phyllis will deny herself, will scrimp and save—all to the end that she may offer her husband and children the luxuries that her low self-esteem does not permit her to give herself.

What verb expresses what Phyllis does?

to self-abnegate

4. repetition

You have delivered a long, complicated lecture to your class, and now, to make sure that they will remember the important points, you restate the key ideas, the main thoughts. You offer, in short, a kind of brief summary, step by step, omitting all extraneous details.

What verb best describes what you do?

to recapitulate

5. no joie de vivre

Perhaps you wake up some gloomy Monday morning (why is it that Monday is always the worst day of the week?) and begin to think of the waste of the last five years. Intellectually, there has been no progress—you've read scarcely half a dozen books, haven't made one new, exciting friend, haven't had a startling or unusual thought. Economically, things are no better—same old debts to meet, same old hundred dollars in the bank, same old job, same old routine of the eight-to-five workdays, the tuna fish or chicken salad sandwich for lunch, the same dreary ride home. What a life! No change, nothing but routine, sameness, monotony —and for what? (By now you'd better get up—this type of thinking never leads anywhere, as you've long since learned.)

What verb describes how you think you live?

to vegetate

454

6. pretense

Your neighbor, Mrs. Brown, pops in without invitation to tell you of her latest troubles with (a) her therapist, (b) her hairdresser, (c) her husband, (d) her children, and/or (e) her gynecologist.

Since Florence Brown is dull to the point of ennui, and anyway you have a desk piled high with work you were planning to light into, you find it difficult to concentrate on what she is saying. However, you do not wish to offend her by sending her packing, or even by appearing to be uninterested, so you pretend rapt attention, nodding wisely at what you hope are the right places.

What verb describes this feigning of interest?

to simulate

7. slight hint, no more

You are an author and are discussing with your editor the possible avenues of publicity and advertising for your new book. At one point in the conversation the editor makes several statements which might—or might not—be construed to mean that the company is going to promote the book heavily. For example, "If we put some real money behind this, we might sell a few copies," or "I wonder if it would be a good idea to get you on a few talk shows . . ." No unequivocal commitments, no clear-cut promises, only the slight and oblique mention of possibilities.

What verb expresses what the editor is doing?

to intimate

8. helpful

Aspirin doesn't cure any diseases. Yet this popular and inexpensive drug is universally used to lighten and relieve various unpleasant symptoms of disease: aches and pains, fever, inflammations, etc.

What verb expresses the action of aspirin?

to alleviate

455

9. when the bell tolls

John Donne's lines (made famous by Ernest Hemingway):

> *No man is an* Iland, *intire of it selfe; every man is a peece of the* Continent, *a part of the* maine; *if a* Clod *bee washed away by the* Sea, Europe *is the lesse, as well as if a* Promontorie *were, as well as if a* Mannor *of thy friends or of thine owne were; any mans* death *diminishes me, because I am involved in* Mankinde; *And therefore never send to know for whom the* bell *tolls; It tolls for* thee.

are truer than you may think; any person who views another's pain with complete detachment or indifference is shutting off important feelings.

When people have suffered a bereavement (as through death); when they have been wounded by life or by friends; then is the time they most need to feel that they are not alone, that you share their misery with them even if you cannot directly alleviate their sorrow. Your sympathy and compassion are, of course, alleviation enough.

What verb signifies this vicarious sharing of sorrow with someone who directly suffers?

to commiserate

10. when two men propose

Should you marry John or George? (You're strongly and equally attracted to both.) John is handsome, virile, tender; George is stable, reliable, dependable, always there when you need him. George loves you deeply; John is more exciting. You decide on John, naturally.

But wait—marrying John would mean giving up George, and with George you always know where you stand; he's like the Rock of Gibraltar (and sometimes almost as dull). So you change your mind—it's George, on more mature reflection.

But how happy can you be with a husband who is not exciting? Maybe John would be best after all. . . .

The pendulum swings back and forth—you cannot make up your mind and stick to it. (You fail to realize that your indecision proves that you don't want to marry either one, or perhaps don't want to give either one up, or possibly don't even want to get married.) First it's John, then it's George, then back to John, then George again. *Which is it, which is it?*

What verb describes your pendulum-like indecision?

to vacillate

USING THE WORDS

Can you pronounce the words?

1.	*enervate*	EN'-ər-vayt'
2.	*castigate*	KAS'-tə-gayt'
3.	*self-abnegate*	self-AB'-nə-gayt'
4.	*recapitulate*	ree'-kə-PICH'-ə-layt'
5.	*vegetate*	VEJ'-ə-tayt'
6.	*simulate*	SIM'-yə-layt'
7.	*intimate*	IN'-tə-mayt'
8.	*alleviate*	ə-LEE'-vee-ayt'
9.	*commiserate*	kə-MIZ'-ə-rayt
10.	*vacillate*	VAS'-ə-layt

Can you work with the words?

1.	enervate	a.	deny oneself
2.	castigate	b.	stagnate
3.	self-abnegate	c.	suggest; hint
4.	recapitulate	d.	sympathize
5.	vegetate	e.	waver
6.	simulate	f.	exhaust
7.	intimate	g.	lessen; lighten
8.	alleviate	h.	summarize

457

9. commiserate
10. vacillate

i. pretend
j. censure; scold; slash at verbally

KEY: 1–f, 2–j, 3–a, 4–h, 5–b, 6–i, 7–c, 8–g, 9–d, 10–e

Do you understand the words? (I)

1.	Should you feel *enervated* after a good night's sleep?	YES	NO
2.	Do motorists who have been caught speeding sometimes start *castigating* the traffic officer?	YES	NO
3.	Do people who are completely *self-abnegating* say "No!" to their needs and desires?	YES	NO
4.	When you *recapitulate,* do you cover new material?	YES	NO
5.	Do people possessed of *joie de vivre* usually feel that they are *vegetating?*	YES	NO
6.	When you *simulate* alertness, do you purposely act somnolent?	YES	NO
7.	When you *intimate,* do you make a direct statement?	YES	NO
8.	Does aspirin often have an *alleviating* effect on pain?	YES	NO
9.	Do we naturally *commiserate* with people who have suffered a bereavement?	YES	NO
10.	Do decisive people often *vacillate?*	YES	NO

KEY: 1–no, 2–yes, 3–yes, 4–no, 5–no, 6–no, 7–no, 8–yes, 9–yes, 10–no

---

Do you understand the words? (II)

1.	enervated—exhilarated	SAME	OPPOSITE
2.	castigate—praise	SAME	OPPOSITE
3.	self-abnegate—deny oneself	SAME	OPPOSITE
4.	recapitulate—summarize	SAME	OPPOSITE
5.	vegetate—stagnate	SAME	OPPOSITE
6.	simulate—pretend	SAME	OPPOSITE
7.	intimate—hint	SAME	OPPOSITE
8.	alleviate—make worse	SAME	OPPOSITE
9.	commiserate—sympathize	SAME	OPPOSITE
10.	vacillate—decide	SAME	OPPOSITE

KEY: 1–O, 2–O, 3–S, 4–S, 5–S, 6–S, 7–S, 8–O, 9–S, 10–O

Can you recall the words?

1.	pretend	1. S_____
2.	scold	2. C_____
3.	sacrifice one's desires	3. S_____
4.	waver	4. V_____
5.	exhaust	5. E_____
6.	sympathize	6. C_____
7.	summarize	7. R_____
8.	lighten	8. A_____
9.	hint	9. I_____
10.	stagnate	10. V_____

KEY: 1–simulate, 2–castigate, 3–self-abnegate, 4–vacillate, 5–enervate, 6–commiserate, 7–recapitulate, 8–alleviate, 9–intimate, 10–vegetate

(End of Session 42)

SESSION 43

ORIGINS AND RELATED WORDS

1. more than fatigue

When you are *enervated,* you feel as if your nerves have been ripped out—or so the etymology of the word indicates.

Enervate is derived from *e- (ex-),* out, and Latin *nervus,* nerve. *Enervation* (en'-ər-VAY'-shən) is not just fatigue, but complete devitalization—physical, emotional, mental—as if every ounce of the life force has been sapped out, as if the last particle of energy has been drained away.

Despite its similar appearance to the word *energy, enervation* is almost a direct antonym. *Energy* is derived from the Greek prefix *en-,* in, plus the root *ergon,* work; *erg* is the term used in physics for a unit of work or energy. *Synergism* (SIN'-ər-jiz-əm)—the prefix *syn-,* together or with, plus *ergon*—is the process by which two or more substances or drugs, by working together, produce a greater effect in combination than the sum total of their individual effects.

Alcohol, for example, is a depressant. So are barbiturates and other soporifics. Alcohol and barbiturates work *synergistically* (sin'-ər-JIS'-tik'-lee)—the effect of each is increased by the other if the two are taken together.

So if you're drinking, don't take a sleeping pill—or if you *must* take a pill for your insomnia, don't drink—the combination, if not lethal, will do more to you than you may want done!

Synergy (SIN'-ər-jee), by the way, is an alternate form of *synergism.*

2. verbal punishment

Castigate is derived from a Latin verb meaning *to punish;* in present-day usage, the verb generally refers to verbal punishment, usually harsh and severe. It is somewhat synonymous with *scold, criticize, rebuke, censure, reprimand,* or *berate,* but much stronger than any of these—*rail at, rant at, slash at, lash out at,* or *tongue-lash* is a much closer synonym. When candidates for office *castigate* their opponents, they do not mince words.

Can you construct the noun form of *castigate?* _____

3. saying "No!" to oneself

Abnegate is derived from Latin *ab-,* away (as in *absent*), plus *nego,* to deny—*self-abnegation* (ab'-nə-GAY'-shən), then, is self-denial. *Nego* itself is a contraction of Latin *neg-,* not, no, and *aio,* I say; to be *self-abnegating* is to say "No!" to what you want, as if some inner censor were at work whispering, "No, you can't have that, you can't do that, you don't deserve that, you're not good enough for that. . . ."

To *negate* (nə-GAYT') is to deny the truth or existence of, as in "The atheist *negates* God"; or, by extension, to destroy by working against, as in, "His indulgence in expensive hobbies *negates* all his wife's attempts to keep the family solvent." Can you write the noun form of the verb *negate?* _____

Negative and *negativity* obviously spring from the same source as *negate.*

4. heads and headings

Latin *caput, capitis* means *head.* The *captain* is the *head of* any group; the *capital* is the *"head* city" of a state or nation; and to *decapitate* (dee-KAP'-ə-tayt') is to chop off someone's *head,* a popular activity during the French Revolution after the guillotine was invented. Write the noun form of *decapitate:* _____

Latin *capitulum* is a little head, or, by extension, the heading, or title, of a chapter. So when you *recapitulate,* you go through the chapter headings again (*re-*), etymologically speaking, or you summarize or review the main points.

Remembering how the noun and adjective forms are derived

from *adulate* (Chapter 9), can you write the required forms of *re-capitulate*?

NOUN: _____

ADJECTIVE: _____

When you *capitulate* (kə-PICH′-ə-layt′), etymologically you arrange in headings, or, as the meaning of the verb naturally evolved, you arrange conditions of surrender, as when an army *capitulates* to the enemy forces under prearranged conditions; or, by further natural extension, you stop resisting and give up, as in, "He realized there was no longer any point in resisting her advances, so he reluctantly *capitulated*." Can you write the noun form of *capitulate*? _____ .

5. mere vegetables

Vegetable is from Latin *vegeto,* to live and grow, which is what vegetables do—but that's *all* they do, so to *vegetate,* is, by implication, to do no more than stay alive, stuck in a rut, leading an inactive, unstimulating, emotionally and intellectually stagnant existence. *Vegetation* (vej′-ə-TAY′-shən) is any dull, passive, stagnant existence; also any plant life, as the thick *vegetation* of a jungle.

REVIEW OF ETYMOLOGY

PREFIX, ROOT, SUFFIX	MEANING	ENGLISH WORD
1. *e-* (*ex-*)	out	_____
2. *nervus*	nerve	_____
3. *en-*	in	_____
4. *ergon*	work	_____
5. *syn-*	with, together	_____
6. *-ic*	adjective suffix	_____
7. *-ion*	noun suffix	_____
8. *ab-*	away	_____
9. *nego*	to deny	_____

10. *caput, capitis*	head	_____
11. *de-*	negative prefix	_____
12. *capitulum*	little head, chapter heading	_____
13. *re-*	again	_____
14. *-ory*	adjective suffix	_____
15. *vegeto*	to live and grow	_____

USING THE WORDS

Can you pronounce the words?

1.	*enervation*	en'-ər-VAY'-shən
2.	*synergism*	SIN'-ər-jiz-əm
3.	*synergy*	SIN'-ər-jee
4.	*synergistic*	sin'-ər-JIS'-tik
5.	*castigation*	kas'-tə-GAY'-shən
6.	*self-abnegation*	self-ab'-nə-GAY'-shən
7.	*negate*	nə-GAYT'
8.	*negation*	nə-GAY'-shən
9.	*decapitate*	dee-KAP'-ə-tayt'
10.	*decapitation*	dee-kap'-ə-TAY'-shən
11.	*recapitulation*	ree-kə-pich'-ə-LAY'-shən
12.	*recapitulatory*	ree-kə-PICH'-ə-lə-tawr'-ee
13.	*capitulate*	kə-PICH'-ə-layt'
14.	*capitulation*	kə-pich'-ə-LAY'-shən

Can you work with the words?

1.	enervation	a. tongue-lashing
2.	synergism, synergy	b. denial; destruction
3.	castigation	c. a lopping off of one's head
4.	self-abnegation	d. summary; review of main points
5.	negation	e. self-denial
6.	decapitation	f. utter exhaustion; mental, emotional, and physical drain

463

7. recapitulation

g. a working together for greater effect

8. capitulation

h. surrender

KEY: 1–f, 2–h, 3–a, 4–e, 5–b, 6–c, 7–d, 8–g

Do you understand the words?

1. enervating—refreshing	SAME	OPPOSITE
2. synergistic—neutralizing	SAME	OPPOSITE
3. castigation—scolding	SAME	OPPOSITE
4. self-abnegation—egoism	SAME	OPPOSITE
5. negate—accept	SAME	OPPOSITE
6. decapitate—behead	SAME	OPPOSITE
7. recapitulatory—summarizing	SAME	OPPOSITE
8. capitulate—resist	SAME	OPPOSITE

KEY: 1–O, 2–O, 3–S, 4–O, 5–O, 6–S, 7–S, 8–O

Can you recall the words?

1. to give in   1. C_____

2. working together for greater effect (*adj.*)   2. S_____

3. total fatigue   3. E_____

4. for the purpose of summarizing or review (*adj.*)   4. R_____

5. self-denial   5. S_____ -A_____

6. deny; render ineffective; nullify   6. N_____

7. process by which two or more substances produce a greater effect than the sum of the individual effects   7. S_____
                                                    or S_____

8. to cut off the head of   8. D_____

464

9. strong censure   9. C_____
10. to surrender   10. C_____

(End of Session 43)

SESSION 44

ORIGINS AND RELATED WORDS

1. not the real McCoy

Simulate is from Latin *simulo,* to copy; and *simulo* itself derives from the Latin adjectives *similis,* like or similar.

Simulation (sim'-yə-LAY'-shən), then, is copying the real thing, pretending to be the genuine article by taking on a similar appearance. The *simulation* of joy is quite a feat when you really feel depressed.

Genuine pearls grow inside oysters; *simulated* pearls are synthetic, but look like the ones from oysters. (Rub a pearl against your teeth to tell the difference—the natural pearl feels gritty.) So the frequent advertisement of an inexpensive necklace made of "genuine *simulated* pearls" can fool you if you don't know the word—you're being offered a genuine fake.

Dissimulation (də-sim'-yə-LAY'-shən) is something else! When you *dissimulate* (də-SIM'-yə-layt'), you hide your true feelings by making a pretense of opposite feelings. (Then again, maybe it's not something completely else!)

Sycophants are great *dissimulators*—they may feel contempt,

465

but show admiration; they may feel negative, but express absolutely positive agreement.

A close synonym of *dissimulate* is *dissemble* (də-SEM'-bəl), which also is to hide true feelings by pretending the opposite; or, additionally, to conceal facts, or one's true intentions, by deception; or, still further additionally, to pretend ignorance of facts you'd rather not admit, when, indeed, you're fully aware of them.

The noun is *dissemblance* (də-SEM'-bləns).

In *dissimulate* and *dissemble,* the negative prefix *dis-* acts largely to make both words pejorative.

2. hints and helps

The verb *intimate* is from Latin *intimus,* innermost, the same root from which the adjective *intimate* (IN'-tə-mət) and its noun *intimacy* (IN'-tə-mə-see) are derived; but the relationship is only in etymology, not in meaning. An *intimation* (in'-tə-MAY'-shən) contains a significance buried deep in the innermost core, only a hint showing. As you grow older, you begin to have *intimations* that you are mortal; when someone aims a .45 at you, or when a truck comes roaring down at you as you drive absent-mindedly against a red light through an intersection, you are suddenly *very sure* that you are mortal.

Alleviate is a combination of Latin *levis,* light (not heavy), the prefix *ad-,* to, and the verb suffix. (*Ad-* changes to *al-* before a root starting with *l-.*)

If something *alleviates* your pain, it makes your pain lighter for you; if I *alleviate* your sadness, I make it lighter to bear; and if you need some *alleviation* (ə-lee'-vee-AY'-shən) of your problems, you need them made lighter and less burdensome. To *alleviate* is to relieve only temporarily, not to cure or do away with. (*Relieve* is also from *levis,* plus *re-,* again—to make light or easy again.) The adjective form of *alleviate* is *alleviative* (ə-LEE'-vee-ay'-tiv)—aspirin is an *alleviative* drug.

Anything light will rise—so from the prefix *e-* (*ex-*), out, plus *levis,* we can construct the verb *elevate,* etymologically, to raise out, or, actually, raise up, as to *elevate* one's spirits, raise them up, make them lighter; or *elevate* someone to a higher position, which is what an *elevator* does.

Have you ever seen a performance of magic in which a person or an object apparently rises in the air as if floating? That's *levitation* (lev'-ǝ-TAY'-shǝn)—rising through no visible means. (I've watched it a dozen times and never *could* figure it out!) The verb, to so rise, is *levitate* (LEV'-ǝ-tayt').

And how about *levity* (LEV'-ǝ-tee)? That's lightness too, but of a different sort—lightness in the sense of frivolity, flippancy, joking, or lack of seriousness, especially when solemnity, dignity, or formality is required or more appropriate, as in "tones of *levity*," or as in, "Levity is out of place at a funeral, in a house of worship, at the swearing-in ceremonies of a President or Supreme Court Justice," or as in, "Okay, enough *levity*—now let's get down to business!"

3. sharing someone's misery

Latin *miser*, wretched, the prefix *con-* (which, as you know, becomes *com-* before a root beginning with *m-*), together or with, and the verb suffix *-ate* are the building blocks from which *commiserate* is constructed. "I *commiserate* with you," then, means, "I am wretched together with you—I share your misery." The noun form? _____.

Miser, miserly, miserable, misery all come from the same root.

4. swing and sway

Vacillate—note the single *c*, double *l*—derives from Latin *vacillo*, to swing back and forth. The noun form? _____.

People who swing back and forth in indecision, who are irresolute, who can, unfortunately, see both, or even three or four, sides of every question, and so have difficulty making up their minds, are *vacillatory* (VAS'-ǝ-lǝ-tawr'-ee). They are also, usually, *ambivalent* (am-BIV'-ǝ-lǝnt)—they have conflicting and simultaneous emotions about the same person or thing; or they want to go but they also want to stay; or they love something, but they hate it too. The noun is *ambivalence* (am-BIV'-ǝ-lǝns)—from *ambi* both. (Remember *ambivert* and *ambidextrous* from Chapter 3?)

Ambivalence has best been defined (perhaps by Henny Youngman—if he didn't say it first, he should have) as watching your mother-in-law drive over a cliff in your new Cadillac.

To *vacillate* is to swing mentally or emotionally. To sway back and forth physically is *oscillate*—again note the double *l*—(OS'-ə-layt'), from Latin *oscillum*, a swing. A pendulum *oscillates*, the arm of a metronome *oscillates*, and people who've had much too much to drink *oscillate* when they try to walk. The noun? _____
_____.

REVIEW OF ETYMOLOGY

PREFIX, ROOT, SUFFIX	MEANING	ENGLISH WORD
1. *simulo*	to copy	_____
2. *similis*	like, similar	_____
3. *dis-*	pejorative prefix	_____
4. *ad- (al-)*	to, toward	_____
5. *levis*	light	_____
6. *-ate*	verb suffix	_____
7. *-ion*	noun suffix	_____
8. *e- (ex-)*	out	_____
9. *intimus*	innermost	_____
10. *miser*	wretched	_____
11. *vacillo*	to swing back and forth	_____
12. *ambi-*	both	_____
13. *oscillum*	a swing	_____

USING THE WORDS

Can you pronounce the words?

1. *simulation*	sim'-yə-LAY'-shən
2. *dissimulate*	də-SIM'-yə-layt'

3. *dissimulation*	də-sim′-yə-LAY′-shən
4. *dissemble*	də-SEM′-bəl
5. *dissemblance*	də-SEM′-bləns
6. *intimation*	in′-tə-MAY′-shən
7. *alleviation*	ə-lee′-vee-AY′-shən
8. *alleviative*	ə-LEE′-vee-ay′-tiv
9. *levitate*	LEV′-ə-tayt′
10. *levitation*	lev′-ə-TAY′-shən
11. *levity*	LEV′-ə-tee
12. *commiseration*	kə-miz′-ə-RAY′-shən
13. *vacillation*	vas′-ə-LAY′-shən
14. *vacillatory*	VAS′-ə-lə-tawr′-ee
15. *ambivalent*	am-BIV′-ə-lənt
16. *ambivalence*	am-BIV′-ə-ləns
17. *oscillate*	OS′-ə-layt′
18. *oscillation*	os′-ə-LAY′-shən

Can you work with the words? (I)

1. simulation		a.	hint
2. dissemble		b.	flippancy or joking when seriousness is required
3. intimation		c.	a sharing of grief
4. alleviation		d.	physical swaying; swinging action, as of a pendulum
5. levitate		e.	a swinging back and forth in indecision
6. levity		f.	pretense
7. commiseration		g.	conflicted and contrary feelings
8. vacillation		h.	rise in the air (as by magic or illusion)
9. ambivalence		i.	pretend
10. oscillation		j.	a lightening; a making less severe

KEY: 1–f, 2–i, 3–a, 4–j, 5–h, 6–b, 7–c, 8–e, 9–g, 10–d

469

Can you work with the words? (II)

1. dissimulate	a. pretense of ignorance
2. dissemblance	b. a rising and floating in air
3. alleviative	c. having simultaneous and contrary feelings
4. levitation	d. tending to swing back and forth in indecision
5. vacillatory	e. to swing back and forth like a pendulum
6. ambivalent	f. to hide real feelings by pretending opposite feelings
7. oscillate	g. tending to ease (pain, burdens, suffering, etc.)

KEY: 1–f, 2–a, 3–g, 4–b, 5–d, 6–c, 7–e

Do you understand the words?

1. simulated—genuine	SAME	OPPOSITE
2. dissimulate—pretend	SAME	OPPOSITE
3. dissemble—be truthful	SAME	OPPOSITE
4. intimation—hint	SAME	OPPOSITE
5. alleviation—reduction	SAME	OPPOSITE
6. levitate—sink	SAME	OPPOSITE
7. levity—flippancy	SAME	OPPOSITE
8. vacillation—decisiveness	SAME	OPPOSITE
9. ambivalent—confused	SAME	OPPOSITE
10. oscillate—sway	SAME	OPPOSITE

KEY: 1–O, 2–S, 3–O, 4–S, 5–S, 6–O, 7–S, 8–O, 9–S, 10–S

Can you recall the words?

1. to swing back and forth
2. feeling both ways at the same time (*adj.*)
3. to conceal real feelings

4. pretense
5. to pretend ignorance though knowing the facts
6. joking; frivolity; flippancy
7. indecisive

8. to rise in the air, as by illusion
9. tending to ease (pain, etc.) (*adj.*)
10. a sharing of another's grief (*n.*)

1. O_____
2. A_____

3. D_____
   or D_____
4. S_____
5. D_____

6. L_____
7. V_____
   or V_____
8. L_____
9. A_____
   or A_____
10. C_____

KEY: 1–oscillate, 2–ambivalent, 3–dissimulate *or* dissemble, 4–simulation, 5–dissemble, 6–levity, 7–vacillatory *or* vacillating, 8–levitate, 9–alleviative *or* alleviating, 10–commiseration

---

CHAPTER REVIEW

A. Do you recognize the words?

1. Complete exhaustion:
   (a) synergism, (b) enervation, (c) negation
2. Co-operation in producing effects:
   (a) synergy, (b) castigation, (c) capitulation
3. Lop off the head of:
   (a) castigate, (b) capitulate, (c) decapitate
4. deny; render ineffective:
   (a) castigate, (b) negate, (c) recapitulate

5. stagnate:
    (a) intimate, (b) simulate, (c) vegetate
6. concealment of true feelings:
    (a) simulation, (b) dissimulation, (c) dissemblance
7. sympathy:
    (a) levity, (b) ambivalence, (c) commiseration
8. indecisiveness:
    (a) vacillation, (b) oscillation, (c) dissimulation
9. aware of contrary feelings:
    (a) alleviative, (b) dissimulating, (c) ambivalent

KEY: 1–b, 2–a, 3–c, 4–b, 5–c, 6–b *and* c, 7–c, 8–a, 9–c

B. Can you recognize roots?

ROOT	MEANING	EXAMPLE
1. *nervus*		enervate
2. *ergon*		energy
3. *nego*		self-abnegation
4. *caput, capitis*		decapitate
5. *capitulum*		recapitulate
6. *vegeto*		vegetate
7. *simulo*		dissimulate
8. *similis*		similarity
9. *levis*		levity
10. *intimus*		intimation
11. *miser*		commiserate
12. *vacillo*		vacillate
13. *ambi-*		ambivalent
14. *oscillum*		oscillate

KEY: 1–nerve, 2–work, 3–deny, 4–head, 5–little head, chapter
      heading, 6–live and grow, 7–to copy, 8–like, similar,
      9–light, 10–innermost, 11–wretched, 12–swing back and
      forth, 13–both, 14–a swing

TEASER QUESTIONS FOR THE AMATEUR ETYMOLOGIST

We have previously met the Greek prefix *syn-*, together or with, in *synonym* ("names together") and *sympathy* ("feeling with"), and again in this chapter in *synergism* ("working together").

Syn- is a most useful prefix to know. Like Latin *con-*, (together or with) and *ad-* (to, toward), the final letter changes depending on the first letter of the root to which it is attached. *Syn-* becomes *sym-* before *b, m,* and *p.*

Can you construct some words using *syn-*, or *sym-?*

1. Etymologically, Jews are "led together" in a house of worship (*agogos,* leading). Can you construct the word for this temple or place of worship? _____.

2. There is a process by which dissimilar organisms live together (*bios,* life) in close association, each in some way helping, and getting help from, the other (like the shark and the pilot fish). What word, ending in *-sis,* designates such a process?

_____

What would the adjective form be? _____.

3. Using Greek *phone,* sound, write the word that etymologically refers to a musical composition in which the sounds of all instruments are in harmony together. _____

_____. Using the suffix *-ic,* write the adjective form of this word: _____.

4. Combine *sym-* with *metron,* measurement, to construct a word designating similarity of shape on both sides (i.e., "measurement together"): _____.

Write the adjective form of this word: _____

_____.

5. *Syn-* plus *dromos,* a running, are the building blocks of a medical word designating a group of symptoms that occur (i.e., run) together in certain diseases. Can you figure out the word?

_____

6. The same *dromos,* a running, combines with Greek *hippos,* horse, to form a word referring to a place in ancient Greece in

which horse and chariot races were run. The word? _____
_____

7. *Hippos,* horse, plus Greek *potamos,* river, combine to form a word designating one of the three pachyderms we discussed in an earlier chapter. The word? _____.

(*Answers in Chapter 18.*)

PICKING YOUR FRIENDS' BRAINS

You can build your vocabulary, I have said, by increasing your familiarity with new ideas and by becoming alert to the new words you meet in your reading of magazines and books.

There is still another productive method, one that will be particularly applicable in view of all the new words you are learning from your study of these pages.

That method is *picking your friends' brains.*

Intelligent people are interested in words because words are symbols of ideas, and the person with an alert mind is always interested in ideas.

You may be amazed, if you have never tried it, to find that you can stir up an animated discussion by asking, in a social group that you attend, "What does _____ mean?" (Use any word that particularly fascinates you.) Someone in the group is likely to know, and almost everyone will be willing to make a guess. From that point on, others in the group will ask questions about their own favorite words (most people do have favorites), or about words that they themselves have in some manner recently learned. As the discussion continues along these lines, you will be introduced to new words yourself, and if your friends have fairly good vocabularies you may strike a rich vein of pay dirt and come away with a large number of words to add to your vocabulary.

This method of picking your friends' brains is particularly fruitful because you will be learning not from a page of print (as in this book or as in your other reading) but from real live persons —the same sources that children use to increase their vocab-

474

ularies at such prodigious rates. No learning is quite as effective as the learning that comes from other people—no information in print can ever be as vivid as information that comes from another human being. And so the words you pick up from your friends will have an amazingly strong appeal, will make a lasting impression on your mind.

Needless to say, your own rich vocabulary, now that you have come this far in the book, will make it possible for you to contribute to your friends' vocabulary as much as, if not more than, you take away—but since giving to others is one of the greatest sources of a feeling of self-worth, you can hardly complain about this extra dividend.

(End of Session 44)

TAKE THIS SPELLING TEST

Even in the most painstakingly edited of magazines, a silly little misspelling of a perfectly common word will occasionally appear. How the error eluded the collective and watchful eyes of the editor, the associate editor, the assistant editor, the typesetter, and the proofreader, no one will ever know—for practically every reader of the magazine spots it at once and writes an indignant letter, beginning: "Didn't you ever go to school . . . ?"

Even if you went to school, you're going to have plenty of trouble spotting the one misspelled word in each group below. And not one of these words will be a demon like *sphygmomanometer* (a device for measuring blood pressure) or *piccalilli* (a highly seasoned relish), which no one would ever dare spell without first checking with a dictionary. On the contrary, every word will be of the common or garden variety that you might use every day in your social or business correspondence.

Nevertheless, you're letting yourself in for ten minutes of real trouble, for you will be working with fifty particularly difficult spelling words. So put on your thinking cap before you begin.

A half-dozen high school teachers who took this test were able to make an average score of only five proper choices. Can you do better? Six or seven right is *very good,* eight or nine right is *excellent,* and 100 per cent success marks you as an absolute expert in English spelling.

Check the only misspelled word in each group.

A: 1–surprise, 2–disappear, 3–innoculate, 4–description, 5–recommend

B: 1–privilege, 2–separate, 3–incidentally, 4–dissipate, 5–occurence

C: 1–analize, 2–argument, 3–assistant, 4–comparative, 5–truly

D: 1–grammar, 2–drunkeness, 4–parallel, 4–sacrilegious, 5–conscience

E: 1–precede, 2–exceed, 3–accede, 4–procede, 5–concede

F: 1–pronunciation, 2–noticable, 3–desirable, 4–holiday, 5–anoint

G: 1–wierd, 2–seize, 3–achieve, 4–receive, 5–leisure

H: 1–superintendent, 2–persistent, 3–resistant, 4–insistent, 5–perseverence

I: 1–accessible, 2–permissible, 3–inimitable, 4–irresistable, 5–irritable

J: 1–pursue, 2–pastime, 3–kidnapped, 4–rhythmical, 5–exhillarate

---

KEY: A–3 (inoculate), B–5 (occurrence), C–1 (analyze), D–2 (drunkenness), E–4 (proceed), F–2 (noticeable), G–1 (weird), H–5 (perseverance), I–4 (irresistible), J–5 (exhilarate)

16

HOW TO TALK ABOUT
A VARIETY OF
PERSONAL CHARACTERISTICS

(Sessions 45—46)

TEASER PREVIEW

What word, ending in -ous, describes someone who is:

- *fawning, servilely attentive, transparently self-ingratiating?*
- *nagging, dissatisfied, complaining?*
- *snobbish, haughtily contemptuous, arrogant?*
- *noisily troublesome, unmanageable?*
- *habitually short of cash?*
- *attentive and courteous to women?*
- *harmless?*
- *fond of liquor?*
- *pale, gaunt, haggard?*
- *melancholy, sorrowful?*

SESSION 45

There are thousands of English words that end in the letters *-ous* —a Latin suffix meaning *full of.*

The central theme about which the words in this chapter revolve is the idea of "fullness"—and as you will shortly see, you can be full of compliance and servility; full of complaints; full of snobbery; full of noise; full of no money; full of horsemanship; full of harmlessness; full of liquor; full of deathly pallor; and full of sorrows.

For each of these ideas English has a word—and the person with a rich vocabularly knows the exact word to describe what someone is full of.

IDEAS

1. compliance

The Latin root *sequor* means *to follow*—and those who follow rather than lead are usually in a menial, subordinate, or inferior position. People who engage in certain fields of endeavor—waiters, clerks, and servants, for example—are forced, often contrary to their natural temperaments, to act excessively courteous, pleasant, obliging, even subservient and humble. They must follow the lead of their customers or employers, bending their own wills according to the desires of those they serve. They are, etymologically, *full of following after,* or—

obsequious

RELATED WORDS:

1. *obsequies*—In a funeral cortege, the mourners *follow after* the corpse. Hence, *obsequies* are the burial ceremonies, the funeral rites.

479

2. *subsequent*—A *subsequent* letter, paragraph, time, etc. is one that *follows* another.

3. *sequel*—A *sequel* may be a literary work, such as a novel, that *follows* another, continuing the same subject, dealing with the same people or village, etc. or it may be an occurrence that grows out of or *follows* another, as in, "Just wait until you hear the *sequel* to the story!"

4. *sequence*—In order, one item *following* another, as in, "The *sequence* of events of the next few days left him breathless."

Any other word containing the root *sequ-* is likely to have some relationship to the idea of *following*.

2. complaints

The Latin root *queror* means *to complain*—and anyone full of complaints, constantly nagging, harping, fretful, petulant, whining, never satisfied, may accordingly be called—

querulous

3. snobbery

The Latin root *cilium* means *eyelid; super* means *above;* and above the eyelid, as anyone can plainly see, is the eyebrow. Now there are certain obnoxious people who go around raising their eyebrows in contempt, disdain, and sneering arrogance at ordinary mortals like you and me. Such contemptuous, sneering, overbearingly conceited people are called—

supercilious

4. noise

The Latin root *strepo* means *to make a noise*. Anyone who is unruly, boisterous, resistant to authority, unmanageable—and in a noisy, troublesome manner—is

obstreperous

480

5. moneyless

The Latin root *pecus* means *cattle*—and at one time in human history a person's wealth was measured not by stocks and bonds but by stocks of domestic animals, which was a lot more logical, since you get milk and leather and meat from cattle—true wealth —and all you get from the stock market is a headache.

Someone who had lots of *pecus,* then, was rich—someone without *pecus* was indigent, destitute, "broke." And so today we call someone who is habitually without funds, who seems generally to be full of a complete lack of money—

impecunious

This word is not a synonym of *indigent, destitute, or poverty-stricken;* it does not necessarily imply living in reduced circumstances or want, but quite simply being short of cash—habitually.

RELATED WORD:

1. *pecuniary*—pertaining to money, as in, a *pecuniary* consideration, *pecuniary* affairs, etc.

6. horses

The French word *cheval* means *horse;* and in medieval times only gentlemen and knights rode on horses—common people walked. Traditionally (but not, I understand, actually) knights were courteous to women, attentive to female desires, and self-sacrificing when their own interests came in conflict with those of the fair sex. Hence, we call a modern man who has a knightly attitude to women—

chivalrous

RELATED WORDS:

(*Cheval,* horse, comes from Latin *caballus,* an inferior horse. *Callabus* is found in English words in the spelling *caval-*.)

1. *cavalcade*—A procession of persons on horseback, as in a parade.

2. *cavalier*—As a noun, a *cavalier* was once a mounted soldier.

481

As an adjective, *cavalier* describes actions and attitudes that are haughty, unmindful of others' feelings, too offhand, such attributes often being associated with people in power (the military being one of the powers-that-be). Thus, "He answered in a *cavalier* manner" would signify that he was arrogant in his answer, as if the questioner were taking a little too much privilege with him. Or, "After the *cavalier* treatment I received, I never wished to return," signifying that I was pretty much made to feel unimportant and inferior. Or, "After her *cavalier* refusal, I'll never invite her to another party," signifying that the refusal was, perhaps, curt, offhand, without any attempt at apology or courtesy.

3. *cavalry*—The mounted, or "horsed" part of an army.

4. *chivalry*—Noun form of *chivalrous*. Can you write the alternate noun form ending in *-ness*? _____.

5. *chivalric*—Less commonly used adjective form, identical in meaning to *chivalrous*.

Another Latin root for *horse*, as you know, is *equus,* found in words we have already discussed:

1. *equestrian*—A horseman.
2. *equestrienne*—A horsewoman.
3. *equine*—Horselike.

7. no harm done

The latin root *noceo* means to *injure;* someone who need cause you no fear, so harmless is that person, so unable to interfere, so unlikely to get you into trouble, is called—

innocuous

RELATED WORDS:

1. *innocent*—Not guilty of crime or injury.
2. *noxious*—Harmful, poisonous; unwholesome.

8. alcoholic

The Latin root *bibo* means to *drink;* and one who is generally found with one foot up on the brass rail, who likes to tipple beyond the point of sobriety—who, in short, has an overfondness for drinks with a pronounced alcoholic content, is called, usually humorously—

bibulous

RELATED WORDS:

1. *imbibe*—To drink in, soak up, absorb. If we use this verb without specifying what is drunk, as in, "He likes to *imbibe*," the implication, of course, is always liquor; but *imbibe* may also be used in patterns like "*imbibe* learning" or "In early infancy she *imbibed* a respect for her parents."

2. *bib*—Upper part of an apron, or an apronlike napkin tied around a child's neck. In either case, the *bib* prevents what is drunk (or eaten) from spilling over, or dribbling down, on the wearer's clothing.

9. like death itself

The Latin root *cado* means *to fall*—one's final fall is of course always in death, and so someone who looks like a corpse (figuratively speaking), who is pale, gaunt, thin, haggard, eyes deep-sunk, limbs wasted, in other words the extreme opposite of the picture of glowing health, is called—

cadaverous

RELATED WORDS:

1. *cadaver*—A corpse, literally, especially one used for surgical dissection.

2. *decadent*—Etymologically, *"falling down"* (*de-* is a prefix one meaning of which is *down*, as in *descend*, climb down; *decline*, turn down; etc.). If something is in a *decadent* state, it is deteriorating, becoming corrupt or demoralized. *Decadence* is a state of decay. Generally *decadent* and *decadence* are used figuratively—they refer not to actual physical decay (as of a dead body), but to moral or spiritual decay.

10. pain and misery

The Latin root *doleo* means *to suffer* or *grieve*—one who is mournful and sad, whose melancholy comes from physical pain or mental distress, who seems to be suffering or grieving, is called—

dolorous

RELATED WORDS:

1. *dolor*—A poetic synonym of *grief*.

2. *doleful*—A word referring somewhat humorously to exaggerated dismalness, sadness, or dreariness.

3. *condole*—Etymologically, to suffer or grieve with (Latin *con-*, with, together). *Condole* is a somewhat less commonly used synonym of *commiserate,* a verb we discussed in Chapter 15. The noun *condolence* is much more frequently heard than the verb, as in, "Let me offer you my *condolences*," usually said to someone mourning the death of a friend or relative. You have heard of *condolence* cards, and no doubt have sent your share of them. When you *condole* with somebody who has sustained a loss, usually by death, you are saying, in effect, "I am suffering or grieving with you."

REVIEW OF ETYMOLOGY

PREFIX, ROOT, SUFFIX	MEANING	ENGLISH WORD
1. *sequor*	to follow	_____
2. *queror*	to complain	_____
3. *cilium*	eyelid	_____
4. *super*	above	_____
5. *strepo*	to make a noise	_____
6. *pecus*	cattle	_____
7. *-ary*	adjective suffix	_____
8. *im- (in-)*	negative prefix	_____
9. *cheval*	horse	_____
10. *callabus (caval-)*	inferior horse	_____
11. *-ous*	adjective suffix	_____
12. *-ic*	adjective suffix	_____
13. *equus*	horse	_____
14. *-ine*	like, similar to, characteristic of	_____

484

15. *bibo*	to drink	_____
16. *im-* (*in-*)	in	_____
17. *cado*	to fall	_____
18. *de-*	down	_____
19. *-ent*	adjective suffix	_____
20. *-ence*	noun suffix	_____
21. *con-*	with, together	_____

USING THE WORDS

A. THE BASIC WORDS

Can you pronounce the words?

1. *obsequious*	ob-SEEK′-wee-əs
2. *querulous*	KWAIR′-ə-ləs
3. *supercilious*	sŏŏ′-pər-SIL′-ee-əs
4. *obstreperous*	əb-STREP′-ər-əs
5. *impecunious*	im′-pə-KYŌŌ′-nee-əs
6. *chivalrous*	SHIV′-əl-rəs
7. *innocuous*	ə-NOK′-yŏŏ-əs
8. *bibulous*	BIB′-yə-ləs
9. *cadaverous*	kə-DAV′-ər-əs
10. *dolorous*	DOL′-ər-əs *or* DŌ′-lər-əs

Can you work with the words? (I)

1. obsequious	a. snobbish
2. querulous	b. harmless
3. supercilious	c. gaunt
4. obstreperous	d. short of funds
5. impecunious	e. fawning; excessively, ingratiatingly, polite
6. chivalrous	f. sorrowful
7. innocuous	g. addicted to drink
8. bibulous	h. courteous to women

485

| 9. cadaverous | i. complaining |
| 10. dolorous | j. unmanageable |

Can you work with the words? (II)

Match each word in the first column with one from the second column that is *opposite* in meaning.

1. obsequious	a. content; uncomplaining; satisfied
2. querulous	b. affluent
3. supercilious	c. healthy
4. obstreperous	d. rude
5. impecunious	e. sober
6. chivalrous	f. dangerous
7. innocuous	g. humble
8. bibulous	h. misogynous
9. cadaverous	i. happy; cheerful
10. dolorous	j. quiet

Do you understand the words?

1. Do *obsequious* people usually command our respect?   YES   NO
2. Are *querulous* people satisfied?   YES   NO
3. Are *supercilious* people usually popular?   YES   NO
4. Is a person of affluence *impecunious*?   YES   NO
5. Do some women like *chivalrous* men?   YES   NO

6. Are *innocuous* people dangerous?	YES	NO
7. Is a *bibulous* character a teetotaler?	YES	NO
8. Is a *cadaverous*-looking individual the picture of health?	YES	NO
9. Is a *dolorous* attitude characteristic of jovial people?	YES	NO
10. Is an *obstreperous* child difficult to manage?	YES	NO

KEY: 1–no, 2–no, 3–no, 4–no, 5–yes, 6–no, 7–no, 8–no, 9–no, 10–yes

---

Can you recall the words?

1. sorrowful   1. D_____
2. servilely attentive; overly polite   2. O_____
3. haggard; gaunt; pale   3. C_____
4. complaining; whining   4. Q_____
5. addicted to alcohol; likely to   5. B_____
   drink past the point of sobriety
6. arrogant; haughty   6. S_____
7. harmless   7. L_____
8. noisily unmanageable   8. O_____
9. attentive and courteous to   9. C_____
   women
10. short of money; without funds   10. I_____

KEY: 1–dolorous, 2–obsequious, 3–cadaverous, 4–querulous, 5–bibulous, 6–supercilious, 7–innocuous, 8–obstreperous, 9–chivalrous, 10–impecunious

---

(End of Session 45)

SESSION 46

B. RELATED WORDS

Can you pronounce the words? (I)

1. *obsequies* — OB'-sə-kweez
2. *subsequent* — SUB'-sə-kwənt
3. *sequel* — SEE'-kwəl
4. *sequence* — SEE'-kwəns
5. *pecuniary* — pə-KYOO'-nee-air'-ee
6. *noxious* — NOK'-shəs
7. *imbibe* — im-BĪB'
8. *dolor* — DŌ'-lər
9. *doleful* — DŌL'-fəl
10. *cavalcade* — KAV'-əl-kayd'
11. *cavalier (adj.)* — kav-ə-LEER'

Can you pronounce the words? (II)

1. *cavalry* — KAV'-əl-ree
2. *chivalry* — SHIV'-əl-ree
3. *chivalric* — shə-VAL'-rik
4. *condole* — kən-DŌL'
5. *condolence* — kən-DŌ'-ləns
6. *equestrian* — ə-KWES'-tree-ən
7. *equestrienne* — ə-KWES'-tree-en'
8. *equine* — EE'-kwīn'
9. *cadaver* — kə-DAV'-ər *or* kə-DAY'-vər
10. *decadent* — DEK'-ə-dənt *or* də-KAY'-dənt
11. *decadence* — DEK'-ə-dəns *or* də-KAY'-dəns

Can you work with the words?

1. obsequies
2. subsequent
3. sequel

a. proper order
b. drink; absorb; take in
c. harmful, poisonous

4. sequence	d. pain, sorrow (*poetic*)
5. pecuniary	e. coming later or afterward
6. noxious	f. procession of mounted riders
7. imbibe	g. offhand, haughty
8. dolor	h. a following event or literary work
9. doleful	i. horsewoman
10. cavalcade	j. pertaining to money
11. cavalier (*adj.*)	k. mounted military division; soldiers on horseback
12. cavalry	l. funeral rites
13. equestrian	m. exaggeratedly sorrowful
14. equestrienne	n. horselike
15. equine	o. horseman
16. cadaver	p. spiritual decline
17. decadent	q. morally decaying
18. decadence	r. corpse
19. chivalry	s. expression of sympathy
20. condolence	t. gallant courtesy to women

KEY: 1–l, 2–e, 3–h, 4–a, 5–j, 6–c, 7–b, 8–d, 9–m, 10–f, 11–g, 12–k, 13–o, 14–i 15–n, 16–r, 17–q, 18–p, 19–t, 20–s

Do you understand the words? (I)

1.	Are speeches usually made during *obsequies*?	YES	NO
2.	Did Margaret Mitchell write a *sequel* to *Gone with the Wind*?	YES	NO
3.	Are these numbers in *sequence:* 5, 6, 7, 8, 9, 10, 11?	YES	NO
4.	Do banks often handle the *pecuniary* details of an estate?	YES	NO
5.	Is arsenic a *noxious* chemical?	YES	NO
6.	Do children sometimes *imbibe* wisdom from their parents?	YES	NO
7.	If a song is sung in tones of *dolor,* is it a happy song?	YES	NO

8. Is a *doleful* countenance a happy one? YES NO
9. Does a *cavalcade* contain horses? YES NO
10. Does a *cavalier* attitude show a spirit of humility? YES NO

KEY: 1–yes, 2–no, 3–yes, 4–yes, 5–yes, 6–yes, 7–no, 8–no, 9–yes, 10–no

---

Do you understand the words? (II)

1. Is a *cavalry* officer usually a good horseman? YES NO
2. Would an *equestrian* statue of General Grant show him with or on a horse? YES NO
3. Is an *equestrienne* a man? YES NO
4. Do humans possess many *equine* characteristics? YES NO
5. Is a *cadaver* alive? YES NO
6. Is an iconoclast likely to consider religion a *decadent* institution? YES NO
7. Is *decadence* a desirable quality? YES NO
8. Is *chivalry* dead? YES NO
9. Is it appropriate to *condole* with someone who has suffered a loss through death? YES NO
10. Are *condolences* appropriate at a wedding ceremony? YES NO

KEY: 1–yes, 2–yes, 3–no, 4–no, 5–no, 6–yes, 7–no, 8–yes, *or* no, depending on your point of view, 9–yes, 10–no (unless you're misogamous)

Do you understand the words? (III)

1. obsequies—rites SAME OPPOSITE
2. subsequent—preceding SAME OPPOSITE

490

3. pecuniary—financial	SAME	OPPOSITE
4. sequence—order	SAME	OPPOSITE
5. noxious—harmful	SAME	OPPOSITE
6. imbibe—drink	SAME	OPPOSITE
7. dolor—delight	SAME	OPPOSITE
8. doleful—merry	SAME	OPPOSITE
9. cavalier—courteous	SAME	OPPOSITE
10. cadaver—corpse	SAME	OPPOSITE
11. decadent—resurgent	SAME	OPPOSITE
12. chivalry—gallantry to women	SAME	OPPOSITE
13. condolences—congratulations	SAME	OPPOSITE

KEY: 1–S, 2–O, 3–S, 4–S, 5–S, 6–S, 7–O, 8–O, 9–O, 10–S, 11–O, 12–S, 13–O

Can you recall the words?

1. harmful	1. N_____
2. a literary work or an event that follows another	2. S_____
3. drink in	3. I_____
4. poetic word for sorrow	4. D_____
5. burial ceremonies	5. O_____
6. horseman	6. E_____
7. horsewoman	7. E_____
8. horselike	8. E_____
9. following (*adj.*)	9. S_____
10. relating to money (*adj.*)	10. P_____
11. exaggeratedly sad	11. D_____
12. proper order	12. S_____
13. parade of mounted riders	13. C_____
14. offhand; unmindful of another's feelings	14. C_____
15. mounted soldiers	15. C_____
16. a corpse	16. C_____
17. morally deteriorating (*adj.*)	17. D_____
18. spiritual decay	18. D_____
19. expression of sympathy	19. C_____

491

20. gallantry to women   20. C_____

CHAPTER REVIEW

A. Do you recognize the words?

1. Excessively polite and fawning:
     (a) querulous, (b) obsequious, (c) supercilious
2. Noisily troublesome:
     (a) querulous, (b) impecunious, (c) obstreperous
3. Courteous and attentive to women:
     (a) querulous, (b) chivalrous, (c) supercilious
4. Complaining, nagging:
     (a) querulous, (b) supercilious, (c) innocuous
5. Haughtily disdainful:
     (a) supercilious, (b) bibulous, (c) dolorous
6. Gaunt, corpselike:
     (a) noxious, (b) cadaverous, (c) doleful
7. Highhanded:
     (a) supercilious, (b) cavalier, (c) decadent
8. Moral decay:
     (a) decadence, (b) obsequies, (c) sequence
9. Expression of sympathy:
     (a) bibulousness, (b) dolefulness, (c) condolence
10. Courtesy to women:
     (a) dolor, (b) chivalry, (c) decadence

KEY: 1–b, 2–c, 3–b, 4–a, 5–a, 6–b, 7–b, 8–a, 9–c, 10–b

B. Can you recognize roots?

ROOT	MEANING	EXAMPLE
1. *sequor*	_____	subsequent
2. *queror*	_____	querulous
3. *cilium*	_____	supercilious
4. *super*	_____	supervision
5. *strepo*	_____	obstreperous
6. *pecus*	_____	pecuniary
7. *cheval*	_____	chivalry
8. *caballus* (*caval-*)	_____	cavalier
9. *equus*	_____	equine
10. *cado*	_____	decadence

KEY: 1–to follow, 2–to complain, 3–eyelid, 4–above, 5–to make a noise, 6–cattle, ·7–horse, 8–(inferior) horse, 9–horse, 10–to fall

TEASER QUESTIONS FOR THE AMATEUR ETYMOLOGIST

1. In logic, a conclusion not based on the evidence is called a *non sequitur;* by extension, the term is applied to any statement that appears to have no connection or relevance to what was said before. Knowing the root *sequor,* how would you define this term etymologically? _____
_____.

2. *Sequor,* like many other Latin verbs, has another form somewhat differently spelled. (Remember *verto, versus* and *loquor, locutus?*) The other form of *sequor* is *secutus.* Can you define the following words in terms of the root?

        (a) second: _____
        (b) consecutive: _____
        (c) persecute: _____
        (d) prosecute: _____

3. Latin *super,* above or over, is used as a prefix in hundreds of English words. Can you figure out the word starting with *super-* that fits each etymological definition?

 (a) above others (in quality, position, etc.) _____

 _____

 (b) above the surface; not in depth (*adj.*) _____

 _____

 (c) (flowing) above what is necessary; more than needed (*adj.*) _____

 (d) above (or beyond) the natural (*adj.*) _____

 _____

 (e) to oversee; be in charge of (*v.*) _____

 _____

4. *Cado,* to fall, is found in the following English words (sometimes the root is spelled *-cid*). Can you define each word in terms of its etymological parts?

 (a) cadence: _____
 (b) occidental: _____
 (c) deciduous: _____
 (d) incident: _____
 (e) accident: _____
 (f) coincidence: _____

5. The negative prefix *in-* plus *doleo,* to suffer, forms an adjective that *etymologically* means *not suffering (pain),* but *actually* means *idle; lazy; disliking effort or work.* Can you figure out the English word? _____.
Can you write the noun form? _____.

6. What does the feminine name Dolores mean etymologically?

_____

(*End of Session 46*)

ANOTHER CHECK ON YOUR SPELLING

In each line you will find four words—one of them purposely, subtly, and perhaps unexpectedly misspelled. It's up to you to check the single error. If you can come out on top at least fifteen times out of twenty, you're probably a better speller than you realize.

1. (a) alright, (b) coolly, (c) supersede, (d) disappear
2. (a) inoculate, (b) definately, (c) irresistible, (d) recommend
3. (a) incidentally, (b) dissipate, (c) seperate, (d) balloon
4. (a) argument, (b) ecstasy, (c) occurrence, (d) analyze
5. (a) sacrilegious, (b) weird, (c) pronunciation, (d) repitition
6. (a) drunkeness, (b) embarrassment, (c) weird, (d) irritable
7. (a) noticeable, (b) superintendant, (c) absence, (d) development
8. (a) vicious, (b) conscience, (c) panicy, (d) amount
9. (a) accessible, (b) pursue, (c) exhilarate, (d) insistant
10. (a) naïveté, (b) necessary, (c) catagory, (d) professor
11. (a) rhythmical, (b) sergeant, (c) vaccuum, (d) assassin
12. (a) benefitted, (b) allotted, (c) corroborate, (d) despair
13. (a) diphtheria, (b) grandeur, (c) rediculous, (d) license
14. (a) tranquillity, (b) symmetry, (c) occassionally, (d) privilege

15. (a) tarriff, (b) tyranny, (c) battalion, (d) archipelago
16. (a) bicycle, (b) geneology, (c) liquefy, (d) bettor
17. (a) defense, (b) batchelor, (c) stupefy, (d) parallel
18. (a) whisky, (b) likable, (c) bookkeeper, (d) accomodate
19. (a) comparitive, (b) mayonnaise, (c) indispensable,
    (d) dexterous
20. (a) dictionary, (b) cantaloupe, (c) existance, (d) ukulele

---

HOW TO CHECK YOUR PROGRESS

Comprehensive Test III

SESSION 47

⊢—etymology

ROOT	MEANING	EXAMPLE
1. *fluo*	⎯⎯⎯⎯⎯⎯	affluent
2. *pheme*	⎯⎯⎯⎯⎯⎯	euphemism
3. *platys*	⎯⎯⎯⎯⎯⎯	platitude
4. *felis*	⎯⎯⎯⎯⎯⎯	feline
5. *piscis*	⎯⎯⎯⎯⎯⎯	piscine
6. *nostos*	⎯⎯⎯⎯⎯⎯	nostalgia
7. *kakos*	⎯⎯⎯⎯⎯⎯	cacophony
8. *carnis*	⎯⎯⎯⎯⎯⎯	carnivorous
9. *voro*	⎯⎯⎯⎯⎯⎯	voracious
10. *omnis*	⎯⎯⎯⎯⎯⎯	omnivorous
11. *potens, potentis*	⎯⎯⎯⎯⎯⎯	impotent
12. *ubique*	⎯⎯⎯⎯⎯⎯	ubiquity
13. *lupus*	⎯⎯⎯⎯⎯⎯	lupine
14. *doleo*	⎯⎯⎯⎯⎯⎯	dolorous
15. *porcus*	⎯⎯⎯⎯⎯⎯	porcine
16. *thanatos*	⎯⎯⎯⎯⎯⎯	euthanasia

17. *canis*	————————	canine
18. *vulpus*	————————	vulpine
19. *algos*	————————	nostalgic
20. *odyne*	————————	anodyne
21. *logos*	————————	eulogy
22. *sciens, scientis*	————————	omniscient
23. *ursus*	————————	ursine
24. *phone*	————————	euphonious
25. *penuria*	————————	penury

II—more etymology

ROOT, PREFIX		EXAMPLE
1. *nervus*	————————	enervate
2. *ergon*	————————	energy
3. *nego*	————————	negation
4. *caput, capitis*	————————	decapitate
5. *capitulum*	————————	recapitulate
6. *vegeto*	————————	vegetate
7. *simulo*	————————	simulate
8. *similis*	————————	similarity
9. *levis*	————————	alleviate
10. *intimus*	————————	intimate (*v.*)
11. *miser*	————————	commiserate
12. *vacillo*	————————	vacillate
13. *ambi-*	————————	ambivalent
14. *oscillum*	————————	oscillate
15. *sequor, secutus*	————————	obsequious
16. *queror*	————————	querulous
17. *cilium*	————————	supercilious
18. *super-*	————————	superior
19. *strepo*	————————	obstreperous
20. *pecus*	————————	impecunious
21. *equus*	————————	equine
22. *caballus (caval-)*	————————	cavalier
23. *loquor, locutus*	————————	circumlocution
24. *cado*	————————	decadence
25. *vanesco*	————————	evanescent

498

III—same or opposite?

1. penury—affluence   S   O
2. vicarious—secondhand   S   O
3. ephemeral—evanescent   S   O
4. badinage—persiflage   S   O
5. cacophony—euphony   S   O
6. clandestine—surreptitious   S   O
7. parsimonious—extravagant   S   O
8. indigent—opulent   S   O
9. destitute—impecunious   S   O
10. euphemistic—indirect   S   O
11. cliché—bromide   S   O
12. platitudinous—original   S   O
13. voracious—gluttonous   S   O
14. omniscient—ignorant   S   O
15. omnipresent—ubiquitous   S   O
16. carnal—libidinous   S   O
17. carnage—slaughter   S   O
18. enervated—exhilarated   S   O
19. castigate—condone   S   O
20. simulate—pretend   S   O

IV—matching

WORDS	DEFINITIONS
1. alleviating	a. excessively polite or servile
2. cavalier (*adj.*)	b. gaunt, corpselike
3. vacillating	c. noisy
4. obsequious	d. poisonous
5. querulous	e highhanded
6. obstreperous	f. sad
7. innocuous	g. nagging; complaining
8. cadaverous	h. harmless
9. dolorous	i. soothing
10. noxious	j. constantly changing one's mind

V—more matching

1.	condolence	a.	a rising into the air
2.	decadent	b.	harsh sound
3.	levity	c.	powerlessness
4.	levitation	d.	a return to life in a new form
5.	surreptitious	e.	devouring all; eating every-thing
6.	cacophony	f.	expression of sympathy
7.	reincarnation	g.	cowlike; phlegmatic; stolid
8.	omnivorous	h.	morally deteriorating
9.	impotence	i.	joking
10.	bovine	j.	stealthy; secret

VI—recall a word

1. lionlike   1. L_____
2. doglike   2. C_____
3. catlike   3. F_____
4. piglike   4. P_____
5. foxlike   5. V_____
6. bearlike   6. U_____
7. horselike   7. E_____
8. all-powerful   8. O_____
9. in the flesh   9. I_____
10. to stagnate   10. V_____
11. secret   11. C_____
12. meat-eating (*adj.*)   12. C_____
13. lasting a very short time   13. E_____
14. stingy; tight-fisted   14. P_____
                                          or P_____
15. feeling contradictory ways at   15. A_____
    the same time (*adj.*)
16. speech of praise   16. E_____
17. a feeling of well-being, both   17. E_____
    physical and emotional
18. statement intended to allay   18. A_____
    pain or anxiety

500

19. mercy death
20. science of speech sounds
21. all-powerful
22. to give in; to stop resisting
23. a working together for greater effect
24. to behead
25. relating to, pertaining to, or involving money (*adj.*)
26. harmless
27. tending to drink a lot (*adj.*)
28. to express sympathy; to share suffering, pain, or grief (with)
29. snobbish; contemptuous; haughty; arrogant
30. mounted soldiers

19. E_____
20. P_____
21. O_____
22. C_____
23. S_____
or S_____
24. D_____
25. P_____

26. I_____
27. B_____
28. C_____
or C_____
29. S_____

30. C_____

KEY: A correct answer counts one point. Score your points for each part of the test, then add for a total.

I

1–to flow, 2–voice, 3–flat, broad, 4–cat, 5–fish, 6–a return, 7–harsh, bad, ugly, 8–flesh, 9–to devour, 10–all, 11–powerful, 12–everywhere, 13–wolf, 14–to suffer, grieve, 15–pig, 16–death, 17–dog, 18–fox, 19–pain, 20–pain, 21–word, speech, 22–knowing, 23–bear, 24–sound, 25–want, neediness

Your score: _____

II

1–nerve, 2–work, 3–to deny, 4–head, 5–little head, chapter heading, 6–to live and grow, 7–to copy, 8–like, similar, 9–light, 10–innermost, 11–wretched, 12–to swing back and forth, 13–both, 14–a swing, 15–to follow, 16–to complain, 17–eyelid, 18–above, 19–to make a noise, 20–cattle, 21–horse, 22–(inferior) horse, 23–to speak, 24–to fall, 25–to vanish

Your score: _____

III

1–O, 2–S, 3–S, 4–S, 5–O, 6–S, 7–O, 8–O, 9–S, 10–S, 11–S, 12–O, 13–S, 14–O, 15–S, 16–S, 17–S, 18–O, 19–O, 20–S

Your score: _____

IV

1–i, 2–e, 3–j, 4–a, 5–g, 6–c, 7–h, 8–b, 9–f, 10–d

Your score: _____

V

1–f, 2–h, 3–i, 4–a, 5–j, 6–b, 7–d, 8–e, 9–c, 10–g

Your score: _____

VI

1–leonine, 2–canine, 3–feline, 4–porcine, 5–vulpine, 6–ursine, 7–equine, 8–omnipotent, 9–incarnate, 10–vegetate, 11–clandestine, 12–carnivorous, 13–ephemeral, 14–penurious *or* parsimonious, 15–ambivalent, 16–eulogy, 17–euphoria, 18–anodyne, 19–euthanasia, 20–phonetics, 21–omnipotent, 22–capitulate, 23–synergism *or* synergy, 24–decapitate, 25–pecuniary, 26–innocuous, 27–bibulous, 28–condole *or* commiserate, 29–supercilious, 30–cavalry

Your score: _____

Your total score: _____

Significance of Your Total Score:

100–120:	Masterly
80–99:	Good
65–79:	Average
50–64:	Barely acceptable
35–49:	Poor
0–34:	Terrible!

Record your score in the appropriate space below as well as your scores from Chapters 8 and 13. You will then have a comparison chart of all three achievement tests.

SCORES

TEST I (Chapter 8): _____ out of 120.
TEST II (Chapter 13): _____ out of 120.
TEST III (Chapter 17): _____ out of 120.

(*End of Session 47*)

18

HOW TO CHECK
YOUR STANDING AS
AN AMATEUR ETYMOLOGIST

*(Answers to Teaser Questions in Chapters 3–7, 9–12,
and 14–16)*

CHAPTER 3:

1. *Anthropocentric* (an′-thrə-pə-SEN′-trik), an adjective built
on *anthropos,* mankind; Greek *kentron,* center, and the adjective
suffix *-ic,* describes thinking, assumptions, reasoning, etc. that see
mankind as the central fact, or ultimate aim, of the universe. The
noun forms are either *anthropocentrism* (an′-thrə-pə-SEN′-triz-
əm) or *anthropocentricity* (an′-thrə-pō′-sən-TRIS′-ə-tee).

2. *Andromania* (an′-drə-MAY′-nee-ə), a combination of
andros, man (male), plus *mania,* madness, signifies an obsession
with males. Person: *andromaniac,* one who is mad about men; adjective: *andromaniacal* (an′-drə-mə-NĪ′-ə-kəl).

3. *Gynandrous* (jī-NAN′-drəs), combining *gyne,* woman, with
andros, man (male), describes:

a. plants in which the male and female organs are united in the
same column; *or*

b. people who physically have both male and female sexual organs, often one or both in rudimentary form; *or*

c. (*a more recent meaning*) people who exhibit, or are willing
to own up to, the male *and* female *emotional* characteristics that
everyone possesses.

The word may have the roots in reverse, becoming *androgynous* (an-DROJ'-ə-nəs), with all three meanings identical to those of *gynandrous.*

Hermaphroditic (hur-maf'-rə-DIT'-ik), a combination of *Hermes,* the Greek god who served as messenger or herald (in Roman mythology, this god was known as *Mercury,* and is conventionally pictured with wings on his heels), and *Aphrodite,* the Greek goddess of love and beauty (in Roman mythology, *Venus*), has either of the first two meanings of *gynandrous.*

The noun form of *gynandrous* is *gynandry* (jī-NAN'-dree); of *androgynous, androgyny* (an-DROJ'-ə-nee); of *hermaphroditic, hermaphroditism* (hur-MAF'-rə-dī'-tiz-əm).

The individual plant is an *andrognye* (AN'-drə-jin); plant or person, a *hermaphrodite* (hur-MAF'-rə-dīt').

4. *Monomania* (mon-ə-MAY'-nee-ə), combining *monos,* one, and *mania,* madness, is an obsession with one thing, or obsessiveness in one area. Person: *monomaniac;* adjective: *monomaniacal* (mon'-ə-mə-NĪ'-ə-kəl).

5. A *misandrist* (mis-AN'-drist), combining *misein,* to hate, with *andros,* man (male), hates men. Noun: *misandry* (mis-AN'-dree). Adjective: *misandrous* (mis-AN'-drəs).

Check your learning

ROOT	MEANING	EXAMPLE
1. *anthropos*	_____	anthropocentric
2. *kentron*	_____	anthropocentrism
3. *andros*	_____	andromania
4. *mania*	_____	andromaniac
5. *gyne*	_____	gynandrous
6. *Hermes*	_____	hermaphrodite
7. *Aphrodite*	_____	hermaphroditic
8. *monos*	_____	monomania
9. *misein*	_____	misandry

KEY: 1–mankind, 2–center, 3–man (male), 4–madness, 5–woman, 6–Hermes, the messenger of the gods, 7–Aphrodite, goddess of love and beauty, 8–one, 9–to hate

CHAPTER 4:

1. *Pedodontia* (pee-də-DON'-shə) is the specialty of child dentistry—*paidos,* child, plus *odontos,* tooth. Specialist: *pedodontist.* Adjective: *pedodontic.*

2. *Cardialgia* (kahr'-dee-AL'-jə), heart pain—*kardia,* heart, plus *algos,* pain.

3. *Odontalgia* (ō'-don-TAL'-jə), toothache.

4. *Nostalgia* (nos-TAL'-jə). Adjective: *nostalgic.*

Check your learning

PREFIX, ROOT	MEANING	EXAMPLE
1. *padios* (*ped-*)	_____	pedodontia
2. *kardia*	_____	cardialgia
3. *algos*	_____	odontalgia
4. *odontos*	_____	pedodontist
5. *nostos*	_____	nostalgia

KEY: 1–child, 2–heart, 3–pain, 4–tooth, 5–a return

CHAPTER 5:

1. Eighty to eighty-nine years old. From Latin *octoginta,* eighty. People of other ages are as follows:

    (a) 50–59: *quinquagenarian* (kwin'-kwə-jə-NAIR'-ee-ən)

    (b) 60–69: *sexagenarian* (seks'-ə-jə-NAIR'-ee-ən)

    (c) 70–79: *septuagenarian* (sep'-chōō-ə-jə-NAIR'-ee-ən)

    (d) 90–99: *nonagenarian* (non'-ə-jə-NAIR'-ee-ən)

    (e) 100 and over: *centenarian* (sen'-te-NAIR'-ee-ən)

2. *Cacophony* (kə-KOF'-ə-nee). Adjective: *cacophonous* (kə-KOF'-ə-nəs).

3. *Cacopygian* (kak'-ə-PIJ'-ee-ən).

4. *Telescope* (*tele-* plus *skopein,* to view) or *telebinoculars; telephone; television.*

Check your learning

PREFIX, ROOT	MEANING	EXAMPLE
1. *octoginta*	_____	octogenarian
2. *quinquaginta*	_____	quinquagenarian
3. *sexaginta*	_____	sexagenarian
4. *septuaginta*	_____	septuagenarian
5. *nonaginta*	_____	nonagenarian
6. *centum*	_____	centenarian
7. *kakos*	_____	cacophony
8. *phone*	_____	cacophonous
9. *pyge*	_____	cacopygian
10. *tele-*	_____	television
11. *skopein*	_____	telescope

KEY: 1–eighty, 2–fifty, 3–sixty, 4–seventy, 5–ninety, 6–one hundred, 7–ugly, harsh, bad, 8–sound, 9–buttock, 10–distance, from afar, 11–to view

CHAPTER 6:

1. *Sophomore;* from *sophos* plus *moros,* foolish, the word etymologically designates one who is half wise and half foolish. The adjective *sophomoric* (sof-ə-MAWR'-ik) describes people, attitudes, statements, writings, etc. that are highly opinionated, self-assured, and coming off as if wise, but which in reality are immature, inexperienced, foolish, etc.

2. *Sophisticated* (sə-FIS'-tə-kay'-təd). The verb is *sophisticate,* the noun *sophistication.* One who is worldly-wise is a *sophisticate* (sə-FIS'-tə-kət).

Sophisticated has in recent years taken on the added meaning of *highly developed, mature, or complicated; appealing to a mature intellect; or aware and knowledgeable.* Examples: *sophisticated* machinery, electronic equipment; a *sophisticated* approach; a *sophisticated* audience, group, staff, faculty, etc.

3. One who is obsessed with books, especially with collecting books.

· 4. (a) speaking one language, (b) speaking two languages, (c) speaking three languages.

Multilingual (*multus*, many, plus *lingua*)—speaking many languages.

A *linguist* is one who is fluent in many languages, or else an expert in *linguistics* (or both).

Multus, as indicated, means *many*, as in *multitude, multiply, multiple, multicolored, multifarious, multilateral*, etc., etc.

5. (a) France, (b) Russia, (c) Spain, (d) Germany, (e) Japan, (f) China.

6. (a) *androphile*, (b) *gynephile* (or *philogynist*), (c) *pedophile*, (d) *zoophile*, (e) *botanophile*.

But *pedophilia* (pee'-də-FIL'-ee-ə) is another story. A *pedophiliac* sexually molests young children—such love little kids can do without!

Check your learning

PREFIX, ROOT	MEANING	EXAMPLE
1. *sophos*	_____	sophomore
2. *moros*	_____	sophomoric
3. *biblion*	_____	bibliomaniac
4. *mania*	_____	bibliomania
5. *lingua*	_____	linguist
6. *monos*	_____	monolingual
7. *bi-*	_____	bilingual
8. *tri-*	_____	trilingual
9. *multus*	_____	multilingual
10. *Franco-*	_____	Francophile
11. *Russo-*	_____	Russophile
12. *Hispano-*	_____	Hispanophile
13. *Germano-*	_____	Germanophile

14. *Nippono-*	_____	Nipponophile
15. *Sino-*	_____	Sinophile
16. *andros*	_____	androphile
17. *gyne*	_____	gynephile
18. *philein*	_____	philogynist
19. *paidos (ped-)*	_____	pedophile
20. *zoion*	_____	zoophile
21. *botane*	_____	botanophile

KEY: 1–wise, 2–foolish, 3–book, 4–madness, 5–tongue, 6–one, 7–two, 8–three, 9–many, 10–France, 11–Russia, 12–Spain, 13–Germany, 14–Japan, 15–China, 16–man (male), 17–woman, 18–to love, 19–child, 20–animal, 21–plant

CHAPTER 7:

1. A *notable* is someone well-*known.*

2. To *notify* is, etymologically, to make *known—notus + -fy,* a derivation of *facio,* to make.

Notice, as a noun, is what makes something *known; to notice,* as a verb, is to observe (something or someone) so that it, he, or she becomes *known* to the observer.

-Fy, as a verb suffix, means *to make.* So *simplify* is to make simple, *clarify,* to make clear; *liquefy,* to make liquid; *putrefy,* to make (or become) rotten or putrid; *stupefy,* to make stupid, or dumb, with astonishment (note the *-e* preceding the suffix in *liquefy, putrefy, stupefy*); *fortify,* to make strong; *rectify,* to make right or correct; etc., etc.

3. *Chronograph* (KRON′-ə-graf′) is an instrument that measures and records short intervals of time.

4. To *generate* is to give birth to, figuratively, or to create or produce, as a turbine *generates* power, a person's presence *generates* fear, etc. The noun is *generation,* which, in another context, also designates the people born and living about the same time (the older, previous, or next *generation,* the Depression *genera-*

tion, etc.), or a period, conventionally set at about thirty years, between such groups of people.

To *regenerate* is to give birth to again, or to be born again. Some creatures can *regenerate* new limbs or parts if these are lost or cut off—or the limbs or parts *regenerate.*

Re- means, of course, *again;* or, in some words, as *recede, regress,* etc., *back.*

5. *Omnipotent* (om-NIP'-ə-tənt)—all-powerful; *omnis* plus *potens, potentis,* powerful.

Omnipresent (om'-nə-PREZ'-ənt)—present all over, or every-where.

Nouns: *omnipotence, omnipresence.*

6. *Anaphrodisiac* (ən-af'-rə-DIZ'-ee-ak')—both a noun and an adjective. Saltpeter is supposedly an *anaphrodisiac;* so, some people say, is a cold shower, which is highly doubtful. The best emporary *anaphrodisiac* is probably sexual intercourse. Some women who were teen-agers when Elvis Presley was at the height of his popularity have told me that the young man's gyrating hips were *aphrodisiacal*—I will take their word for it, as Elvis has ever turned me on. On the other hand, if you want to talk about Diane Keaton or Raquel Welch . . . or especially Marilyn Monroe . . .

heck your learning

PREFIX, ROOT	MEANING	EXAMPLE
. *notus*	_____	notify
. *chronos*	_____	chronograph
. *graphein*	_____	chronographic
. *genesis*	_____	generate
. *re-*	_____	regenerate
. *omnis*	_____	omnipotent
. *potens, potentis*	_____	omnipotence
. *an-*	_____	anaphrodisiac

KEY: 1–known, 2–time, 3–to write, 4–birth, 5–again, 6–all, 7–powerful, 8–not (negative)

CHAPTER 9:

1. *Magnanimity* (mag'-nə-NIM'-ə-tee). Adjective: *magnanimous* (mag-NAN'-ə-məs).

2. *Bilateral* (bī-LAT'-ər-əl), as in a *bilateral* decision, i.e., one made by the two sides or two people involved. On the other hand, a *unilateral* (yōō-nə-LAT'-ər-əl) decision is made by *one* person, without consultation with others.

3. *Transcribe.* Noun: *transcription.* A stenographer *transcribes* shorthand notes into English words, or a musical *transcriber* arranges or adapts a musical composition for an instrument, group, etc. other than the one for which the work was originally written.

4. *Malaria* was once thought to have been caused by the "bad air" of swamps; actually, it was (and is) transmitted to humans by infected anopheles mosquitoes breeding and living in swamps and other places where there is stagnant water.

5. *Confection.* The word is hardly used much today with this meaning, except perhaps by members of an older generation who remember *confectioner's* shops and *confectionery* stores. Now such places are called *ice cream stores* (or *ice cream parlors*) and are run, at least on the west coast, by Baskin-Robbins or Farrell's; or they are called *candy shops;* or, when I was growing up, *candy stores,* where the kids all hung out, and candies could be bought for a penny apiece, with Hershey bars selling for a nickel (that's why they are called "the good old days").

Check your learning

PREFIX, ROOT	MEANING	EXAMPLE
1. *magnus*	_____	magnanimous
2. *animus*	_____	magnanimity
3. *bi-*	_____	bilateral
4. *unus*	_____	unilateral
5. *latus, lateris*	_____	unilateral
6. *trans-*	_____	transcribe
7. *scribo, scriptus*	_____	transcription

8. *malus*	_____	malaria
9. *con-*	_____	confection
10. *facio* *(fec-)*	_____	confectionery

CHAPTER 10:

1. *Modus operandi.* Method (or mode) of working (or operating). Pronounced MŌ′-dəs op′-ə-RAN′-dī, the word is not, of course, restricted to the special methods used by a criminal, but may refer to the method or style of operating characteristic of any other professional. *Modus vivendi* (MŌ′dəs və-VEN′-dī), etymologically "method of living," is the style of life characteristic of a person or group.

2. *Circumscription.* To *circumscribe* also means, figuratively, to write (a line) *around* (*one's freedom of action*), so that one is restricted, limited, hemmed in, as in, "a life *circumscribed* by poverty, by parental injunctions, or by an overactive conscience, etc.," or "actions *circumscribed* by legal restraints." The noun *circumscription* has the figurative meaning also.

3. *Somniloquent* (səm-NIL′-ə-kwənt). Noun: *somniloquence* (səm-NIL′-ə-kwəns) or *somniloquy* (səm-NIL′-ə-kwee), the latter noun also designating the words spoken by the sleeper. One who habitually talks while asleep is a *somniloquist* (səm-NIL′-ə-kwist).

4. An *aurist* is an ear specialist, more commonly called an *otologist* (ō-TOL′-ə-jist), from Greek *otos,* ear. Noun: *otology.* Adjective: *otological* (ō-tə-LOJ′-ə-kəl).

It is difficult at this point to resist telling a well-known story about medical specialists. In fact it's impossible to resist, so here it is:

A dentist, doing his first extraction on a patient, was understandably nervous. When he got the molar out, his hand shook, he lost his grip on the instrument, and the tooth dropped down into the patient's throat.

"Sorry," said the doctor. "You're outside my specialty now. You should see a laryngologist! [lair'-ing-GOL'-ə-jist—a larynx or throat specialist]."

By the time the unfortunate victim got to the laryngologist, the tooth had worked its way much further down.

The laryngologist examined the man.

"Sorry," said the doctor, "You're outside my specialty now. You should see a gastrologist! [gas-TROL'-ə-jist—a stomach specialist]."

The gastrologist X-rayed the patient. "Sorry," said the doctor, "the tooth has traveled into your lower intestines. You should see an enterologist! [en'-tə-ROL'-ə-jist—an intestinal specialist]."

The enterologist took some X rays. "Sorry, the tooth isn't there. It must have gone down farther. You should see a proctologist! [prok-TOL'-ə-jist—a specialist in diseases of the rectum; from Greek *proktos*, anus]."

Our patient is now on the proctologist's examining table, in the proper elbow-knee position. The doctor has inserted a proctoscope and is looking through it.

"Good heavens, man! You've got a tooth up there! You should see a dentist!"

5. *Aural* (AWR-əl) refers to the ears or to the sense or phenomenon of hearing. *Monaural* reproduction, as of music over a radio or by a phonograph record, for example, has only one source of sound, and technically should be called *monophonic* (mon'-ə-FON'-ik)—*monos,* one, plus *phone,* sound. *Binaural* may mean *having two ears* or *involving the use of both ears,* or, recently, *descriptive of sound from two sources,* giving a *stereophonic* (steer'-ee-ə-FON'-ik) effect—*stereos,* deep, solid, plus *phone.*

6. A *noctambulist* (nok-TAM'-byə-list) walks at night—*nox, noctis,* night, plus *ambulo,* to walk. Noun: *noctambulism* (nok-TAM'-byə-liz-əm).

7. *Somnific* (som-NIF'-ik): *a somnific lecture, movie, effect,* etc.

513

8. *Circumambulate* (sur'-kəm-AM'-byə-layt'). To *circumnavigate* is to sail around—*circum,* around, plus *navis,* ship.

Check your learning

PREFIX, ROOT	MEANING	EXAMPLE
1. *modus*	_____	*modus operandi*
2. *operandi*	_____	*modus operandi*
3. *vivo*	_____	*modus vivendi*
4. *circum-*	_____	circumscribe
5. *scribo, scriptus*	_____	circumscription
6. *somnus*	_____	somniloquent
7. *loquor*	_____	somniloquence
8. *aurus*	_____	aurist
9. *otos*	_____	otology
10. *proktos*	_____	proctologist
11. *stereos*	_____	stereophonic
12. *phone*	_____	stereophonic
13. *monos*	_____	monaural
14. *bi-*	_____	binaural
15. *nox, noctis*	_____	noctambulist
16. *ambulo*	_____	noctambulism
17. *facio (fic-)*	_____	somnific

KEY: 1–mode, method, 2–of working, 3–to live, 4–around, 5–to write, 6–sleep, 7–to speak, to talk, 8–ear, 9–ear, 10–anus, 11–deep, solid, 12–sound, 13–one, 14–two, 15–night, 16–to walk, 17–to make

---

CHAPTER 11:

1. *Matronymic* (mat'-rə-NIM'-ik). Or, if you prefer to use the Greek root for mother (*meter, metr-*), *metronymic*. The Greek word *metra,* uterus, derives from *meter,* naturally enough, so *metritis* is inflammation of the uterus; *metralgia* is uterine pain; *endometriosis* (en'-dō-mee'-tree-Ō'-sis) is any abnormal condi-

tion of the uterine lining—*endo,* inside; *metra,* uterus; *-osis,* abnormal condition.

2. (a) An *incendiary* statement, remark, speech, etc. figuratively enflames an audience, sets them afire, gets them excited, galvanizes them into action, etc.

  (b) *Incense* (IN'-sens) is a substance that sends off a pleasant odor when burned—often, but not necessarily, to mask unpleasant or telltale smells, as of marijuana smoke, etc.

  (c) To *incense* (in-SENS') is to anger greatly, i.e., to "burn up." "I'm all burned up" is etymologically an accurate translation of "I'm *incensed.*"

3. (a) *Ardent* (AHR'-dənt)—burning with zeal, ambition, love, etc., as an *ardent* suitor, worker, etc.

  (b) *Ardor* (AHR'-dər)—the noun form of *ardent*—burning passion, zeal, enthusiasm, etc. Alternate noun: *ardency* (AHR'-dən-see).

4. *Megaphone.*

5. *Megalopolis* (meg'-ə-LOP'-ə-lis).

6. *Police. Politics.*

7. *Bibliokleptomaniac* (bib'-lee-ō-klep'-tə-MAY'-nee-ak): one who has an obsession for stealing books. Not too many years ago, an author titled his book, *Steal This Book!,* perhaps hoping to appeal to *bibliokleptomaniacs;* if the appeal was successful enough, his royalty statements must have been minuscule indeed!

Gynekleptomaniac.
Pedokleptomaniac.
Androkleptomaniac.
Demokleptomaniac.

If you prefer to use shorter words, *compulsive kidnapper* or *obsessive abductor* will do as well for these words.

8. *Acromaniac.*
Agoramaniac.
Claustromaniac.

9. *Kleptophobe; pyrophobe; gynephobe; androphobe; demophobe.*

Triskaidekaphobia (tris'-kī-dek'-ə-FŌ'-bee-ə) is the morbid

515

dread of the number 13, from Greek *triskai*, three, *deka*, ten, and *phobia*.

10. *Gnosiology* (nŏ'-see-OL'-ə-jee), the science or study of knowledge.

11. *Amadeus* is love (Latin *amor*) God (Latin *deus*). *Theophilus* is love (Greek *philos*) God (Greek *theos*). *Gottlieb* is love (German *Lieb*) God (German *Gott*).

Perhaps this explains why he started composing at the age of four and wrote forty-one symphonies.

12. *Cellophane*—cellulose made to be transparent, i.e., to *show* what's wrapped in it.

13. *Hypoglycemia* (hī-pŏ-glī-SEE'-mee-ə)—low blood sugar, a common ailment today, though I believe the AMA has called it a "non-disease" (Greek *hypos*, under; *glykys*, sweet; *haima*, blood).

Haima, blood, is found in many English words, the root spelled either *hem-* or *-em*. Here are a few, with their etymological interpretations:

- (a) *Hemorrhage*—excessive blood flow.
- (b) *Anemia*—"no blood"—actually a pathological reduction of red blood corpuscles.
- (c) *Hematology*—science of blood (and its diseases).
- (d) *Hemophilia*—"love of blood"—actually a hereditary condition, occurring in males, in which the blood clots too slowly.
- (e) *Hemoglobin*—"blood gobules"—actually the red coloring matter of the red blood corpuscles.

Hyperglycemia is the opposite of *hypoglycemia*.

14. (a) *Pantheon* (PAN'-thee-on')—a temple built in Rome in 27 B.C. for "all the gods."

   (b) *Pandemonium* (pan'-də-MŌ'-nee-əm)—a word supposedly coined by poet John Milton in *Paradise Lost* to signify the dwelling place of all the demons; now any wild and noisy disorder.

   (c) *Panorama* (pan'-ə-RAM'-ə *or* pan'-ə-RAH'-mə)—a view (or a picture of such a view) all around—*pan*, all, plus *horama*, view. The adjective: *panoramic* (pan'-ə-RAM'-ik).

15. *Monarchy*—rule by one person.

Check your learning

PREFIX, ROOT	MEANING	EXAMPLE
1. *mater, matris*	_____	matronymic
2. *onyma*	_____	metronymic
3. *meter*	_____	metronymic
4. *metra*	_____	metritis
5. *endo-*	_____	endometriosis
6. *incendo, incensus*	_____	incendiary
7. *ardo*	_____	ardent
8. *megalo-*	_____	megalopolis
9. *polis*	_____	police
10. *demos*	_____	demokleptomaniac
11. *akros*	_____	acromaniac
12. *agora*	_____	agoramaniac
13. *claustrum*	_____	claustromaniac
14. *triskai*	_____	triskaidekaphobia
15. *deka*	_____	triskaidekaphobia
16. *gnosis*	_____	gnosiology
17. *amor*	_____	Amadeus
18. *deus*	_____	deity
19. *theos*	_____	Theophilus
20. *philos*	_____	hemophilia
21. *phanein*	_____	cellophane
22. *hypos*	_____	hypoglycemia
23. *glykys*	_____	hypoglycemia
24. *haima*	_____	hemorrhage
25. *an-*	_____	anemia
26. *hyper-*	_____	hyperglycemia
27. *pan*	_____	Pantheon
28. *horama*	_____	panorama
29. *archein*	_____	monarch
30. *monos*	_____	monarchy

KEY: 1–mother, 2–name, 3–mother, 4–uterus, 5–inside, 6–to set
on fire, 7–to burn, 8–big, large, great, 9–city, 10–people,
11–highest, 12–market place, 13–enclosed place,

14–three, 15–ten, 16–knowledge, 17–love, 18–God, 19–God, 20–love, 21–to show, 22–under, 23–sweet, 24–blood, 25–not, negative, 26–over, 27–all, 28–view, 29–to rule, 30–one

---

CHAPTER 12:

1. *Survive.* Noun: *survival.*

2. *Vivarium* (vī-VAIR′ee-əm)—enclosed area in which plants and (small) animals live in conditions resembling their natural habitat. The suffix *-ium* usually signifies *place where—solarium,* a place for the sun to enter, or where one can sunbathe; *aquarium,* a place for water (Latin *aqua,* water), or fish tank; *podium,* a place for the feet (Greek *podos,* foot), or speaker's platform; *auditorium,* a place for hearing (or listening to) concerts, plays, etc. (Latin *audio,* to hear).

3. *Vita* (VĬ′-tə), etymologically, *life,* is one's professional or career résumé.

4. (a) *Unicorn* (Latin *cornu,* horn).
   (b) *Uniform.*
   (c) *Unify* (*-fy,* from *facio,* to make).
   (d) *Unity.*
   (e) *Unicycle* (Greek *kyklos,* circle, wheel).

5. *Anniversary*—a year has turned.

6. (a) *Universe*—everything turning as one.
   (b) *University*—highest institute of education—universal subjects taught, learned, etc., i.e., the curriculum covers the universe, is in no way restricted, etc.

7. (a) *Interstate.*
   (b) *International.*
   (c) *Intermediate.*
   (d) *Interrupt* (Latin *rumpo, ruptus,* to break).
   (e) *Interpersonal.*

8. (a) *Intrastate.*
   (b) *Intranational.*
   (c) *Intrapersonal* or *intrapsychic.*
   (d) *Intramuscular.*

Check your learning

PREFIX, ROOT	MEANING	EXAMPLE
1. *vivo*	_____	survive
2. *podos*	_____	podium
3. *vita*	_____	*vita*
4. *cornu*	_____	unicorn
5. *kyklos*	_____	unicycle
6. *annus*	_____	anniversary
7. *verto, versus*	_____	universe
8. *unus*	_____	university
9. *inter-*	_____	interstate
10. *intra-*	_____	intrapsychic

KEY: 1–to live, 2–foot, 3–life, 4–horn, 5–circle, wheel, 6–year, 7–to turn, 8–one, 9–between, 10–within

---

CHAPTER 14:

1. "View of Death."

2. *Thanatology.*

3. (a) *Prophesy* (PROF'-ə-sī').
   (b) *Prophecy* (PROF'-ə-see).
   (c) *Prophet* (PROF'-ət).

4. (a) *Predict.*
   (b) *Prediction.*

5. *Nostopathy*—"disease" (tensions, insecurities, conflicts) on returning home after leaving the service. Some veterans could not face the freedom and responsibilities of being on their own. The

Army, Navy, or Air Force had fed and clothed them and made
decisions for them; now they had to readjust to civilian life.

6. (a) *Vulpicide.*
   (b) *Lupicide.*
   (c) *Felicide.*
   (d) *Ursicide.*
7. (a) *Piscivorous* (pǝ-SIV'-ǝr-ǝs).
   (b) *Insectivorous* (in'-sek-TIV'-ǝr-ǝs).
8. *Canaries,* what else?
9. *Potentiate* (pǝ-TEN'-shee-ayt').

Check your learning

PREFIX, ROOT	MEANING	EXAMPLE
1. *thanatos*	_____	thanatology
2. *logos*	_____	thanatology
3. *opsis*	_____	*Thanatopsis*
4. *pheme*	_____	prophecy
5. *pro-*	_____	prophet
6. *pre-*	_____	predict
7. *dico, dictus*	_____	predict
8. *nostos*	_____	nostopathy
9. *pathos*	_____	nostopathy
10. *vulpus*	_____	vulpicide
11. *lupus*	_____	lupicide
12. *felis*	_____	felicide
13. *ursus*	_____	ursicide
14. *piscis*	_____	piscivorous
15. *voro*	_____	insectivorous
16. *caedo (-cide)*	_____	insecticide
17. *canis*	_____	canary
18. *potens, potentis*	_____	potentiate

KEY: 1–death, 2–science, study, 3–view, 4–voice, 5–beforehand
     6–before, 7–to say or tell, 8–a return, 9–disease, 10–fox,
     11–wolf, 12–cat, 13–bear, 14–fish, 15–devour, 16–to kill
     (killing), 17–dog, 18–powerful

CHAPTER 15:

1. *Synagogue.*

2. *Symbiosis* (sim′-bī-Ō′-sis). Adjective: *symbiotic* (sim′-bī-OT′-ik).

People (for example lovers, spouses, parent and child, etc.) also may live in a *symbiotic* relationship, each depending on the other for important services, emotional needs, etc.; each also providing these for the other.

3. *Symphony; symphonic.*

4. *Symmetry* (SIM′-ə-tree); *symmetrical* (sə-MET′-rə-kəl) or *symmetric* (sə-MET′-rik).

5. *Syndrome* (SIN′-drōm).

6. *Hippodrome* (HIP′-ə-drōm′); the word today is often used as the name of a movie theater or other place of entertainment.

7. *Hippopotamus.*

Check your learning

PREFIX, ROOT	MEANING	EXAMPLE
1. *syn-*	_____	synagogue
2. *agogos*	_____	synagogue
3. *bios*	_____	symbiosis
4. *phone*	_____	symphonic
5. *metron*	_____	symmetry
6. *dromos*	_____	syndrome
7. *hippos*	_____	hippodrome
8. *potamos*	_____	hippopotamus

KEY: 1–with, together, 2–leader, leading, 3–life, 4–sound, 5–measurement, 6–a running, 7–horse, 8–river

CHAPTER 16

1. *Non sequitur* (non SEK'-wə-tər)—"it does not follow."
2. (a) *Second*—following after the first.
   (b) *Consecutive*—following in proper order
   (c) *Persecute*—to follow (i.e., pursue) through and through; hence to annoy, harass continually for no good reason.
   (d) *Prosecute*—to follow before; hence to pursue (something) diligently or vigorously in order to complete it successfully (*prosecute* a campaign); or to start, or engage in, legal proceedings against, especially in an official capacity.
3. (a) *Superior.*
   (b) *Superficial.*
   (c) *Superfluous* (sə-PUR'-floo-əs). Noun: superfluity (soo'-pər-FLOO'-ə-tee).
   (d) *Supernatural.*
   (e) *Supervise.*
4. (a) *Cadence* (KAY'-dəns)—fall and rise of the voice in speaking; hence inflection, rhythm beat, etc. of sound or music. Adjective: *cadent* (KAY'-dənt).
   (b) *Occidental* (ok'-sə-DEN'-təl)—etymologically, falling. Hence relating to western countries, since the sun falls in the west; also, a native of such a country. Noun: *Occident* (OK'-sə-dənt). The sun rises in the east, so Latin *orior,* to rise, is the origin of the *Orient, oriental,* etc., and also of the verb *orient* (AW'-ree-ent'). To *orient* is to adjust to a place or situation; etymologically, to turn, or face, east. Noun: *orientation.* "I'm finally *oriented*" does not mean that I'm easternized or facing east, but that I have become familiar with, and comfortable in, a place, job, situation, etc. So to *disorient* (dis-AW'-ree-ent') is to remove (someone's) *orientation,* or to confuse or bewilder, especially in reference to locality, direction, etc. Noun: *disorientation.*

(c) *Deciduous* (də-SIJ′-ōō-əs)—falling down (Latin prefix *de-*). This adjective refers to trees whose leaves fall (down) every autumn.

(d) *Incident*—that which falls upon, befalls, or happens.

(e) *Accident*—that which falls to (*ac-* is a respelling of *ad-*, to, toward) someone or something (by chance).

(f) *Coincidence*—*co-* is a respelling of *con-*, together. A *coincidence* occurs when two things befall, or happen, together, or at the same time, and by chance.

5. *Indolent* (IN′-də-lənt). Noun: *indolence* (IN′-də-ləns).

6. *Dolores*—from Spanish *María de los Dolores,* Mary of the Sorrows; hence, I guess, someone who is generally sorrowful, though the few Doloreses I have known do not live up to their etymology.

Check your learning

PREFIX, ROOT	MEANING	EXAMPLE
1. *sequor, secutus*	_____	non sequitur, second
2. *per-*	_____	persecute
3. *pro-*	_____	prosecute
4. *super-*	_____	superior
5. *fluo*	_____	superfluous
6. *cado*	_____	cadence
7. *orior*	_____	Orient
8. *dis-*	_____	disorient
9. *ad-* (*ac-*)	_____	accident
10. *doleo*	_____	indolent
11. *in-*	_____	indolence

KEY: 1–to follow, 2–through, 3–beforehand, 4–above, 5–to flow, 6–to fall, 7–to rise, 8–negative prefix, 9–to, toward, 10–to suffer, to grieve, 11–negative prefix

19

HOW TO KEEP BUILDING YOUR VOCABULARY

At commencement exercises, whether in elementary school, high school, or college, at least one of the speakers will inevitably point out to the graduates that this is not the end—not by a long shot. It is only the beginning; that's why it is called "commencement," etc., etc.

Of course the speaker is right—no educative process is ever the end; it is always the beginning of more education, more learning, more living.

And that is the case here. What has happened to you as a result of your reaction to the material and suggestions in this book is only the beginning of your development. To stop increasing your vocabulary is to stop your intellectual growth. You will wish, I am sure, to continue growing intellectually as long as you remain alive. And with the momentum that your weeks of hard work have provided, continuing will not be at all difficult.

Let me offer, as a summary of all I have said throughout the book, a recapitulation of the steps you must take so that your vocabulary will keep growing and growing.

STEP ONE. *You must become actively receptive to new words.*

Words won't come chasing after you—you must train yourself to be on a constant lookout, in your reading and listening, for any words that other people know and you don't.

STEP TWO. *You must read more.*

As an adult, you will find most of the sources of your supply of new words in books and magazines. Is your reading today largely restricted to a quick perusal of the daily newspaper? Then you will have to change your habits. If your aim is to have a superior vocabulary, you will have to make the time to read at least one book and several magazines *every week*. Not just this week and next week—but every week for the rest of your life. I have never met a single person who possessed a rich vocabulary who was not also an omnivorous reader.

STEP THREE. *You must learn to add to your own vocabulary the new words you meet in your reading.*

When you see an unfamiliar word in a book or magazine, do not skip over it impatiently. Instead, pause for a moment and say it over to yourself—get used to its sound and appearance. Then puzzle out its possible meaning in the context of the sentence. Whether you come to the right conclusion or not, whether indeed you are able to come to any intelligent conclusion at all, is of no importance. What is important is that you are, by this process, becoming superconscious of the word. As a result, you will suddenly notice that this very word pops up unexpectedly again and again in all your reading—for you now have a mind-set for it. And of course after you've seen it a few times, you will know fairly accurately not only what it means but the many ways in which it can be used.

STEP FOUR. *You must open your mind to new ideas.*

Every word you know is the translation of an idea.

Think for a few minutes of the areas of human knowledge that may possibly be unknown to you—psychology, semantics, science, art, music, or whatever. Then attack one of these areas methodically—by reading books in the field. In every field, from the simplest to the most abstruse, there are several books written for the average, untrained lay reader that will give you both a good grasp of the subject and at the same time add immeasurably to your vocabulary. College students have large vocabularies because they are required to expose themselves constantly to new areas of learning. You must do the same.

STEP FIVE. *You must set a goal.*

If you do *nothing* about your vocabulary, you will learn, at most, twenty-five to fifty new words in the next twelve months. *By conscious effort you can learn several thousand.* Set yourself a goal of finding several new words *every day*. This may sound ambitious—but you will discover as soon as you start actively looking for new words in your reading, and actively doing reading of a more challenging type, that new words are all around you—that is, if you're ready for them. And understand this: vocabulary building *snowballs*. The results of each new day's search will be greater and greater—once you provide the necessary initial push, once you gain momentum, once you *become addicted* to looking for, finding, and taking possession of new words.

And this is one addiction well worth cultivating!

APPENDIX

SOME ESOTERIC PHOBIAS

(You will recognize many of the Greek roots on which these words are constructed)

air: aerophobia
animals: zoophobia
beauty: callophobia
birth: genophobia
blood: hematophobia
breasts: mastophobia
burglars: scelerophobia
burial alive: taphephobia
cats: ailurophobia
change: neophobia
childbirth: maieusiophobia
children: pedophobia
colors: chromophobia
crowds: ochlophobia
darkness: nyctophobia
death: thanatophobia
depths: bathophobia
disease: pathophobia
doctors: iatrophobia
dogs: cynophobia
dying: thanatophobia
emptiness: kenophobia

everything: pantophobia
eyes: ophthalmophobia
fear: phobophobia
feces: coprophobia
feet: podophobia
female genitals: eurotophobia
filth: mysophobia
fire: pyrophobia
fish: ichthyophobia
fog: homichlophobia
food: cibophobia
foreigners: xenophobia
freaks: teratophobia
frogs: batrachophobia
ghosts: phasmophobia
hands: chirophobia
hair: trichophobia
healers or healing: iatrophobia
heat: thermophobia
hell: stygiophobia
horses: hippophobia
insects: entomophobia

knives: aichmophobia
knowledge: gnosiophobia
large things: megalophobia
light: photophobia
lightning: astrophobia
males: androphobia
many things: polyphobia
marriage: gamophobia
medicine: pharmacophobia
mice: musophobia
mirrors: spectrophobia
mobs: ochlophobia
motherhood: metrophobia
motion: kinesophobia
nakedness: gymnophobia
needles: belonophobia
newness: neophobia
night: nyctophobia
oceans: thalassophobia
odors: osmophobia
old age: geraphobia
old men: gerontophobia
pain: algophobia; odynophobia
people: demophobia
plants: botanophobia
pleasure: hedonophobia
poison: toxicophobia
poverty: peniophobia
prostitutes: pornophobia
punishment: poinophobia
rain: ombrophobia
red: erythrophobia
rivers: potamophobia
robbers: harpaxophobia
sameness: homophobia
sex: genophobia
sexual intercourse: coitophobia
sinning: peccatophobia
skin: dermatophobia
sleep: hypnophobia
small things: microphobia
smothering: pnigerophobia

snakes: ophidiophobia
snow: chionophobia
solitude: autophobia; mono-
    phobia
sounds: acousticophobia
speaking: lalophobia
speaking aloud: phonophobia
speech: logophobia
spiders: arachneophobia
stairs: climacophobia
stars: siderophobia
stealing: kleptophobia
stillness: eremiophobia
strangers: xenophobia
strength: sthenophobia
study: logophobia
sunlight: heliophobia
tapeworms: taeniophobia
taste: geumophobia
teeth: odontophobia
thieves: kleptophobia
thinking: phronemophobia
thirteen (the number): triskaidek-
    aphobia
thirst: dipsophobia
thunder: brontophobia
time: chronophobia
togetherness: synophobia
travel: hodophobia
ugliness: cacophobia
voices: phemophobia
vomiting: emetophobia
walking: basiphobia
watching: scoptophobia
water: hydrophobia
weakness: asthenophobia
wealth: plutophobia
wind: anemophobia
women: gynephobia
words: logophobia
work: ergophobia
writing: graphophobia

?????

INFORMATION IS POWER

With these almanacs, compendiums,
encyclopedias, and dictionaries at your fingertips,
you'll always be in the know.
Pocket Books has a complete list of essential
reference volumes.

162

123